Sod ha-Shabbat
(The Mystery of the Sabbath)
from the *Tola^c at Ya^c aqov* of R. Meir ibn Gabbai

SUNY Series in Judaica: Hermeneutics, Mysticism, and Religion
Michael Fishbane, Robert Goldenberg, and Arthur Green, Editors

Sod ha-Shabbat
(The Mystery of the Sabbath)

from the *Tola^c^at Ya^c^aqov* of

R. Meir ibn Gabbai

Translated and with a critical commentary by
ELLIOT K. GINSBURG

State University of New York Press

Published by
State University of New York Press, Albany

Printed in the United States of America

For information, address State University of New York
Press, State University Plaza, Albany, N.Y., 12246

Library of Congress Cataloging-in-Publication Data

Ginsburg, Elliot Kiba.

Gabbai, Meir ben Ezekiel ibn, 1480-ca. 1540.
[Sod ha-Shabat. English]
Sod ha-Shabbat = The mystery of the Sabbath : from the Tolaᶜat Yaᶜaqov of Meir ibn Gabbai / translated and with critical commentary by Elliot K. Ginsburg.
p. cm. — (SUNY series in Judaica)
Translation of: Sod ha-Shabat.
Bibliography: p.
Includes index.
1. Sabbath. 2. Siddur. Sabbath. 3. Cabala. 4. Gabbai, Meir ben Ezekiel ibn, 1480-ca. 1540. Sod ha-Shabat. I. Ginsburg, Elliot Kiba. II. Title. III. Title: Mystery of the Sabbath. IV. Series.
BM685.G2813 1989
296.4'1—dc19 87-26765
CIP

10 9 8 7 6 5 4 3 2 1

Contents

Preface

The present volume is a translation of, and critical commentary to, *Sod ha-Shabbat,* a treatise on the mystical Sabbath by the influential Spanish-Turkish Kabbalist, R. Meir ibn Gabbai (1480/81-after 1543). Ibn Gabbai's text is part of a larger composition, the *Tolaᶜat Yaᶜaqov,* which he completed in 1507. The merit of *Sod ha-Shabbat* is two-fold: 1) it is the most systematic treatment of the Sabbath in classical Kabbalah; 2) it is a summary work: standing at the end of a Kabbalistic era, composed on the eve of the Safed Renaissance, it brings together many disparate strands from the classical mystical tradition.

The present volume assumes the following structure: The translation is preceded by an Introduction to Meir ibn Gabbai's life and work, and followed by extensive critical notes which serve three major functions: to clarify philological problems arising from manuscript variants and general problems of translation; to place the work in broader historical context by mapping influences and noting significant parallels; and to raise certain broader theoretical issues regarding myth and the ritual process.

This is the second book in my two-volume study of the mystical Sabbath prior to the Safed Renaissance. The first volume, *The Sabbath in the Classical Kabbalah* (SUNY Press: Albany, 1989) is a synthetic study of the Sabbath drawn from a full range of mystical sources. In it the conceptual canvas was deliberately stretched wide; here it is kept smaller, more tightly circumscribed. Yet what variety lurks within Meir ibn Gabbai's text! *Sod ha-Shabbat* is a rich and sometimes difficult work, replete with legal dialectic, encoded mystical allusions and multiple layers of meaning. One "opens" a text and enters a world, *ᶜolam u-melo'o.* So this book is not, perhaps, to be read so much as studied: to be eyed keenly, puzzled over, contemplated and—slowly savored.

Acknowledgements

It is a pleasure to be able to acknowledge a debt of gratitude to the many people who have contributed to this work, who have challenged and encouraged me and brought me to this season.

An earlier version of the present study, here substantially revised, was part of a doctoral dissertation under the direction of Arthur Green. Art has been a teacher and friend for many years; it is difficult to express how much I have learned from him. He introduced me to the field of Kabbalah and its symbolic universe, and helped me refine my skills in textual interpretation. I thank Art for his painstaking and insightful reading of this work, for warmly but firmly pushing me to clarify my ideas, for his numerous helpful suggestions. He has given valiantly of his time, thought, and effort; I am ever grateful.

Several colleagues have been especially helpful in the recent stages of writing. Dr. Elliot Wolfson has made several helpful comments on Zoharic precursors and Profs. Moshe Idel, Joseph Hacker, Daniel Matt, and Mark Verman have called important sources to my attention. My good friends Jeffrey Dekro and Dr. Morris Faierstein also deserve a note of gratitude. I thank Jeffrey for introducing me to the *Tolaʿat Yaʿaqov,* and for his comments in the early stages of writing. I have learned much from studying with him. I thank Moishele for sharing his vast knowledge and for his special brand of humor, which both enlightened and helped put matters in perspective.

Much of this book was written at Oberlin College. I am grateful to my colleagues in the Department of Religion and the Judaic and Near Eastern Studies Program, and to the wonderful students there, as well. Together they helped create a thoroughly enjoyable and stimulting intellectual environment, ideally suited to productive work.

Thanks are also due to the Jewish Theological Seminary of America, the Bibliothèque Nationale in Paris, the Schocken Institute in Jerusalem, and the Jewish National and University Library at Hebrew University for use of manuscripts and first editions of key works.

The Memorial Foundation for Jewish Culture, by granting me a dissertation fellowship for 1981-1983, enabled me to lay the groundwork for this study. Two generous research grants from Oberlin

College in the summers of 1985 and 1986 permitted me to travel to research libraries, here and abroad. Finally, a fellowship from the National Endowment for the Humanities enabled me to complete this and several related studies, while the National Foundation for Jewish Culture supplied a subvention grant facilitating publication. I acknowledge their support with gratitude.

William Eastman, my publisher at SUNY Press, has been consistently supportive and understanding, and Francis Richardson, Judy Block, and Marilyn Semerad, my editors at SUNY Press, precise and discerning. Luis Fernandez—dear friend and computer-*maven*—shared his time and expertise just when it was most needed.

Five people have contributed to this study in unique ways. My wife Terri has shared with me this labor from beginning to end. She has proof-read significant parts of this work and helped me with organization. But those not inconsiderable tasks are but a small measure of her contribution. Without her understanding, her patience and her love, this work would be unthinkable. Without her sense of humor and her wisdom, it would have been far less bearable.

My two little boys, Jacob Uri and Noah Eitan, were born while this book was being composed; they have been a constant source of renewal and delight *ᶜerev va-voqer ve-ẓahorayim!*

And finally, *sof maᶜaseh be-maḥashavah teḥillah.* My parents, Bernard and Rose Ginsburg, kindled within me the desire to learn and taught me the virtues of perseverance. Their love and untold sacrifice have cheered and sustained me. It is in love and gratitude that I dedicate this book to them.

Tam ve-nishlam, done and completed
21 October 1988
ᶜErev Shabbat Parashat Lekh-Lekha 5749
Oberlin, Ohio

Illustrations

Abbreviations

Abud.	David Abudraham, *Sefer 'Abudraham*
AJS Review	*Association for Jewish Studies Review*
AQ	Meir ibn Gabbai, *ʿAvodat ha-Qodesh*
ARN	*'Avot de-Rabbi Natan*
BḤ	Joel Sirkes, *Bayit Ḥadash*
BY	Joseph Karo, *Beit Yosef*
EJ	*Encyclopedia Judaica* (Jerusalem)
EJB	*Encyclopedia Judaica* (Berlin)
Guide	Moses Maimonides (RaMBaM), *Guide for the Perplexed*
HUCA	*Hebrew Union College Annual*
JJS	*Journal of Jewish Studies*
IR	*Zohar, 'Idra' Rabba'*
IZ	*Zohar, 'Idra' Zuṭa'*
JAAR	*Journal of the American Academy of Religion*
KS	*Kiryat Sefer*
"Le-Qorot"	Meir Benayahu, "Le-Qorot ha-Yehudim be-Tiria."
Legends	Louis Ginzberg, *Legends of the Jews*, 7 vols.
M.	*Mishnah*
Major Trends	Gershom Scholem, *Major Trends in Jewish Mysticism*
Manhig	Avraham ben Nathan of Lunel, *Sefer ha-Manhig*
Meḥqarim	Efraim Gottlieb, *Meḥqarim be-Sifrut ha-Qabbalah*
Mekh.	*Mekhilta' de-Rabbi Ishmael*
Mid. R	*Midrash Rabbah* (including Gen. R for *Genesis Rabbah;* Ex. R For *Exodus Rabbah;* etc.)
MN	*Zohar, Midrash ha-Neʿlam*
MT	Moses Maimonides (RaMBaM), *Mishneh Torah*
MZ	Isaiah Tishby with F. Lachover, *Mishnat ha-Zohar,* 2 vols.
n	note(s)
OK	Ṭodros ha-Levi Abulafia, *'Oẓar ha-Kavod*
OZ	David ben Judah he-Ḥasid, *'Or Zaruʿa*
PR	Moses Cordovero, *Pardes Rimmonim*
PRE	*Pirqei de-Rabbi 'Eliʿezer*

PRK	*Pesiqta' de-Rav Kahana'*
R.	Rabbi
R. Goetschal	Roland Goetschal, *Meir ibn Gabbai: Les Discours de la Kabbale Espagnole*
RM	*Ra^caya' Meheimna'*
SCK	Elliot Ginsburg, *The Sabbath in the Classical Kabbalah*
ShA	Joseph Karo, *Shulḥan ^cArukh*
SHeLaH	Isaiah Horowitz, *Shenei Luḥot ha-Berit*
SRA	*Siddur Rav ^cAmram Ga'on*
ST	*Zohar, Sitrei Torah*
SṬM	Joseph of Hamadan, *Sefer Ṭa^camei ha-Miẓvot*
Tanḥ	*Tanḥuma'*
TB	Babylonian Talmud *(Talmud Bavli)*
TJ	Palestinian Talmud *(Talmud Yerushalmi)*
Tos.	*Tosefot*
Ṭur	Jacob ben Asher, *'Arba^cah Ṭurim*
TY	Meir ibn Gabbai, *Tola^cat Ya^caqov*
TZ	*Tiqqunei ha-Zohar*
TZḤ	*Tiqqunei Zohar Ḥadash*
Viṭri	Simḥah ben Samuel, *Maḥzor Viṭri*
YS	*Yalqut Shim^coni*
Z	*Zohar*
ZḤ	*Zohar Ḥadash*

Note on Transliteration and Orthography

א	'	ל	l
בּ	b	מ	m
ב	v	נ	n
ג	g	ס	s
ד	d	ע	ᶜ
ה	h	פּ	p
ו	v	פ	f
ז	z	ק	q
ח	ḥ	צ	ẓ
ט	ṭ	ר	r
י	y, i	שׁ	sh
כּ	k	שׂ	s
כ	kh	ת	t

◌ָ ◌ַ ◌ֲ	a	◌ִ	i
◌ֵ ◌ֶ ◌ֱ	e	◌ֹ וֹ ◌ֳ	o
◌ְ	only *sheva' na*ᶜ is transliterated	◌ֻ וּ	u

Dagesh ḥazaq (forte) is indicated by doubling of the letter, except for the letter שׁ. Certain Hebrew nouns frequently used in English are spelled in accord with common English usage, most notably, Kabbalah. Diacritical marks for the *'alef* and *ᶜayin* have been omitted from names set in roman type. The letter ו , generally transliterated as *v*, has been rendered as *w* in exceptional cases, e.g., when indicating the Tetragammaton, commonly notated in English as YHWH. Finally, in several instances the letter ב has been transliterated as a single *b*: שׁבת, e.g., has been rendered *shabat* to enable the non-Hebrew reader to more readily see the etymological connection between that term and שׁבּת, i.e., *shabbat*.

Introduction

Sod ha-Shabbat, Meir ibn Gabbai's treatise on the mystical Sabbath, lies at the heart of his *Tolaᶜat Yaᶜaqov* (TY), completed by the author in the spring of 1507. *Sod ha-Shabbat* is perhaps the most comprehensive and systematic treatment of Sabbath celebration in the classical Kabbalah. From a literary point of view, it has the advantage of being more focused than the sprawling, albeit richer, Zoharic treatment and more complete than the earlier systematic discussions found in Moshe de Leon's *Sefer ha-Rimmon* and David ben Judah he-Ḥasid's *ᶜOr Zaruᶜa,* to cite two leading examples. Moreover, as a largely synthetic text, Meir ibn Gabbai's work brings together many disparate strands from the classical tradition; standing at the end of a Kabbalistic era, on the very eve of the Safed Renaissance, it is essentially a work of summation. For these reasons *Sod ha-Shabbat* is an ideal point of entry for exploration of the classical Sabbath-mythos and the course of its development.

Before turning to the actual translation and interpretation of this text, it is useful to set it in a broader context. The purpose of this chapter is to orient the reader to:

(1) Meir ibn Gabbai: his life and work

(2) The TY as a whole: its structure and purpose; the influences it absorbed and the influence that it, in turn, exerted; and

(3) the structure of *Sod ha-Shabbat, per se,* and the methodological concerns informing its translation and interpretation.

BIOGRAPHICAL NOTES

R.J. Zwi Werblowsky has commented that for centuries Jews chose to remember their greatest sons by the titles of their books,

> if possible every one by the title of his *magnum opus.* Even when authors were referred to by their actual names, these did not so much represent individual personalities as literary figures. Every

> name, it might almost be said, functioned like a pen-name. Who, after all, was the RaMBaN if not the author of the talmudic novellae *ḥiddushey ha-RaMBaN* or of the commentary on the Pentateuch *perush ha-RaMBaN?* No doubt the book often hid a distinct and unique personality, but the author was never allowed to protrude, as it were, from his work.[1]

Such is the case of the author of the TY, Rabbi Meir ben Yeḥezqel ibn Gabbai. To the historian, he has essentially become his books; the bare bones of his biography are all that can be uncovered. Meir ibn Gabbai was born in Spain in 1480/81,[2] underwent the trauma of the Expulsion as a youth, and ultimately resettled in the Ottoman Empire. The precise order of his perigrinations has been the subject of scholarly debate. Based on circumstantial evidence, he was commonly thought to have spent much of his adult life in Turkey, proper,[3] though certain scholars averred that he may have lived in Egypt, as well; G. Scholem and R. Goetschal maintain that he may have died in *'Ereẓ Israel,* though neither provides documentation for this.[4] These historians have apparently overlooked the persuasive evidence presented by Meir Benayahu some forty years ago,[5] locating Meir ibn Gabbai in the Turkish town of Tire (Thyrea)[6] from at least 1516. According to the *She'elot u-Teshuvot* of the esteemed R. Elijah Mizraḥi of Istanbul,[7] responsum 24, one R. Meir ibn Gabbai served as a member of the rabbinical court of Tire at this time.[8] Given the likely Turkish provenance of our Kabbalist's writings and the halakhic (legal) expertise evident in them,[9] there is little doubt that judge and mystic are one and the same.

Meir Benayahu suggested that ibn Gabbai served in Tire for an extended period; there is no independent evidence, unfortunately, to confirm this view. Benayahu did show that ibn Gabbai, in his later years, lived in Manissa (Magnesia), a city north-east of Izmir that was home to Jewish refugees from Lorca and Toledo.[10] Here, too, the responsa literature is revealing. A query addressed to the eminent R. Levi ibn Ḥabib of Jerusalem in the summer of 1540 indicates that Meir ibn Gabbai served as head of the Manissa rabbinical court.[11] Ibn Gabbai is again mentioned in the Responsa of Moshe ben Joseph Ṭrani (the MaBiṬ) of Safed, having corresponded with the latter in the fall of 1543.[12] Ibn Gabbai died sometime thereafter, at any event later than the 1540 date suggested by most scholars.[13]

Of the conditions of Meir ibn Gabbai's life, little is known. In the colophon to TY, completed when he was 26, ibn Gabbai indicate that his young adult years were lived under difficult material circumstances:

> The sins of my youth forced me to fend for myself; so I was caught up in earning an income to support myself and my household.

This evidently rendered the holy task of writing difficult for "this requires free time and a clear mind." It is known that he had at least one son, R. Ḥayyim, the author of the Kabbalistic work, *Sefer Pesaḥ La-'Adonai,*[14] and one daughter, who married R. Shneur ben Judah Falqon of Istanbul.

Meir ibn Gabbai wrote three major works, all of which attained a relatively wide audience: the TY, a kabbalistic commentary on the prayers and assorted rituals (1507); the *Derekh 'Emunah* (1539) on the ten *sefirot,* which was specially written for his disciple, one Joseph ha-Levi; and his *magnum opus, 'Avodat ha-Qodesh* (AQ) (1531), a book that ibn Gabbai wrote between the ages of 42 and 50. Gershom Scholem has called it "perhaps the finest account of Kabbalistic speculation before the resurgence of Kabbalah in Safed."[15] The focus here will be on the TY.

CONTENT AND STRUCTURE OF THE *TOLAᶜAT YAᶜAQOV*

The TY is best placed in that genre of Kabbalistic literature devoted to mystical prayer or more specifically, to the mystical interpretation of the traditional liturgy. As G. Scholem notes "such interpretations were less commentaries in the ordinary sense than systematic manuals for mystical meditation in prayer."[16] The very title of the work underscores the extraordinary power Meir ibn Gabbai accorded Kabbalistic prayer. Israel is the *Tolaᶜat Yaᶜaqov,* the "silkworm Jacob," who by the power of his mouth, i.e., prayer, can weave a silken "garment of holiness," a cloak of great beauty, for divinity.[17] Nonetheless, it would be mistaken to see the TY as solely concerned with prayer, narrowly construed. Meir Ibn Gabbai devoted a good deal of space to other ritual acts: to Torah-study, fasting, dwelling in a *Sukkah,* sacramental eating, marital intercourse, Sabbath-speech, the *miẓvah* of returning a pledge to its owner at night, and many others. The book thus takes on some of the characteristics of the mystical *Ṭaᶜamei ha-Miẓvot* literature. Although prayer constitutes the central focus of the work, the TY aims to provide its readers with an idealized road map for the devotional journey, as a whole.[18]

Structurally, the TY is composed of a preface and a body consisting of three major divisions. The preface focuses on the spiritual function of the human being as divine Microcosm and underscores the power of the *miẓvot,* in general, and mystical prayer, in particular, "to order the [divine world] and to draw the Creator's will unto the created beings." According to ibn Gabbai, the life of devotion has two complementary aspects: it both promotes *devequt,* the joyous "union [*ḥibbur*] of the form of the seeker to the Sought" (6b), and promotes divine restoration *(tiqqun ha-kavod),* whereby

> one renews and strengthens the structure of the Great Person and adorns the House of Glory, filling it with light. (7a)[19]

The rest of the book is a Kabbalistically oriented guide to 1) the daily prayers; 2) the prayers and attendant rituals of the Sabbath and the major holy days; and 3) the meaning of miscellaneous blessings, including the so-called "blessings of enjoyment," the Grace after Meals, Circumcision, Marriage, and the blessing recited upon the initial act of sexual coupling.[20] Although the focus is always on the *sodot* or mystical meanings of these prayers and rituals, Meir ibn Gabbai often included Rabbinic interpretations, both Aggadic and halakhic, as a kind of prelude.[21]

INFLUENCES: MEIR IBN GABBAI'S LIBRARY

Ibn Gabbai relied on a wide array of sources in composing this work, revealing an impressive knowledge of the classical Rabbinic and Kabbalistic literature. In contrast to the AQ, however, the influence of philosophical texts is minimal here. This may be due more to the subject matter of the book and its non-polemical tone than to a lack of familarity with this tradition.[22] It is perhaps more noteworthy that the Gerona tradition, so central to the AQ, plays a minor role here.[23]

The TY as a whole stands firmly within the Zoharic stream of Kabbalah. Indeed, the influence of the *Zohar* and its ancillary works, which he generally termed "The Midrash of R. Shimon bar Yoḥai,"[24] is paramount: hundreds of Zoharic references—both explicit and unstated—populate the TY's pages.[25] Ibn Gabbai readily acknowledged his debt. Writing the book was an act of homage which he hoped would give the *Zohar*'s words new life and facilitate their incorporation into devotional life. He attested to the *Zohar*'s unique status by quoting the good book itself (TZḤ: 93d–94a)!

> This book boldly reveals the hidden meanings of the Torah, something granted to no other work. It is like Noah's ark which contained all species. In it are gathered all the souls of the righteous. Of this

> book it is said, "This is the gateway to the Lord; the righteous shall enter it." [Ps. 118:29]

From his citations, it is clear that Meir ibn Gabbai had access to virtually all strata of the *Zohar*, including the *Zohar Ḥadash*.

Although the *Zohar* formed what ibn Gabbai called the "Great Tamarisk"(8a; cf. TZḤ 103d), i.e., the central source of inspiration, it stood in good company. As R. Goetschal has noted, the TY is practically an anthology of classical sources, "a montage of his own language and quotations."[26] The following is a list of the works and authors explicitly cited by Meir ibn Gabbai. I have omitted those standard sources, such as the Bible, TB, TJ, and the *Zohar* which appear with great frequency. I have traced his many uncited sources for *Sod ha-Shabbat* elsewhere[27] (in the notes to the translation and in the indices at the end of this book). The TY citations, printed below, follow the 1876 Warsaw pagination.

Midrashic literature
Mekhilta' (= TY 49a)
Midrash Rabbah (45a; 56a; 58b)
Pesiqta' Rabbati (56a)
Pirqei de-R. 'Eliᶜezer (52a; 59a)
Yelammedenu (47a)

Biblical exegesis
RaSHI (15a)

Halakhah and liturgy
Abraham b. Nathan of Lunel (ff. its citation in Abudraham) (47b)
David Abudraham, *Sefer 'Abudraham* (40a; 47b; 48a-b)
Isaac Alfasi (15a and 87b)
R. Amram Gaon (15a)
Jacob ben Asher, *Ṭur* (32b; 48a; 85b [uncited])
Joseph Yaaveẓ (39a)
Judah ben Barzilai of Barcelona (24b)
Meir of Rothenburg (24b)
RaMBaM (26a; 68a; 91b)
Saadiah Gaon [?] (32a)
R. Tam (15a and 85b)
Tosafot (82b)
Ibn Yaḥya (47a)
Ẓemaḥ Gaon (40a)

Philosophical literature

RaMBaM, *Moreh Nevukhim* [Guide for the Perplexed] (3ab; 5a; 9b; 15a)

Rabbinic Mysticsm

Sefer Heikhalot (21b and 71a)
Sefer Yeẓirah (82a)

Ḥasidei 'Ashkenaz

Anonymous (34b)
Eleazar of Worms, *Sefer Razi'el* (3b)

Kabbalistic Sources

Late twelfth to early thirteenth century

Abraham ben David of Posquieres (68a)
Sefer ha-Bahir (41a; 54a; 56b)

Late thirteenth to early fourteenth century

David ben Judah he-Ḥasid, *'Or Zaruᶜa* (18b; 31b)
Joseph Angelino, *Livnat ha-Sappir* (28b)
Menaḥem Recanati, *Ṭaᶜamei ha-Miẓvot* (33a)
Moshe de Leon, *Sefer ha-Rimmon* (66b; 75b)—referred to generically as *Sitrei ha-Ḥokhmah*[28]
————. *'Orḥot Ḥayyim*—also known as *Ẓavva'at R. 'Eliᶜezer ha-Gadol*, cited anon. (71a)[29]
Ṭodros ha-Levi Abulafia, *'Oẓar ha-Kavod* (49b)

Mid-fourteenth century until the Expulsion

Joseph Alcastiel, cited anonymously as *'eḥad me-ḥakhmei ha-'emet* (30b)
Sefer ha-Qanah (10b; 31a)
Sefer ha-Peli'ah [cited as *Sefer ha-Qanah!*][30] (46a)

PURPOSE OF THE BOOK

Why did Meir ibn Gabbai write the book? Or to pose a more readily answerable question: What reasons did the author give for writing the TY? In the preface (8a–b), he mentioned three reasons for so doing. Although there is no reason to doubt their veracity, it must be recalled that cultural convention precluded articulation of certain rationales that might be seen as self-aggrandizing, especially for a writer so young.[31] Ibn Gabbai's first two reasons are inner directed:

(1) To enrich his current devotional life:

> So that the secrets of the prayers and their hidden meanings may be before my eyes constantly.

In several instances ibn Gabbai implied a certain lack of satisfaction with his own spiritual condition. He hoped that through the act of writing he would be able to internalize and integrate the various Kabbalistic teachings he had studied, and to preserve the insights God had vouchsafed unto him:

> I saw the need to press beyond the bounds, to enter inside, to gather from the bounty of those who had previously harvested this "apple orchard"[32] . . . and to write in this book the secret meanings of prayer which God gave into my hands.

By synthesizing these scattered sources of inspiration, Meir ibn Gabbai hoped that his devotional life would be made whole.

(2) For the sake of his future life. He hoped that the book would serve as a source of spiritual nourishment enabling him to merit life in the World-to-Come. Moreover, he hoped, this book would serve as his defending attorney on the day of his death.

(3) The third reason is outer-directed. He hoped to reach those wavering souls, attracted to philosophical rationalism but open to the path of Kabbalah. Thus, he wrote:

> I hope to convince an outsider or two, who may be likened to a "rose among the thorns" [Cant. 2:2], who is willing to trod the well-paved path, ready to appear before God and serve Him.

(4) Although he did not include this in his articulated rationale, we may safely assume a fourth reason. From his previous remarks (8a), it is clear that ibn Gabbai hoped to reach other Kabbalists. He nurtured the hope that his manual—with its collation of scattered, often arcane sources—would make Kabbalistic teachings more vital and accessible:

> I will gather their banished words, joining them one to another till they become whole again. Then perhaps, I will be worthy of being counted among these men's numbers, if only in a small measure. I know that many of the surviviors of the Chosen People will

> recognize the value of this book and will remember me for good in that I will have lessened the burden of their wandering [from source to source], seeking out God hither and yon.[33]

THE *TOLA^cAT YA^cAQOV'S* INFLUENCE

Despite being addressed to a limited audience, the TY's influence radiated beyond its intended sphere. Clearly, it was known to some of the Safed mystics in the mid- to late sixteenth century. In his introduction to *Re'shit Ḥokhmah* (end), Elijah de Vidas judged the TY most favorably:

> I have refrained from writing . . . about the significance of prayer, because the book TY has preceded me. While "there is no interpretation without new insights" [TB Ḥag. 3a], still I will desist lest I [unnecessarily] prolong the book.[34]

In his subsequent *Toẓe'ot Ḥayyim,* de Vidas explained that:

> All the esoteric meanings of the Prayer, in general and in specific, have already been established by Meir ibn Gabbai, of blessed memory, in his holy works, the TY and *Mar'ot 'Elohim* [AQ].[35]

According to G. Scholem,[36] another Safed authority, Joseph Ashkenazi ha-Tana', also exhibited familiarity with the TY; it may safely be assumed that these two were not the only Safed figures who made use of it.

Perhaps the highest compliment paid Meir ibn Gabbai was that of the Polish-*'Ereẓ Israeli* Kabbalist, Isaiah Horowitz (1550-1630). In his *Two Tablets of the Convenant* (*Shenei Luḥot ha-Berit* or SHeLaH), he ranked the TY's author as one of the three great Kabbalists of the later era, along with Moses Cordovero and Isaac Luria.[37] The SHeLaH made frequent use of the TY and extensively quoted ibn Gabbai's teachings on Shabbat, in particular.[38] Via the SHeLaH, surely one of the most influential books among the Jews of Eastern Europe, ibn Gabbai's interpretations became widely known, even entering *qiẓẓurim* (popular abridgements and adaptations) and compendia of *dinim u-minhagim* (ceremonies and customs).[39]

Seventeenth century Italian Kabbalists and their antagonists were familiar with the TY, as well. Joseph ben Solomon Del Medigo, Aaron Berakhiah of Modena, and Leone of Modena all mentioned it, the first two in praise and the latter in censure.[40] The TY also influenced the great Yemenite poet and Kabbalist, Shalem Shabbazi,[41] and made a positive impact on certain ex-*Marrano* circles in Holland at this time.[42]

The publication history of the TY is perhaps the best indicator of its strong appeal, which might be traced to three factors: the high regard in which it was held by certain influential authorities; the TY's succinct[43] and systematic style; and finally, its useful nature as a guide to daily devotion.

Some eleven editions of the work have been printed to date: the first is the Istanbul, or Constantinople, edition from 1560; the second through tenth editions are all Eastern European, the earliest dating from 1581 and the others from 1797–1876; the most recent printing was in Jerusalem in 1967.[44] Moreover, the large number of Yemenite manuscripts of the TY attests to the significance accorded this book by Jews in that region.[45] The Jewish National and University Library [JNUL] in Jerusalem lists some thirty-one extant manuscripts, at least twenty-three of Yemenite provenance.[46] The publishing history suggests that the TY was most intensively studied in the mid- to late sixteenth century in the Ottoman setting, from the seventeenth through twentieth centuries in Yemen, and throughout the nineteenth century in Eastern Europe.

ON *SOD HA-SHABBAT*

Finally, it is useful to say a few words about the structure of *Sod ha-Shabbat* itself, and about the mechanics of translating and interpreting it. *Sod ha-Shabbat* opens the second major section of the TY, filling over sixteen closely printed pages (44a–60a) in the Warsaw edition. Meir ibn Gabbai organized the rich variety of Sabbath-ritual into twenty-two central categories, which more or less follow a chronological order. Beginning with the sundry preparatory acts and concluding with *Havdalah,* these rituals first pave the way for, then dramatize, and, finally, prolong the Sabbath-cosmos, extending it into the week. A complete listing of these twenty-two items may be found in the Table of Contents and on page 15 below.

My translation is based on three MS sources—JNUL Heb. octo 3913 (written in Adrianople [Edirne] in 1546), the earliest extant source; and JTSA Mic. 1553 and 1646, Sefardic texts from the late sixteenth century—and upon the first printed edition (= e.p., Istanbul, 1560). In general, the two most reliable sources are the Adrianople MS and the e.p. Most of the discrepancies are minor; all are noted in the commentary.[47]

The commentary (or notes) to the translation serves three major functions:

(1) **Clarification of philological issues,** including the notation of textual variants and problems of translation, and most commonly, the elucidation of Meir ibn Gabbai's Kabbalistic terminology. The critical question here is, "How is the text to be 'read' "?

(2) **Placing the work in historical context.** Technically, this involves mapping influences and noting parallels. The underlying questions here are: How and when did given Kabbalistic traditions develop? What influences are discernible? And most pointedly: What sources did Meir ibn Gabbai read and how did he read (or re-read) them?

These more technical concerns will pave the way for:

(3) **Broader discussions on Sabbath myth and ritual.** These may be either historical-comparative in nature, e.g., analyzing the Kabbalistic contribution to Sabbath-celebration and its relation to earlier traditions, or phenomenological, focusing on issues of religious experience and signification, especially, the ritual process and the creation of symbolic meaning. Such analyses are generally prefaced by the bold-face **Discussion.**

Sod ha-Shabbat: The Translation

Prologue

The Holy One, blessed be He, has given us the Sabbath as our inheritance and it is equal to the entire Torah, as it is said: "And You came down upon Mount Sinai . . . And You made known to them Your Holy Sabbath." [Neh. 9: 13–14] This passage teaches us [via parallel structure] that the Sabbath is equal to the entire Torah.[1]

There is a hidden meaning in the fact that *Shabbat* is sometimes treated as a masculine form and sometimes as a feminine form[2]—namely, to hint at the "Two Faces," the mystery of "Remember" and "Keep."[3] As [an allusion] to this mystery both terms are included in the Decalogue, for the entire Torah is included in these two; the *miẓvot* of commission are contained within "Remember" and the miẓvot of omission, within "Keep."[4] And so, the Sabbath esoterically represents the entire Torah.[5]

Know that during the six days of Creation the six levels of the [Divine] Structure[6] were engaged in their activities, turning all things from potential into actual, until the twilight of the seventh day. When the seventh day[7] arrived, they all rested. This was *shebitat ha-ᶜolam,* the cessation of the world from creative labor. Thus, the seventh day was called *Shabbat,* Cessation.

Know that each level causes the cessation of the preceding one. For example, the Light[8] that emanated the first level of the Structure ceased after it had completed actualizing its potential. And the same was true down through the seventh level, at which point, they all rested.[9]

Regarding this mystery we read in TB *Shabbat,* chapter "A Great Principle" (69b):

> Said R. Huna: "If one is travelling in the wilderness and does not know when it is the Sabbath, he must count seven days and observe that day as the Sabbath,"[10]

The reason [that any one of the days may be treated as Shabbat] is that they are all called "Sabbaths of the Lord."[11] [Lev. 23:38]

According to the secrets of the Torah, why is it called Shabbat? Because [on Shabbat] *Bat-ᶜAyin,* the daughter of Abraham, is separated from the profane days of the week, the mystery of the Narrow Straits, and is reintegrated in the mystery of the Patriarchs on high.[12] This totality is called *ShaBbaT*[13] and it is the mystery of Coupling. Once again [*Shekhinah* and the Patriarchs] stand face-to-face, for the Community of Israel [*Shekhinah*] was given to the Sabbath,[14] to be its mate.

We read in *Genesis Rabbah* (11:8):[15]

> R. Shimon bar Yoḥai taught: "The Sabbath came before the Holy One, and she said; 'Sovereign of the Universe. All the other (days of the week) have a mate, am I to be without one?!"

[The text then brings us up short, treating the Sabbath as masculine:]

> The Holy One said to *him* [*lo*]: "The Community of Israel will be your mate [*ben zugekh].*"[16] When Israel stood before Mount Sinai, God said to them: "Recall those words which I said to Shabbat: 'The Community of Israel is your mate." As it is written: "Remember the Sabbath day, *le-qaddesho,* to wed it."[17] [Ex. 20:8]

[Meir ibn Gabbai now attempts to solve the implicit difficulty in the preceding text: the apparent androgyny of Shabbat:][18]

Before the diminution of the moon, the "[two] Kings used one crown" and Shabbat had no mate parallel to it, like the other essences.[19] For this reason, [the Midrash says]: "And Sabbath, *'amrah,* she spoke," referring to the Sabbath as a feminine form, but said thereafter, "God spoke *lo,* to *him*" [the masculine Shabbat], the mystery of the Supernal Light, saying: The Bride, "the Community of Israel [*Shekhinah*] will be your mate."[20] This relationship is similar to that described in the verses: "They are joined one to another" [Job 41:9] and *"ke-maʿar 'ish ve-loyot"* [I Kings 7:36], meaning: even as a man embracing his mate.[21]

The Bride said: "Sovereign of the Universe, you gave the rest of them a mate, am I to be without one?" Said the Holy One: "The Community of Israel"—the corporeal Israel—"will be your mate [*bat zugekha*] and you will be ruler and king over them." And when Israel stood upon Sinai, the Holy One said to them: "Recall those words which I said to Shabbat: The Community of Israel will be your mate."[22]

And so, we must observe the Sabbath properly and be a mate to it below. In so doing, we will merit to be its mate in the World-to-Come. We must therefore know those activities through which the Sabbath may be properly observed:

1. Each person[23] should take pains to personally prepare for the needs of the Sabbath, to honor it.
2. Complete reading the Torah portion together with the congregation, reciting the Hebrew text once and the [Aramaic] Targum once.
3. Pare one's nails.
4. Prepare Sabbath-fusions [*ᶜeruvin*] in one's courtyard.
5. Wash one's body.
6. Change one's garments.
7. Add to the holy by taking from the profane [by beginning the Sabbath early].
8. Candle-lighting.
9. The evening prayers.
10. Sanctify the day over wine on Friday night.
11. The Friday night feast.
12. The prescribed "time" for scholars.[24]
13. The morning prayers and Torah-reading.
14. [Desist from] prohibited labor.
15. Delight in the Sabbath.
16. [Refrain from] mundane speech.
17. The mystical meaning of one who is engaged in a dream-fast.
18. Engage in Torah-learning.
19. The afternoon prayers.
20. The mystery of the three festive meals.
21. Add to the holy by taking from the profane at Sabbath's end [i.e., by prolonging Shabbat].
22. The mystery of "May the Pleasantness" and the mystery of *Havdalah*.

I will now enter into the explanation of these twenty-two items. Your mnemonic is "We will delight and rejoice [in the Sabbath] *BaKH*" [Cant. 1:4], through these twenty-two![25] I do so with the help of the One who teaches humanity wisdom; I ask that He guide me on the proper path, so that I may not utter even one word that is counter to His will. May He fulfill in me the dictum, "I shall be with your mouth and teach you what you shall speak." [Ex. 4:12]

SECTION 1

On Friday morning one should take pains to personally prepare whatever is necessary for the Sabbath, even if one happens to have several servants.[26] Consider the example of the sages of Israel, the holy ones on high, as it is said in chapter "All Sacred Writings" (TB Shab. 119a):

> [In preparation for the Sabbath] R. Naḥman b. Isaac carried in and carried out, saying, "If R: Ammi and R. Asi visited me, would I not carry for them?" Others state: R. Ammi and R. Asi carried in and out, saying "If R. Joshua visited us, would we not carry for him?"

In doing the carrying themselves these holy men [invoke] the hermeneutical principle of "from minor to major," indicating that if they would do this when [hosting] each other, how much more so when they are hosting the King of the Universe, amid the mystery of Shabbat. For the Sabbath is the entirety of the holy rungs, the mystery of the Faith of Israel, She who comes and rests on the Holy People.[27]

One who honors the Sabbath is considered one who honors God. Of him Scripture says, "For them that honor Me, I will honor." [I Samuel 2:30] We read in Tractate *Beiẓah,* chapter "Festival" (15b–16a):

> R. Taḥlifa, the brother of Rabinai of Ḥozaah learned: "One's yearly sustenance is fixed between New Year's and the Day of Atonement, except for the expenditure for Sabbaths and for Festivals, and the expenditure for the teaching of his children Torah. [If he spends less, he is given less, if he spends more], then he is given more."

And it is also said there [TB *Beiẓah* 15b]:

> "Neither be grieved; for the joy of the LORD is your strength." [Neh. 8:10] . . . The Holy One, blessed be He, said unto Israel:

"My Children, borrow on My account and celebrate the holiness of the day; trust in Me and I will repay."

The relationship of the sixth day to Shabbat is as the relationship of this world to the World-to-Come. For one should prepare for all one's Sabbath-needs on the eve of Shabbat; one is forbidden to prepare thereafter. Indeed, without prior preparation, what shall he eat on the Sabbath? Thus, our Sages said: "He who took trouble [to prepare] on the eve of Shabbat can eat on Shabbat . . ." [TB AZ 3a]

Similarly, one who upholds Torah and performs good deeds in this world will eat of his reward in the World-to-Come;[28] but he who has not prepared, what shall he eat? In this spirit, our Sages continued, "But he who has not troubled [to prepare] on the eve of Sabbath, what shall he eat on the Sabbath?" [Ibid.][29]

Carefully note their words! It is written, *mah yo'khal,* "**what** shall he eat?" and not, *lo' yo'khal,* "he shall **not** eat!" Had they said the latter it would seem that eating would be within the realm of possibility and that not eating was (merely) his punishment. However, by saying "What shall he eat?", they wished to make clear that it was impossible to eat; because "the reward for a miẓvah is a miẓvah,"[30] and he has not prepared properly. Therefore, the text states: *Mah yo'khal,* "what shall he eat?!"

The point of the teaching that "one's sustenance is fixed, etc." is similar to that made [elsewhere in the Talmud] concerning [the fate of] "this new drop of life, what will become of it?"[31] For God decrees ["whether he will be weak or strong, wise or weak, rich or poor"] in this world until the day of Judgment, his death.

It is said that "one's yearly sustenance is fixed between New Year's and the Day of Atonement, etc." [However], by excluding "the expenditures for Shabbat" i.e., sustenance in Torah and good deeds, [the Sages are teaching] that these depend on the actions of the person. Similarly, [in the second case], "whether he be righteous or wicked is not decreed," for that choice lies in the hands of the individual. It is up to him whether to add [to the good] or to subtract from it.

Each person holds the scales of justice. If he inclines to the side of good, this is an enhancement "and he is given more," for according to the fruit of his deeds will he be sated and "the reward for a miẓvah is a miẓvah!" But if he inclines to the side of evil, he detracts, and therefore, "he is given less," for "what shall he eat" if he has not prepared properly? As the verse says: "[On the sixth day] they shall prepare what they have brought in."[32] [Ex.16:5]

When a person prepares Torah and miẓvot he gives joy to God. Doing so requires that he not think of a reward. This is the path of those who serve God out of love, even though they still hope that, in the end, God "will give them their due."[33] All their strength and being is directed into giving Him joy. They promote peace between the two Lovers and crown them with a diadem of grace.[34] Of this it is said, "The joy of YHWH is your strength." [Neh. 8:10] and also, "Said the Holy One: 'Borrow on my account, etc."[35] [TB *Beiẓah* 15b]

In this fashion a person should prepare the necessities for Shabbat. Just as one must always see himself as hanging in the balance and should add a miẓvah so as to weight himself to the side of Good, so must he view himself when preparing the Sabbath necessities,[36] [realizing that] he can still do more to honor God, to give joy to the Guest who is coming to his home.

One must intend to impart this [joy] both when preparing for Shabbat and when rejoicing at the festive table. Such[37] was the intention of the Sage when he said: "So I commended joy, that a man has no better thing under the sun than to eat and to drink and to be merry and *hu' yilvennu*—it will accompany him—in his labor all the days of his life which God has given him under the sun." [Eccles. 8:15]

He said: **"So I commended joy":** This is the joy of the Kingdom of Heaven that dominates the world on Sabbaths[38] and holidays. **"That a man has no better thing . . . than to eat, drink and to be merry:"** during the time of Her rule so that he will have a portion in the World-to-Come. **"And *hu' yilvennu*": The Holy One, blessed be He, will accompany him** and usher him into the World-to-Come.

Another interpretation: ***Hu' yilvennu***. *Hu'* refers to the one who eats and drinks and rejoices. Everything that he eats and drinks with the proper intention, *MaLVeH:* he **lends** unto the Holy One[39] and "He will repay him for his kindness." [Prv. 19:17] A person can lend unto God in two ways: [First], in his preparations for Sabbaths and holidays, as we previously mentioned; and [second], in being gracious to the poor—for one must give priority to their Sabbath-needs. For this reason, the holy children of Israel have always been accustomed to give [to the poor] on the eve of Sabbaths and holidays.[40] Thus, it is said: "Whoever is gracious unto the poor lends unto the Lord; and he will repay him for his kindness."[41] [Ibid.]

SECTION 2

To complete the weekly portion together with the congregation, [reading] the Hebrew text twice, and the *Targum* once.[42] As it is written in the chapter "From what time?" (TB Ber. 8b):

> Everyone who completes his portions together with the congregation, his days and years are prolonged.

This [directive] may be rendered as an acronym: *Ve-'elleh* ***SHMoWT*** [a play on Ex. 1:1], meaning, "and these are ***SHenayim Miqra' We-'eḥad Targum*** [lit., the Text twice and the *Targum* once]." For a man must go over the portion twice in the Hebrew and once in the *Targum*. There are those who say that the law permits recitation in one's native tongue, because the purpose of [reading] the *Targum* is to understand the meaning of the text; and there are those who say that *Targum* [*'Onqelos*] must specifically be read, and that is the proper opinion.[43]

The reason for this is that it was given at Sinai, as it is said in the first chapter of *Megillah* (3a),

> R. Jeremiah—or some say, R. Ḥiyya b. Abba—also said: "The *Targum* of the Torah was composed by Onqelos the proselyte under the guidance of R. Eleazar and R. Joshua" . . . But did Onqelos the proselyte compose the *Targum* to the Torah? Has not R. Iqa said in the name of R. Ḥananel who had it from Rav: "What is meant by the verse, 'and they read in the book, in the law of God, with an interpretation, and they gave the sense, and caused them to understand the reading' [Neh. 8:8]? **'And they read in the book in the law of God':** This indicates the Hebrew text; **'with an interpretation':** this indicates the *Targum*; **'and they gave the sense':** This indicates the verse stops; **'And caused them to understand the reading':** This indicates the cantillation, or according to others, the masoretic notes. These had been forgotten, and were now established again [by Onqelos]."

So the *Targum* must be read exactly as it was given.[44]

There is an underlying reason for [including] the *Targum*. For it functions like the hair of the *tefillin*, which is a law given to Moses at Sinai.[45] Indeed, the Torah descended wrapped in [the covering of] the *Targum*, just as "the curtains of goat hair for the tent cover the Tabernacle."[46] [Ex. 26:7 and 36:14] Because this [combination] promotes wholeness, one's days and years are prolonged and the Accuser is given no opportunity to open his mouth in dissent. Your mnemonic is "These men are made whole through us."[47] [Gen. 34:21]

The esoteric reason for "the Hebrew text twice" is to parallel *Torei Zahav*, the "circlets of gold."[48] [Cant. 1:11] In the *Book Qanah* I saw "the Hebrew text twice" to parallel the *Vav* [the 3rd letter of the Tetragrammaton, i.e., *Tif'eret*] and its continuation [*Yesod*], and "the *Targum* once" to parallel the Crown [*Malkhut*].[49]

SECTION 3

To pare one's nails.[50] Know that the garment that Adam wore was from the mystery of the Chariots called the *'Aḥorayim*, or Rear Ones. According to our Sages of blessed memory, they were garments of nail.[51] When Adam was in the Garden all these chariots surrounded him and no evil thing could draw near him. When he sinned these lights left him and he was divested of the garment of that Inclination.[52] Nothing of that [primordial garment] remains except for [the nails] at the tips of the fingers and toes, and they are surrounded by filth.

And since one must not bring an impurity into the Sanctuary, one must pare them on Friday afternoon, so that the sacred is not profaned on account of this impurity. Nor should one [merely] throw away [the parings,] thereby denigrating [the Left Side]. For [the proper balance between the forces of *Din* and divinity] constitutes the perfection of the cosmos, and "God has made [the Left Side] so that people men fear Him."[53] [Eccles. 3:14]

We read in [TB] *Mo^ced Qaṭan*, chapter "These are Permitted to Shave" (18a):

> Three things were said in reference to nails: One who buries them is just [*ẓaddiq*]; one who burns them is pious [*ḥasid*]; and one who throws them away is a villain [*rasha^c*]!

The reason for this is that nails intimate *Din*. One who removes [*Din* by burning the nails] promotes Peace and Compassion in the world. This constitutes *middat ḥasidut*, pious conduct, that benefits both the person and others.

"One who buries them is just." Even though he did not remove *Din* from the world totally, still he impedes *Din* and quiets it. However, this falls short of [the actions of] the *ḥasid*.[54]

"One who throws them away is a villain": For he causes *Din* to flow into the world. And in *Mo^ced Qaṭan* [Ibid.] it is said:

> What is the reason [that one should not throw away nails]? Lest a pregnant woman should step over them and miscarry.

And perhaps this is Woman's punishment, because she caused Adam to be divested of his precious garment.[55]

And so, the remnants of this garment became a place where this filth would adhere. And this [susceptibility to miscarriage] is her punishment. And for this reason "Rabbi Yoḥanan used to throw them away in the House of Study," as it says there (MQ 18a) [because women did not frequent the place].[56]

And God will show us further marvels from His Torah!

SECTION 4

To make Sabbath-fusions in the courtyards [*ᶜeruvei ḥaẓerot*].[57] The Torah only proscribes [carrying] from the private domain [*Reshut ha-Yaḥid*] to the public domain [*Reshut ha-Rabbim*], and vice-versa. *Reshut ha-Yaḥid* is an enclosed place whose width is [not less than] four [handbreaths] and whose height is [not less than] ten [handbreaths]. *Reshut ha-Rabbim* refers to wilderness, forests, fields, vineyards and open alleys so long as they are [at least] sixteen cubits wide and have no cross-beams above them.

According to the path of truth,[58] *Reshut ha-Yaḥid* refers to the final *He'* of the Divine Name, **"whose height is *ten*,"** for [*Malkhut*] is crowned with the mystery of ten holy rungs. **"Whose width is *four*"** esoterically refers to the four letters of the Divine Name. In this regard it is said, "Let no man go from His Place" [Ex. 16:29] for ["His Place"] contains the mystery of holiness. But beyond it lies the *Temurot*,[59] the Counter-World called *Reshut ha-Rabbim* [the Realm of Multiplicity], for in that realm there is no unity. One who brings from *Reshut ha-Rabbim* profanes the Shabbat and causes a profanation above, by effecting a transfer from the sacred realm to the profane.

Of one who carries from *Reshut ha-Rabbim* to *Reshut ha-Yaḥid* it is said, "Everyone that profanes it shall be put to death" [Ex. 31:14], for he has brought a handmaiden[60] into [*Malkhut's*] domain, "a profane woman, a harlot." [Lev. 21:14] He thereby renders Her profane.

According to the Torah, one is permitted to carry in a courtyard onto which houses open,[61] but by scribal enactment it is prohibited [to transfer objects] unless an *ᶜeruv* has been prepared.[62] For an *ᶜeruv* is the symbol of the perfect Bride [*Malkhut*], the locus at which [sacred and profane] domains meet.

Everything should be in accord with the supernal paradigm. King Solomon, peace be upon him, ordained these Sabbath-fusions.[63] This is the inner meaning of the verse, "A throne was set for the king's mother."[64] (IK 2:19)

SECTION 5

To wash one's body.[65] The reason for this is that during the week Another Causality [*Siṭra' 'Aḥra'*] holds sway over the world, but [on Sabbath eve] the holy People must get out from under that dominion. They must cleanse themselves of this [impurity] to enter into the mystery of the Holy Faith. For this reason they must immerse themselves in the river, enabling the Mother of the Children to rest upon them. Then will they be crowned with an additional-soul as will be explained later.

SECTION 6

To change one's garments so as to emulate one's Creator.[66] For during the days of the week the Holy One is garbed in the Ten Lower Crowns and on Shabbat He is divested of them and cloaked in multiple garments of Light. To emulate this example, one should have nice clothing to change into for Shabbat—all in accord with one's means. Thus, one may be seen before the King dressed in accord with the celestial paradigm.

SECTION 7

To add to the holy by taking from the profane, [by beginning the Sabbath early].[67] In so doing one expands the boundaries of the sacred, the mystery of *Shekhinah*. One should set back the border[68] of the profane in order to curtail the rule of "another god."[69] For [on Sabbath eve], *Shekhinah* separates from the Left Side, the mystery of "the days of the week," and unites on high with her beloved [*Tif'eret,*], the one who lights up Her eyes. For this reason, Israel, Her children, begin the sanctification of Shabbat early, while it is still day.[70] One who scrupulously observes this mizṿah will be given ample reward by God in his hour of need; as he meted out, so will he be rewarded. Of this [reward] Scripture says, "I will walk in amplitude."[71] [Ps. 119:45]

We read in chapter "All Sacred Writings" (TB *Shabbat* 119a):

> R. Ḥanina robed himself and stood at sunset of Sabbath eve and said: "Come, let us go forth to welcome the Queen Sabbath." R. Yannai [put on his robes] and exclaimed: "Come, O Bride, come O Bride!"

These two holy men meant one and the same thing. For Queen Esther and the Bride in the Song of Songs both connote the Glory of the Night.[72] So it was their custom to welcome Her, to go forth to greet the Bride and usher Her in with joy.

SECTION 8

To light candles on Sabbath [eve]. This is incumbent on all women as we learned in the chapter "With What May We Kindle?"[73] According to the path of truth, souls which are [called] cosmic Candles issue from the Tabernacle of Peace and rest on those people who are worthy of them. Sabbath night [*Shekhinah*] distributes an additional-soul to each of them, for these [souls] are Her "candles."[74] To symbolize this mystery, the responsibility of lighting the Sabbath candles devolves upon the woman.[75] This [miẓvah] affords her a great privilege for through it she will merit holy sons, shining lights of Torah and piety, who will promote peace in the world.[76] Moreover, she thereby grants her husband length of days.

She must light two wicks to represent both "Remember" and "Keep."[77]

SECTION 9

The evening prayers for Shabbat.[78]

We previously mentioned that the Work of Creation was completed at twilight of the first Sabbath. But know that the evil spirits were not completed [then], for when their vital soul was created, the holy day began and God never did fashion bodies for them.[79] These evil spirits are the very ones that are mentioned in *Midrash Yelammedenu*, chapter "Bere'shit,"[80] and [their unfinished state] is esoterically referred to in the verse "The snake was *ᶜarum*, naked."[81] [Gen. 3:1]

Indeed, these spirits remained naked because of the creation of the human being. For this reason the snake was jealous of Adam and caused him to be stripped of his precious garments.[82] And should you say: Was it not possible for the Holy One to delay the arrival of the holy day until He had created bodies for those [spirits] and cloaked them?[83] In *Midrash Yelammedenu,* the Sages reply that this comes to teach us that if a person was walking along the way and had some coins in his hand or was engaged in [labor] when the holy day began, he should cast those [items] out of his hand. This he should learn from [the example of] the Holy One, blessed be He.[84]

The Holy Lamp, may peace be upon him,[85] replied that these creatures were from the aspect of Evil in the Tree of Knowledge, the mystery of the Alien Cause [*Siṭra' 'Aḥra'*]. When God saw that they wished to take root and be built up in the world—and had this happened, the world could not have survived their powerful onslaught—He gave priority to the aspect of Compassion and Holiness and began the holy day [early].[86]

Instead of the Evil Side becoming the dominant power in the world, as it intended, the Side of Holiness was built up on that night, as [additional] sacred bodies and spirits were established then. This is the inner meaning of the new souls that are added to the Holy People [on Friday night].[87] It is only proper that such a formation take place within the Aspect of Good within the Tree of Knowledge, and not in the Aspect of Evil.

When the Accuser saw that his intention was not carried to fruition, "he vanished" [Cant. 2:11], "and the city of Shushan exulted and rejoiced." [Esth. 8:15] For the face of wrath had passed away and shining face had come, and Her children were wreathed with additional-souls.[88]

To symbolize this we begin the holy day early. We enter the synagogue[89] and open with the prayer, "Bless the Lord who abounds in blessing," as was explained above.[90]

On weeknights we [first] recite the prayer, *Ve-Hu' Raḥum*: "But He, being full of compassion."[91] On this matter, Abraham ben Nathan ha-Yarḥi wrote:[92]

> Since sinners are punished with lashes between afternoon and evening, and since they recite this prayer thrice over the flogging, the Prayer-Leader proclaims: "But He, being full of compassion, forgives iniquity and destroys not. . . ."[93]

But I do not accept his rationale [for reciting the prayer] for it is an extraneous one.[94] He wrote further that:

> this is a refutation of the custom of Spain whose fashion it is to recite this prayer on Sabbaths and festivals[95]

—however, it is not fitting to recite it [then] because—

> the holy day has already arrived and a sinner may not be lashed any more.[96]
>
> But consider what was said in the Midrash:[97] "Righteousness lodged in her [Jerusalem].' [Isa. 1:21]. . . No man who lodged in Jerusalem for a full day could stay possessed of his sin. How so? The morning offering made atonement for transgressions committed at night, and the offering at dusk made atonement for transgressions committed in the daytime."
>
> The prayers were instituted to replace the daily offerings, [the morning prayer corresponding to the morning offering, and the afternoon prayer to the offering at dusk],[98] but the evening prayer has no such basis, for there was no offering at night. As it says, "In the *day* that he commanded the children of Israel to present their offerings." [Lev. 7:38]
>
> The Rabbis correlated the evening service with the limbs and fat which were not consumed before evening. Of them it is said: "This is the burnt offering: it is that which goes up on its firewood upon the altar *all night* unto the morning."[99] [Lev. 6:2] However, if they were consumed by evening, they were consumed, and [thus] there is no [firm] sacrificial basis for the evening prayer. Therefore, it is customary to say 'But He, being full of compassion,' for we have no firm sacrificial basis for the evening prayers, and so must seek atonement [by means of this prayer]. For this reason, the Spanish custom is well and good.

Thus far, the words of ha-Yarḥi.

I am astounded at this! For this prayer was established[100] to correspond to the limbs and fat that were not consumed during the daytime; and which could be brought all night. Now, if they [happened to] be consumed before evening, this did not trouble the Sages; so how can we be troubled by it and recite "But He, being full of compassion" for this reason even on Shabbat?

Rather, since the morning prayer replacing the morning offering atones for transgressions committed at night and since the afternoon prayer replacing the daily offering at dusk atones for transgressions committed during the day, as stated in the midrash which ha-Yarḥi brings in to buttress and maintain the Spanish rite, [recitation of] "But He, being full of compassion" is extraneous [as a means for atonement].[101]

But the truth of the matter is that this verse was not established to seek the welfare of the living. Rather, it was established to be said during the week to ask for mercy on those souls [of the deceased] that are judged every night by three groups of destructive angels: Mashḥit [the Destroyer], Af [Fury] and Ḥemah [Wrath] who are mentioned in this verse.[102] It contains thirteen words corresponding to the thirteen attributes of Mercy.[103] We ask God that He show mercy to the souls of his creatures for the sake of His thirteen attributes, lest the attribute of *Din* vent its wrath upon them.[104]

On the Shabbat, when *Din* departs from the world, it is forbidden to say this prayer. Indeed, it is a false plea. For on Shabbat, there is "rest, quietude and safety."[105] One who recites the prayer commits a great sin, for he causes *Din* to be aroused after it had vanished. Through his influence, the Realm of Holiness and Compassion recede into the distance. For all that is aroused below brings about a similar arousal on high, and one should not promote *Din* on the Sabbath.[106]

In the Midrash of Ruth [ZḤ (79b)] it is stated:

> Three forces rule Gehinnom under the aegis of the [angel] Dumah,[107] and they are Mashḥit, Af and Ḥemah; all the other forces are under their command. They punish the souls of the wicked. The entire company of destructive angels fill Gehinnom with a din, and their voices reach up to the firmament. The voices of the wicked are [heard] among the din, as they shriek and scream with cries of woe. But no one has mercy upon them.
>
> During the week these angels of destruction rule from the time of the evening prayer and punish those whose deeds were in the dark and who hatched [evil] thoughts on their beds. Of these people it is said: "Their deeds are in the dark, and they say 'Who sees us?' and 'Who knows us?' " [Isa. 29:15] and "Woe to them that devise[108] iniquity and design evil on their beds." [Mic. 2:1]
>
> Once begun, the [angels] continue punishing them during the day. But since the meting out of justice begins with nightfall, the [angels of destruction] are called 'Nights'. R. Alexander said: "From the dread of night' [Cant. 3:8]: From the dread of *Gehinnom* which is similar to the night."[109]
>
> Therefore, it was established that throughout the week "But He, in His compassion" be recited; because from the time of nightfall the wicked are judged by the three angels of destruction, Mashḥit, Af and Ḥemah, who are included in this verse. But when Sabbath enters, *Din* vanishes from the world and the wicked in Gehinnom rest. The angels of destruction cease ruling over them from the moment the holy day arrives. Therefore, one must not say "But He, in His compassion" on Shabbat, lest the angels of destruction be aroused.

> [Moreover], it is forbidden to recite it on Shabbat because of the honor of the King who protects the wicked on the Sabbath, and to show that *Din* has already withdrawn from the world and that these destroyers have no authority on which to act. [A parable.] There are guards that beat the sinners until the king comes to defend them. Once a servant stands before the king, if he was to threaten a sinner with a beating, would this not be a insult to the king?[110]

For this reason, as well, we do not conclude [the prayer *Hashkivenu* with the blessing] "He who protects His people Israel."[111] For it is said in the Midrash that on the Sabbath there is no need for protection, for the Sabbath itself protects;[112] and it is stated in the Jerusalem Talmud, in the first chapter of *Berakhot*:[113]

> Since the miẓvah of *ẓiẓit* does not apply at night, [the prayer] "He who protects his People Israel" should be added. R. Levi said: "This may be said during the weekdays, but on Shabbat one should say: 'He who spreads over us a *Sukkah* [Tabernacle] of Peace."[114]

This is the position of the Holy Lamp, Rabbi Shimon bar Yoḥai,[115] who added that when Israel recites the *Barekhu* [the opening blessing] on Sabbath eve, a *bat-qol* [oracular voice] goes out among the heavenly hosts and proclaims: "Happy are you, O holy People, for you offer your blessings below so that the holy camps may be blessed on high. Happy are you in this world and in the World-to-Come!" Israel should not offer this blessing until they are crowned with an extra-soul.[116]

Then, the *Qeri'at Shema*ᶜ and its benedictions are recited [as during the week] until one reaches the phrase "Save us, soon, for the sake of Your Name."[117] The benediction is completed with the words: "He who spread over us a *Sukkah* of Peace." The Sukkah of Peace is a hidden reference to the Sukkah of David [*Malkhut*] that is spread over the cosmos [on Shabbat]. It is called the Sukkah of Peace because peace is everywhere:[118] "He who spreads peace over us, over His People Israel and over Jerusalem." [Jerusalem refers to] the abode of the Sukkah of Peace. We invite Her into our midst that She might rest upon us, like a mother [bird] sheltering her fledglings.[119]

We then recite the prayer *'Attah Qiddashta* [You sanctified the seventh day]. The hidden meaning is that the seventh day [*Malkhut*] is sanctified and appointed to be wed[120] to the groom, the mystery of *Tif'eret Yisra'el*. For the woman belongs to her husband and she is off-limits to the rest of the world, and no alien forces [*Siṭra' 'Aḥra'*] can draw nourishment from Her.[121] And so, this prayer is framed in marital terms.[122]

[After the *ᶜAmidah* is completed] the prayer-leader recites *Va-Yekhullu:* "and the heaven and the earth were completed. . . ." [Gen. 2:1–3]

> Even[123] though the congregation recited it during the *ᶜAmidah* it was established that it be said a second time in a raised voice and while standing. For this prayer attests that the Holy One created heaven and earth in six days, and that on the seventh day He rested. One may only bear witness while standing, as it is said: "then both men [who are testifying] shall stand." [Dt. 19:17] And it is interpreted that "these are the witnesses" [TB Shev. 30a] means they must testify *together* and while standing.

Thus wrote R. David Abudraham, may peace be upon him; and so too, wrote R. Jacob, son of the Ro'SH.[124]

But I find this [argument] difficult to understand, for we have already recited "The Children of Israel shall keep the Sabbath. . . it shall be a sign for all time between Me and the Children of Israel. . . ." [Ex. 31:16–17] There is no testimony greater than this.[125] Moreover, we should not be concerned about standing [to bear witness] because no judgment may be rendered at night, nor evidence accepted.[126] So, this is no reason to be scrupulous about standing.[127]

[Abudraham] gave another reason [for reciting *Va-Yekhullu* after the *ᶜAmidah*]:

> When a holiday falls on Shabbat, *Va-Yekhullu* is not recited during the *ᶜAmidah* because "You have chosen us" is said in its stead. Therefore, one needs to recite *Va-Yekhullu* after the *ᶜAmidah*. On account of the Sabbaths on which it *must* be recited afterwards, it was ordained to be recited [there] every Sabbath.[128]

But neither does this explanation seem [adequate] to me. On a holiday that occurs on Shabbat could one not [simply] recite *Va-Yekhullu* [after the *ᶜAmidah*]? This [infrequent necessity] does not justify having to recite it [afterwards] throughout the year!

It seems to me that there is a [better] reason [for doing so]. *Va-Yekhullu* contains thirty-five words; one must repeat it after the *ᶜAmidah* in order to complete the quorum, which is seventy, to correspond to the seventy crowns that the Bride takes from the seven rungs above Her on this night.[129] The word *sheviᶜi*—seventh—occurs in this passage thrice—[which, when repeated] makes a total of six—a hidden allusion to the six Sabbaths below the "Mother of the Children" [*Binah*] for *Ẓaddiq* and *Ẓedeq* (the Righteous One and Righteousness) form one Shabbat.[130] Consequently, the *Va-Yekhullu* must be repeated after the *ᶜAmidah,* for all the holy rungs, the mystery of the "Work of Creation," are included in it. And for this reason, as well, it must be recited while standing: [to show that] it corresponds to the celestial world.[131]

It is said in chapter "All Sacred Writings" [TB Shab. 119b]:

> R. Hamnuna said: "He who prays on the eve of Sabbath and says *Va-Yekhullu,* Scripture considers him as though he had become a partner with the Holy One, blessed be He, in the Work of Creation, for it is said *'va-yekhullu'*: Read not *va-yekhullu*: 'they were completed,' but *va-yekhallu*: 'they completed,' meaning the Holy One and that person."

It was the Sages' intention [to show] that through this completion, wherein the holy rungs are linked and united, the [supernal] entities are gladdened. The Spirit of Knowledge and the Fear of the Lord unite, as in primordial Creation. Indeed, one who completes this becomes a partner with the Holy One in the very enterprise of Creation.[132] He who does so with the proper intention has the miẓvah within his account; through it he is forgiven and will merit life in the World-to-Come. This is indicated in that same chapter [TB Shab. Ibid.]:

> R. Ḥisdai said in the name of Mar Uqba: "He who prays on Sabbath eve and and recites *Va-Yekhullu,* the two ministering angels who accompany people place their hands on his head and say to him: 'and your iniquity is taken away, and your sin purged." [Isa. 6:7]

The prayer-leader then recites the benediction "Shield of Our Fathers" which is an embodiment of the seven blessings [in the *ᶜAmidah*]. It was instituted on account of the danger,[133] as is mentioned in the chapter "With What May We Kindle?" [TB Shab. 24b]:

> On a festival that falls on Shabbat, the prayer-leader who comes before the ark at the evening Service need not make mention of the festival

while reciting the blessing embodying the seven. It was determined that

> "Shield of Our Fathers" is not logically required even on a Sabbath, and it was the Rabbis who instituted it on account of danger.

That which they instituted has been established [for us], and that which they did not, has not been.[134]

According to the path of truth, this blessing was established to correspond to *Bat-Sheva*[c135] who is Shabbat, the Glory of the Night. She is called "the embodiment of seven" because She is the embodiment of the seven celestial spheres. For everything is in Her and She is composed of all of them. Since, on this night, there is peace everywhere[136] and division nowhere, this blessing was instituted, according Her honor. [This act of singling Her out] entails no heresy for the Community of Israel is given to the celestial Shabbat as a mate.[137] Therefore, we conclude [the prayer "Be Pleased with Our Rest"] on Sabbath night with the phrase, "And you shall rest *BaH*: in Her," to correspond to the feminine Sabbath.[138] May God lead us on the path of truth.

We read in chapter "All Sacred Writings" [TB Shab. 119b]:

> It was taught. R. Yose, son of R. Judah, said: "Two ministering angels accompany a person on Sabbath eve from the synagogue to his home, one a good [angel], and one an evil [one]. [When he returns home] and finds the candles burning and the table set and the bed covered [with a spread],[139] the good angel exclaims, 'So may it be on another Shabbat [too] and the evil angel unwillingly responds' 'Amen.' "

This teaching is clearly explained in the Midrash of R. Shimon bar Yoḥai:[140]

> When one returns home from the synagogue on Sabbath eve, he is accompanied by angels on either side, with the *Shekhinah* [arching] over all, like a mother [bird] encompassing her children. At that moment, "a thousand may fall at your side and ten thousand at your right hand; but it shall not reach you. Only with your eyes shall you see and witness the recompense of the wicked. Because you took the Lord, my Refuge, the Most High as your haven, no harm will befall you, no disease touch your tent." [Ps. 91:7][141] All this holds true when one [joyously][142] returns to his home and receives his Guest in joy.
>
> When the *Shekhinah* sees the candles burning and the angels behold the set table and when the husband and wife are filled with joy, the *Shekhinah* says: "This [household] is mine, 'O Israel, through

> you will I be glorified." [Isa. 49:3] But if [the candles are not burning, the table is not set and the husband and wife are not rejoicing], the *Shekhinah* leaves, taking the angels with Her. [In their stead] the Evil Inclination [*Siṭra' 'Aḥra'*] arrives along with its forces, and they bind themselves to the husband and wife. The [Evil Inclination] proclaims: "This [household] belongs to me and to my forces." At once, the spirit of defilement rests upon them and the *Yod* [the letter Y] withdraws from *'iYSH* [the man] and the *He'* [the letter H] leaves *'iSHaH* [the woman], and they are left as *'eSH 'eSH*: fire, fire.[143]
>
> Furthermore, their food[144] is rendered impure. Of this it is said: "Eat not the food of him that has an evil eye." [Prov. 23:6] And "their tables are covered with vomit and filth." [ff. Isa. 28:8]

Therefore, one must take care to receive Shabbat in joy, with lit candles, a set table and a bed covered [with a spread], so that one may honor the presence of the *Shekhinah*.

SECTION 10

To recite the Sanctification [*Qiddush*] over the wine. We read in *Mekhilta'* [to Ex. 20:8]:

> "Remember the Sabbath; to keep it holy": to sanctify it with a blessing. On the basis of this passage the Sages said: "At the entrance of the Sabbath we consecrate it by [reciting] the sanctification over the wine. From this I know only about the *Qiddush* for the night. Whence do we know that the day [also requires a *Qiddush*]?[145] Scripture says: 'You shall keep *'et ha-Shabbat,* the [*entire*] Sabbath.' "[146] [Ex. 31:14]

We also read in the chapter "On the Eve of Passover" [TB Pes. 106a]:

> Our Rabbis taught, "Remember the Sabbath day; to keep it holy": . . . . Remember it over wine at its inception. I know only about the [*Qiddush*] for the night; whence do we know that the day [also requires a santification]? Scripture says: "Remember the Sabbath *day*; to keep it holy."

According to the path of truth, we are obligated to sanctify [the Sabbath] over wine because when the Bride enters the bridal canopy, She must be gladdened.[147] The emanation of the holy spirit must be brought to Her from the source of Her nourishment, the mystery of the Fear of Isaac [*Gevurah*]; for therein lies the mystery of "the wine that brings joy to *'Elohim* and humankind."[148] [Judges 9:13] As it says in the chapter "How Do We Bless?" [TB Ber. 35a]:

> R. Samuel B. Naḥmani said in the name of R. Jonathan: "Where do we know that a song of praise is sung only over wine? Because it says, 'And the vine said unto them: Should I leave my wine which gives joy to God and humankind?' [Jud. 9:13] If it cheers people, how does it cheer God? From this we learn that a song of praise is sung only over wine."[149]

On this night, the Bride [*Shekhinah*] is wreathed with seventy supernal crowns and therefore, there are thirty-five words in *Va-Yekhullu* and thirty-five in ". . . Who has sanctified us through Your miẓvot and has taken pleasure in us," the [two paragraphs] that constitute the *Qiddush* recited at night.[150] [These seventy words] indicate that the [Bride] is "consecrated with the thirty-two paths of Wisdom and the three rungs of Apples."[151] In this consecration we must invoke the totality of Creation [by reciting] "Heaven and earth were completed."[152] For it contains the mystery of the thirty-two paths and the three rungs which are [represented by] the three occurrences of the word *shevi^ci* ("seventh") in the passage and the three occurences of the word *'Elohim* ("God") therein. For *'Elohim* is the hidden meaning of the entirety of Faith and [its three-fold repetition] corresponds to "the Mother of the Children [*Binah,*] the Fear of Isaac [*Gevurah*] and the Lower Court [*Shekhinah.*] So have I found it written in the Midrash of R. Shimon bar Yoḥai.[153]

Therefore, one must recite the *Qiddush* at night with unbroken concentration and extreme care. If one lacks wine, it is sufficient to make the sanctification over bread.[154] This may be done because the Bride is already secured in a position of strength and joy is found there.[155] However, [making the Sanctification over] wine is one of the choicest ways of fulfilling this miẓvah [*miẓvah min ha-muvḥar*]; it is an enhancement of the Holy Spirit.

According to the Midrash, one must recite the *Va-Yekhullu* three times on Shabbat: one time during the *^cAmidah*, a second time after it, and a third time over the cup [of wine].[156]

SECTION 11

The festive meal of Sabbath night. In the fourth Palace, which is called *Zekhut* (Merit) there presides a certain *Ḥayyah* or living creature, and under it are four seraphim who are appointed to watch over those who rejoice on the Sabbath.[157] This *Ḥayyah* and the seraphim beneath it enter that station in the Palace called *ᶜoNeG*, Delight, because [each Shabbat] festive tables are arranged there for the children of the King's Palace. Thousands upon thousands stand at their tables and this *Ḥayyah* who is above the seraphim watches over each table, observing their celebration. When it sees that those present at a [certain] table are rejoicing in honor of the Sabbath, it blesses them. The [celebrants], in turn, answer "Amen."[158]

The blessing the *Ḥayyah* offers them is: "Then shall you delight in the Lord and I will make you to ride upon the high places of the earth and I will feed you with the heritage of Jacob your father, for the mouth of the Lord has spoken."[159] [Isa. 58:14] All those present respond: "Then shall you call and the Lord will answer. You shall cry and He will say, 'Here I am." [Isa. 58:9]

But should the *Ḥayyah* see that one is not rejoicing in proper fashion, then it, the seraphim and the other celebrants force him outside and usher him into an antipodal realm, realm, into [that Palace] called *NeGaᶜ*, Harm.[160] They say:[161] "Yea, he loved cursing; may a curse come upon him. He is not delighted in blessing; may blessing be far from him. . . . May the creditor seize all his possessions, may strangers plunder his wealth. May no one show him mercy; may none pity his orphans." [Ps. 109:17, 11–12]

For rejoicing in the Sabbath is God's glory and those who partake in that joy are protected by the seraphim, who see to it that the River of Fire shall not overcome them.[162]

Therefore, one must grace [the table] with plenty and show great joy at the festive meal on Sabbath night, so as to point to the Bride, the Glory of the Night, who is filled with all good and who is encompassed by Supernal Eden.[163] To [partake of] this mystery, one should sample all the foods prepared for Shabbat, [further] alluding to the Bride who is encompassed by All. One should only take care not to detract from the festive meal during the day.[164]

We read in Tractate *Berakhot*, chapter "How Do They Bless" [39b] and in Tractate *Shabbat*, chapter "All Sacred Writings" [117b]:

> R. Abba said: "On Shabbat one is obligated to break bread [and recite the blessing] over two loaves, as it is said: 'They gathered twice as much bread." [Ex. 16:22] R. Ashi said: "I saw that R. Kahana held two [loaves] but broke bread over one."

"Twice as much bread": [the two loaves] correspond to "Remember" and "Keep."[165] I received a tradition that **"but broke bread**

over one" is a reference to the bottom loaf. R. Ṭodros ha-Levi, may his memory be for a blessing, explained this [custom] in accord with the verse: "No one can see My face, for no man shall see Me and live."[166] [Ex. 33:20]

SECTION 12

The prescribed "time" for scholars[167] [to engage in marital intercourse] is on Sabbath nights. Our Sages expounded on this matter in Tractate *Bava' Qamma'*, chapter "There Is More Frequently Occasion" [!] [TB 82a]:

> "That brings forth its fruit *in its season*" [Ps. 1:3.] . . . . This refers to the time for the scholar [to perform his marital duty]: on each Sabbath night.[168]

According to the path of truth this is [mandated] because the "Garden is locked" [Cant. 4:12] during the six days of the week, as it is said: "The gate of the inner court that faces the east shall be closed on the six working days; but on the Sabbath day and on the day of the new moon it shall be opened." [Ezek. 46:1] For the six days of Creation are garbed in the Profane Days, [those impure forces] that dwell outside the encampment.[169]

Therefore, during the week there should be no coupling, for the man is not in his house.[170] However, on the day of the Throne, the mystery of the Seventh Day, the Sabbath, unites with His mate, because at that time, the Profane Days have passed away, the days of impurity and separation are gone, and the wife is permitted to her husband. This is [truly] a veiled mystery.[171]

And so, "when a righteous man couples with his wife during the week, the child who comes forth [from that union] is one of whom it is said: *ẓaddiq ve-raᶜ lo,* a righteous person who is in adversity."[172] For the child is conceived at a time when the Evil Days reign and [the father] has made the sacred profane. But on Shabbat "the gate of the inner court" is open so as to receive the souls which She distributes to Her children.[173] Since this is the moment of coupling above, the sages engage in marital intercourse [at this time].[174]

Of them it is said: "These are words of the Lord: Concerning the eunuchs that keep my Sabbaths . . ." [Isa. 56:4] 'Eunuchs' refers to those scholars who abstain from sex during the week.[175] For the rest of the people may engage in marital intercourse daily from midnight onwards, but the scholars arise at [midnight] to immerse themselves in Torah study.[176] They proceed in this fashion until Sabbath night, which is their [appointed] time [for intercourse].[177] For then they are crowned in the mystery of the additional soul which wafts downs from its supernal source onto the Final Light [*Shekhinah*] bestowing upon it eternal rest. From there, "the soul descends and bathes in the spices of the Garden of Eden" [continuing its descent until] it rests upon those worthy sages and righteous persons[178] "'*asher yiSHMeRu*—who keep—my Sabbaths." [Isa. 56:4] [The root *SHMR*, here, is used] as in the verse, "His father *SHaMaR*, kept the matter in his heart" [Gen. 37:11], [that is, he waited].[179]

They [eagerly] await the arrival of Shabbat and prepare for the [moment of] celestial coupling. They choose [to have sexual relations] when it is the desire of their Creator[180]—during the time of celestial coupling, the union of the Bride with Her Beloved—and avoid [marital relations] during the profane working days. Rather, the scholar must "strengthen His covenant" and power, so that the Holy Essence may spread throughout the world by means of a holy seed. But this "seed of peace and truth"[181] is not of the essence of the Weekday. It is through [this proper coupling] that Israel is called "children to the Lord" [ff. Dt. 14:1], children of the living God. And it is written: "Yet I had planted you as a noble vine, altogether a seed of truth." [Jer. 2:21] The Holy One looks upon these children when Israel is amidst travail and has mercy upon them.[182]

Of the sages it is said: "Unto them will I give in My house [and within My walls a portion and a memorial better than sons and daughters; I will give them an everlasting memorial that shall not be cut off]." [Isa. 56:5] What is meant by **"in My house"?** As it is said [of Moses]: "He is trusted in all My house."[183] [Num. 12:7] And **"within Your walls?"** As it is said: "Upon your walls, O Jerusalem . . .," the mystery of the celestial Jerusalem [*Malkhut*.] **"A portion and a memorial:"** This signifies that they will bring forth holy souls from this [celestial] sphere and this "portion," in its fullness and wholeness, "is full of sons and daughters."[184] **"I will give him an everlasting memorial:"** This refers to the one who fathoms the mystery [of coupling] and knows how to concentrate on it with the proper intention.[185]

And since the true sages who are called the true scholars know these awesome mysteries, they abstain from sex and immerse themselves in Torah during the week. But on Sabbath night they diligently [engage in marital intercourse] and parallel the celestial coupling. Of these men it is said: "He said to me: 'You are My servant, Israel, in whom I will be glorified.'" [Is. 49:3]

SECTION 13

The morning prayers [*Shaḥarit*] and the Torah-reading.[186]

In the morning we enter the synagogue and recite the [preliminary] blessings and the selections on the sacrifices as we do during the week.[187] [On the Sabbath] it is forbidden to concern oneself even with the needs of the synagogue. Rather, one must engage only in songs of praise, in prayer and in words of Torah.[188] One who concerns himself with other matters profanes the holy Sabbath. And the two angels appointed over this matter place their hands on the [offender's] head and say: "Woe to so-and-so who has no portion in the God of Israel." Therefore, one must engage in songs and praises of one's Master.[189]

We open [the *Shaḥarit* service] with "Give thanks to the Lord; call upon His name."[190] The sun offers this praise as it travels its course to illumine the world. It recites this song in a lovely and sweet voice,[191] and Israel joins the sun in praise of the Holy One, as it is said: "Let them revere You together with the sun."[192] (Ps. 72:5)

You undoubtedly know that David, may peace be upon him, ordained that this praise be said daily in front of the Ark. The Levites, below, chant it in front of the Ark.[193] Even the Levites above chant [this prayer] before the Ark of the Covenant, the Master of the whole earth. For all is symbolic.[194]

[Next we recite] "For the Choir Master; a psalm of David. The heavens proclaim the glory of God; the sky declares His handiwork, etc." [Ps. 19] The heavens referred to here are the heavens of which Solomon said: "Then hear you, O heavens!" [I Kings 8:32, 34, et al.], the mystery of the Name of the Holy One, blessed be He [*Tiferet*.] The text says *meSaPpeRim* (proclaim). But [here] it should be read "illumine,"[195] for the heavens receive this light and splendid radiance from the luminaries so that they [i.e., the heavens] may give light to all that lies below.

With this light the Moon shines forth;[196] it is wreathed with fifty Gates in the likeness of the celestial Mother [*Binah*]. This is expressed [in the verse]: "The Lord's Torah is perfect, refreshing the soul." [Ps. 19:8] *Torah* refers to the Oral Torah [*Shekhinah*] which is complete, encompassed by the mystery of the five lights above Her which comprise the fifty [gates].[197] Therefore, each [of the six] phrases [in verses 8–10] contains five words. One may find six citations [of God's name, therein] to correspond to the Six Points, that constitute the mystery of the Great Name.[198]

On the Sabbath day the Moon is full, completed in the mystery of the supernal wholeness. Therefore it was established that this praise be recited on the Sabbath.

Afterwards we say: "Rejoice in YHWH, you righteous."[199] [Ps. 33] The heavens receive [the supernal light] first and illumine the other rungs [below]. Through this [process] the Righteous One receives the light, which it, in turn, conveys to the conveys to the Moon, enabling Her to be illumined by the Sun, [as well].[200]

This is [alluded to in]: "A song of David, when he changed his demeanor before Avimelekh, and he [David] drove him away and departed."[201] [Ps. 34] For [*Shekhinah*] separated Herself from the dross of the gold[202] to unite with Her beloved. This is what is meant by "drove him away." This song of praise is arranged [alphabetically], composed of the twenty-two letters that the Sun emanated into the Moon.[203] The Oral Torah is encompassed by the Written Torah once it has separated itself from the dross. This song of praise contains Her separation from the dross and the union with Her beloved,[204] and this is [the meaning of]:

"A prayer of Moses, the man of *'Elohim*." [Ps. 90:1] ["Man" here means husband], as it is said: "The man of Naomi" [Ruth 1:3]. For the lover spreads out both his right hand and his left to receive her, as in the verse, "His left hand was beneath my head and with his right hand he embraced me."[205] [Cant. 2:6] And now, that they are face-to-face, "man" and "wife," the supernal Mother [*Binah*] showers them with *No^caM*, the pleasing radiance of Her blessings. Then the blessings rests on this perfect entity. This is stated [in the verse]:"May your *No^caM*, Lord our God, rest on us" [Ps. 90:17], which is a hidden reference to the supernal radiance which comes from *Na^coMi*.[206]

It is our custom to [then] recite the Song against Demons, which will be explained, with God's help, in the liturgy of Sabbath's departure.[207]

Afterwards, we recite: "A Psalm. O sing unto the Lord a new song . . ." [Ps. 98] It is written, "And the kine *YeSHaRna:* took the straight way, by the way of Bet-Shemesh."[208] [I Sam. 6:12] Our Sages of blessed memory interpreted: This text teaches us that "the kine *'ameru SHiRaH,* rendered song. . . and what song did they sing. . .? 'A Psalm. O sing unto the Lord a new song.' "[209]

According to the path of truth, the Sages alluded to the mystery of the *Ḥayyot*, the Holy Living Creatures, who bore aloft the Throne.[210] You undoubtedly know that the twelve cattle are the cows of the Bashan who issued from a perfect red heifer. They lie under the Sea of Bronze, three in each direction. As they bear aloft the Ark of the Covenant [*Shekhinah*] and join with the one who is above, they chant this song of praise.[211]

The reason the Psalm speaks of a "new" song, even though it is constant, is that it is a hidden reference to the New Moon which chants this song as it is illumined by the Sun.[212] It is renewed "as the eagle [renews] its youth" [Ps. 103:5] and this is the inner meaning of a new [song].[213]

[The verse continues:] "His right hand, His holy arm, has brought it salvation." [Ps. 98:1] This refers to the arousal of the right and left hands to receive the Ark just as its bearers raise it aloft to Bet-Shemesh, a veiled reference to the "Lord [of hosts] who is sun and shield."[214] Because the Sabbath contains the mystery of the rising of the moon and its union with the sun, the [Sages] established that this song of praise be recited on the Sabbath.[215]

There are communities where it is customary to add four more songs at this point. They are: "I lift my eyes to You" up through "Had not the Lord been on our side." [Psalms 121–24] This is their hidden meaning:

"I lift my eyes to the mountains; whence will my help come?": This song of praise is anonymous. It is the song of the Bride to the rungs above Her. She chants this song sweetly: "I lift my eyes to the mountains." You [undoubtedly] already know the teaching of the Sages: "The mountains are the Patriarchs" for Her longing is for them.[216] "*Me-'ayin* [from where] will my help come?" [*Me-'ayin*] is a veiled reference to [*Keter*, as in] "Wisdom will come from *'Ayin*."[217] [Job 28:20]

In this song of praise the root *SH-M-R* [guard] is mentioned six times,[218] corresponding to the six Points that esoterically represent the Great Name. For on the Sabbath, [*Shekhinah*] is united above in the mystery of the Patriarchs, and the World of Compassion[219] showers them with an abundance of divine blessings from above. Through this, [*Shekhinah*] is protected from all evil, for She is encompased on all sides. [Indeed],"the uncircumcized and unclean [*Siṭra' 'Aḥra'*] shall not come into Her" [ff. Isa. 52:1], for the profane days have passed and the holy day has arrived.[220]

"A song of ascent by David. I was glad when they said to me, 'Let us go to the house of the Lord." [Ps. 122] David, may peace be upon him, recited this song of praise about his kingdom. Therefore, he said, "Jerusalem that is built like a city joined together."[221] [Ibid.:3] And in chapter one of Tractate *Ta^canit* [5a], "He replied. . . Is there a heavenly Jerusalem? Yes, for it is written: 'Jerusalem that is built like a city joined together."

"For the tribes of the Lord [YaH] ascended there."[222] [Ibid.:4] They are the mystery of "the twelve springs of water" [Ex. 15:27] that issue forth from the Spring of Justice, and corresponding to them below are the twelve cattle.[223]

"There, indeed, were set the Thrones of Justice and the Thrones of the House of David."[224] [Ps. 122:5] For all is in union: "And Righteousness and Peace—*Ẓedeq ve-Shalom*—kissed" [Ps. 85:11] and then "there is peace within your walls."[225] [Ps. 122:7] [Peace] refers to the Righteous One—the *Ẓaddiq*—who is called *Ṭov*, "good." "I seek your good" [Ibid.:9], as it is said, "Shall I not seek rest for you?"[226] [Ruth 3:1] Since there is peace everywhere,[227] we recite the following song of praise:

"A song of ascent. To You I lift my eyes, [You who dwell in the Heavens]." [Ps. 123] This song, too, is anonymous. It corresponds to the [relationship between] the Bride and Israel. Israel below offers this praise to the one "who dwells in the heavens."[228] For the Ark has been borne aloft to Bet-Shemesh, the house of the sun, and all is in unity on the Sabbath.

Therefore, we ask the Lord our God that He "have compassion on us" [Ibid.:4] for "we are full-sated with contempt" [Ibid.] for those who say "Where. . .is your God [*'Elohim*]? Our God [*Malkhut*] is in the heavens [*Tif'eret*]!" [Ps. 115:2–3]

"A song of Ascent by David. Had not the Lord been on our side, says Israel, [. . .they would have swallowed us alive when their anger blazed forth against us.]" [Ps. 124] David recited this song of praise referring to the future Redemption; for at that time Israel will thank and praise God, saying "Had not the Lord been on our side"—in the Exile—"when the man[229] rose up against us" [Ibid.:2], that is, *'Adam ha-Beliyya^cal*, the Wicked Man[230] and his nation. They are "the insolent waters"[231] mentioned later [Ibid.:5].

At that [future] time, [Israel] will extol [God]: "Blessed be the Lord, who did not give us as prey to their *SHiNaYiM*: teeth." [Ibid.:6] It is written: *SHiNaYiM*, [meaning, to those two].[232] "Our souls are like a bird escaped from a fowler's snare, the snare is broken and we have escaped." [Ibid. :7] Solomon referred to the [pre-Messianic situation], saying: "While one man"—that is, *'Adam ha-Beliyya^cal*—"still had authority over other men to do them evil" [Eccles. 8:9];

"Over other men": that is, over Israel [who are called "men"][233] as in the verse, "For you, My flock, flock that I tend, are men."[234] [Ezek. 34:31]

But in that [future time] Scripture will be fulfilled, as it is written: "He will swallow up death forever."[235] [Isa. 25:8] And so too: " 'Therefore will I give *'aDaM:* a man for you.' [Ibid. 43:4] Read not *'aDaM* [a man] but *'eDoM* [Sammael]."[236]

Since the Sabbath is a symbol of that [future] world, we recite this song of praise on Sabbath. People will offer this praise in the World-to-Come, "a world that is entirely Shabbat" [Mekh. "Beshallaḥ"], as they go forth from the darkness of Exile and the rule of strangers, and behold the light of the Living. And so it is said: "Had not the Lord been on our side when the Man rose up against us" [Ps. 124:2] and "the insolent waters" [Ibid.:5] that sought to banish us from the Great Light.[237] "Blessed be the Lord, who did not give us as a prey to those two; We are like a bird escaped from a fowler's snare, etc." [Ibid.:6–7] This is indeed a veiled mystery. Since this song of praise is to be recited in the World-to-Come, we say it on the Sabbath as well, for [the Sabbath] is the symbol of the World-to-Come. This [psalm] also contains an allusion to the Bride, the Community of Israel. For when the holy day arrives on Sabbath eve, She escapes from those that beset Her. She leaves their domain and enters the domain of holiness.[238]

Thereafter we recite [Psalm 135 which begins] "Halleluyah": i.e., Praise *YaH*. For this word contains both praise [*hallel*] and the [supernal] Name.[239] This phrase is a hidden one, anonymous,[240] but [thereafter] we say "Praise the name of the Lord" referring to the Great Name; and it is [specified that] "the servants of YHWH" [Ps. 135:2] who know this mystery are the ones "who praise Him." [Ibid.] They are the ones who "stand in the House of the Lord" [Ibid.],[241] as it is said: "That one is trusted in my House" [Num. 12:7] "and in the courtyards" [Ps. 135:2] of that house, as it is said: "Happy is the one You choose and bring near; that he may dwell in Your courtyards." [Ps. 65:5]

On the Sabbath day all Israel are like holy ministering angels; their only concern is the praise and exaltation of their Creator.[242] For God has chosen them and has bestowed upon them this day which is God's prized possession, hidden within his Treasury. Thus Scripture says: "Surely the Lord has chosen Jacob to be His, and Israel as His prized possession." [Ps. 135:4] And it is stated in Tractate *Beiẓah*, chapter two [16a]:

> That you may know that I am the Lord who sanctifies you" [Ex. 31:13]: The Holy One, blessed be He, said unto Moses: "Moses, I have a precious gift in My Treasury, and its name is Sabbath, and I wish to give it to Israel. Go and tell them."

This teaching is also presented in Tractate *Shabbat,* chapter one [10b].

Most assuredly, the Sabbath is a precious gift for it is a foreshadowing of the World-to-Come, hidden in God's supernal Treasury [*Binah*]. No [other] nation or tongue has a portion in it, for the [Sabbath] is "between Me and the Children of Israel."[243] [Ex. 31:17]

For this reason, we recite this praise on Shabbat. We also do so because it invokes the essence of *Maᶜaseh Bere'shit* which is *ḥiddush:* Creation *ex nihilo.*[244] The signs and wonders that the Holy One wrought in Egypt attest to the creation of the world as well.[245] The Sabbath teaches us all this.[246]

[As stated in this Psalm,] God banished the seven [Canaanite] nations and gave His treasured people their land as a heritage.[247] This teaches us of God's providence and power. Now, the maintenance of the Land[248] depends on the observance of the Sabbath; as it says in chapter "All Sacred Writings" [TB Shab. 119b]:

> Abbaye said: "Jerusalem would not have been destroyed had Israel not profaned the Sabbath in it."

For the profanation of the Sabbath causes the destruction of celestial Jerusalem [*Malkhut*] and through this [process] earthly Jerusalem was destroyed.[249]

This song of praise contains hope for the future, as it is said: "O Lord, Your name endures forever; Your repute, O Lord, through all generations." [Ps. 135:13] For the name and repute that He acquired of old when He wrought His wonders in Egypt and when He led his treasured people out from [that land]—this very name and repute He will acquire in the future world. So Scripture says: "For the Lord will champion His people, and have compassion on His servants" [Ibid.:14] as of old. The underlying reason is that "The idols of the nations are silver and gold, the work of human hands . . ." [Ibid.:15ff.], but such is not the case for Israel. Rather, they "cleave to the Lord their God" while "He will make a full end of these nations."[250]

"Give thanks to the Lord, for He is good." [Ps. 136] This psalm is comprised of 26 verses of thanksgiving to the Great Name [YHWH] which is numerically equivalent to 26.[251] Thus, it was called the

Great Hallel in the teachings of our Sages[252] for "the Lord is great and much praised." [Ps. 96:4, et al.]

The [Great Hallel] alludes to the celestial Sabbath [*Binah*] and so we recite it on Shabbat. Through this song of praise we recall the Creation of the World and the Exodus from Egypt that attests to that Creation.[253] The Sabbath teaches us of all this, as we mentioned [above].

Thereafter, this [psalm] recalls the inheritance of the land[254] [whose meaning] we explained previously. At this point we recite "Who took note of us in our degradation." [Ps. 136:23] Perhaps, this is an allusion to the Second Redemption.[255] In saying "He rescued us from our enemies" [Ibid. :24] the [psalm also] alludes to the Future Redemption. Concerning that era, it continues: "He gives food to all creatures." [Ibid.:25]. This [food] is the intimate knowledge of the Lord, as it is written: "For then I will make the peoples pure of speech, that they may call upon the name of the Lord and serve Him with one accord."[256] [Zeph. 3:9] In this spirit the [psalm] proceeds: "Give thanks to the God of heaven"[257] [Ps. 136:26] which is an allusion to the World-to-Come, after the Resurrection. For then, all [of Creation] will return to its [primordial] Sheath, and "the Lord alone shall be exalted on that day."[258] [Isa. 2:11, 17] This is the "cosmos that is entirely Shabbat; rest in life everlasting."[259]

Thus it is said: "Give thanks to God in heaven," meaning the sublime and lofty God. Since the Sabbath intimates this [future] cosmos, we recite this song of praise on Shabbat.[260]

We then recite "Blessed be He who spoke and the world came into being" through [the closing phrase] "Extolled with hymns of praise,"[261] and thereafter recite "A Psalm; a song of the Sabbath day." [Ps. 92]

It is written in *Pirqei de-Rabbi 'Eli^c^ezer,* chapter 19:

> The Sabbath entered and became the defending attorney for Adam. . . .Through the merit of the Sabbath, Adam was saved from the rigors of Gehinnom [Hell]. When Adam saw the power of the Sabbath, he began to chant a hymn to the Sabbath: "A Psalm for[262] the Sabbath day." The Sabbath said to him: "Why are you chanting a hymn to me? Let us both chant a hymn to the Holy One, blessed be He," as it is said: 'It is good to give thanks to the Lord.' "[263] [Ps. 92:2]

It was the [Sages'] intent [to indicate] that this praise is offered by the Bride in the Song of Songs who is called "Shabbat" to "the

King whose is the peace."[264] This is what is meant by [the prayer] "The seventh day itself offers praise, saying: 'A psalm; a song of[265] the Sabbath day.' "

And in the Midrash,[266]

> R. Judah said: "No praise and acclaim before the Holy One, blessed be He, can compare with that of the Sabbath.[267] Those above and those below praise Him as one; even the Sabbath day actually offers Him praise, as it is written: 'A psalm; a song of the Sabbath.' "

Thus far, [the Midrash].

Therefore, the psalm is presented anonymously, without mentioning its author, as in [the Biblical verses]: "And ____ spoke unto Moses" and "____ called unto Moses."[268] In the chapter "If the Festive Day of New Year Fell on the Sabbath" [TB RH 31a] [it is written]:

> On the seventh day what did they say? "A psalm; a song for the Sabbath day": for a day that is entirely Sabbath, a day of rest everlasting.[269]

This is a veiled mystery to which we have alluded previously.[270]

We then read the songs of praise until *Yishtabbaḥ:* "Praised be Your Name forever" and recite *Nishmat Kol Ḥai:* "The soul of every living being [shall bless Your Name]." This is a hidden reference to the souls which sail forth from the Eternal Life [*Yesod*] and which bless the honored Name [*Shekhinah*] below. [Meanwhile] the [earthly] *ẓaddiq* blesses [the Name] above. Thus, the Bride is encompassed in the mystery of the supernal *Ẓaddiq* and that of the lower *ẓaddiq* who is crowned with an extra soul.[271]

During the week, [*Shekhinah*] is blessed by the souls below, but on the Sabbath, She is [also] blessed by those souls that come forth from the Eternal Life. Thus, She is encompassed by All.[272] We bless her with *MaH:* with the 45 words [that constitute the first paragraph of this prayer],[273] and they are:[274]

> The soul of every living being shall bless Your name, Lord our God; the spirit of all mortals shall ever glorify and extol Your fame, our King. From eternity to eternity You are God. Besides You we have no King who redeems and saves, ransoms and rescues in all times of woe and stress. We have no King but You. To You alone we give thanks.

Thus, there are MaH: 45 words [here] and MaH in the [numerology called] *'aT-BaSH* is *YeẒ*, whose numerical value is 100,[275] the [number] that represents the entirety of the [supernal] rungs.[276]

[In the second paragraph], from "Were our mouths filled with song" until "Of yore [You did deliver us]," there are *MiY*—50—words corresponding to the Primordial Sea [*YaM*], a hidden reference to the 50 Gates of *Binah*.[277] It reads:

> Were our mouth filled with songs as the sea [is with water], and our tongue with ringing praise as the roaring waves; were our lips full of adoration as the wide expanse of heaven; and our eyes sparkling like the sun or the moon; were our hands spread out in prayer as the eagles of the sky, and our feet as swift as the deer—we should still be unable to thank You and bless Your name, Lord our God, for one-thousandth of the countless millions of favors, miracles and wonders, which You have conferred on us and on our ancestors.

[The prayer] concludes with another praise composed of 100 words which represent the entirety of the ten rungs;[278] they are:

> Of yore, You did deliver us from Egypt, Lord our God, and redeem us from slavery. You have nourished us in famine and provided us with plenty. You have rescued us from the sword, made us escape the plague, and freed us from severe diseases. Until now Your mercy has helped us, and Your kindness has not abandoned us.
>
> Therefore, the limbs which You have apportioned in us, the breath and spirit which You have breathed into our nostrils, and the tongue which You have placed in our mouth, shall ever thank and bless, praise and glorify Your name, our King. Indeed, every mouth shall praise You; every tongue shall vow allegiance to You; every eye shall look hopefully to You; every knee shall bend to You; every one shall worship You alone. [All] hearts shall revere You, and People's innermost being shall sing Your name, as it is said: "All my being shall say: O Lord, who is like You? You save the poor person from one that is stronger, the poor and needy from one who would rob him." [Ps. 35:10] You hear the cry of the oppressed; You pay heed to the cry of the poor and bring deliverance.

The remaining words [until *Yishtabbaḥ*] form the likeness of the Chariot, [a throne] for the rungs mentioned above. This is the opinion of R. Shimon bar Yoḥai, may peace be upon him; for this reason I have enumerated the words [of this prayer].[279]

At this point, the prayer leader rises and recites the portion of the service containing the *Shema*ᶜ:[280] "[Blessed are You, Lord our God. . .] who forms light and creates darkness [who makes peace and creates all things]." The text of this section is lengthier [during the Sabbath] than during the week, as the [weekday recitation] is a restitution of the lower world, while the [Sabbath prayer] is a restoration of the upper world.[281] [Indeed], it is a song of praise directed to the supernal rung, the mystery of the sun that gives light to all.[282] And this is "Who forms light": the hidden meaning of the luminary through which the Chariots, the stars and constellations, and all the cosmic forces are illumined and maintained.[283]

[We then recite] *'El 'Adon:* "God is the Lord of all Creation."[284] This song of praise is an acrostic, written with a large interval between each [successive] letter to show that [this hymn] corresponds to that world where all souls exist in amplitude, namely, the World of Souls which is called the Great Sabbath [*Binah*].[285]

The [verses containing] the first two letters each contain five words, parallel to the fifty Gates of *Binah*, while the [verses containing] the final two letters each contain six words, parallel to the Six Entities that emanated from the Mother of the Cosmos.[286] The [verses containing] the intervening letters all contain four words, corresponding to the Chariot, the Chariot of "the One who rides in the ancient highest heavens."[287] [Ps. 68:34] In the [verses containing] the first two and final two letters there are twenty-two Great Letters, the mystery of the Great Alphabet that corresponds to the first *He'* [in God's name, *Binah*].[288] In [the eighteen] intervening verses[289] there are seventy-two letters[290] with which the Holy One [*Tif'eret*] crowns Himself. And it is with this [Name] that the Crown of Solomon [*Shekhinah*] is wreathed.[291] One who properly attends [to this prayer] merits to praise Him in the World-to-Come.

The Holy Lamp, R. Shimon bar Yoḥai, said that when this praise ascends on high, sixty chariots take it and bear it aloft as a crown for the many [supernal] lights.[292] The righteous ones in the Garden of Eden are wreathed with this praise and they [too][293] ascend [with it] to the Throne of Glory [*Shekhinah*]. There all remains until the *Qedushah* [Sanctus] of *Musaf* is recited.[294] At that point all these lights and souls rise up to be nourished by the supernal splendor; and so, this prayer [*'El 'Adon*] is considered great and lovely on high.[295]

[We then complete] the prayer "Creator [of lights]" and [recite the first three blessings of the ᶜ*Amidah*:]: The Patriarchs, the Acts of Might, and the *Qedushot*.[296] We [then] recite the Sanctification of the

Day, the middle blessing [of the *ᶜAmidah*].[297] This [passage] corresponds to the mystery of the holy Palace of Light, which is situated in the middle.[298]

The hidden meaning of "Moses rejoiced": This [prayer refers to] the joy experienced by that rung which is the essence of the Patriarchs, the Written Torah [*Tif'eret*], when "its gift"[299]—the Oral Torah—"is bestowed upon it." The two Lovers "sweeten" the mystery of "the two stone tablets"[300] "upon which was engraved the command to observe the Sabbath."

"[The Sabbath] is a sign between Me and the Children of Israel:"[301] so that no stranger may interfere in their midst for strangers have no portion in it whatsoever. For it is entirely holy unto the Lord. Therefore, it was established that we recite: "You, Lord our God, have not given the Sabbath day to the nations of the world." For neither the nations below nor their [cosmic] powers above have a portion in the sanctity of the Sabbath. And so it was said in Tractate *Beiẓah*, chapter "A Festival Day" [16a]:

> R. Shimon Bar Yoḥai said:[302] "Every miẓvah which the Holy One, blessed be He, gave unto Israel, He gave to them publicly, except the Sabbath which He bestowed upon them in privacy, as it is said: '[It is a sign] between Me and the Children of Israel.'"[303] [Ex. 31:17]

Know that for this reason a sin-offering of a goat is not required [on the Sabbath] as it is on the other festivals. It is not needed for the Community of Israel is given as a partner to the Sabbath and peace is everywhere. Neither Satan nor demonic forces are to be found.[304] But since it is a time for lovers, a time of grace,[305] we [may] approach God on our own behalf and recite: "O God and God of our fathers, be pleased with our rest."[306] [We then say] "We ever thank You" and "Grant us peace." Thus, the [*ᶜAmidah*] contains seven blessings in all, corresponding to the Cosmic Days.[307]

Thereafter, as the Torah-scroll is removed [from the Ark,] the prayer-leader recites "Unto you it was shown, that you might know [that the Lord alone is God; there is none else besides Him.]" [Dt. 4:35] For this verse refers to the receiving of the Torah, and the Torah was given on the Sabbath.[308] This [passage] contains eight verses, [the first seven] corresponding to the seven *qolot* with which the Torah was given and the seven men who ascend to read [each Sabbath] and the seven days of Creation, while the eighth verse corresponds to the concluding portion, the *mafṭir*.[309] These verses are [excerpted from] the Torah, the Prophets, and the Writings, for all is in complete union on the Sabbath. The passage opens with [a verse from] the Torah, continues with [a verse from] the Writings and thereafter, with one from the Prophets to show how the Bride is guarded by all.[310] She is properly positioned, as it is written, "And I Myself, declares YHWH, will be a wall of fire around it, and I will be a glory inside it."[311] [Zech. 2:9]

The esoteric meaning of the verse [Dt. 4:35] is as follows: When Israel received the Torah, they were shown, and came to know, that "the Lord [YHWH] alone is God [*'Elohim*]," that these two divine Names [*Tif'eret* and *Shekhinah*] form one inseparable unity. They are the hidden meaning of the Written and Oral Torah which Israel received. When Israel takes heed of the Torah, they unify these two Names. While standing upon Mount Sinai, they saw this and grasped this truth, for so it is said: "Face to face the Lord spoke to you on the mountain out of the fire." [Dt. 5:4] From this they knew that "there is none else besides Him." Furthermore, this verse [Dt. 4:35] contains ten words, corresponding to the Decalogue and to the ten divine utterances that are contained in the two Names mentioned here.[312]

The Torah-scroll is then taken out [from the Ark]. It is a symbol of the supernal [Torah] and so, its holiness is of the highest degree. [The text] is not vocalized, nor is it written with accentuation or Masoretic notes, although all was transmitted to Moses at Sinai. As our Rabbis of blessed memory said in the first chapter of TB *Megillah* [3a]: "What is meant by the text, 'And they read in the book, in the Torah of God, with an interpretation. . .' [Neh. 8:8], etc."[313]

There is a reason [for having an unpointed text]: When the Bride is joined with Her beloved, the mystery of the Written Torah, all the accentuations and Masoretic notes are recorded *in Her*. She is impregnated with them, through the mystery of the Written Torah, as a woman is impregnated by the male. This shows that the Oral Torah is blessed through the Written Torah: For the latter emanates all those accentuations and Masoretic notes, symbols of the supernal entities, into the Oral Torah. Through them, the Oral Torah is sanctified.[314] Thus, it is customary to show the entire congregation the Torah-script which contains only the letters in their holiness. The proof for this may be found in Scripture: "Cursed be he who will not uphold—that is, hold up—the words of this Torah and observe them" [Dt. 27:26], so that the people may take unto their hearts the faith of Israel.[315]

Seven portions are read, parallel to the seven days of Creation and to the seven *qolot* with which the Torah was given.[316] A Kohen reads first for he is [at] the head; a Levite follows and thereafter, a Yisrael.[317] The sixth reader represents the [supernal] *Ẓaddiq*. He must be a worthy person of whom it may be said: "The name of the Lord is a tower of strength, the *ẓaddiq* runs [*yaRUẒ*] in it and is set up on high." [Prv. 8:10] "In it" refers to the Torah-scroll, whose words this *ẓaddiq yaRUẒ*: recites fluently![318] He is "set up on high," sheltered from the fear of the Angel of Death, so that his days may be lengthened and he never know harm.[319]

The one who completes the portion receives a reward equal to that of all who preceded him, for he [is a symbol of] the Bride who completes the quorum and Herself receives a reward comprising all that lies above Her, "for all streams flow into the Sea."[320] [Eccles. 1:7]

We read in [Tractate] *Soṭah*, chapter "The Following May be Recited" [39a]:

> When the Torah-scroll is unrolled, it is forbidden to converse even on matters concerning the law, as it is said, "And when he opened it, all the people stood up."[321] [Neh. 8:5] [And standing up] signifies nothing other than silence, as it is said, "And I wait because they speak not, because they stand still and answer no more." [Job 32:16]

There is a reason [why conversation is forbidden]: When the Torah was given, there was but one Speech and one Speaker, as it is said: "God spoke all these words, saying" [Ex. 20:1], He being above and the people below, as it is said: And they stood at the foot of the mountain."[322] [Ex. 19:17] Should there be heard more than one voice during the Torah reading, it would be a lessening of the mystery of Faith and of the glory of the Torah.[323]

The reader must direct his heart to that which he says and must maintain an awareness that he is the intermediary[324] between Israel and their Father in Heaven. Thus, he must prepare the portion beforehand. We learn of this from God's Speech [at Sinai]. Before He spoke to the people, Scripture says: "Then did He see it and declare it; He prepared it, yea, and searched it out." [Job 28:27] Only afterwards does it say: "And He spoke unto man."[325] [Ibid. :28]

It is forbidden for the reader to break off anywhere save where Moses indicated a pause. Neither may he conflate next week's portion with this week's, for the Holy One, blessed be He, apportions each Lesson, saying, "You [are read] on Sabbath X, and you, on Sabbath Y." He appoints [the angel] Yofiel and the fifty-three holy Chariots under his charge to minister to the secrets of Torah.[326] Each Chariot is [assigned] to its own Sabbath and ministers to that week's Lesson. It is forbidden to confound the weekly portions, disarranging so much as a word or letter, thereby causing the Chariots to overlap. Rather, each [Lesson should be read] within the limits set by the Holy One; each [Chariot] will stand guard over its appointed Lesson, as determined by Him.

When Israel completes the portion below, the words ascend. They are gathered up by their appointed Chariot which lifts them up before the Holy One, blessed be He. The words stand before Him and form a crown for the Throne of Glory [*Shekhinah*]. With this [crown] the Bride ascends to join [the rungs] above and all becomes one totality. And so, happy is the one who completes his weekly portion in the proper manner, in accordance with the divisions fixed on high.[327]

Thereafter, the [Lesson] is completed through reading [a selection] from the Prophets, for [the Hafṭarah] reflects the Torah portion,[328] even as the Bride reflects the Written Torah: Everything is included in Her. [Through reading the Hafṭarah] honor is bestowed upon *Malkhut*.[329]

At this point, the Torah is returned [to the Ark]. As this is being done, it is customary to recite "A Psalm of David. Ascribe unto the Lord, O heavenly beings" [Ps. 29], for it contains seven *qolot*, "Voices." It is customarily recited on the Sabbath, for on that day the seven entities, the mystery of the seven Voices, become one.[330]

[This psalm] contains eighteen citations of the Divine Name, by means of which the Holy One "courses through 18,000 worlds." As it is said:

> "The chariots of God are myriads [*ribbotayim*], thousands [*'alfei*] *SHiN'aN*." [Ps. 68:18] [Do not read *SHiN'aN*, but *SHe'eiNaN*: that are not.][331]

The inner meaning of these worlds will be clear to the enlightened person who merits such knowledge.[332]

Thereafter, we add "Lift up your heads, O Gates." [Ps. 24:7] Solomon recited this when he brought the Ark into the Holy of Holies,[333] thereby symbolizing the supernal process. For the Sabbath is the time of returning the supernal Torah into the mystery of the Ark, into the Treasury of the Holy One.

Then the celestial Living Creatures who are called by the name of *YHWH*[334] exclaim, "Lift up your heads, O Gates, [up high, everlasting Doors]" so that "the King of glory may come in" [Ibid.] to his Palace [*Binah.*]

Thus, we recite this psalm as we place the Torah in its Palace. This teaches us further of the reabsorption of the Holy [into its primal Source] and ascension of the Glory, as it rises from height to height unto the place from which it unfolded, unto a "world that is entirely Shabbat."[335] This is a veiled teaching.[336]

***Musaf,* the Additional prayer,** corresponds to the pillar upon which the world rests,[337] the mystery of *Zakhor,* "Remember." [The prayer] "Remember and Keep" is recited, corresponding to the two Sabbaths that are united in the Additional Service.[338] For the *Musaf* contains an additional portion [*tosefet*] of the holy spirit.

During the reader's repetition of the Prayer, we recite the *Qedushah Rabbah,* [**"A Crown of Glory, Lord our God, is given You"**]; for as our Rabbis of blessed memory have long expounded, all the prayers are formed into a crown [to adorn] the head of the Holy One, blessed be He.[339] According to the path of truth, this crown esoterically refers to the source of the [divine] essences [*Keter,*] with which the "Lord our God," the letters Y[*od*] H[*e'*] in the divine Name, crown the Middle Column. Thus wrote R. Shimon bar Yoḥai, may peace be upon him.[340]

"The countless angels on high together with Your People Israel assembled beneath": All offer praise, those above and those below. As this praise, offered **"in unison,"** ascends on high, there is an awakening: "The fine oil" descends "upon the head" [Ps. 132:2] and from there onto the remaining "aspects" [Ibid.] and the divine Glory is perfected on all sides.[341]

[The prayer continues:] **"Holy, holy, holy"** [Isa. 6:3]: corresponding to the three Patriarchs. **"The Lord of hosts"** [Ibid.]: referring to the *Ẓaddiq* of the Cosmos together with the "Disciples of the Lord" called Hosts. **"The entire earth ['areẓ] is filled [with His Glory]"** [Ibid.]: That is, *'Ereẓ Yisra'el,* the Land of Israel, is filled with the Lord's Glory, as it is written: "And the land was lit up by His glory."[342] [Ezek. 43:2]

"His glory fills the cosmos; His ministering angels ask one another, 'Where ['aYeH] is the Place of His Glory?" The Place from which the Glory emanates is [called] *'aYeH* by those who understand.[343] The Glory ascends from height to height unto its home on high, where it is brought into union.[344] **["The angels] respond with praise and say: 'Blessed be the Glory of the Lord from His Place."** [Ezek. 3:12]

In the Midrash of R. Neḥunya ben ha-Qanah (*Bahir* 130–32) [it is written]:

And what is the meaning of "the entire earth is filled with His Glory"? This is the earth that was created on the first day [*Shekhinah*]. It is a supernal [realm], filled with the Glory of God's Name; it parallels the Land of Israel [below]. What is [this Glory]? It is Wisdom, as it is written: "The wise shall inherit the Glory." [Prv. 3:35] It is also said: "Blessed be the Glory of the Lord from His Place."[345] [Ezek. 3:12]

What is "the Glory of the Lord"? To what may this be compared? To a king who had a lady in his chamber in whom all his hosts delighted. He had sons who came daily to behold the king and bless him. They asked him: "Where is our mother?" He replied: "You cannot see her now." They said: "Let her be blessed wherever she might be."[346]

And why is it written "from His Place"? Because "there is no one who knows His Place." [Ḥag. 13b] A parable. There once was a princess who came from a distant place. No one knew whence she came, but it was seen that she was a woman of valor, lovely and refined in all her ways. So they said: "Surely, this one is taken from the Realm of Light, for through her deeds she illumines the world." They asked her: "From where do you come?" She replied: "From my place." They said: "If so, the people from her place are great. Blessed be she! And may she be blessed from her place!"[347]

"From[348] His Place may He turn with compassion to His People." So too, if we lift up the Divine Glory to its home on high, compassion will well up in fullness there and love will be bestowed upon those children who cleave to Him.[349]

In the Midrash of R. Shimon bar Yoḥai [it is written]:[350]

"But You, O Lord, be not far off." [Ps. 22:20] "You" esoterically refers to the union of the Bride with Her Lover.[351] Thereafter, they are bound above with *'Ein Sof*, and so [it is said]: "be not far off": do not abandon us. As it is said: "The Lord has appeared to me from afar [*me-RaḤoQ*]." [Jer. 31:3][352] But through the mystery of this prayer the [Bride's] children are included with Her; they do not let Her grow distant.[353]

"My Gazelle, [hasten to my aid]" [Ps. 22:20]: A gazelle or a hart may traverse great distances, yet soon it returns to the place it left. So too, with the Holy One, blessed be He. Even as he ascends to *'Ein Sof* on high, He soon returns to His place for the sake of Israel. For they cleave to Him and do not let Him go too far from them. Thus [it is said]: "My Gazelle, hasten to my aid."[354]

Now it is the time to pray for compassion.[355] Indeed, this is a time of grace, for the Compassionate One appears and the wide streams of the river nourish the saplings in the Garden.[356] We invoke before Him the Merit of the Unification[357] that is recited twice [every day], for with this merit He will have compassion upon us. So we say: **"From His Place may [He turn in compassion to His People] who acclaim His Oneness. . ."**

SECTION 14

To cease from labor in accord with the mystery of Creation. This is alluded to in [the verse] "For on it He rested." [Gen. 2:3] Know that it was through the Bride that the six rungs above Her functioned in the lower world, as it is written, "And all His work is done through Faithfulness." [Ps. 33:4] She served as the emissary of those on high.[358]

On the first day She initiated the activity deriving from the Right Crown, [proceeding] in accord with the other rungs.[359] So it occurred each day until the seventh, when She completed the Work of Creation with the energy She received from the grades above;[360] as it is written, "For the Lord made six days." [Ex. 31:17] These six days esoterically refer to the entire Work of Creation. Thus, it is written "six" and not "in six."[361] [*Malkhut*] carries Creation to fruition, [acting] as an emissary of those on high, for She lacks the wherewithal to independently bring forth a new creation, one that is viable.[362] [During the six days] when She brought forth Her Chariots, Her Hosts and Palaces of Light,[363] through whom She acted upon the lower entities, behold, these [intermediaries] were viable; for *Malkhut* was then an emissary of each rung within the Tree of Life. Now, however, on the seventh day, it is *Her* moment to reign. Were She to act through Her external agencies, which are profane, and so be their leader without, God forbid, the authority of Her husband upon Her, there would be two domains.[364]

Therefore, whoever performs an act which causes the natural world to function in a profane modality, swelling the latter's influence, this person "cuts off the shoots" and is deserving of death.[365] [On Shabbat] the Tree of Knowledge is sovereign and he has left off inclining it to the side of Good and has turned it to Evil. The [offender] has brought about his own death, for he has roused the aspect of Death and removed the aspect of Life.[366]

Since God, may He be blessed, wanted living things to exist, He included *Malkhut* in the sixth divine aspect so as to appease Her and light up Her face. Now, the sixth [*sefirah*] is also the seventh, for [*Yesod*] is the sixth in the Structure, counting from the Right Arm and below, while it is the seventh when reckoning from *Binah*.[367] Through this [union] the spiritual world flourishes while the physical world is at rest. Holiness is enlarged and the profane rungs shrink and shut down; for now they do not draw [nourishment] from their celestial counterparts.[368]

Instead, the "Unbounded Inheritance" appears and the two cherubim reign. From the power they generate, the days of rest are ever renewed.[369] The holy rungs are refreshed there, while the profane rungs are annulled. The "Wings"—those constraining boundaries which cling to the [holy rungs]—hide their heads and the seventh rung, the perfect Bride, adorned in holy raiment, is revealed.[370]

For this reason, the [Sabbath sacrificial] service was required in the Sanctuary, but forbidden in the provinces;[371] "You shall kindle no fire in your settlements on the Sabbath day," [Ex. 35:3] so as not to arouse the profane rungs and incline the Tree of Knowledge to the side of evil. But in the Sanctuary, the domain of the Bride, "on the Sabbath-day, two perfect yearling male lambs" [Num. 28:9ff.] [are to be offered]; for there, *Malkhut* reigns.[372] One who engages in profane labor takes away from the Glory and makes Her into a separate authority. He is like the rest of the heretics.[373]

Know that the Sabbath alludes to the [era of] desolation, which is the seventh millenium, a time that is altogether a Sabbath unto the Lord. Thus our Rabbis of blessed memory stated in Tractate *Ro'sh ha-Shanah*, chapter "A Festival" [31a]:

> On the Sabbath they used to say, "A Psalm. A song for the Sabbath day" [Ps. 92]: for a cosmos that is entirely Sabbath; rest in life everlasting.[374]

For then all profane activity will have ceased. In accord with this paradigm, we rest from work on the Sabbath and so allude to this great matter.

[Sabbath-rest] also refers to the World of Souls.[375] There "the righteous sit with crowns on their heads, feasting on the radiance of the *Shekhinah*." [TB Ber. 17a] They eat that which they prepared on "Sabbath eve" and rest on that Sabbath. Whoever wishes to be in their company must do his work on the six days of activity and rest on the seventh day.[376]

SECTION 15

To delight in the Sabbath. We read in [TB *Shabbat*], chapter "All Sacred Writings" [118 a–b]: "He who delights in the Sabbath is given an unbounded heritage, etc."[377] It is known that on Saturday Saturn holds sway,[378] but it has no influence over the Holy People, for they are not subject to any star or constellation. They are solely under the dominion of the Holy One, blessed be He.[379] All those under Saturn's rule must afflict themselves and grieve; they must dress in black and keep from any semblance of joy.[380] Thus R. Shimon bar Yoḥai remarked:

> Of Saturn, it is said: "'And the pit was empty, there was no water in it.' [Gen. 37:24] Rather, it contains snakes and scorpions." That is, thirst, lamentation and wailing. This [pit] is the exile of Israel.[381]

On Saturn's day it behooves Israel to make certain changes: to eat and drink sumptuously, to wear fine raiment, to enjoy themselves, to set the home in order and arrange a festive table, and to display abundant mirth. When [Saturn] realizes that there is no resting place for it, it flees.[382] This is the mystical meaning of "I am fleeing from Sarai my mistress."[383] [Gen. 16:8]

This [Sabbath-rejoicing] contains a further sublime and recondite mystery concerning that additional spirit which rests upon the Holy People.[384] During the six working days, the [spirit] basks in the supernal splendor, but on the Sabbath it descends to sojourn with Israel, taking pleasure in their pleasures, delighting in their delights, so as to be perfected on all sides.

Know that this spirit spreads forth from the End Point of the Supernal Thought.[385] It contains an abundance of holiness and blessing. [On Shabbat] it is divided into two portions, one luxuriating in the celestial light above while the other takes pleasure in Israel's pleasures below. Thus, it is written, "It is between Me and Israel," [Ex. 31:17] meaning "Israel and I are partners; together we perfect this Point. Through them and Me it is crowned, above and below." When the lower portion experiences pleasure and delight through Israel, as is fitting, it ascends and unites with the supernal portion. The Bride is crowned by them, perfected by those on high and those below.

He who delights in the Sabbath causes blessing to emanate from its supernal Source: from the Wide Streams of the River, the mystery of "Jacob's heritage," the "unbounded heritage."[386] His reward is meted out measure for measure. As it is written: "Then shall you delight in the Lord . . . And I shall feed you with the heritage of Jacob your father, for the mouth of the Lord has spoken."[387] [Isa. 58:14]

SECTION 16

Concerning mundane speech,[388] it is written: "Not finding your own affairs, nor speaking your own words." [Isa. 58:13] Our Rabbis of blessed memory gave the following interpretation:

> Your speech on the Sabbath should not be like your speech on weekdays. [TB Shab. 113a–b]

The reason is that there is no uttered word that does not have a "Voice." Now, a [profane] Voice ascends on high and rouses that which is called *ḥol,* Profane. When the Profane is roused on the holy Sabbath, it is a great denigration. He who does so "separates friends." [Prv. 6:28] The Holy One, blessed be He, and the Community of Israel ask: "Who is this who seeks to break up our union?" For the Supernal Holy One does not dwell amidst the profane.[389] This matter contains a deep mystery. As the [profane] entity is aroused on high, "It defiles the sanctuary of the Lord." [Num. 19:20] Now if this occurs because of an insignificant word, it would certainly occur in the case of a more serious deed, which defiles the upper and lower [worlds].[390]

"Thought [about mundane matters] is permitted" [TB Shab. 113b] for a thought has no Voice. But should a person utter words of Torah, words of holiness, a voice is produced. It rises up and rouses the holy entities. Concerning this, it is written, "go forth, daughters of Zion, etc."[391] [Cant. 3:11]

SECTION 17

The hidden meaning of keeping a dream-fast on the Sabbath. We read in the first chapter of [Tractate] *Shabbat* [11a]:

> Rabba bar Meḥasseya said in the name of R. Ḥama bar Gurya in Rav's name: Fasting is as potent against an [ominous] dream as fire

> against straw." R. Ḥisda said: "Providing it is on that very day." And R. Joseph added: "And even on the Sabbath."[392]

We read in [TB] *Berakhot,* chapter "One Should Not Stand" [31b]:

> R. Yoḥanan said in the name of R. Yose ben Zimra: "If one keeps a fast on the Sabbath, a decree of seventy years standing against him is annulled: [turned] from evil to good."
> R. Naḥman ben Isaac said: "Yet all the same he is punished for neglecting to make the Sabbath a delight. What is the remedy? Let him keep another fast to atone for this one."[393]

Out of God's love for him, a person is alerted in a dream. Through it he may turn in repentance, so that compassion may be sought for him, on high. Woe to the person who is not warned. Of him, it is said: "One who rests satisfied and is not visited [in a dream] is evil."[394] [Prv. 19:23]

[R. Ḥisda stated:] **"Providing it is on that very day,"** and not thereafter. For the dominion of a Day does not extend to another. A Day can only request compassion on behalf of that which occurred on it. Therefore, a Day does not leave until the [dream's] decree has been annulled, through fasting thereon.[395] However, **"a decree of seventy years"** cannot be abrogated [through fasting], except on the Sabbath.[396]

The reason the text states: **"And even on the Sabbath"** is that one is attended to by Providence more closely on that day, and the [dream-faster] more so than other people. For on the Sabbath rest and joy fill the world; on this day even the sinners in Gehinnom rest.[397] So when this one sits in sorrow all those on high inquire after him, asking: "why is this one grieving when the whole world is rejoicing?" This one's prayer ascends to the Compassionate One, who annuls the decree which had been approved by the celestial Court, the mystery of the Seventy Places.[398] For when the Supernal Light is disclosed, the gates of Compassion open and the entire cosmos is gladdened.[399] Those forces of *Din* cower before Him.

To what may this be likened? To a king who married off his son and enjoined all his subjects to rejoice. All were indeed joyous except for one man who was bound in chains and was sad. When the king arrived to regale his son, he saw that everyone was rejoicing. But when he lifted his eyes, he saw that sad-faced man bound in chains.[400] The [king] said: "All my subjects are rejoicing in my son's time of joy, while this one is bound in chains." Straightway, he ordered that the man be released. Thus, the [Gemara'] states: **"A decree of seventy years standing against him is annulled,"** esoterically referring to the seventy supernal Years, the mystery of the celestial Court.[401]

"Yet all the same he is punished for neglecting to make the Sabbath a delight." Why? Because the portion [of the spirit] that descends to experience pleasure with Israel, below, is not properly completed; it ascends less fulfilled than [the portion partaking of] the Supernal Delight. Because the portion below is not completed neither is the one above, for the one depends on the other. Since this person causes a diminution on high, he is subject to punishment. Thus, [the Gemara' continues]: **"What is the remedy? Let him keep another fast to atone for this one."**[402]

Concerning this matter, the Exegetes, of blessed memory, explained that one need not fast immediately thereafter, on Sunday.[403] But hearken unto the truth as it was received by thsoe who "beheld the King's face" [Esth. 1:14] and stood in his innermost chamber![404] Know that one who fasts on the Sabbath does away with the Supernal Delight. He violates the territory of the Community of Israel which holds sway on this sacred day.[405]

Should this person take delight immediately thereafter, on Sunday, when the Profane Days hold sway, he would be according greater honor to Another Force [*Siṭra' 'Aḥra'*] than he did to the Holy One, blessed be He. He would be denigrating the mystery of Holy Faith, while enhancing the external entities. Concerning this, Scripture says: "Say not, I will enhance Evil." [Prv. 20:23] For this sin he will be called to account in this world and the World-to-Come.

Therefore, one must fast immediately [after Shabbat], on Sunday, when the Profane Spirit holds away. Since the aspect of Good was not enhanced, neither should the aspect of Evil. This [second fast] provides healing, as is indicated in the verse, "He shall restore that which he took away by robbery."[406] [Lev. 5:23] Thereafter, no further punishment may be exacted. [. . .] But the Holy One [may] punish him in this world and in the next.[407]

Happy is he who cleaves to the Holy Faith and who strives to always do what is right in his eyes when serving Him; cleaving to Him, as it is said, "but you who did cleave unto the Lord your God are alive, every one of you, this day." [Dt. 4:4]

SECTION 18

To study Torah. Know that the Written Torah mystically connotes *Tif'eret Yisra'el,* the Beauty of Israel, "the king in his beauty, whom your eyes shall behold." [Isa. 33:17] It is also called the "Torah of Truth" as Scripture says, "Ascribe Truth unto Jacob" [Micah 7:20] and "The Torah of Truth was in his mouth."[408] [Mal. 2:6] The Oral Torah is the Bride mentioned in the Song of Songs [*Shekhinah*].

While[409] the Oral Torah is called *Torah she-be-ʿal peh,* literally, "the Torah that is upon the mouth," the Written Torah is called *Torah she-bi-khtav,* "the Torah that is in writing." "In" writing, and not "upon" it: The underlying reason is that the supernal Torah is veiled and hidden, within "Writing," the mystery of the Celestial Palace.[410] This [Torah] is concealed within, and together they[411] form an indivisable unity. From this [Palace] the [Written Torah] is revealed [to those] below. Thus, it is written:[412] "[These are . . . the Torah and the miẓvah] which I have written *le-HWRTM.*" [Ex. 24:12] One should not read *le-HoWRoTaM,* "that you may teach them," but *le-HoWRaTaM,* "belonging to Her that conceived them," that is, the one who brought forth the Torah and the miẓvah mentioned in the verse.[413] [She is also referred to in the verse]: "And into the chamber *HoWRaTiY:* of her that conceived me."[414] [Cant. 3:4] [She is] the mystery of the "Wine preserved in its grapes," the place where the Supernal Book resides.[415] The Torah issues forth from this point. Thus, it is called *Torah she-bi-khtav,* the Torah that is in Writing.[416]

Why is the Oral Torah called "the Torah that is upon the Mouth"? Because it rests upon the lower Chariots which stand below [the sefirotic world].[417] Concerning them it is said: "From this point on, there is Separation." [Gen. 2:10] For these [entities] are not included within the Sphere of Unity, nor do they serve as a Palace [sheltering this Torah].[418] Therefore, we use the phrase, "[the Torah] that is upon the Mouth."

To allude to these mysteries, we call these [Teachings], "the Torah that is in Writing" and "the Torah that is upon the Mouth."[419] They are the mystery of the two lovers, "the two fawns that are twins of a gazelle." [Cant. 4:5][420]

In this vein, our Rabbis of blessed memory taught in *Midrash Ḥazita* and in *Pesiqta'* [*Rabbati*], chapter "This Month Shall Be for You":

> "My dove, my undefiled one [TaMmaTiY]." [Cant. 5:2] R. Yannai said: "[The word TaMmatiY], when vocalized *Te'oMaTiY,* means 'my twin,' 'my equal': I am not greater than she; nor is she greater than I."[421]

But since the Written Torah is hidden and veiled, it stands in need of the Oral Torah to explain its mysteries and to shed light upon its hidden meanings; the [Oral Torah] serves as its celestial symbol. For the supernal lights are [only] disclosed and made known through the Bride. It is she who actualizes their potential power.[422] The Sage had this in mind when he said: "Her husband is known through the gates," [Prv. 31:23] meaning: Through the Gates of Righteousness the Supernal Name may be known in the world.[423]

[We read] in the Midrash of R. Neḥunya ben ha-Qanah [*Bahir* 149]:

> R. Reḥumai said: This teaches us that [the Torah] is Israel's light and lamp. Thus, it is written: "For the mizvah is a lamp and the Torah is a light." [Prv. 6:23] It is said that "lamp" connotes mizvah and mizvah refers to the Oral Torah. The "light" refers to the Written Torah.[424] But since the light [of the Written Torah] is sustained through [the Oral Torah], the latter also is called "Light."
>
> A parable. To what may this be compared? To a room hidden away at the end of a house. Even though it is day and the world is filled with bright light, no one can see in this room unless he brings along a lamp. So it is in the case of the Oral Torah. Even though it is [but] a lamp, the Written Torah needs it, so that the problems therein may be solved and its mysteries explained.[425]

When Israel studies these two *Torot* for their own sake, their celestial counterparts [are aroused]: "They are joined one to another" [Job 41:9] through a kiss, and "the Tabernacle becomes one."[426] [Ex. 26:6] Then blessing descends upon them from on high and peace fills the world.[427] This is the meaning underlying that which our Rabbis, of blessed memory, taught in the chapter "These Are the Knots" [TB Shab. 114a]:

> What are *banna'im*, builders? Said R. Yoḥanan: They are scholars, who are engaged all their days in building up the world.

This [building up] refers to the union of the Torah on high and the Holy One; upon [such activity] the existence of the world depends.[428]

In the Midrash of R. Neḥunya ben ha-Qanah [*Bahir* 196] [it is said]:

> How was David able to overcome [the Evil Inclination]? Through his studying, for he did not desist from it day or night.[429] He would perform acts of unification, binding the Torah on high to the Holy One.[430] For whenever a person studies the Torah for its own sake, the Torah on high is bound up with the Holy One, blessed be He.

> Thus, it is said: "A person should always study Torah, even if he does not do so for its own sake; for out of learning with an ulterior motive, he will come to learn it for its own sake." [TB Pes. 50b]

Now, when Israel learns Torah for its own sake, their Mother on high sings unto Her lover, chanting: "Let him kiss me with the kisses of his mouth." [Cant. 1:2] For it is the way of lovers to kiss each other mouth-to-mouth, visibly affirming that they have one spirit [between them], so great is their love. This [supernal love] is symbolized by the two lovers in the Song of Songs who unite through a kiss.[431] Thus, [the Bride] says: "If only he were to kiss me with the kisses of his mouth,"[432] speaking in the third person before the kiss. But once the man has entered his home,[433] she addresses [him directly]: "How good is your love *mi-yayin:* through the wine," [Cant. Ibid.] meaning: how sweet and good is your love unto me when Israel is studying Torah, which is compared to wine.[434] For through [such activity] the divine structure is completed. So it is that Israel strengthens the love between the Holy One and the Community of Israel whenever its people learn Torah for its own sake.[435]

Know that when the adept studies Torah he becomes like an angel of the Lord of hosts.[436] In his contemplation he resembles them, for their activity is purely contemplative.[437] This [experience] is a taste of the World-to-Come, for "the righteous sit with crowns on their heads basking in the splendor of the *Shekhinah*."[438] This refers to a wondrous attainment, something that was beyond them as long as their souls were still in fetters. The Sabbath is a symbol of this [future] world. It is devoid of bodily concerns, for it is the World of Souls.[439] Thus, one must perfect one's soul on this day.[440]

[The way to] perfection is [through] Torah-study, engaged in for its own sake. We have already explained [our Sages'] intent in saying *li-shmah,* "for its own sake." But this phrase has an additional meaning: namely, [through Torah-study] the spirit that sojourns with us this day is made whole.[441] One who attains this [rung] will merit to "be enlightened in the light of Life." [Job 33:30] Of him, it is said: "And He said unto me: 'You are my servant, Israel, through whom I am glorified.' "[442] [Isa. 49:13]

SECTION 19

The mystery of *Minḥah,* the prayers of Sabbath afternoon.[443] We recite *'Ashrei* and thereafter, *U-va' le-Ẓion:* [A Redeemer] Shall Come to Zion. This order [of Biblical verses] is recited because from

Minḥah onwards the aspect of *Din* is aroused.[444] Through this Sanctification, Compassion is bestirred.[445] There is no need to recite [this prayer] on Sabbath mornings because the aspect of Compassion holds sway then. During the week, however, this prayer is recited in the morning, for then the Days of Evil prevail.

Now, "since the Temple was destroyed . . . the curse of each day is greater than than of its predecessor," as R. Shimon ben Gamliel said in the name of R. Joshua.[446] For the Temple sustained the world, and the merit of the Temple Service brought it blessing. Indeed, such Service is one of the pillars upon which the world rests.[447]

Nowadays, it is incumbent on us to recite this Portion in order to perfume the world, [to restore it even] in a small way. As it says in the conclusion of Tractate *Soṭah* [49a]:

> How can the world endure? Through the *Qedushah* of the Biblical Portion and [the response]: "Amen. May His great Name [be blessed]" which follows the homily.[448]

Thereafter, we recite "I offer my prayer to You, O Lord, at a time of Grace." [Ps. 69:14] This verse is not recited during the weekly *Minḥah* service, for then the aspect of harsh Judgement prevails; it is not a "time of Grace." But on Sabbath afternoons, even though *Din* is empowered, it is a "time of Grace."

At this hour the Light of Compassion is disclosed before all things and "the king's fury abates." [Esth. 7:10][449] Prayer is particularly welcome because peace now pervades the cosmos. Indeed, this verse attests to the divine unity; and so it was established that we recite it at this time.[450]

"I offer my prayer": "I" esoterically refers to the Bride, the Community of Israel; "my prayer" to the "prayer of Moses." **"A time of Grace"** alludes to the union of the Bride, the so-called "time of Peace" with the supernal Grace which is revealed at this hour.[451]

The Torah-scroll is then taken [from the Ark]. On Shabbat we read the Torah twice: in the morning we read the Portion in its entirety, for "[God's] love persists the entire day" [Ps. 52:3] and [daytime] signifies wholeness.[452] But at dusk we read ten verses or [perhaps a few] more, but not the entire portion for the complete portion is of the Right, and [the Right] prevails only till the hour of *Minḥah*. Thereafter, the aspect of Judgment prevails. We read from the Torah at *Minḥah* in order to subsume the Left in the Right.[453] Indeed, [the Torah] proceeded from the fusion of these two, as it says: "From His Right, [and from] the Fire, the Teaching came unto them."[454] [Dt. 33:2]

[Upon completing the reading], the Torah-scroll is returned to its place.

We then pray "You are One and Your name One." This prayer is the consummation of the Sabbath liturgy,[455] for at this moment all the supernal lights, mystically invoked in the four Prayers, unite.[456] The evening prayer ["You sanctified"] corresponds to the perfect Bride who is betrothed to the Groom. The morning prayer, "And Moses rejoiced" esoterically refers to the Groom who rejoices "when he is given his Portion" which ascends to unite with him. In this prayer ["Groom"] implicitly includes the supernal Arms, as well. The *Musaf* prayer mystically denotes the Cosmic *Ẓaddiq*, including the two pillars, *Yakhin* and *Boᶜaz*, upon which the House is firmly established.[457] Hence, [at *Musaf*] all seven [lower] rungs band together in intimate union.[458] But now, [as we recite "You are One"], He and His Name "are one."[459]

In the Midrash of RaSHBI it is written:[460]

> The three [daily] services are recited on the Sabbath, along with a fourth, *Musaf*. The evening prayer, "You sanctified [the seventh day]" refers to the lower *Shekhinah*. She comes from the Left side, the abode of the Levites of whom it is said: "You shall sanctify the Levites."[461]
>
> [Next comes] the morning prayer, "And Moses rejoiced when he was given his Portion." This [Portion] is the "Soul of every living thing" namely, the Supernal Mother,[462] of whom it is said: "When you lie among the Lips."[463] [Ps. 68:14] Do not read *'iM*, "when you" but *'eM*, "Mother". [. . .][464]
>
> [The third prayer] "You are One and Your Name One" refers to YHWH, the Central Column, which brings together the two others.[465]
>
> They correspond [. . .][466] *Neshamah yeterah*, the additional soul [called] *nishmat kol ḥai*, the soul of every living thing, corresponds to "And Moses rejoiced when he was given his portion." *Ruaḥ yeterah*, the additional spirit, corresponds to "You are One and Your name One."[467] Happy is he who recites these three prayers on the Sabbath, for they symbolize all this.[468]
>
> The *Musaf* prayer corresponds to the *Ẓaddiq* who encompasses all [the rungs].[469] It is of him we say in the *Musaf* prayer, "A crown is given unto You, [Lord our God]" etc.[470]

"An ornament of distinction [*Tif'eret Gedullah*]":[471] Here the prayer describes the union of the supernal entities, [beginning with] the mystery of *Ḥesed* and *'Emet*.[472] **"A diadem of salvation":** meaning that the Woman of Valor, the crown of Her Husband, is perfected through the Right, as in the verse, "His right hand has wrought this one salvation."[473] [Ps. 98:1] At this moment, all is united on high, as is intimated in the [phrase], **"rest and holiness have You given Your people."**[474]

Thereafter, we move from the upper realm to the lower, so as to bring down the fragrant oil onto the Head and unite the supernal Chariot:[475] **"Abraham took delight, Isaac sang joyously,"** alluding to the mystery of the Levite's song.[476] **"Jacob and his children rested thereon; it is a rest given in love and generosity, a true and faithful rest":** indicating that Truth and Faith are now in perfect union.[477] [Only] after this point may we entreat God on our own behalf, reciting "Please accept our rest, etc."[478]

Now, ["You are One"] also contains allusions to that world where "the Lord will be one and His Name one."[479] [Zech. 14:9] At that time Israel, too, will be **"a singular People on earth."** "No stranger will be found in their midst."[480] [Prv.14:40] The text implies that in this epoch **"Abraham will take [full] delight, Isaac will [truly] rejoice, and Jacob and his children will find [perfect] rest.[481] For [then] your children shall perceive [and know that their rest is from You, etc.]":** We pray that this season arrive, when "your children shall directly know"!

It is customary to recite "Your Righteousness."[482] Mar Sar Shalom[483] claimed that:

> It is recited as an acknowldgement of the divine justice rendered Moses, who passed away at this hour.[484] It is also customary to refrain from public study at this time, for when a scholar dies, the Houses of Study suspend their activity. Our ancestors' custom is binding Law [*Torah*] for us.[485]

If some have raised objection to this interpretation,[486] consider that the Midrash of RaSHBI supports it, clearly stating that Moses, the Lord's servant, died on Sabbath afternoon and that Israel must acknowledge the divine justice by praising Him, saying "Your righteousness is like the mountains of God, etc."[487] [Ps. 36:7]

Three such acknowledgments are made here, because three [great souls] departed from the world at this hour. And all were included in Moses, peace be upon him! They are: Moses himself, Joseph the *Ẓaddiq*, and King David.[488] The first verse is directed to Joseph the *Ẓaddiq*, because he was the first one historically. This is:

"Your righteousness is like the mountains of God," [Ps. 36:7] a reference to Joseph the *Ẓaddiq* who is compared to the supernal mountains, for "the mountains are the Patriarchs."[489] [The verse continues:] **"Your judgments [come from] the endless Deep,"** the place where the infinite waters abide.[490]

The verse **"Your righteousness, O God, reaches the heights"** [Ps. 71:19] is directed to Moses our Teacher, as it is said: "You are the heights."[491] [Ps. 92:9] [The verse continues]: **"You have done great things [gedolot],"** for great and wondrous things are within his compass.[492]

The [third verse], **"Your righteousness is everlasting [ẓedeq le-ᶜolam] and Your Torah is truth"** [Ps. 119:142] is directed to King David, the mystery of the lower *Ẓedeq*.[493]

In this hour [those that represented] both the Written and Oral Torah died. For this reason, the Houses of Study suspend their activity.[494]

When Joseph died, the wellsprings dried up. No sooner had the *Ẓaddiq* been gathered up than the Tribes sank into Exile.[495] The [heavenly beings] broke forth, saying: "Your righteousness is like the mountains of God." When Moses died the sun faded and the Written Torah, the mystery of the luminous glass, gathered up its light. When David died, the Oral Torah lost its normal lustre and "the moon no longer caused its light to shine."[496] [Isa. 13:10]

To hint at this [three-fold] mystery it was established that we acknowledge the divine Justice thrice on Sabbath afternoon.[497]

SECTION 20

The mystery of the three festive meals.[498] R. Isaac said:[499] It is written: "And God blessed the seventh day" [Gen. 2:3] and "Six days shall you gather [manna, but on the seventh day there shall be none]." [Ex. 16:26] One might wonder: Since there is no food on the Sabbath, where is its blessing? But it is taught: All blessings depend on the seventh day.[500] And it is further taught: Why is there no manna on the seventh day? Because all the supernal Days receive [their blessings] from it.[501] Each one sustains the world on its appointed day, imparting that which it received on the seventh.[502]

Hence, every member of the community of Israel[503] must set his table with bread and fine food on Friday night and on the Sabbath day as well,[504] so that his table may be blessed every day of the week. For at this time, blessing is present, by which the weekdays may be blessed; but no blessing may be found at an empty table.[505]

Know that the supernal dew and the Great Light descend from the head of the Holy One unto the Field of Apples thrice each Sabbath, forming the mystery of the King's feasts.[506] For this reason our Sages of blessed memory enjoined us to partake of three festive meals each Sabbath; for they reflect the supernal paradigm. According to the Holy Lamp the [symbolic] structure of the meals is as follows:[507]

Concerning the nighttime feast it is written: **"I will cause you to ride upon the high places of the earth."** [Isa. 58:14] This is an esoteric reference to the Bride who is blessed on this night. This is the time of Her joy and so, the night meal corresponds to Her. Concerning the daytime feast, it is written: **"Then shall you delight yourself above the Lord."** [Ibid.] This alludes to the Ancient of Days who is disclosed at this hour.[508] Concerning the third meal, it is written: **"I will feed you with the heritage of Jacob,"** [Ibid.] an allusion to *Tif'eret Yisra'el*. Since *Tif'eret* connotes completeness, we complete the meal cycle with it.[509]

However, we find that in his dying hour, the Holy Lamp structured the meals in another fashion:[510]

> I attest before all those assembled here, that in all my days I never neglected the three festive meals.[511] Because of them I had no need to fast on Shabbat. Indeed, I had no need to do so on weekdays, much less on the Sabbath![512] For whoever is privileged to partake of these feasts, partakes of Perfect Faith.[513] The [first] meal is that of the Lady; [the second], the meal of the King, and [the third], the meal of the Holy Ancient One, the mystery of all mysteries.

It is clear from his words that the daytime meal is that of the King, the mystery of the Central Column while the late afternoon meal is that of the Ancient of Days. This order is the better one, for it is at *Minḥah* that the supernal Lamp, the mysterious Ancient of Days, is revealed.[514]

This proves that one should make the third meal at *Minḥah* and not in the morning as some do. After the daytime meal they recite the Grace, and then spread a table-cloth and proceed to make the third.[515] No honor is shown the Sabbath festivites when a meal is divided into two. Such an act in no way makes for a Third Meal, which should only take place in the late afternoon.[516] For this meal corresponds to the Ancient of Days who is disclosed at that hour.

Further proof may be adduced from the teaching in the chapter "All Sacred Writings" [TB Shab. 117b]:

> If a fire breaks out on Friday night, food for three meals may be saved; if in the morning, food for two meals may be saved; if in the late afternoon, food for one meal.[517]

And the passage in the first chapter of TB *Pesaḥim* [13a] provides still more corroboration:

> If the 14th [of Nisan] falls on a Sabbath, all [leaven] must be removed before the Sabbath . . . and food for two meals is left over [so as to eat till the fourth hour].[518]

One must leave food for precisely two meals, for leavened food is forbidden from the sixth hour on. Consequently, the time for the third meal can only be at *Minḥah*.[519]

Whenever[520] the 14th of Nisan would fall on the Sabbath, Rabbenu Tam would eat an enriched *maẓẓah*, kneaded with oil and honey, for the Third Meal. The Rabbinic saying, "Whoever eats maẓẓah on the eve of Passover is like one who has intercourse with his betrothed at his father-in-laws's house," applies only to the "bread of affliction" (unenriched maẓẓah)![521] Enriched maẓẓah is permitted, as the obligation to eat specifically unenriched maẓẓah does not go into effect until evening.[522]

It is written in the Midrash of RaSHBI that whenever the fourteenth day fell on a Sabbath, he would arrange the table and contemplate the Construction of the Chariot, instead of [eating] the Third Meal.[523] He would say, "This is the Banquet of the King." This is a veiled mystery.[524]

The mnemonic for these meals is "You shall call the Sabbath *ᶜoNeG*, a Delight." [Isa. 58:13] To wit: "A River [*Nahar*] went forth from Eden [*ᶜeden*] to water the Garden [*Gan*]." [Gen. 2:10] This may be arranged ᶜeden, Nahar, Gan, forming the acronym ᶜoNeG.[525] The evening meal corresponds to the Bride who is called "a locked Garden; my sister, my bride." [Cant. 4:12] The morning meal corresponds to "the River coming forth from Eden," [Gen. 2:10] the mystery of the Beauty [*Tif'eret*] of Israel. The afternoon meal corresponds to the celestial Eden.[526]

THE MYSTERY OF SABBATH'S DEPARTURE

SECTION 21

To add to the holy [by taking] from the profane at the Sabbath's departure.[527] We prolong the Sabbath by extending it into Saturday night, thereby showing that we do not like to see the departure of the holy Guest; indeed, its parting evokes a deep feeling of regret. So we detain it[528] and, in our great affection, escort it with song and [choruses of] praise, as in the teaching, "We will send you off with joyous song."[529]

It is said in the Midrash:[530] "[The Sabbath] may be compared to a Bride and Queen who is escorted with song and verses of praise." We have already alluded to the high mystery of Shabbat as Bride and Queen,[531] as mentioned in the chapter "All Sacred Writings."[532] In *Genesis Rabbah* [it is said]:

> "And God completed His work on the seventh day" [Gen. 2:1]: The Holy One said: "Go forth and chant a song for a new guest has arrived."[533]

This refers to the advent of Shabbat, the Bride who has just arrived.[534]

That is to say, when the Sabbath arrives we must usher it in with songs and choruses of praise; and when the Sabbath departs, we must escort it in like fashion.[535] So is our custom!

We then recite the evening prayer, using the weekday format, but including the *Havdalah* in the Standing Prayer [*Tefillah*].[536] The mystery of the *Havdalah* will, with God's help, be elucidated a bit later.[537] After [the *Tefillah* we recite] "May the Lords' Pleasantness" [the series of verses beginning with Ps. 90:17].

SECTION 22

The mystery of "May the Lords's Pleasantness" and the mystery of *Havdalah*.[538] Why do we recite "May the Pleasantness"?[539] As we have explained, *Din* is banished on Sabbath eve, departing from even the sinners in Gehinnom. For Shabbat protects the cosmos.[540] But on Saturday night, *Din* is restored to its station. A herald cries out: "Return, o you wicked, to She'ol!" [Ps. 9:18], for *Din* is aroused at this hour.[541]

We recite [the verse] "May the Pleasantness [*No^cam*] of *YHWH* our God [come unto us]," alluding to the pleasing [radiance] that is *No^cam*. It is the Great Light which perpetually shines upon us, streaming forth from *Na^comi* without end.[542] Recitation of the psalm delivers us from the dread of Gehinnom and the harshness of unmitigated *Din*.[543] Scripture says "Gaze upon the Pleasantness of YHWH, and you shall frequent His Sanctuary."[544] [Ps. 27:4]

[Concerning] "He who dwells in the shelter of the Most High" [Ps. 91]: This is the "Song against demons."[545] We recite this to be delivered from evil spirits which seek to rule over us. For when they see us immersed in [holy] song and choruses of praise they withdraw beyond the inhabited world.[546] Finally, we recite the *Seder Qedushah* so that we might arouse divine Compassion, as noted above.[547]

When Israel completes the [evening] prayers, the wicked in Gehinnom cry out: "Happy are you, Israel! Happy are the righteous who uphold the Torah! But woe to them who have not merited this!" Straightaway, Dumah proclaims: "Return, o wicked, to She'ol!"[548] [Ps. 9:18] To delay their return to Gehinnom, we recite "May the Pleasantness" slowly, lingering over it.[549]

No fire may be lit before these prayers are concluded, for such an act causes the flames of Hell to be kindled prematurely. The wicked in Gehinnom curse the one who does so, saying: "The Lord is about to shake you severely, fellow!"[550] [Isa. 22:17] But when one waits till the prayers are concluded, the wicked acknowledge the divine justice and confirm for him all those blessings recited: "May God give you [of the dew of heaven and the fat of the earth]"; [Gen. 27:28] "Blessed shall you be in the city and blessed shall you be in the country." [Dt. 28:3] "Blessed shall you be in your comings and blessed shall you be in your goings."[551] [Ibid. 28:16]

Thereafter, the *Havdalah* is [publicly] recited. This *Havdalah* must be made over wine.[552] For at this time a person's Sabbath-soul departs and one enters the days of toil and privation, diminished and saddened.[553] So one makes *Havdalah* over wine, for it rejuvenates; it brings down strength from *Gevurah* and stimulates good cheer.[554]

Next one makes the blessing over fragrant herbs to regain serenity of spirit, for the Sabbath-soul has left him.[555] As it says in Tractate *Beiẓah*, chapter "A Festival" [16a]:

> On Sabbath eve the Holy One gives the human being an extra soul and on Saturday night He takes it away. Thus R. Shimon ben Laqish said: Why is it written, "He ceased from work and rested, *shabat va-yinnafash*" [Ex. 31:17]? This may be read: once the rest has ceased, *vay-nefesh:* woe! that soul is gone.[556]

This teaching is also found in Tractate *Taᶜanit,* in the chapter "Three Times a Year" [27b].

An objection was raised in the Midrash of R. Shimon bar Yoḥai:[557] "Should not the verse end *vay la-guf:* 'Woe to the body'? For it is the body that has lost the Sabbath-soul!"[558] But it was explained: a person's soul [*nefesh*] takes in[559] this spirit [*ruaḥ*] on Sabbath eve and houses it. The spirit resides there all Sabbath long, and the soul is elevated and enlarged, greater than before.

For this reason we learn: All souls of Israel are crowned on the Sabbath, adorned by this indwelling spirit.[560] When the Sabbath departs, *vay la-nefesh* woe to the soul, for it has lost its crown.[561] Hence, the verse: *Shabat:* when the rest ceased—i.e., when the Sabbath departs, *vay nefesh*: woe to the soul that has lost so much! Thus far, the *Zohar*.[562]

We have already mentioned that the Sabbath is the symbol of the World-to-Come.[563] It is written in the first chapter of Tractate *Megillah* [15b]:

> R. Eleazar said in the name of R. Ḥanina: The Holy One will, in the the time to come, be a crown upon the head of each righteous person, as it says: "On that day, the Lord of hosts shall become a crown of beauty and a diadem of glory [*ẓefirat tif'eret*]" [Isa. 28:5] . . . for those who do His Will and await His Glory [*meẓappin le-tif'arto]*.

On this holy day God wishes to wreathe us with the symbol of that Crown with which He will adorn us in the time to come. But I cannot speak of this at greater length.[564]

One must smell the fragrant spices as Sabbath departs and the choicest way of fulfilling this miẓvah is with myrtle.[565] For myrtle brings to mind the soul's abode: from its souls depart to sojourn with us each Shabbat and to it they return; from it they draw sustenance. The Tree from which these souls flower forth is called *Hadas,* Myrtle.[566] Thus, Scripture says: "It was standing among the myrtles."[567] [Zech. 1:8] Queen Esther was named Hadassah in its honor.[568]

We then recite the blessing over the fire.[569] Know that on Sabbath eve the Fire of the North is hidden away and concealed. Lest we rouse it in the slightest, it is written, "You shall not kindle a fire."[570] [Ex. 35:3] As Israel makes the blessing over the fire on Saturday night, this [Fire] goes out to stand guard as before.[571]

Four Camps are illumined by the candlelight. They are called the "lights of the fire."[572] We bend the four fingers of our right hand and hold them up to the candle.[573] The fingers symbolize these Camps, the mystery of the Lower Chariots, which are illumined by the [supernal] Candle, the Bride. She, the Community of Israel, holds sway over them; She lights them up and sustains them.[574]

One may only gaze upon the backs of the fingers, which symbolize the Lower Lights. As it is said, "You shall see My back." [Ex. 33:23] But one may not gaze upon the inner side which symbolizes the Supernal Lights. Of them it is written, "But My Face may not be seen."[575] [Ibid.] So we never let the inner part of the fingers catch the light, for they are inward and not illumined by the Lower Candle; rather, they are illumined by the Supernal Lamp on high.[576] But since the "Backside" [*'Aḥorayim*] is lit up by the Lower Candle, we bend down the outer part of the fingers[577] and hold them up to the flame. Thus we dramatize whence they derive their light.[578]

There is another reason that we gaze upon the fingernails. For they allude Another Causality, as we mentioned above.[579] This is the mystery of "the wicked encircling the righteous."[580] [Hab. 1:4] Because this realm expands as the Sabbath departs, we gaze upon the fingernails to sap its strength and be spared harm during the coming week.[581] One should make sure, however, that use is made of the candle's light.[582]

After [we have made use of it], we bless the One who created [fire],[583] that He may deliver us from all distress. In chapter twenty-one of *Pirqei de-Rabbi 'Eliᶜezer* it is written:[584]

> At twilight [on Saturday night][585] Adam sat down and pondered his situation. "Woe is me," he said. "I fear that the snake that led me astray will come and 'strike my heel' [ff. Gen. 3:5]" [At that moment] he was sent a pillar of fire to light up [the way] and protect him from evil. When Adam saw the pillar of fire, he rejoiced and said: "Blessed are You, *'Adonai,* Creator of the lights of fire."[586]

Surely you already know that on Saturday night we may bless light which issues from tinder [*ᶜeẓim*] and stones [*'avanim*], but on Yom Kippur we may not. So it is ruled in [TB] *Pesaḥim,* in the chapter "Where It Is The Custom" [54a].[587] The reason for this is that Shabbat is within the Structure called *ᶜeẓim,* "the Woods." Concerning it Scripture says, "The Trees [*ᶜaẓei*] of the Lord *yisbeᶜu,* are sated."[588] [Ps. 104:16] Moreover, Diadem is called *'Even Yisra'el,* the Cornerstone of Israel, and those above Her are called Stones, for together they comprise the Structure [*binyan*].[589]

And so, on Saturday night we bless the light created from tinder and stones. But since Yom Kippur is above the Structure, we may only make a blessing over pre-existent light when it departs.

"O House of Jacob! Come let us walk by the light of the Lord!"[590] [Isa. 2:5]

Thereafter we recite the blessing, "who makes a distinction between the sacred and the profane [between light and darkness, between Israel and the other nations, between the seventh day and the six working days.]" These four acts of separation were established to parallel the four "husks" or "shells" [*qelippot*] that surround the divine emanation. They are called *ruaḥ seᶜarah* [the Stormy Wind], *ᶜanan gadol* [the Great Cloud], *'esh mitlaqqaḥat* [the Flashing Fire], and *nogah lo saviv* [the Encompassing Brightness].[591]

Those initiated into the esoteric wisdom know that they are the hidden meaning of the Ten Lower Crowns, called *qelippot*.[592] When sins are committed, these shells form a barrier between Israel and their Father in Heaven. Hence, Scripture says: "But your iniquities have been a barrier between you and your God."[593] [Isa. 59:2] During the week *Shekhinah* is garbed in them, thus upholding the dicta, "His Kingdom [*malkhuto*] rules over all" [Ps. 103:19] and "*'Elohim* reigns over the Nations."[594] [Ibid. 47:9] It is the hidden meaning of "In all their troubles He was troubled" [Isa. 63:9] and "I will be with him in distress" [Ps. 91:15]; it is the underlying meaning of: "When [Israel] was exiled into Egypt, *Shekhinah* went with them." All this in order to protect His children.[595]

Now the [*qelippot*] may be likened unto the axe in the woodcutter's hand.[596] They are the evil in the Tree of Knowledge.[597] This is a veiled teaching.[598]

Know that on Sabbaths and holy days the Holy One is cloaked in the portion of Good within the Tree of Knowledge. This is the mystery of "holy garments."[599] But on Saturday night, this garment is removed and [divinity] is clad in the four aforementioned shells so as to direct the world.[600] The garments of Shabbat are in the mode of *Beri'ah* and the four *qelippot* can mix with—and contaminate—them.[601] Hence it was established that we make a ritual separation as Sabbath departs.[602]

This is the hidden meaning of the forbidden junction of kinds [*kil'ayim*] and the prohibition against mixing wool and linen [*shaᶜaṭnez*].[603] Whoever mixes them, Scripture says: "He has defiled my Sanctuary."[604] [Num. 19:13,20] However, no impurity may reach the supernal lights, for they are in the mode of Emanation and the [*qelippot*] cannot mix with them.[605]

This is the Kabbalistic meaning of the *Havdalah* itself: [Blessed are You. . .] **"who makes a separation between the sacred and the profane,"** for the supernal lights are garments of holiness and the lower realms, profane.[606]

"Between light and darkness": the former referring to the supernal lights and the latter, to the four *qelippot*. **"Between Israel and the Nations"**: Israel laid claim to the summit of the Tree, the holy Place, and the idolatrous nations, to the four "shells."[607] One must make a distinction between them. **"Between the seventh day,"** which is sacred, **"and the six working days,"** which are profane.[608] Whoever makes a distinction between them does good in the eyes of the Lord.

The great worth of *Havdalah* is attested[609] in the [chapter], "On Passover eve" [TB Pes. 113a]:

> R. Yoḥanan said: Three types will inherit the World-to-Come: He who dwells in the Land of Israel; he who brings his sons to the study of Torah; and he who recites *Havdalah* over wine at the termination of Shabbat.[610]

Polish your mind's eye and you shall see how the three instances mentioned by the hallowed [master] point to one thing: the knowledge that "the Lord [*Tif'eret*] is *'Elohim* [*Malkhut*]; there is no other."[611] [Dt. 4:39]

You undoubtedly already know the dictum of our Rabbis:[612]

> Whoever dwells outside the Land of Israel it is as if he had no God, as it is said: "For they have driven me out today, so that I cannot have a share in the Lord's possession, but am told, 'Go and worship other gods.' " [Lev. 25:38] But whoever dwells in the Land of Israel, it is as if he has a God, as it says: "to give you the land of Canaan, to be your God."[613] [1 Sam 26:19]

The reason for this is that whoever dwells in the Land of Israel is under the dominion of the sacred, the mystery of the Holy Faith. Indeed, he dwells in *'Elohim's* abode, for the supernal Glory rests in the Land of Israel.[614]

So one makes the distinction between the sacred and the profane, between the impure and pure.[615] As he metes out, so is he measured. He will not enter the Exile of the *Temurot*, the realm of evil. Rather, he will mount up from peak to peak till he is bound up in the bond of life, the mystery of the World-to-Come.[616]

Next let us consider the one who brings his children to the study of Torah. For the Torah is "the law of the God of the Land."[617] [2K 17:26,27] One can only come to revere the Name, glorious and awesome, through His perfect Torah. Whoever studies it, is engaged in building up the world. For the existence of the world depends on this [on Torah-learning].[618] He binds the supernal Torah to the Holy One so that "Righteousness [*Ẓedeq*] and Peace [*Shalom*] kiss."[619]

[Ps. 85:11] Then the Hidden Lamp, the World-that-is-Coming, pours forth the fine oil, for blessing rests on that which is whole.[620] [And so] "royalty joined forces; they advanced together" [Ps. 48:5] "and no outsider can share in [their] joy."[621] [Prv. 14:10]

As the devotee metes out, so is he measured. Whoever promotes this [union] is granted a place in the World-to-Come, for "from the fruit of his work will he be sated."[622]

The father provides the impetus[623] for this for he brought his children to the study of Torah, which in turn, brought about the [divine union]. By the same token, it is stated in the first chapter of *Qiddushin* [30a]:

> He who teaches his son Torah, Scripture regards him as though he had received it [directly] from Mt. Sinai, for it is said: "and you shall make them known to your children," [Dt. 4:9] which is immediately followed by "The day that you stood before the Lord your God at Ḥoreb."[624] [Ibid.:10]

Moreover, the entire generation that stood at Mt. Sinai attained life in the World-to-Come;[625] whoever teaches his children Torah is included in their midst.

As for "the one who makes *Havdalah* over wine," this we have explained previously.[626]

You undoubtedly recall the opinion of our Rabbis that the tree at which Adam sinned was a grape vine.[627] They said that this teaches "that [Eve] squeezed the grapes and gave it to him,"[628] namely, "the fermented juice of the alien vine," [Jer. 2:2] "the bowl, the cup of reeling. . .the cup of his wrath."[629] [Isa. 51:17] [In punishment] for this, women came to have menstrual blood,[630] the residue of the polluting substance that the snake injected in Eve.[631] Since she sought to separate [*HiBbaDeL*] herself from Adam through this wine,[632] women customarily do not partake of the *Havdalah* wine.[633]

In the time to come the Holy One will be divested of the constraining shell [*qelippah*].[634] He will be disclosed to Israel face-to-face, without any barriers. As it is written, "Then your Guide will no longer be kept under wraps, but your eyes shall behold your Guide."[635] [Isa. 30:20] This will come to pass in the age when the sacred Word will be fulfilled: "Death shall be utterly consumed."[636] [Isa. 25:8] "Then shall the moon be ashamed and the sun abashed," [Ibid. 24:23] referring to the renowned prince and his mate.[637] Then the [prophecy] will be fulfilled regarding the two Lovers, so that "the light of the moon shall be like the light of the sun, and the light of the sun shall increase sevenfold, like the light of the seven days, when the Lord binds up His people's wounds and heals the injuries it has suffered."[638] [Isa. 30:26]

With this we have completed "The Mystery of the Sabbath" and its many attendant concerns. May God grant us "to be enlightened in the Light of Life,"[639] [Job 30:26] that we may revel in the delights of the World-to-Come, a world that is entirely Shabbat. Amen, may it be His will.

"Blessed be 'Adonai forever. Amen and amen!" [Ps. 89:53]

Notes to the Introduction

1. *Joseph Karo: Lawyer and Mystic* (Oxford, 1962): 1.

2. On his Spanish origin, see TY (Warsaw ed., 1876): 8a. On his birthdate see the colophons to both TY and *ᶜAvodat ha-Qodesh* (hereafter, AQ).

3. That is, his daughter—and likely his son—lived in Istanbul in the mid-1500's. Cf. A. Yaari, "Sefer Pesaḥ la-'Adonai le-R. Ḥayyim ben Meir ibn Gabbai" in KS 9 (1933).

4. In EJ 7:233, G. Scholem writes: "The details of his life are not known. Apparently he lived in Turkey and possibly died in *'Ereẓ Israel.*" Elsewhere (*Sabbatai Ṣevi* [Princeton, 1973]: 47) he avers that AQ was written either in Egypt or in Palestine. Similar views are found in R. Goetschal, *Meir ibn Gabbai: Le Discours de la Kabbale Espagnole* (Leuven, 1981): 34. Among the older generation of scholars G. Karpeles (*Geschichte der Judischen Literatur* [Berlin, 1921], Vol. 2: 258–59) and S. A. Horodetsky (EJB 6:1219) specify Egypt as Meir ibn Gabbai's home, whereas I. Zinberg avoids the problem by simply suggesting the "Turkish Empire" (*History of Jewish Literature* [New York, 1974] Vol. 5:40).

There seems to be no firm basis for J. H. A. Wijnhoven's recent claim that "Meir ibn Gabbai came to Safed from Asia Minor." (*Bibliographic Essays in Medieval Jewish Studies* [New York, 1976]: 288).

5. See Meir Benayahu, "Le-Qorot ha-Yehudim be-Tiria" [hereafter, "Le-Qorot"], *Zion* 12 (1948): 37–48. Also see Joseph Hacker's recent article, "Ha-Peᶜilut ha-'Inṭeleqṭu'alit be-Qerev Yehudei ha-'Impiriah ha-ᶜOthemanit," *Tarbiẓ* 53 (1984): 592. I would like to thank Prof. Hacker for calling Benayahu's article to my attention.

6. Tire is located southeast of Izmir (Smyrna) and was home to a community of *Sefardim*, especially from the late fifteenth to the mid-sixteenth centuries. Many ultimately moved to Izmir, though Jews have continued to live in Tire to the present day. A *yeshivah* was established in the sixteenth century and, as late as the early seventeenth century, Tire was known among Turkish Jews as "Katchuk Safet" (little Safed), apparently in reference to the piety of its inhabitants. See M. Benayahu, "Le-Qorot": 48. For more on Tire, see idem, "Taqqanot Tiria," *Qoveẓ ᶜal Yad* n.s. 4 (1946): 193–268; *Encyclopedia Judaica* (EJ) 16:1549; and Nicholas de Lange, *Atlas of the Jewish World* (New York, 1984): 47.

7. Circa 1450–1526, perhaps the greatest halakhic authority in the Ottoman Empire at the time. Over 110 of his *Responsa* were published in two editions, the *editio princeps* [e.p.] from Istanbul (1560–61) and the second from Jerusalem, 1937–38. Others remain in manuscript form. (See J. Hacker, EJ 12:182ff.)

8. See Jerusalem edition, esp. fol. 63a–65a. In "Le-Qorot": 38, M. Benayahu added:

> Two famous men served as the heads of the rabbinical court in Tire: R. Meir ben Yeḥezqel ibn Gabbai and R. Joseph ibn Gaqon. Two other *ḥakhamim* also served on the court, R. Moshe Israel and R. Samuel Aluri.

Like Meir ibn Gabbai, Joseph Gaqon was a Kabbalist of note. Gaqon was extensively quoted and praised in Solomon Alqabeẓ's commentary on the five *megillot*. See "Le-Qorot": 41 n22 for details.

9. On his halakhic activity, also see his personal attestation in the colophon to TY. Apologizing for the shortcomings of the TY, he stated:

> Thirdly, "I did not cease reciting" [TB Shab. 30b] in the dark and deep of night the words of Abbaye and Rabba. As it is said in *Sanhedrin* [24a] "'He has let me dwell in darkness' [Lam. 3:6], meaning, in [the hidden depths of] the Babylonian Talmud." According to the Midrash, "those who walked in darkness"—i.e, who learned Talmud—"they shall see a brilliant light"—the World-to-Come; "On those who dwelt in a land of deep dark, light shall dawn." [Isa. 9:1]

10. On Manissa, see EJ 11:878.

11. See Levi ibn Ḥabib's *She'elot u-Teshuvot me-ha-RaLBaḤ* (Venice, 1565) fol. 124d. The query was signed on the ninth of Tammuz 5300 (1540). Joining ibn Gabbai were Moshe ben Qish and Binyamin ha-Kohen.

12. See *She'elot u-Teshuvot ha-MaBiṬ* (Lwow, 1861), part 1 section 84 (fol. 24b–c). This issue at hand was the attempt of several residents to establish a third recognized community in Manissa, alongside the Lorca and Toledo emigre *qehillot*. The query was signed on the first day of Ḥeshvan 5304 (1543) by six rabbis, with Meir ibn Gabbai at their lead.

13. R. Goetschal concluded that ibn Gabbai died "sometime around 1540, possibly in the Holy Land." G. Scholem cautiously suggested: "after 1540." The *terminus ad quem* for ibn Gabbai's demise is 1560. His first books were printed in that year and refer to the author "of blessed memory."

14. Cf. A. Yaari as cited in n3.

15. Cf. G. Scholem, *Kabbalah* (Jerusalem, 1973): 69. The AQ was first printed in 1566–68 under the title *Mar'ot 'Elohim*. The AQ is comprehensively analyzed in R. Goetschal's recent *Meir ibn Gabbai: Le Discours de la Kabbale*

Espagnole (Leuven, 1981) [hereafter, R. Goetschal]. However, he treats the TY only in passing.

16. *Kabbalah:* 179.

17. To appreciate the significance of the title, it is helpful to consider Meir ibn Gabbai's own explanation and to draw out some of its implications. The author commenced:

> And I shall call my book *Tola^cat Ya^caqov,* "The Worm Jacob," in honor of Israel, who is likened to a worm [ff. Isa. 41:14]. Just as a worm has strength only in its mouth, so Israel has strength only in its people's mouths. . .

But this humbling evaluation is dialectically turned on its head: the worm's very weakness is revealed to be its underlying source of strength. Citing a midrash in *Tanḥuma'* ("Beshallaḥ" 9), he wrote:

> As the worm is soft and weak but can strike the hard and mighty, as a worm can only fell cedars by its mouth, so too, Israel has only prayer. For the heathen nations may be compared to cedars, as it is said: "Behold the Assyrian was a cedar in Lebanon." [Ezek. 31:3]

Here, the worm is a kind of "termite," or alternatively, like the legendary *shamir,* the miraculous worm who split rocks for Solomon's Temple. Prayer is seen as Israel's secret weapon, able to undermine and overcome the physical might of those who seek to harm it. However, prayer is not only—or even primarily—a spiritual weapon but also an outpouring of love for God. To dramatize this notion, ibn Gabbai shifted attention from Israel's persona as termite or shamir to that of gentle silkworm. He wrote:

> In *Genesis Rabbah* [source not extant] it says: What is a worm? That creature which brings forth silk from its mouth, from which are fashioned precious garments, royal garb. So too, Israel prays with their mouths, giving praise to the Holy One, coronating Him over them.

In other words: Israel, a politically weak community in Exile, may *only* have "the power of the mouth" but it is *all* the power it needs: for it is through prayer that God is adorned and redemption ultimately brought about.

Having established the dialectical meaning of the *tola^cat Ya^caqov* through midrashic sources, Meir ibn Gabbai then offered a distinctively Kabbalistic explanation. Focusing on the image of the Jew as silkworm, the image he deemed primary, ibn Gabbai described the harmonious effect mystical prayer has on the divine world:

> When Israel prays with proper intention this causes the Spring to gush forth so that the Great Light [the divine efflux or *shefa^c*] may flow into the holy forms. Then all the branches [lower *sefirot*] unite with their Source.

The consummation of divine restoration is described through imagery of kingly enrobement and coronation, thereby refocusing attention on Israel, the silkworm. As the *tola^cat Ya^caqov* spins a silken garment of holy letters and words,

> The Mother of the Cosmos [*Binah*] crowns King Solomon [*Tif'eret*] and garbs him in raiment of salvation composed of all the colors in the spectrum. This is the mystery of "And Mordechai [*Tif'eret*] went forth before the presence of the king in royal apparel of blue and white, with a magnificent diadem of gold and with a robe of gleaming linen and purple, and the city of Shoshan"—the lily of the valley, the city of David [*Malkhut*]—"exulted and was glad." [Esther 8:15]

Newly crowned and robed in a multi-hued sefirotic light, *Tif'eret* draws near *Malkhut:* "Mordechai the Groom extends his right and left hands to embrace Her"; they unite and the divine world is filled with joy.

The divine harmony promoted by mystical prayer causes blessing to flow onto the People below. Reciprocity is now complete:

> The worm brings forth silk from its mouth to make raiment for the King and the Holy One reciprocates in kind: As Israel dresses Him in precious garb, His face lights up; the Bride and the Groom rejoice and are glad. So too, "the Jews had light and gladness, joy and honor." [Esth. 8:16]

Israel emerges from prayer "victorious." For it is they who are bathed in divine light and who are theurgically empowered. In ibn Gabbai's words, "they have bested their enemies through the power of the mouth."

It should be noted that this dialectical empowerment of the "weak" Jew recalls V. Turner's theoretical writings on liminal castes, i.e., small nations "who fall within the interstices of the social structure" or "are on its margins." Such "powerless" groups are sometimes accorded uncanny mystical power (though in this case it is the powerless caste which is claiming it for itself). Turner writes:

> The structurally inferior [is often] the morally and ritually superior, and secular weakness. . . sacred power. (*The Ritual Process* [Ithaca, 1969]: 125)

For a Zoharic variant on the motif of *tolaʿat Yaʿaqov,* cf. Z 1:177b–78a.

18. It should be recalled that the TY is written within a firmly halakhic viewpoint. New insights universally confirm the authority of tradition by showing a given *halakhah* to be cosmically neccessary. Mystical novellae are employed to determine (rather than merely legitimate) praxis only in matters of *minhag* (custom) and on infrequent occasion, to settle a halakhic debate. (For an example, see *Sod ha-Shabbat,* pp. 25–26 above and the accompanying note, n104 below.) In general, ibn Gabbai exemplified what Scholem has called the "conservative" impulse in mystical life. For further discussion, see G. Scholem's *On the Kabbalah and its Symbolism* (New York, 1965): chapter 1, "Religious Authority and Mysticism" and idem, "Mysticism and Society" in *Diogenes* 58 (1967): 1–24. Also see S.T. Katz, "The Conservative Character of Mystical Experience" in idem (ed.), *Mysticism and Religious Traditions* (NY, 1983): 3–60.

19. On the often radical nature of Meir ibn Gabbai's theurgy, see M. Idel, "The Magical and Theurgic Significance of Music in Jewish Texts from the Renaissance to Hasidism" in *Yuval* Vol. 4 (1982). Also see my *The Sabbath in the Classical Kabbalah* (Albany, 1989) [hereafter, SCK], pp. 194 and 209 n30.

20. This final blessing, termed *birkat 'asher ẓag*, specifically refers to the piercing of the hymen.

21. The preface to the first printed edition (written by his son-in-law, Shneur b. Judah Falqon) maintains:

> This book illumines the prayers for the entire year according to the four-fold method—literal-contextual [*Peshaṭ*], allegorical [*Remez*], legal [*Din*], and mystical *Sod*—whose acronym is *PaRDeS*.

It must be pointed out that Meir ibn Gabbai never made such a claim himself and that this four-fold hermeneutic was not systematically employed. *PaRDeS* may be viewed, however, as a general rubric for the multiplicity of readings—the multi-tiered "truth"—articulated by ibn Gabbai in the TY.

22. The AQ contains detailed polemics against rationalist philosophy, in general, and the RaMBaM (Moses Maimonides) in particular. (Ibn Gabbai obviously knew the RaMBaM's writings very well). In the TY, however, polemical arguments are confined to the Preface. Ibn Gabbai therein refuted RaMBaM's intellectualist rationales for prayer, the priestly blessing, and *ẓiẓit*, and underscored their theurgic power. Following the lead of Shem Ṭov b. Shem Ṭov he contrasted Philosophy (whose source is "in the supernal Ṛealm of Defilement") with Kabbalah, which emanates from the divine realm.

Nevertheless, he did agree with RaMBaM on several points elsewhere in the TY and makes occasional use of the philosophical terminology: *ᶜolam ha-ẓuriyyi, sibbat kol ha-sibbot,* etc. More generally, R. Goetschal has noted that Meir ibn Gabbai's Hebrew style reflects a Tibbonite influence (R. Goetschal: 40).

23. An exception is ibn Gabbai's subscription to the theory of *shemiṭṭot* or Cosmic Cycles in the TY. See *Sod ha-Shabbat*, pp. 49–50 above, where the influence of R. Baḥyya ben Asher is evident. (Also cf. the accompanying note, n336 below.) On the strong influence of Gerona Kabbalah in the AQ, see R. Goetschal: 35 and 501.

24. On occasion, ibn Gabbai did refer to it as *Sefer ha-Zohar*. Cf. TY: 33a.

25. The Zoharic references may be divided into three categories: quotations of the Aramaic original; and two forms of Hebrew paraphrase: explicit citations (usually introduced by: "As it says in the Midrash of RaSHBI" or the like) and indirect borrowings. The former tend to be closer renderings of the Aramaic original.

An issue worthy of mention here is the evolution of Meir ibn Gabbai's style of Zoharic citation. In the first section of the book, he tended to quote the *Zohar* in the original: Twenty-eight such cases may be found in pages 8–40 (Warsaw ed.). In the next eighteen pages, there are but three direct quotations: a brief parable on p. 48a and two passages on pp. 57–58, one of which seems to be a late addition or afterthought (See the notes to *Sod ha-Shabbat*, n460 below.) In the last thirty-six pages, no Aramaic quotations are found. It is hard to know what to make of this stylistic evolution. The two most likely options are that he came upon a translation of the *Zohar* at some point in his writing or that the shift merely represents a "slide" within his own developing style.

The former option merits serious consideration in light of Moshe Idel's recent assertions. In a series of articles published in *ʿAlei Sefer* (1980–81), M. Idel suggests that in AQ Meir ibn Gabbai incorporated the Hebrew translations of the *Zohar* made by David ben Judah he-Ḥasid. I have not been able to procure all the necessary MSS of R. David ben Judah's work to assess its possible influence on the TY. My initial assessment, however, is that they had little, and probably no, influence:

a) Even when explicitly citing the *Zohar*, ibn Gabbai generally employed a looser form of paraphrase than R. David did, at least in the examples I have seen;

b) In his indirect borrowings, ibn Gabbai often interwove several *Zohar* passages at once and did so with a great deal of freedom. These passages are undoubtedly his own; and, finally,

c) Ibn Gabbai employed a Hebrew paraphrase for sections of the *Zohar* that presumably were not translated by R. David, e.g., the TZ!

Given this evidence, it seems likely that the shifts in the patterns of citation reflect a purely internal development within ibn Gabbai's literary style. This merits further investigation.

26. Cf. R. Goetschal: 52–53.

27. I will provide a single example here. Meir ibn Gabbai made unacknowledged use of Israel Al-Naqawa's *Menorat ha-Ma'or* (ca. 1391). See the list of quotations in Hyman Enelow's edition of *Menorat ha-Ma'or* Vol. 4 (New York, 1932): 91–92.

28. Cf. *Sefer ha-Rimmon* (MS Oxf. Bodleian Opp. 344) fol. 51a–b. Meir ibn Gabbai referred only to its author in the TY:

> I wished to include what R. Moshe de Leon wrote on the Mystery of Fasting in accord with what he saw in the Secrets of Wisdom [*sitrei ha-ḥokhmah*.]

This refers not to a specific text (e.g., *Ha-Nefesh ha-Ḥakhamah* as R. Goetschal [p. 36] suggests), but rather to Moshe de Leon's sources of vision and contemplation. My thanks to Prof. Daniel Matt for calling the *Rimmon* passage to my attention.

29. This work was probably written by a member of Moshe de Leon's circle.

30. Although ibn Gabbai attributed his source to the *Qanah* (see my translation, p. 20 below), it clearly came from the *Peli'ah:* 36a. These two works, written by the same anonymous author in northern Greece, ca. 1410, were frequently confused. The problem was especially pronounced in MS editions. According to Michal Oron, the *Peli'ah* was frequently termed "Sefer ha-Peli'ah which is Sefer ha-Qanah" or "Sefer ha-Qanah which is Sefer ha-Peli'ah." On several occasions, the *Peli'ah* is actually titled "Sefer ha-Qanah" or "Sefer ha-Qanah ha-'Arokh." For details see M. Oron's *Ha-Peli'ah ve-ha-Qanah* [!] (Jerusalem, 1980): 31.

Interestingly, in his later AQ 1:18 (36a), ibn Gabbai did mention the *Peli'ah* by name.

31. For example, see Meir ibn Gabbai's disclaimer on 8b: "Please do not blame me, for I wrote the book for myself." He assured his readers that he did not write the book to gain prestige or to benefit materially from his sacred labor. Echoing M. *'Avot* 4:7, he wrote, "I did not compose this book 'for self-aggrandizement, as a crown for my head, nor as a spade with which to dig.' "

Ibn Gabbai apologized for his youth on both p. 8b and in the colophon.

32. That is, those who had derived mystical insight by cleaving unto *Shekhinah,* the divine Apple Orchard or Apple Field. See, e.g., Abraham Azulai in *'Or ha-Ḥammah* to *Zohar* 3:106a:

> The Reapers of the Field are the Comrades, masters in wisdom because *Malkhut [Shekhinah]* is called the Apple Field, and She grows sprouts of secrets and new flowerings of Torah. Those who constantly create new interpretations of Torah are harvesting Her. (Trans. by D. Matt in his *Zohar: The Book of Enlightenment* [NY, 1983]: 29–30.)

33. It is probable that many of these sources were hard to come by in Turkey in the years just after the Spanish Expulsion for the indigenous Jewish community had exhibited little interest in the Sefardic Kabbalistic tradition. See I. Zinberg *A History of Jewish Literature* 5:18 and J. Hacker, "Ha-Peᶜilut ha-'Inṭeleqṭu'alit," cited in n5 above, esp. pp. 587–93.

34. This and several other sources mentioned in this section have been brought to my attention by R. Goetschal: 485ff. Also see *Re'shit Ḥokhmah,* "Shaᶜar ha-Qedushah" 6:48, where de Vidas quoted the TY on *sod ha-ẓiẓit.*

When de Vidas subsequently wrote about prayer in his *Toẓe'ot Ḥayyim,* he made substantial use of TY. See n35 below for examples.

35. *Toẓe'ot Ḥayyim* sec. 205. He explicity quoted from the TY on *Sod ha-Qedushah* (in sec. 209) and on *Sod Nefilat 'Appayim* (in sec. 214).

36. Cf. G. Scholem, "Yediᶜot Ḥadashot ᶜal R. Yosef 'Ashkenazi ha-Tana' mi-Ẓefat" in *Tarbiẓ,* 28 (1958): 59–89 and 201–209.

37. Cf. SHeLaH, Intro.: 2a.

38. A partial list of TY citations in the SHeLaH may be found in R. Goetschal: 491 n18. It is worthwhile noting that fully half of the SHeLaH's mystical interpretations on Shabbat come from the TY. Prominent examples include the preparatory nail-paring, candlelighting, the blessing over the *ḥallot,* the "Mystery of the Three Festive Meals," *Havdalah,* and marital intercourse. For details see SHeLaH, "Tractate Shabbat": *Pereq Torah 'Or.*

39. On the popularization of Kabbalah through *qiẓẓurim* and popular compendia, see Z. Gries' seminal article, "ᶜIẓẓuv Sifrut ha-Hanhagot ha-ᶜIvrit be-Mifneh ha-Me'ah ha-16 u-ve-Me'ah ha-17 u-Mashmaᶜuto ha-Hisṭorit." *Tarbiẓ* 56 (1987): 527–81.

For an example of the early modern dissemination of the TY's teachings, see Yehiel Mikhl Epstein's enormously popular *Qiẓẓur SHeLaH* (e.p., 1683), on the mystical significance of the benediction over the fire at Sabbath *Havdalah.* (This may be found on p. 173a in the 1969 Jerusalem ed.) For a latter-day example of the popularization of the TY see A. Sperling's *Sefer Ṭaᶜamei ha-Minhagim u-Meqorei ha-Dinim* (Lwow, 1895–96): index, s.v. "To-laᶜat Yaᶜaqov." Sperling also cites teachings which he attributes to later sources, but which were originally stated in the TY. Cf. Sperling sec. 254 with *Sod ha-Shabbat,* section 3 (s.v. "to pare one's nails").

40. See R. Goetschal: 491–92.

41. Shalem Shabbazi cited the TY in his commentary to the Torah, *Ḥemdat Yamim.* See R. Goetschal: 492 and G. Scholem's citation in "Sefer Ḥemdat Yamim le-R. Shalem Shabbazi," KS Vol. 5 (1927/28): 272. Prof. Yosef Tobi of Jerusalem recently showed me a MS edition of Shabbazi's unpublished liturgical commentary, *Sefer Beit Tefillah.* Its first words: *Katuv be-Tolaᶜat Yaᶜaqov*—it is written in the TY.

42. The TY is cited in the *Puerto del Cielo* of Avraham ha-Kohen Herrera and in Menasheh ben Israel's *Conciliator.* See R. Goetschal: 494. On the influence of ibn Gabbai's interpretation of prayer on Sabbatcanism, see Ibid.

43. The TY need only be compared with other manuals such as the *Peri ᶜEẓ Ḥayyim* to appreciate its brevity.

44. *Beit ᶜEqed Sefarim* [BES] (Tel Aviv, 1954) Vol. 4: 1067 lists nine editions; the second through ninth editions are the Krakow (1581), Shklov (1797), Lwow (1799), Zolkiew (1817), Boguslav (1820), Lwow (1850), Lwow (1858), and Warsaw (1876). (The tenth edition in this reckoning, the Jerusalem reprint of the Warsaw ed., appeared after BES's publication.)

The Jewish National and University Library in Jerusalem lists nine editions in its catalogue of holdings. It does not have the 1797 Shklov or 1850 Lwow editions. The other variations from the BES include a 1799 Zolkiew edition (presumably the same as BES's "1817" ed.); and the addition of an 1859 edition from Koenigsberg (presumably intended for Lithuanian Jews). This Koenigsberg version would seemingly make eleven editions in all.

45. It should be recalled that printed books were not readily available in Yemen. On the spread of Kabbalah to Yemen in the late sixteenth to early seventeenth centuries, see M. Ḥallamish's introduction to his *Le-Toledot ha-Qabbalah be-Teiman be-Re'shit ha-Me'ah ha-17* (Ramat Gan, 1984).

46. As of 1987, the following MSS were on file in the JNUL Institute of Microfilmed Hebrew Manuscripts:

1) JNUL octo 3913: Adrianople 1546

2) JNUL Mic. 10651 (JTSA Mic. 1553): Sefardic hand with Italian glosses, sixteenth century (According to JTSA cataloguers the text itself was written in an Oriental—i.e., Near Eastern—setting.)

3) Mic. 23211 (NY Lehman 36): Sefardic, sixteenth century (copied from Istanbul e.p.)

4) Mic. 9789 (Sassoon 435/568): Yemen, sixteenth century

5) Mic. 10744 (JTSA Mic. 1646): Sefardic, sixteenth century (Censor: 159[7?])

6) Mic. 9206 (Sassoon 947): n.p., 1601

7) JNUL quarto 949: Yemen, 1607 (MS includes "Tikhlal *Seder Tefillot ha-Shanah be-niqqud ʿelyon* with the TY and *ḥiddushim*.")

8) Mic. 9618 (Sassoon 1189): n.p., 1648

9) Mic. 31118 (NYPL Heb. MS 116/1): Yemen, 1659

10) Mic. 21084 (Rav Kook 242): Yemen, 1666

11) Mic. 10864 (JTSA Mic. 1766): Yemen, seventeenth century

12) Mic. 10846 (JTSA Mic. 1748/1) Yemen, seventeenth century (copied from e.p.)

13) Mic. 9789 (Sassoon 169): Yemen, seventeenth to eighteenth century

14) Mic. 10838 (JTSA Mic. 1740) Yemen, seventeenth to eighteenth century

15) JNUL octo 1301: Yemen, seventeenth to eighteenth century (incomplete)

16) Mic. 31119 (NYPL Heb. MS 117): Saana, Yemen, seventeenth to eighteenth century (incomplete)

17) Mic. 10854 (JTSA Mic. 1756): Yemen, eighteenth century

18) Mic. 30655 (Brooklyn Hebrew College): Yemen, eighteenth century

19) Mic. 24126 (JTSA Mic. 1019): Yemen, eighteenth century (copied from e.p.)

20) Mic. 29149 (JTSA 3112): Yemen, eighteenth century

21) Mic. 36758 (Bar Ilan 295): Yemen, eighteenth century

22) Mic. 10861 (JTSA 1763): Yemen, eighteenth to nineteenth century (Copied from e.p.)

23) JUNL (Yahuda Heb. MS 84): Yemen, eighteenth to nineteenth century

24) Mic. 10849 (JTSA 1751): Yemen, 1871

25) Mic. 40726 (Montreal Elberg 180/2): Ṣaʿadah, Yemen, nineteenth century (copied from e.p.)

26) Mic. 9215 (Sassoon 198/1137): Yemen, nineteenth century

27) no photocopy (Adler 467): no information given

Curiously, JTSA has catalogued entries #2 and #5 as dating from 1507, even suggesting that MS 1646 is a possible autograph. However, as G. Scholem noted in the margin of the text: "It most certainly is not!" Evidently, the cataloguer confused Meir ibn Gabbai's colophon ("completed in 1506/07") with that of the scribe.

By the fall of 1988, as this book was going to press, JNUL had added four more listings, making a total of thirty-one MSS. The new listings, which had not yet been assigned a JNUL Mic. number, were all of Yemenite provenance. They included: JTSA Mic. 1723: seventeenth century; Ben-Ẓvi 3139: seventeenth century; Benayahu 14/2: eighteenth century; and Benayaḥu 363/1: seventeenth to eighteenth century.

47. The Istanbul edition reads very smoothly and has the advantage of having been published by Meir ibn Gabbai's son-in-law, R. Shneur Falqon (who likely had access to the autograph). As is shown later, the Adrianople MS provides the most plausible readings for several problematic passages.

The most readily available edition of the TY (Jerusalem, 1967) is based on the 1876 Warsaw edition, which suffers from intermittent, though mostly minor, typographical errors.

Notes to Sod ha-Shabbat

1. Meir ibn Gabbai begins his exposition by stressing the supreme importance of Shabbat.

The notion that Sabbath-observance might be counted the equivalent of the rest of the *mizvot* is implied in the Biblical corpus. See M. Greenberg, EJ 14:562. This idea was stated more pointedly by the Rabbis. See TJ Ber. 1:1 and 1:5; and TJ Ned. 3:9; as well as the later rendering in Ex. R 25:12. Midrash *Tanhuma'* "Ki Tissa' " was the first to explicitly equate the institution of Shabbat with the entirety of *Torah*, the TY's claim here. Making use of the hermeneutical principle of *gezerah shavah* (comparison of similar expressions) to underscore the equivalence, *Tanhuma'* states:

> R. Joshua b. Nehemiah said: The Holy One spoke unto Israel, saying: "Keep the Sabbath" for it is equal to the entire Torah. Of the Sabbath it is written "*Keep* [*shamor*] the Sabbath day" [Dt. 5:12] and of the Torah, "If you *keep* [*shamor*] it." [Dt. 11:22]

"via parallel structure." Ff. Ex. R 25:12, RaSHI to Num. 15:41 and Moshe de Leon's *Sefer ha-Mishqal* (ed., J. Wijnhoven [hereafter, *Mishqal*]): 110, ibn Gabbai employs the hermeneutical principle of *semukhin* (the juxtaposition of two laws in adjacent verses) to show the equivalence of Shabbat and Torah. The midrash reads:

> R. Eleazer ben Avina said: We have found that Scripture equates the Sabbath with the all the mizvot. . . . How do we learn this in the Hagiographa? It is written: "And you came down upon Mount Sinai and spoke unto them." [Neh. 9:13]. What is written therafter? "And you made known to them Your holy Sabbath." [Ibid.: 14]. The Holy One said to Israel. If you merit to keep the Sabbath, I will consider it as though you kept all the mizvot in the Torah.

2. **"masculine form . . . feminine form."** *Shabbat* is treated as a masculine form in Ex. 20:8, 11 and Isa. 56:2, 6, et al.; and as a feminine form in Lev. 16:31, 23:3 and Jer. 17:24. At least two Midrashic sources—Gen. R 11:8 and the parallel *Pesiqta' Rabbati* 23:7 preserved this ambiguity. See n16 below for details.

Shabbat's grammatical androgyny was given hidden—i.e., theosophical—significance by various Kabbalists. Cf., e.g., *Mishqal:* Ibid; *Sefer ha-Rimmon* [*Rimmon*], MS Brit. Mus. 29a; Bahyya ben Asher to Ex. 20:8; and Menahem Recanati ad loc. This last source reads:

> Because it is said concerning Shabbat "Remember" [Ex. 20:8; kabbalistically, a cipher for *Yesod* or *Tif'eret*] and "Keep" [Dt. 5:12; sefirotically *Malkhut*], it is male and female. Thus, Scripture says:

"Who keeps the Sabbath and does not *meḥallelo*—profane *him.*" [Isa. 56:2] and "Those *meḥalaleha*—who profane *her*—shall be put to death." [Ex. 31:14]

3. **"Two-faces."** (Aramaic, *du-parẓufin*): a reference to the primordial unity of the divine Male and Female, which is renewed each Shabbat. For discussion of this sefirotic or metaphysical state of Shabbat see E. Ginsburg, *The Sabbath in the Classical Kabbalah* [SCK]: 71–74; and I. Tishby, *Mishnat ha-Zohar* (Jerusalem, 1957–61) [hereafter, MZ] 2:493–94.

"Remember" and "Keep." According to TB Shev. 20b, the two versions of the Sabbath Command in the Decalogue "were spoken as one." As intimated above, the Kabbalists interpreted this teaching as a veiled reference to the union of the supernal "Remember" and "Keep." While "Keep" was associated exclusively with *Shekhinah,* the term "Remember" was linked with both *Yesod* and with *Tif'eret* in classical Kabbalah. See, e.g., *Bahir* 180–82; RaMBaN to Ex. 20:8, 31:13; Lev. 19:30; and Dt. 5:15; Baḥyya ben Asher to Ex. 20:8; J. Giqatilia, *Shaᶜarei 'Orah* 1:107; and *Peli'ah* 85c-d, all of which associate "Remember" with *Yesod.* And see Ṭodros Abulafia, *'Oẓar ha-Kavod* [hereafter, OK] to Shab. 33b; Zohar 1:48b, 2:138a, 162a; and 3:115b, etc.; Z 2:92a (*Raᶜaya Meheimna'* [RM]); and *Tiqqunei ha-Zohar* [TZ] Intro (23b), all of which associate "Remember" with *Tif'eret.* (For further discussion, see SCK: 69–71 and E. Wolfson, *The Book of the Pomegranate* [Atlanta, 1988]: 66–67.) Ibn Gabbai has drawn on virtually all of these works in the TY and, not surprisingly, it is not clear which of the two sefirotic options he intended here. In favor of a link with *Tif'eret* is the fact that ibn Gabbai generally followed Zoharic theosophy in the TY and the fact that he tended to associate the apposite term, *du-parẓufin,* with *Tif'eret.* Supporting evidence may also be drawn from ibn Gabbai's later work, AQ, where "Remember" was clearly identified with *Tif'eret.* (See Goetschal: 43, 293.) In favor of a link with *Yesod* is the fact that ibn Gabbai borrowed closely from the *Peli'ah* throughout his prologue (see n11, n15, and n20 below) and more crucially, the fact that "Remember" is linked with *Yesod* in the one annotated use of the term in *Sod ha-Shabbat.* See the text at n337 above (but note the alternate reading contained in n338 which allows for a link with *Tif'eret* as well).

In light of the contradictory evidence, it is entirely possible that ibn Gabbai never consciously chose *between Tif'eret* and *Yesod* here, but read "Remember" more loosely as the "divine Male."

4. This teaching, though perhaps implied in Ex. R 25:12, reached articulation only well into the Middle Ages. TB ᶜEruv. 96a and Mekh. "Yitro" and "Mishpaṭim" linked the miẓvot of omission with "Keep" but no parallel associations were made with the miẓvot of commission and "Remember." Full articulation was likely stimulated by the systematic attempts, from the eleventh century onwards, to subsume all 613 miẓvot under the Ten Commandments. The inclusion of the miẓvot under "Remember" and "Keep" is seemingly an outgrowth of this larger enterprise. (For discussion see E.

Urbach, *HaZaL* [Jerusalem, 1971]: 318ff.) The earliest examples I have been able to locate are those of the Gerona Kabbalists. Cf., e.g., RaMBaN to Ex. 20:8 and Ezra ben Solomon's *TaRYaG Mizvot ha-Yoze'ot me-ᶜAseret ha-Dibberot (Kitvei RaMBaN 2:548).* M. Meier ("A Critical Edition of the Sefer Taᶜamey ha-Mizwoth," Ph.D. diss., Brandeis Univ., [1974], p. 48 n24) has tentatively identified the latter "as the first to associate *Zakhor*/Remember and *Shamor*/ Keep with positive and negative precepts, respectively." R. Ezra wrote:

> These are the 613 mizvot, both of commission and of omission, which are implied in the Ten Commandments via *Remember* and *Keep*. For this reason our Rabbis, of blessed memory, stated: "Remember and Keep were uttered as one" [TB Shev. 20b] . . . referring to the [mizvot] *of commission and omission.*

As is clear from his *Perush le-Shir ha-Shirim* (to Cant. 4:11), R. Ezra derived all 613 mizvot from the *sefirotic* "Remember" and "Keep." See *Kitvei RaMBaN* 2:496–97 for details. Also see Bahyya ben Asher to Ex. 20:8, as well as *Mishqal:* Ibid.

5. Meir ibn Gabbai finds a Kabbalistic secret in the exoteric equation of Shabbat and Torah, for their archetypes (the "divine Shabbat" and the supernal Torah) both connote divine perfection, the union of *Tif'eret/Yesod* and *Shekhinah.*

Earlier Kabbalistic versions of this teaching are numerous. Cf., e.g., *Zohar* [Z] 2:47a, 89a, 151a; 2:92a (RM); TZ 19 (40b) and 21 (54a–b and 57a); and *Tiqqunei Zohar Hadash* [TZH] 12lb, as well as *Sefer ha-Mishqal*: 110, which forms the closest parallel to the TY here. Also see *Me'irat ᶜEinayim:* 108; Menahem Recanati, *Taᶜamei ha-Mizvot* 10a; Bahyya ben Asher, *Kad ha-Qemah* (*Kitvei* 2:391); and David ben Judah he-Hasid's expansive claim (OZ 46a): "Whoever keeps the Sabbath it is as though he kept the entire Torah, for the Torah, Shabbat and the [supernal] reality are all one."

6. Here ibn Gabbai begins a second interpretation of the divine "Shabbat," one which derives from *illo tempore,* the primordial Week of Creation.

"the six levels . . . Structure." That is, the six *sefirot*, from *Hesed* to *Yesod,* active in the work of Creation. See the discussion in SCK: 32, 72, and 146 n48; and in I. Tishby, MZ 1:143.

7. Under the sway of the seventh of the active rungs, *Shekhinah.*

8. *Binah.*

9. **"they all rested."** That is, attained the state of Shabbat, of completion. The origins of this teaching may be found in R. Asher ben David's *Sefer ha-Yihud* (published in *Ha-Segullah* [1937], p. 4):

> In the six days all the rungs performed their function and when the seventh day arrived, they all ceased; the seventh day [*Shekhinah*] performed its function and completed that which was lacking: namely, cessation from labor, rest. . . . Each rung caused the rung below

> it to cease, and it proceeded until the seventh, which is *Shabbat* [cessation] for them all.

Also cf. Baḥyya ben Asher's recasting of this source, ad Num. 15:32. For discussion, see SCK: 72ff.

10. The printed version of the TB reads: "he must count six days and observe one." However, Meir ibn Gabbai's variant was not uncommon in medieval manuscripts. Cf., e.g., Ṭodros Abulafia, OK to TB Shab. 69b.

11. On the notion that all seven lower *sefirot* are "Shabbat," see SCK: 72 and esp. 146 n48.

Throughout this section—from n9–11—the TY seems to be building on expositions found in Menaḥem Recanati to Ex. 16:26 and *Peli'ah* 85d (Part 1, end). The Recanati source reads:

> "Six days shall you gather it; on the seventh day, Shabbat, there shall be none." [Ex.16:26]: . . . Know that all six Points transform things from the potential to the actual . . . and the rungs are sustained by the *shefa*[c] coming from the "Source of Life"; the divine flow comes from *'Ein Sof* unto the first of the six Points [*Ḥesed*], proceeding until it reaches the final *sefirah*, called "Shabbat" [*Shekhinah*]. She is filled with blessing by all [the rungs]. This is the cessation [*shebitah*], the delight and rest that is equal to all. Hence this is called "Shabbat" for She is *shabbat* [cessation] unto them all and delight and rest unto Herself, by means of the inner light that spreads through Her from the rungs above. Because each rung comes to a halt as it completes transforming the potential into the actual, our Rabbis claimed: "If one is lost in the desert and does not know when Shabbat is, he should count six days and cease working on the seventh," for all the rungs are Shabbat [i.e., at rest].

12. ***Bat-*[c]*Ayin.*** Lit., "the daughter of the eye"; idiomatically, "the apple of the eye," i.e., the pupil. According to Moses Cordovero, *Pardes Rimmonim* [PR] Gate 23: "[*Malkhut*] is called *Bat-*[c]*Ayin* when She is surrounded by the three hues [of the eye] which are the Patriarchs," i.e., when She is reintegrated into the divine realm.

On this eye-imagery see *Zohar* 1:226a and 2:23a–b, where the three Patriarchs are likened to the white sclera, the colored iris and the dark outer portion of the pupil. *Shekhinah* is the center of the pupil, the darkest hue of all. See the discussion in PR 23: [c]*Ayin* and D. Matt, *Zohar* (NY, 1983): 243–44.

On *Shekhinah*'s liberation from the demonic realm ("the Narrow Straits") each Shabbat, see the extended discussion in SCK, chaps. 1 and 3.

13. That is, the entire active divine realm is now in perfect harmony. Here Meir ibn Gabbai is following Z 2:204a where the re-integration of the divine Daughter [*BaT*] into the Patriarchs (symbolized by the three-pronged

ש) is said to "spell" *SHaBbAT* [ת ב ש]. See the explanation in SCK: 73–74. For parallel sources, see Z 3:28lb (RM); TZ 21 (45b and 55b) and 22 (67a).

14. Here the so-called male Sabbath. On this connotation of Shabbat, see SCK: 69–70.

15. From here through the end of n22, Meir ibn Gabbai is clearly drawing on *Peli'ah* 85c–d. Compare! The *Peli'ah* source explicitly identifies the male Sabbath with *Yesod* here, and it is likely that ibn Gabbai is following suit.

16. **"!"** Aramaic, *'etmeha'*, an expression of astonishment.

"brings us up short." For ibn Gabbai the astonishment deepens as the formerly feminine Sabbath is suddenly rendered in the masculine form, *'amar lo.* Thereafter, the text reverts to the feminine form for Shabbat, speaking of *ben zugekh, her* masculine mate. It may be noted that ibn Gabbai's version of the midrash was not unusal in medieval sources; cf. R. Isaac of Acco, *Me'irat ᶜEinayim:* 20 (line 30); *Be'ur Sodot ha-RaMBaN* to Gen. 2:3; Shem Ṭov ibn Gaon, *Keter Shem Ṭov:* 25a and 38a; and of course, *Peli'ah* 85c.

17. Although *le-qaddesho* is conventionally rendered "to sanctify it," it may also connote betrothal. On this midrash and its Kabbalistic interpretations, see SCK: 102–03, 109–11, etc.

18. From a critical standpoint, the grammatical androgyny of Shabbat in this midrash may have resulted from a scribal error; however, for the Kabbalist it is a cipher alluding to a primordial mystery.

19. The quotation is from TB Ḥul. 60b. The extended text reads:

> R. Shimon ben Pazzai pointed out a contradiction [in a Biblical verse]. The verse opens, "And God made the two great lights" [Gen. 1:16] and immediately continues, "the greater light . . . and the lesser light." The moon said unto the Holy One: "Sovereign of the Universe! Is it possible for two kings to wear one crown?" He answered, "Go then and make yourself smaller," etc.

Legends of the moon's diminution abound in the Aggadic literature. Cf. TB Pes. 68a, Shev. 9a; Gen. R 6:3; and the sundry sources discussed in L. Ginzberg, *Legends of the Jews* [*Legends*] (Philadelphia, 1968) 5:34–36. Kabbalistically, the *Ḥullin* legend is understood to connote the primordial unity and equality of the divine Male (the Sun) and *Malkhut* (the Moon). Before *sod ha-nesirah*—the cosmic bifurcation—they constituted one undifferentiated "Shabbat." For details see *Zohar* 1:169b, 2:252a; *Zohar Ḥadash* [ZḤ] 18b; *Peli'ah* 85c; as well as pp. 73–74 above.

"Shabbat had no mate . . . other essences." The other cosmic days of the week—the six *sefirot* from *Binah* through *Hod*—were paired while the undifferentiated Shabbat remained alone. In addition to the *Peli'ah* source, cf. *Be'ur Sodot ha-RaMBaN* to Gen. 2:3 (translated in SCK: 111); Menaḥem

Recanati ad loc.; and Joseph Albo's interpretation ff. the "Sages of Kabbalah" in *ᶜIqqarim* (Husik ed.) Vol. 3:64–65.

It may be noted that the diminution of the moon is generally seen as a tragic development in the Kabbalistic literature, a way of symbolizing *Shekhinah*'s Fall, the onset of Her Exile. (See pp. 73–74 above and n638.) But here it has more positive connotations: it is an act of separation that dialectically facilitates a more meaningful or profound union.

20. Kabbalistically, the gender change in the midrash alludes to a momentous change within the Godhead. The initial feminine form refers to the undifferentiated Shabbat prior to separation. Since Shabbat lacks a partner below to whom it can convey *shefaᶜ*, it can only receive blessing. In its passivity/receptivity it is considered—ff. regnant philosophical convention—to be "feminine."

In the *Peli'ah* source ibn Gabbai is utilizing, the masculine form refers to *Yesod*, the distinctively "male" Sabbath, after the separation. Shabbat can now actively convey blessing to a mate, *Shekhinah*, below. As noted, separation must precede fully realized union.

Again cf. *Be'ur Sodot ha-RaMBaN* to Gen. 2:3; Joseph Albo, *ᶜIqqarim* 3:63–64; *Peli'ah* 85c; and the more concise version found in Menaḥem Recanati to Gen. 2:3:

> Before the diminution of the Moon, when "two kings made use of one crown," Shabbat had no mate [below] to receive [divine energy] as did the other entities. But when the Moon was diminished, He gave [Shabbat/*Yesod*] the supernal Community of Israel as His mate, as in "they are joined to one another" [Job 41:9] and "even as a man embracing his wife." [I K 7:36 ff. TB *Yoma'* 54a–b]

21. These Scriptural verses are taken as references to the cherubim in the Holy of Holies, which according to Talmudic tradition (TB BB 99a) "were male and female, united as one." In the Rabbinic interpretation, the male cherub was considered the symbol of God whereas the female cherub, nestled in his embrace, represented the Community of Israel. Cf., e.g., TB *Yoma'* 54a:

> Rabbi Qaṭṭina said: Whenever Israel came up for the Festival, the curtain would be removed for them and the cherubs were shown to them. [The cherubs'] bodies were intertwined with one another, and they would be addressed: "Look, you are beloved before God as the love between man and woman."

Also see BB 99a and RaSHBaM ad loc.; Lam. R, Intro: 9; PRK 19 and YS to Isa., sec. 474.

In the TY (as elsewhere in the Kabbalistic tradition) it is the *divine* Male and Female—the Holy One and the supernal Community of Israel—who are the embracing cherubim. For a sampling of Zoharic sources see Z 1:154b, 2:176a, 278a, 3:59a–b; 3:229a (RM), ZḤ Terumah 53b; and TZḤ 149b–50b. Also see the discussion in n426.

"ke-ma^car 'ish ve-loyot [לויות]." This verse was the subject of Rabbinic speculation. Although Biblical scholars render the problematic term לויות as wreaths (hence "with wreaths all around"), TB *Yoma'* 54a–b vocalized לויות as *levayot,* hence: "a man embracing his mate [*levayah shelo*]." The TY's interpretation follows this Talmudic reading:

> What is the meaning of this verse? Rabba bar Rav Shilah said: "Even as a man embraces his mate." Resh Laqish said: ". . . the cherubs' bodies were interwined with one another. . . ."

Also see RaSHI ad loc.: "The cherubs were joined together, and were cleaving to and embracing each other, like a man who embraces the female." For extended discussion of the cherubim in the Jewish religious imagination, see R. Patai, *Man and Temple* (NY, 1967): 91–94; idem, *Hebrew Goddess* (NY, 1978): Chap. 3; and M. Idel, *Kabbalah: New Perspectives,* (New Haven, forthcoming), Chap. 6, "Kabbalistic Theosophy," s.v. "Du-parẓufim."

22. **"the corporeal Israel."** E.p. and the MSS all read *Keneset Yisra'el ha-gashmi.* The Warsaw ed. of the TY mistakenly reads *Keneset Yisra'el ha-neshamah*! Meir ibn Gabbai is here clearly following *Peli'ah* 85d verbatim: *Keneset Yisra'el ha-gashmi tehe' bat zugekh ve-tihyeh sar ve-nagid ᶜaleihem.*

Discussion: Here ibn Gabbai looks at the midrash a second time. Previously, it was *Yesod* that was the primary (or active) Shabbat whereas *Shekhinah* was the receptive "Community of Israel." Now it is *Shekhinah*—the Bride—that is the primary Shabbat and the earthly Community of Israel that is Her mate. *Shekhinah* may be said to lack a mate in the sense that She has no one below Her to receive Her blessing and be subject to Her. By divine decree, the People Israel step into the breach. Note that the People Israel are termed *bat zugekha,* the female companion for *Shekhinah,* which now assumes the dominant "masculine" role!

The TY's extended interpretation of Gen. R 11:8 illustrates the multivocality of Kabbalistic symbolism. On the one hand the primary midrashic stage has been moved to the intradivine world: each Shabbat, the divine Groom and *Shekhinah* are betrothed unto each other. But on another level *Shekhinah* and the People Israel are said to exist in a special relationship. And on a third level, the exoteric Rabbinic meaning has been preserved. That is, by keeping the Sabbath day, the Jew is consecrated unto it. But this exoteric meaning now takes on a sacramental quality; Sabbath-observance is the outward sign of the intradivine process.

23. In the ensuing list I have translated Meir ibn Gabbai's words in rather literal fashion, not attempting to impose a uniform grammatical structure where none exists. With the exception of categories 14–18, the list follows a chronological order, beginning with Sabbath-preparation and ending with *Havdalah.* Categories 14–16 and 18 refer to activities which are desirable throughout Shabbat. Category 17 deals with an exceptional (i.e., rarely occurring) case.

24. Heb., *ᶜonat talmidei ḥakhamim:* Rabbinic idiom connoting marital intercourse. See TB BQ 82a.

25. A play on words. *BaKH* (lit., "in it" is equivalent to the number 22 in gematria. Cf. TZ 70 (132b).

Kabbalistically: Through proper Sabbath observance one regales and delights in one's Beloved. On this motif see Joseph Giqatilia's *Sodot*, section 3 (discussed in SCK, Appendix I).

26. The emphasis here is on making provisions for the festive meals. Meir ibn Gabbai provides two basic rationales for this custom: a standard eschatological explanation (enabling one to attain life in the World-to-Come; and a specifically Kabbalistic-theurgic rationale (enabling the devotee to augment divinity). He concludes by providing a mystical-ethical rationale for providing for the poor before Shabbat.

27. **"the entirety of the holy rungs":** i.e., the most inclusive principle, the sefirotic totality. See, e.g., Z 2:92a (RM):

> The Sabbath is the mystery of the Whole Faith [the sefirotic totality] which issues from the Supernal Head [*Keter*] and stretches onto the final rung. Shabbat is All.

For further discussion, see SCK: 72–74.

"she who . . . rests." Kabbalistically, an allusion to *Shekhinah*, the most immanent divine Sabbath; On Shabbat She is commonly called *kol*, the Totality, for She absorbs the fullness of the divine world.

On *Shekhinah*/Shabbat as honored guest see SCK: 218–19, 256 and 286. On *Shekhinah*/Shabbat as numinous presence, see Ibid.: 243 and the ZḤ passage cited on p. 30 above.

28. Ff. M. *Pe'ah* 1:1 and TB Shab. 127a.

29. **"what shall he eat?"** Heb., *mah yo'khal*. Printed version of TB reads *me-heikhan yo'khal*, "whence shall he eat?"

For the *Zohar*'s treatment of this AZ passage see 1:196b: "Whoever does not prepare provisions for the journey in this world will not eat in the other world."

30. M. *'Avot* 4:2. That is, that which sustains one in the World-to-Come.

31. TB *Niddah* 16b. The text continues: "Will it be strong or weak, wise or foolish, rich or poor? Whether it be righteous or wicked is not decreed."

32. A reference to the injunction to gather an extra portion of manna on Friday for use on the Sabbath. On the TY's image of each person holding the scales of justice, see n36.

33. Heb., *hu' poreʿa*, ff. TB Beiẓ. 15b. In other words, any reward is an epiphenomenon. The underlying intention must be theurgic, *le-ẓorekh gavoha*.

For detailed discussion of "service from love" see Meir ibn Gabbai's later AQ 1:27–28. Briefly, this "inner [dimension of] Love" is service whereby one "gives of one's entire being, with no thought of a reward." This is service *li-shmah*, conventionally "for its own sake" but here read, "for the sake of the Name." Ibn Gabbai explains: "One who serves from true love unifies . . . His Name [i.e., the sefirotic world]." (AQ 1:28).

34. **"promote peace between the two Lovers."** Unite *Shekhinah* and *Tif'eret.*

"Diadem of grace." Heb., *livyat ḥen,* ff. Prv. 1:9.

On ritual life as a means of unifying and coronating divinity, see SCK: 200–01.

35. **"Borrow on my account."** Heb., *levu ᶜalai.* It is conceivable that ibn Gabbai is here reading the phrase as "Join" or "Unite Me," in accordance with an alternate meaning of the root *LVH.*

36. Here ibn Gabbai's imagery recalls RaMBaM, *Mishneh Torah* [MT] "Hilkhot Teshuvah" 3:4:

> Everybody should, therefore, regard himself throughout the year as half innocent and half guilty; so too, he should consider the entire world as half innocent and half guilty. If, then, he commits one additional sin he presses down the scale of guilt against himself and the entire world, and causes his destruction; if, on the other hand, he performs a miẓvah he presses down the scale of merit in his favor and that of the entire world, and causes deliverance and salvation to reach him and his fellows.

37. Here Meir ibn Gabbai begins a paraphrase of Z 2:255a. See n41 for details.

38. "Kingdom of Heaven." *Malkhut* or more generally, the divine realm which directly sustains the world on Shabbat. Cf., e.g., Z 1:48a, 2: 135a–b, Z 3:273b (RM), TZ 21 (57a) and many others.

39. That is, imbues divinity with joy. This interpretation underscores the theurgic valence of Kabbalistic ritual.

40. On the custom of providing for the poor on Sabbath eve see the allusions in M. *Pe'ah* 4:8 and 8:7; and TB Ket. 67b. Also see the more detailed codifications in MT "Hilkhot Mattenot ᶜAniyyim" 9:1–3, 6 and Ṭur YD 256. A noteworthy description of this custom is found in Moshe ibn Makhir's *Sefer Seder ha-Yom* (late sixteenth century); it is worth quoting from here. While setting forth the guidelines for Sabbath-preparation, ibn Makhir stated:

> Even if one eats simply during the week, [on Shabbat] he should try to be like a prince and his household, like royalty. One should share the bounty with the local poor, giving them either a cooked

> meal or a loaf of bread, or that failing, money to the town treasury, to be distributed to the needy.
> But it is best to give a portion of that which one prepares so that they be equal in dining, he and the poor person. One should have neither more nor less. The *ẓedaqah* should be given so that the poor person need not be bothered and have to go out again to obtain sufficient food. And who knows whether he will find it or not . . .? No sensitive [*baʿal nefesh*] or God-fearing person should eat on Friday night till he has given a portion of his choicest food to a poor person living near him, whether by inviting the poor man to one's own table or by sending the food to his home. . . . The point is not to impoverish oneself and one's household, but to give a portion to a poor soul, even one-sixtieth of the meal, for he is poorer than you. Each person must look out for those who are less well-off. And so all Israel are compassionate and gracious with one another, and the Holy One the most of all, for He is the Compassionate Father at all times. (38a)

41. For Rabbinic interpretation of this verse, cf. TB BB 10a.

The notion that by being gracious to the poor one is "lending unto the Lord" takes on special theurgic meaning in the Zoharic tradition. As I. Baer has noted, the poor are commonly seen as the worthiest of souls in both the *Zohar* and TZ/RM. (See his *History of the Jews in Christian Spain* [Philadelphia, 1961]: "Mysticism and Social Reform," 1:261ff. for sources and socio-historical analysis.) Not infrequently, *Shekhinah* is symbolized as the Poor One, "without anything of Her own." The human poor are seen as Her most worthy symbols. See, e.g., Z 3:113b and 2:86b: "Anyone who mistreats a poor person mistreats *Shekhinah*." Conversely, divinity rejoices—and is strengthened by—acts of kindness on behalf of the poor. See *Ẓavva'at R. 'Eliʿezer*, sec. 27 and ZḤ Ruth 87b (MN): "The Holy One enjoys the food that one gives to the poor person because that food satisfies the poor person." Elsewhere, Moshe de Leon claimed that it is the poor who enable divine blessing to be directed into the world. See, e.g., Z 3:103b–04a (on the *Sukkot 'Ushpizin*).

As noted above, ibn Gabbai has been relying on Z 2:255a (*Heikhalot di-Qdushah*) in this last section. The *Zohar* reads:

> It is written: "So I commended joy that a man has no better thing under the sun than to eat and drink and to be merry, and it will accompany him in his labor all the days of his life which God has given him under the sun." [Eccles. 8:15]
>
> "So I commended joy": Did King Solomon commend this [i.e., this seemingly indulgent position]? Rather, this joy refers to the Joy of the Holy King during the time of His reign, namely on Sabbaths and holy days. For of all the good deeds that a person can do, "none is better under the sun than to eat and drink," and to show joy before that Realm, that he may attain the World-to-Come. "*Hu'*

will accompany him in his labor": Who? None other than the Holy One who will usher him into the World-to-Come.

Another interpretation: *Hu' yilvennu. Hu'* refers to the person who eats, drinks and rejoices. For with whatever [*kavvanah* or intentionality] he expends in his eating and drinking, he lends unto [theurgically affects] the Holy One. He will be repaid many times over for his expenditure.

There are two ways in which a person can lend unto the Holy One: [first] when he treats the poor with compassion; second, when he prepares for the Sabbath and holidays. For both lend unto the Lord, as it is written: "Whoever is gracious to the poor lends unto the Lord; and He will repay him for his kindness." [Prv. 19:17]

42. Ff. TB Ber. 8a. As part of the spiritual preparation for Shabbat.

43. Both opinions are stated in Tos. to TB Ber. 8a–b:

> Some say that it should be recited in one's vernacular . . . for just as the *Targum* explained passages for the unlettered [*ᶜammei ha-'areẓ*], so may the [current] vernacular be used so that all may understand the text. But this ruling is not sound, for the *Targum* explains that which one [i.e., even a great scholar] could not understand from the Hebrew alone. . . . Hence, [the Torah Portion] must be recited a third time specifically in the *Targum*.

Interestingly, certain Kabbalists were also divided on the issue of studying *Targum 'Onqelos:* I suspect that Meir ibn Gabbai has them in mind, as well. Although the *Zohar* mandates its recitation (see below), the *Peli'ah* (from which ibn Gabbai later quotes; see n49) holds: "If one does not understand *Targum* [*'Onqelos,*] he may recite the text in Greek [i.e., the local vernacular] or in some other language or in Hebrew a third time." (36a)

44. That is, because the *Targum* is of Sinaitic origin, it mandates the same formal respect accorded the Hebrew text.

45. **"the hair of the *tefillin*."** According to TB Shab. 28b and 108a, the Scriptural portions which are placed in the apertures of the tefillin "are to be tied around with the hair. . . . of a clean animal." Like the other laws concerning the composition of tefillin, the TB asserts that "this too is a law given to Moses at Sinai [*halakhah le-Mosheh mi-Sinai.*]" (This is the Rabbinic term for those Oral laws possessing Biblical authority but which are neither stated in the Bible nor derived via hermeneutical principles.)

The first extant source to give a specific rationale for this law was *Shimmusha' Rabba'* (ca. late twelfth century Languedoc, but containing much older material) which required that the hair be that of a calf "that we might recall the Incident of the (Molten) Calf and not sin." RaMBaM (MT "Hilkhot Tefillin" 3:8) simply reports that "it is the universal custom nowadays to tie around a hair from a calf's tail." The thirteenth century French work, *Sefer Miẓvot Qaṭan* also mandates calf-hair, specifically "as *atonement* for the

Incident of the Calf." However, other medieval authorities permit other types of hair, so long as they come from a kosher animal. See Ṭur OḤ 32:47 and BY ad loc. for details.

The Kabbalists reshaped this halakhah in line with specifically magical concerns. In doing so they undoubtedly drew on the popular understanding of tefillin as a kind of amulet. (See J. Trachtenberg, *Jewish Magic and Superstition* [NY, 1939]: 145.) According to *Zohar* 2:237b, e.g., one calf-hair must protrude from the tefillin as a kind of offering of appeasement to *Siṭra' 'Aḥra'* [*piyyus ha-din.*] Also see *Sefer ha-Qanah* 31a–33b and 67a; and Menaḥem Recanati, *Ṭaʿamei ha-Miẓvot* sec. 67 and idem., *Perush ʿal ha-Torah,* "Bo'" (end; 42b). The latter reads:

> You should be alert to the mystery of the calf's hair which is tied around the Scriptural portions of the tefillin, for it is a great mystery. It is a miẓvah that there be a loop protruding from the box in order to appease the aspect of *Din,* and to grant it a portion in our holy [act]. . . .

As I noted in SCK: 226 and 230 hair is a marginal—hence, dangerous—entity, susceptible to pollution and symbolically associated with *Siṭra' 'Aḥra'.* In the words of ZḤ Yitro 37a, "hair is *Din.*" But when utilized in minute quantities, in the controlled context of ritual life, it may serve as a kind of "vaccine": a modicum of evil that may ward off a much greater, indeed cosmic, evil. The aforementioned Zohar source (2:237b) relates that by placing a calf-hair in the tefillin, the demonic realm may be bribed or assuaged and harm thereby averted. Although *Din* has a legitimate place in the pre-Messianic world, one must strive to limit and neutralize its ruinous power:

> R. Shimon said: Even though [Evil is a destructive, polluting force] as you suggest, the Holy One accords it some power; hence, the Spirit of Defilement must be defeated in every possible manner. Come and I will reveal to you another mystery, one that may only be revealed to supernal holy ones. Come and see! . . . The Holy One has granted the Spirit of Pollution control over the world in several areas. It may therefore injure us, and we have no right to treat it cavalierly; we must take care lest [*Siṭra' 'Aḥra'*] inveigh against us in our holy acts. We have, therefore, a secret [device]: to assign the Accuser a little portion within our holy acts, since he derives his power from Holiness [the sefirotic world].
>
> For this reason, we are enjoined to place a calf-hair inside the tefillin, with one end jutting out so that it is visible. This hair is incapable of communicating defilement, since it is smaller than a grain of barley. . . . We give this hair a place within our sacred [instrument], lest [the Accuser] inveigh against us. . . . When *Siṭra' 'Aḥra'* beholds this hair within the supremely holy, and finds that he has a portion therein, he will not inveigh against [the wearer] and will be powerless to cause him harm on high or below; for he has given [Evil] a place.

The *Zohar* interprets several other rituals in this light, e.g., the scapegoat offered on Yom Kippur, the red heifer, and *mayim 'aḥaronim.* One purpose of sacrifice, in general, was to bribe and appease *Din.* For details see I. Tishby's discussion in MZ 1:290–92 and 2:206–10. For further discussion of the apotropaic power of tefillin also see M. Oron, *Ha-Peli'ah ve-ha-Qanah:* 254–57.

46. **"The Torah . . . Targum."** That is, the *Targum* serves as a *qelippah* or shell which protects the sacred "fruit" of Torah from defilement. For details, see the discussion below.

"curtains of goat-hair . . . Tabernacle." Like *Targum* and the hair in the tefillin, the goat-hair is a modicum of non-virulent evil which protects the divine realm/*Shekhinah* ("the Tabernacle") from more ruinous Evil. Cf. *Zohar* 2:233b and esp. 2:213a. According to the latter, the divine world is surrounded by two protective layers or "curtains." The outer layer is composed of the "curtains of [coarse] goat-hair," i.e., the least harsh aspect of the Other Side, whereas the inner layer is made of more refined curtains [ff. Ex. 26:31], connoting the angelic worlds. The text states:

> "You shall make curtains of goat-hair for a tent over the Tabernacle." For there are curtains and there are curtains. The curtains of the Tabernacle itself are called the firmaments of the Creatures of the Holy Tabernacle. The curtains of goat-hair are other firmaments, from *Siṭra' 'Aḥra'.* They are the firmaments for the Chariots of the holy spirits [the angelic worlds]. . . . The goat-hairs are the from the Side of Defilement . . . and they cover the firmaments within like a shell [*qelippah*] covers the fruit.

Discussion: Ibn Gabbai's ambivalent view of the Targum, and indeed of the Aramaic language itself, stems (oddly enough) from that Aramaic classic, the *Zohar.* On the one hand, Moshe de Leon spoke of the holy power of Aramaic in his interpretation of *Qedushah de-Sidra'* (2:129a). But immediately thereafter, in his discussion of the *Qaddish,* he stated that the power of Aramaic derives from its affinity with *Siṭra' 'Aḥra'.* In a memorable phrase he averred "*Targum* is the language of *Siṭra' 'Aḥra'.*" That is, *Targum* is that aspect of *Din* from the Side of Holiness which girds and protects divinity (symbolized as Hebrew); like a vaccine, Aramaic may be used to counteract its more virulent strain, the "Other Side":

> Through this language [*Targum*] *Siṭra' 'Aḥra'* will necessarily be subjugated and his power sapped, even as the power of the Holy One will ascend. [Reciting the *Targum*] shatters the locks and heavy chains [constraining the holy realm]; it breaks the power of the evil *qelippot.* Thereupon, the Holy One will recall his Name and that of His children. (2:129b)

One wonders how Moshe de Leon understood his own Aramaic writing. For this external language liberated his mystical imagination in a way that the more sacred Hebrew did not. (See D. Matt: 26ff. and SCK: 19.) On the relative importance of Hebrew and Aramaic in the *Zohar,* also see Z 2:132b.

47. **"promotes wholeness."** Only by consciously including (and thereby neutralizing) evil can wholeness be attained. The point is to "detoxify" evil, not to deny it. See p. 20 above and n53, below. And see now E. Wolfson, "Left Contained in the Right: A Study in Zoharic Hermeneutics," *AJS Review* 11 (1986): 27–52. For a psychoanalytic account of this dialectical notion of "wholeness," see C. Jung, "The Relations between the Ego and the Unconscious" in *The Portable Jung* (NY, 1971): 70–138, passim, and his discussion of *conjunctio oppositorum* in "Answer to Job" (Ibid.: 519–650).

"These men . . . whole through us [*shelemim hem 'ittanu.*]" Meir ibn Gabbai's reading of the verse is unusual. A more conventional rendering of *shelemim* is "peaceable." The indirect object *us* refers to the sons of Ḥamor, kabbalistic symbols of the forces of defilement, and the subject, "these men," to the children of Israel—kabbalistically, the divine realm and/or earthly Israel.

48. The "double" recitation is an allusion to the ascent of of *Ḥesed* (here, *gold*) and more generally, to the imminent sefirotic harmony of Shabbat. According to Z 3:143b (1R):

> When the entire [divine realm] is perfumed, forming one body, this is "we will add circlets of gold to your spangles of silver." [Cant. 1:11] Judgment and compassion become entwined, and the Female is perfumed within the Male.

Contrast this rationale of "the Hebrew text twice" with *Zohar* 2:132b.

49. **"Book Qanah."** Actually, *Peli'ah* 36a. On the confusion of these two works, see p. 81 (n30).

Although the initial rationale for reciting the *Targum* on Friday afternoon stresses the apotropaic-separating function of preparatory ritual (see SCK, chap. 2–3), the rationale here is symbolic-unitive, directing attention to the imminent integration of *Targum/Shekhinah* in the divine Male, *Tif'eret* + *Yesod* ("the Hebrew text twice"). The continuation of the *Peli'ah* more clearly stresses the *theurgic* valence of this act:

> "Complete them, *'ashlimu*" [ff. TB Ber. 8b]: create peace, wholeness. "Your portions": the divine rungs. "Together with the congregation": in order to unite them so that all is complete, *be-shalom* . . .

50. Sections 3–6 constitute a "rite of passage" whereby the devotee leaves behind the profane world of the week and gradually enters the unfolding Sabbath-cosmos. All four of these sections have been analyzed in detail in the SCK. The discussion concerning ritual nail-paring may be found on pp. 224–27. I shall limit myself to new material here.

Throughout Section 3 Meir ibn Gabbai is relying on an Edenic myth found in *Zohar* 2:208b. However, he applies it to a new ritual context, specifically integrating nail-paring into Sabbath-preparation.

51. The Adamic garment of nail is first mentioned explicitly (as *levushei ṭufra'*) in *Targum Yerushalmi* to Gen 3:7 and 3:21. Also see PRE 14. According

to an earlier source, Gen. R 20:12,the Edenic garment was "smooth like nails and shone like pearls." The motif of the primordial garment of nails entered the Kabbalah via the *Bahir* (60) and occurs frequently in the Zoharic corpus , e.g., 1:263a, 2:208b and TZ Intro (10b).

The Rabbinic legend of the "horny" Edenic garb may have its roots in various Gnostic speculations on the cloak of Primordial Man. Although this cloak is most frequently imaged as an effulgence of Light, at least one source, attributed to the Persian Mani, speaks of Primal Man's spiritual "armor." For details, see H. Jonas, *The Gnostic Religion* (Boston, 1963): 216ff.

52. **"lights left him."** According to Gen. R 20:12 the Edenic garment was *ketonet 'or,* a garment of light, a word-play on Gen. 3:21, *kotnot ʿor.* See, L. Ginzberg, *Legends* 5:103 for other ancient parallels.

I might note that the *Zohar*—and hence Meir ibn Gabbai—freely mixes nail-, Chariot- and light-imagery when speaking of the primordial garment. See e.g., Z 1: 36b, 261b, and 2:229b which states: "When Adam was in the Garden of Eden he was cloaked . . . in a garment of supernal light" issuing from the divine world. According to Z 1:53a, Adam and Eve were surrounded by an armor of radiant holy letters (*zainei 'atvan nehirin qaddishin*) which protected them from Death. Also see TZ Intro (10b): "Adam was garbed in a cloak of nails which shone like the clouds of glory (ff. PRE 14)."

"that Inclination." That is the Left Side, which in its Edenic state served a protective role.

53. **"perfection of the cosmos."** Here ibn Gabbai is again arguing that Evil has a legitimate—albeit limited—place in the cosmic schema, and that *Din* must be given its due lest it gain excessive influence.

"God has made . . . fear Him." This Scriptural verse is conventionally rendered: "And God has brought to pass that people revere Him." On *Din* as a force encouraging piety and repentance, and ultimately contributing to the "perfection of the cosmos" see Z 1:146b (ST) and 2:183b–84a. The former evinces a relatively harmonistic view of the relations between good and evil:

> Over against [the seven lower *sefirot*] there are seven *havalim* [of *Sitra' 'Aḥra'*], from which all harsh judgment derives. . . . Their function is to lash out against people and keep them on the straight path. . . . They are called *hevel* for they are evil winds. They sustain the world, for because of them people walk on the straight path and fear the Holy One.

The second source stresses the need for dialectical wholeness:

> Light only emerges from darkness . . . for cosmic wholeness is Good and Evil together, though ultimately it is Good which is ascendant, emerging from [and overcoming] Evil.

Discussion: In this section Meir ibn Gabbai unself-consciously oscillates between harmonistic and dualistic views of Evil. According to the former, *Din* is a necessary constituent of the cosmos; indeed, an emissary of divinity. According to the latter, it is a counterforce to divinity, a quasi-independent adversary. Although ibn Gabbai stresses the first view here, he soon moves to the second position; for on Shabbat "perfection of the cosmos" entails not the integration of *Din* but—as shall be seen—its total removal. On these two views of evil, see MZ 1:288–95 and G. Scholem, "Sitra' 'Ahra'" in his *Pirqei Yesod be-Havanat ha-Qabbalah u-Semaleha* (Jerusalem, 1976).

54. The enjoinder to destroy the nail-clippings on Sabbath eve contrasts with the prescription given women after *niddah*. According to RM 3:248b, women are bidden to save their nail-parings: to place them in an out-of-the-way location as an offering to *Sitra' 'Ahra'*. Such acts of appeasement are not needed as Sabbath draws near and the forces of *Hesed* expand.

55. **"And perhaps."** Heb., *ve-'ulai*, indicating that ibn Gabbai is about to offer an original interpretation. (One may assume that Meir ibn Gabbai has the punishment in Gen. 3:16 in mind here.) The TY's interpretation was widely disseminated, and was cited in such sources as SHeLaH "Massekhet Shabbat"; the *Be'er Heitev* to ShA OH 260; *Matteh Mosheh* 4:211; and (without attribution) in A. Sperling's *Ta^camei ha-Minhagim*, sec. 254.

56. But cf. Z 2:208b which counsels one to carefully dispose of parings at all times, "even in an uninhabited place."

Concern over proper disposal of nail-parings is found in many cultures. A salient motive is to guard against their misuse by demons. For discussion, see J. G. Frazer, "Disposal of Cut Hair and Nails" in *The Golden Bough* (3rd ed.; NY, 1935) 3: 267–87 and Bruce Lincoln's critique of Frazer in "Treatment of Hair and Fingernails Among the Indo-Europeans," *History of Religions* 16 (1977): 351–62.

57. For detailed analysis of this ritual and information concerning the TY's sources of influence, see SCK: 221–24 and the germane notes.

58. Heb., *ʿal derekh ha-'emet;* ff. RaMBaN's usage, this phrase always signals a Kabbalisatic interpretation.

59. The *Temurot* is a synonym for *Sitra' 'Ahra'*, employed by such Kabbalists as David ben Judah he-Hasid. Generally it is envisioned as an emanation parallel and opposite to the seven lower *sefirot*. For discussion, see D. Matt, ed., *The Book of Mirrors* (Chico, 1982): 29–31.

60. That is, Lilith, the feminine expression of *Sitra' 'Ahra'*. On Lilith, see G. Scholem, *Kabbalah*: 356–61. For Zoharic parallels to the TY, see 3:69a and 3:272b (RM).

61. On the purported Biblical origin of this ruling, see MT "ʿEruvin" 1:1 and Tur OH 366.

62. "Scribal enactment." Heb., *mi-divrei sofrim*. See MT Ibid. 1:2 (ff. TB ʿEruv. 21b) where Solomon and his *beit din* are said to have promulgated this law.

63. According to TB ᶜEruv. 21b.

64. Kabbalistically, an allusion to the divine harmony that reigns on Shabbat. *Tif'eret* ("King Solomon") unites *Shekhinah* (the throne) with *Binah,* (the King's mother). The courtyard *ᶜeruv* symbolizes this new configuration. Cf., e.g., TZ 24 (69a):

> The *ᶜeruv* delineates the Middle Column . . . stretching from the Supernal *Shekhinah* [*Binah*] unto the Lower One.

65. This ritual is discussed in SCK: 227–31. The TY's contribution is two-fold. 1) It is the first Kabbalistic source to mandate *ṭevilah* or ablution. 2) It is the first source to explicitly link *ṭevilah* with the onset of what may be called "existential Shabbat" i.e., the reception of the Sabbath-soul. As noted to SCK: 230 and 250–51 n42, both points were widely accepted in subsequent generations.

66. For analysis of this rite the TY see SCK: 231–32. On the symbolism of Sabbath-dress eleswhere in classical Kabbalah, see there, pp. 232–42.

67. Sacred Time is thereby "stretched" or expanded. See the comments in SCK: 95 and 256.

This miẓvah has its roots in the Talmudic custom of extending the Sabbath before and aft. Cf. TB Ber. 52a: "The earlier we can commence it [on Friday night] the better; the longer we can defer it [on Saturday night] the better." Also see the dictum of R. Yose on TB Shab. 118b and *Mekhilta'* "Yitro" to Ex. 20:8:

> "Remember" and "Keep": Remember it beforehand and keep it afterwards. Hence we learn to add to the holy by taking from the profane. This may be compared to a wolf vigilantly moving backwards and forwards.

The length of the addition was never specified in Talmudic literature nor did it take on significant halakhic status before the twelfth century. It was the consensus of early authorities, Geonic and Sefardic, that a few minutes of *tosefet* [addition] is sufficient. In Ashkenazic lands, beginning in the twelfth century, a much longer—and halakhically formalized—*tosefet shabbat* of up to two hours was mandated, in part because these northern communities were situated at such a high latitude line that sundown occurred at a very late hour during the summer months. This practice of formally extending Shabbat eventually spread to certain southern communities, as well, and may have stimulated Kabbalistic speculation. It is unclear how long a *tosefet* Meir ibn Gabbai had in mind here.

On the evolution of this miẓvah see I. Ta-Shma's recent "Tosefet Shabbat" in *Tarbiẓ* 52 (1982/83): 309–23.

68. Heb. idiom, *le-hassig gevul,* ff. Dt. 19:14 and 27:7. MS Adrianople and e.p. mispell *HaSiG* with a *sin* whereas MSS JTSA Mic. 1553 and 1646 correctly emend to a *samekh.* Also see n405.

69. Beginning Shabbat early has theurgic significance. It facilitates the proper redrawing of cosmic boundaries, regaining "territory" for *Shekhinah* at the expense of *Sitra' 'Aḥra'* (the "other god."). According to the Zoharic myth (discussed in SCK, on p. 95) this act quashes the threat to the Sabbath-cosmos posed by *Sitra' 'Aḥra'* each Friday afternoon. (Meir Ibn Gabbai cites this myth later in the TY, pp. 23–24 above). More directly related to the TY here is J. Giqatilia's teaching that:

> One should receive the Sabbath while it is yet day; for the Sabbath [*Shekhinah*] is holy, but She is surrounded by profane powers. Therefore one must never narrow the boundaries of the sacred nor bring impurity into the Palace [of Shabbat] . . . Rather, one must expand the boundaries for *Shekhinah*. Whoever begins the Sabbath early and ends it late, prolongs holiness and extends the boundaries of the sacred. . . . This is the mystery of *reḥovot ha-nahar*, the "Expanded River." (*Sodot*, sec. 1)

For other germane sources see Z 3:272b (RM), TZ 48 (85b) and Baḥyya ben Asher to Ex. 31:14.

70. Here the symbolic significance of the ritual is stressed. The adept should align—or synchronize—himself with the changes unfolding on high, taking care not to fall behind their cadence; he should leave Profane Time even as *Shekhinah* is separating from the Profane Realm to rejoin Her Lover.

71. **"Meted out . . . be rewarded."** Meir ibn Gabbai makes use of the Hebrew root RḤB to illustrate the principle of "measure for measure." Because the adept has expanded the boundaries of the sacred [*le-harḥiv gevul ha-qodesh,*] God will grant him [*yarḥiv lo*] amplitude and ease [*reḥavah*]. Again, cf. the parallel in J. Giqatilia, *Sodot:* Ibid.

72. That is, *Shekhinah*/Shabbat. Also cf. *Peli'ah* 36a: "When the Bride enters the Wedding Canopy with the King. . . then She is called Queen."

73. See TB Shab. 21ff., esp. 31b. According to the latter, the commandment to light candles applies to men as well as to women, but it devolves more upon women because they are more closely associated with the home. This rite is one of the key halakhic makers for full Shabbat.

74. **"souls . . . Candles."** Ff. Prv. 20:27: "The soul of man is the candle of the Lord." Here the TY is speaking specifically of the Sabbath-souls, flickering points of divine light brought forth by *Shekhinah* each Sabbath eve and distributed to Israel. On the image of Sabbath-souls as flames of light/enlightenment, see SCK: 129. More generally on the motif of the Sabbath-soul, see the extended discussion in SCK: 121–36.

"Sabbath night." A common appellation for *Shekhinah*. This symbolism was already implicit in the *Bahir* (180) and was used explicitly thereafter. Cf. RaMBaN to Ex. 20:8, *Shaʿarei 'Orah* 1:107, Z 2:92a, et al. Underlying this image is the notion that Friday night is the "time of *Malkhut*," the hour of Her joy. See pp. 30 and 65 above.

75. A mystical rationale is thereby provided for the halakhah. For the woman is held to be the most fitting symbol of *Shekhinah*, the Cosmic *Maṭronita'*. On the micro/macro-cosmic relationship between *Shekhinah* and women, see, e.g., Z 1:228b: "All the females in the world are included in Her mystery." And Z 3:124a: "All the women in the world are included in, and blessed through, Her." This interpretation shows how fluid Kabbalistic symbolism can be, how it stretches to meet different (in this case, halakhic) needs. During the preparatory rituals (nail-paring, ablution, etc.) it was the male devotee who served as *Shekhinah*'s symbol, but now it is his wife who best represents Her. For further discussion see n77.

76. **"holy sons, etc."** Ff. TB Shab. 23b: "Said R. Huna: Whoever regularly lights Sabbath candles will have sons who are scholars, shining with the light of Torah."

On candlelighting promoting peace, see Ibid. (s.v., *shelom bayit.)*

77. **". . . length of days."** In this last section Meir ibn Gabbai has been following Z 1:48b. Note, however, that the souls referred to in the *Zohar* passage are probably not *neshamot yeterot*, but the souls of potential offspring, to be drawn forth during marital intercourse. The *Zohar* thereby highlights the maternal aspects of both *Shekhinah* and the adept's wife:

> Responsibility for lighting the Sabbath candles is given to the women of the Holy People [TB Shab. 31b]. As the Comrades put it: "Woman [Eve] extinguished the light of the world and brought darkness, etc." This is well and good [i.e., it serves as *tiqqun* for Eve's sin; cf. Gen. R 17:7] but there is a deeper rationale. The Canopy of Peace [*Shekhinah*] is the Lady [*Maṭronita'*] of the Cosmos and the souls which are the supernal Candles abide in Her. For this reason, the lady of the house [*maṭronita'*] ought to light [the candles] for she is attached to Her place [i.e., is *Shekhinah*'s symbol] and performs Her function [i.e., brings forth new life]. So she ought to light the candles with the great joy and zest, for it is a high honor for her, one affording her great privilege: through it she will merit holy sons, shining lights of Torah and piety, who will promote peace in the world. She will also grant her husband length of days. Hence, she should observe this [miẓvah] with great care.

"She must light two candles . . . 'Remember' and 'Keep'." Kabbalistically, " 'Remember' and 'Keep' " is an allusion to the union of the divine Male and Female. See n3 above.

The origin of this association is relatively late. TB Shab. 33b had linked the two bunches of myrtle (used to welcome the Sabbath) with "Remember" and "Keep," but no mention was made of the two candles. Indeed, M. Shab. 2:7 and TB Shab. 25b, 32a and 119b all spoke of *ner Shabbat*, implying that one candle was sufficient. One of the earliest sources to mention two candles is *Shibbolei ha-Leqeṭ* (mid-thirteenth century, Rome) which offered the interpretation in the name of RaVYaH. Shortly thereafter, the Provençal works

'Orḥot Ḥayyim and the *Kol Bo* (ca. 1300) recorded a similar view, ascribed to R. Asher ben Saul of Lunel (early thirteenth century). R. Asher attempted to provide a Rabbinic precedent for the custom of using two candles but his argument only underscored its lateness. The *Kol Bo* ("Dinei Shalosh Seᶜudot") reads:

> "In *Tanḥuma'* I found that on Shabbat things are doubled: two lambs (for the offering); two recitations of the Psalm for the Sabbath-day; two portions of bread; and "Remember" and "Keep." This apparently is the source for the custom of lighting two candles for Shabbat." Thus wrote R. Asher [ben Saul].

It should be noted that the number of Sabbath-candles was never firmly fixed in either the halakhic or the Kabbalistic literature. Some Kabbalists found mystical rationales for the custom of lighting more than two. The *Qanah* and *SHoSHaN Sodot,* e.g., offered a rationale for lighting three candles (see SCK: 254–55 n56). The SHeLaH averred that seven is the optimal number "as an allusion to the seventh millenium. . . . when the Moon's light will be like that of the Sun." ("Massekhet Shabbat") For further discussion of the various customs, see Mordecai Ha-Cohen, "Minhagei Leil Shabbat" in *Maḥanayim* 85–86 (1963): 31–32.

78. More than all other rituals, perhaps, it is prayer that enables the adept to partake of the supernal mysteries. For an overview of the multi-tiered significance of prayer in *Sod ha-Shabbat,* see my remarks in n186.

79. **"vital soul."** Heb., *nefesh ḥayyah.* The baser animal aspect of the soul, as opposed to *neshamah,* its loftier spiritual aspect. This two-fold division of the soul was employed less frequently in Kabbalistic literature than the tri-partite model. For Zoharic discussion of the vital soul see Z 1:34a, 2:12a, 3:39b and ZḤ "Bere'shit"18b–19b (MN).

The notion that demons were given souls is midrashic. See below for details.

80. See *Tanḥuma'* (Buber), "Bere'shit" (17):

> ". . . which God created to make [*'asher bara' 'Elohim la-ᶜasot.*]" [Gen. 2:3] It is written "to make" and not "He made" [*ᶜasah*]. For the Sabbath took priority and their workings were never completed. R. Banyya said: " 'Their' refers to the evil spirits. God fashioned their souls but before He could create their bodies, the holy day arrived and He left them as spirits without bodies."

Also see M. *'Avot* 5:8 and Gen. R 7:5. For Kabbalistic treatments of this midrash see RaMBaN to Lev. 17:1; Z 1:14a, 47b, 17a; 178a; 2:155b 3:142b; TZ 59 (93a); and Joseph Alcastiel, *Teshuvot la-She'elot ᶜal Derekh ha-Qabbalah she-Sha'al R. Yehudah Ḥayyaṭ,* published by G. Scholem in *Tarbiẓ* 24 (1954): 192.

81. *ᶜarum* is generally rendered as "cunning" or "sly" in this context; however, it may also mean "naked," as in the word-play in Gen. 3:7.

82. On Adam's precious garments, see SCK: 224–25, 264–67, 281 n29, 282 n33; and p. 20 above.

In this last section Meir ibn Gabbai has clearly been influenced by TZ 59 (93a):

> Only the snake was *ᶜarum,* without this "garment of skin" [*ketonet ᶜor*], for all the other creatures were created with clothing during the six days of Creation. . . . Now the bodies of the demons were yet to be made; and [God] never did make them because the Sabbath arrived. This is "which God created, to make." [Gen. 2:3] For this reason "the snake alone was naked among the creatures that God had made." [re-reading Gen. 3:1] All the other creatures were given clothing, but he was not. . . . Why were he [and his minions] not given clothing? Because He created the human being on Sabbath eve. . . . For this reason the snake grew jealous of Adam, having been left without garments because of him. He therefore caused Adam to be stripped of his garments. . . . using *ᶜormato,* his cunning, to do so.

This Adamic explanation for the demons' nakedness contrasts with the more cosmic one offered in Z 1:14a. See below for details.

83. This question is posed in *Zohar* 1:14a. See there for a different (distinctively Kabbalistic) answer.

84. That is, God provided a moral-halakhic lesson regarding *muqẓeh,* objects that are not to be handled during Shabbat.

"some coins." Heb., *kelum shel meᶜot.* Warsaw ed. misprints: *kelim.*

The source cited here is not found in any extant version of *Yelammedenu.* As noted by Moshe Herr [EJ 15:794 ff.], certain *Yelammedenu* passages known in the Medieval period have apparently been lost. A similar teaching, however, may be found in Gen. R 7:5:

> Rav said: These are the evil spirits that the Holy One created. After He had fashioned their souls, as He was about to created their bodies, the holy Sabbath arrived, and He did not create them. This teaches a moral lesson: If someone has a precious stone or pearl in his hand at dusk on Sabbath eve, they say to him: cast it off! For the One who spoke and brought the world into being . . . was about to create bodies for the spirits, but the holy Sabbath arrived, and He did not create them.

85. That is, Shimon bar Yoḥai. At this point ibn Gabbai begins his paraphrase of Z 1:14a, wherein R. Shimon answered the question posed above (n83). A significant portion of this passage has been discussed in SCK: 95. I will concentrate on new material here.

86. *Siṭra' 'Aḥra'* is here portrayed as the rebellious residue of *Malkhut,* the Tree of Knowledge of Good and Evil. The arrival of Shabbat signals both the triumph of good within *Malkhut* and the victory of divinity/Cosmos

over *Sitra' 'Ahra'*/Chaos. For another account of the cosmic battle that raged on the eve of primordial Shabbat, see Z 2:203a–b, and the discussion in SCK: 268–70.

87. Herein ends ibn Gabbai's parapharase of the Zohar text.

"New souls that are added." Ff. Z 1:14a–b, a reference to the holy offspring conceived on Friday nights:

> Sacred bodies and spirits were built up that [Sabbath] night. It is for this reason that the prescribed time for the marital intercourse of scholars is on Sabbath nights. (ff. TB BQ 82a and Ket. 62a)

The act of bringing forth new and sacred life on Shabbat recalls and re-affirms divinity's triumph in *illo tempore.*

88. **"he vanished."** On the disappearance of *Sitra' 'Ahra'* for the duration of Shabbat, see SCK: 137–38 and 268–70.

"Shushan." Kabbalistically, *Shekhinah.* This word may also be vocallized as *Shoshan,* the Rose or Lily. See the TY passage in my Introduction, p. 78 n17 above and TZ 6 (22a).

"face of wrath . . . shining face." A dramatic portrayal of cosmic restoration as *Shekhinah* is re-united with Her lover, *Tif'eret,* after Her weekday subjection to *Sitra' 'Ahra'.*

89. Although the meaning is clear enough, the Hebrew phrasing is somewhat problematic: *maqdimim be-qiddush ha-yom dugma'; ve-nikhnasin 'el beitah.* Although *dugma'* is the most difficult term, the final phrase is also somewhat ambiguous. A literal rendering yields "we enter Her [*Shekhinah's*] House," i.e., the synagogue. It seems more likely, however, that the term *beitah* is simply an abbreviation of *beit ha-keneset.*

90. Cf. TY 24b–26b, *Sod Barekhu.*

91. Meir ibn Gabbai now enters into an extended discussion of the differences between the weekday and Sabbath liturgies, and the rationales for these differences. He first considers *Ve-Hu' Rahum,* a prayer whose recitation on Shabbat was the subject of considerable debate. After assessing exoteric and esoteric rationales for the prayer's daily recitation, ibn Gabbai determines whether it should be recited on the Sabbath, as well. This prayer reads:

> But He, being full of Compassion, forgives iniquity, and does not destroy; frequently He turns His anger away, and does not stir up all his wrath. [Ps. 78:38] O Lord, save us; may the King answer us when we call. [Ps. 20:10].

92. Abraham ben Nathan ha-Yarhi was a twelth century legalist, born in Lunel (hence his name!) and active in Spain and France. He wrote the influential *Sefer ha-Manhig* (I. Rafael ed., [Jerusalem, 1978] 2 vols.) [hereafter, *Manhig*], a comparative study of rites and ceremonies as practiced in various European communities. His work is important for scholars of Kabbalah, as

well, for he occasionally cites *sefarim penimiyyim,* mystical teachings on prayer from the circles of the RI and RaBaD of Posquieres, two of ha-Yarḥi's teachers. See *Manhig:* 29 and I. Twersky, *Rabad of Posquieres* (Philadelphia, 1980): 243.

It should be noted that ibn Gabbai shifts between exact quotation and paraphrase in his citation of ha-Yarḥi here.

93. Ff. *Manhig* 1:118–19.

"sinner . . . evening." Throughout the Middle Ages it was customary to punish sinners by means of a "symbolic penance (i.e., flogging) at the threshold of the synagogue between the daily afternoon and evening service." See EJ 13:1389, s.v. "Punishment." Ff. M. *Makkot* 3:14, this flogging was accompanied by the recitation of *Ve-Hu' Raḥum.*

"thrice over the flogging." The verse beginning "Ve-hu' raḥum" (Ps. 78:38) is comprised of thirteen words. Its three-fold repetition yields thirty-nine words, each word corresponding to one of the prescribed thirty-nine stripes. See *Siddur RaSHI* and *Maḥzor Viṭri* (Ish-Hurwitz ed. [*Viṭri*]): 77 for details. Ha-Yarḥi claims to be relying on "his French teachers" here, undoubtedly an allusion to these sources.

94. **"extraneous."** Heb., *muttar,* here a synonym for the more common *meyuttar.* Meir ibn Gabbai is disposing of this first rationale for reciting *Ve-Hu' Raḥum,* having found it to be extraneous or incidental. As shall be seen, ha-Yarḥi does not accept this rationale, either.

95. Cf., e.g., Tur OḤ 267, Al-Naqawa *Menorat ha-Ma'or* (Enelow ed.) 2:181, and *Sefer Abudraham* [hereafter, *Abud.*]: 137.

96. In other words, ha-Yarḥi said that if the French rationale for reciting the prayer were the correct one, then there would be no basis for reciting it on the Sabbath. However, he has a more compelling rationale for reciting *Ve-hu' Raḥum,* which he now presents.

97. *Tanḥuma'* "Pinḥas" (13) and PRK 15:7; also see Ibid. 5:7 and 6:4, and *Pesiqta' Rabbati* 15:24.

98. Ff. TB Ber. 26b.

"daily offerings." The *temidim* (continual burnt offerings) which were made twice a day at the Temple. The clarifying phrase (in brackets) is found in the *Manhig.*

99. TB Ber. Ibid. For this reason the evening service could, technically speaking, be said all night.

Incidentally, Lev. 6:2 is not used as a proof-text in any extant versions of the *Manhig.* However, it is included in David Abudraham's citation of the *Manhig* passage (*Abud.*: 137). Textual analysis suggests that ibn Gabbai did not actually have the *Manhig* text in front of him here, but rather relied on Abudraham's quotation. Compare!

100. Heb., *nitqenah.* Warsaw ed. misprints *nithanah.*

101. That is, as the Rabbinic tradition makes clear, the two daily offerings, and the two prayer services that parallel them, provide sufficient atonement. Ibn Gabbai therefore concludes that recitation of *Ve-Hu' Rahum* must serve another, more substantial (Kabbalistically derived) purpose.

102. **"judged every night."** Ff. ZH Ruth (79b):

> The recitation of *Ve-Hu' Rahum* during the evening service was established, because from the time of nightfall, the wicked in Gehinnom are judged.

On these three angels, see ZH Ibid. and Z 1:23b:

> Three deputy [angels] rule in Gehinnom . . . Mashhit, Af, Hemah.

According to this source all three are mentioned in the verse under discussion:

> "And does not destroy [*yashhit*]"; that is Mashhit, "frequently He turns away His anger ['*apo*]": that is Af; "and does not stir up all His wrath [*hamato*]": that is Hemah.

103. God's thirteen attributes—Merciful, Gracious, Long-Suffering, Bountiful, Faithful, etc.—are derived from Ex. 34:6ff. For Rabbinic treatment see RH 17b, et al.

104. Having determined the true basis for recitation of *Ve-hu' Rahum,* ibn Gabbai can now determine whether it ought to be said on Shabbat. His final decision is based on *Zohar* 2:135b and the aformentioned ZH source. As Jacob Katz has noted, the *Zohar* here served as an innovative liturgical force. Moshe de Leon followed the Provençal-French-Ashkenazi custom of not reciting this prayer on Shabbat—for Kabbalistic reasons; his ruling had a great impact on subsequent Sefardic practice. See J. Katz's *Halakhah ve-Qabbalah* (Jerusalem, 1985): 44–45.

105. Heb. *menuhah hashqet va-vetah;* from the Sabbath afternoon prayer, *'Attah 'Ehad* ("You Are One").

106. Recitation of this verse is an example of a counter-transformative act, as discussed in SCK chaps. 2 and 3. See p. 202 and p. 242 where this prayer is alluded to. Our TY passage recalls Z 2:135b:

> One should open the Sabbath prayers with a blessing [i.e., *Barekhu*]. For it is forbidden for the Holy People to commence on a note of *Din,* as in *Ve-Hu' Rahum.* For She [*Shekhinah*] has already separated from the mystery of *Sitra' 'Ahra'* and likewise, all the masters of judgement have separated and been lifted from Her. Whoever rouses [*Din*] below causes it to be roused on high, preventing the Holy Throne from being properly crowned. These masters of judgment had all gone to hide in the maw of the dust of the Great Abyss; but whenever they are roused, they return to their place . . . and press against the Holy Place.

Also see the succinct parallel in *Mishqal:* 111.

107. **"Dumah."** From the Hebrew word for stillness or death. In Rabbinic literature *Dumah* is the angel appointed to oversee the netherworld. Cf. TB Sanh. 94a, et al.

108. All versions of the TY mistakenly read *ḥoreshei* instead of *ḥoshevei.*

109. Ff. TB Yev. 109b and Sanh. 7b where it is attributed to R. Samuel b. Naḥmani in the name of R. Jonathan.

110. This paragraph, presented in the ZḤ as a *mashal,* is left in the Aramaic by Meir ibn Gabbai. On this phenomenon, see my Introduction, p. 80 n25. Despite its elliptical style, the point of the parable is relatively clear. During the week the destructive angels—"the guards"—are empowered to exact punishment on the sinners. But on Shabbat the divine presence extends even unto Hell (see SCK: 137) and hence, no punishment may be exacted. The Jew is the servant of the king. During the week his recitation of *Ve-Hu' Raḥum* arouses Compassion and insures that the sinners not suffer excessively. However, by reciting *Ve-Hu' Raḥum*—"when he is in the presence of the king"—he makes two crucial errors: a) he empowers the guards when they are not needed, thereby threatening the well-being of the sinners; and b) he mocks the protective power of the King.

111. As is done during the week. In skipping ahead to this prayer Meir ibn Gabbai is following the discussion in the ZḤ source (Ruth 79b–c). See *Mishqal:* 111 for the same phenomenon and cf. Baḥyya ben Asher to Ex. 20:8.

112. Cf. *Viṭri:* 81; *Siddur RaSHI:* 24–41; and R. Eleazar of Worms *Perush ha-Tefillot* (MS Oxf. Bodl. 1204): 133a. Cited as an anonymous midrash in Ṭur OH 267; *Abud:* 144, et al. For Kabbalistic interpretations of this notion, see OZ 39a, translated in SCK: 182–83 (n282) as well as *Mishqal:* 111.

113. This quotation does not, in fact, come directly from the TJ. For details see the following note.

114. In attributing this passage to TJ Ber., Meir ibn Gabbai is basing himself on a mistaken attribution found in the commentary of RaVYaH to TB Ber. 20b:

> In the Yerushalmi it is written: "There are three blessings surrounding the morning *Shemaᶜ*; three paragraphs in the *Shemaᶜ* proper; and the [miẓvah] of *ẓiẓit.* [This makes a total of seven sacred acts;] hence,"I praise You *seven* times a day." [Ps. 119:64]

In fact, only the verse from Psalms actually belongs to our version of TJ Ber. 1:5. RaVYaH continued his "quotation":

> But since the miẓvah of *ẓiẓit* does not apply at night, we add 'He who protects His People Israel' [to make the requisite total of seven.] R. Levi said: This may be recited during the week, but on Sabbaths and festivals, one recites "He who spreads a Sukkah of Peace."

R. Ḥayyim Dembitzer (to Mid. Ps. [Buber ed., p.29]) has shed light on the origin of this mis-attribution. He noted, rather delicately:

> Our TJ is missing those words that our teacher [RaVYaH] copied. In my opinion . . . he wrote this as a commentary on TJ [Ber. 1:5] to bring it in accord with the midrash on Ps. 6:1,

where his quotation is actually found. Compare the two sources!

115. See ZḤ Ruth (69b–c).

116. Here Meir ibn Gabbai has been paraphrasing Z 2:135b–136a. On the custom of not beginning the prayers until the Sabbath-soul has been received, also see Ibid. 135b ("Raza' de-Shabbat").

117. **"Qeri'at . . . benedictions."** That section of the evening prayer consisting of the *Shema*ᶜ proper, the two benedictions preceding it, and the two following it. See M. Ber. chap. 1. This sentence appears to have been taken verbatim from *Abud:* 144.

118. **"peace is everywhere."** Heb., *shalom ba-kol.* Kabbalistically, indicating that *Shekhinah* is now in union with Her lover and so embodies the divine totality.

119. See Z 1:48a:

> Why is it [said] "over Jerusalem"? Because it is the abode of this *Sukkah.* We must invite this *Sukkah* to spread over us and rest upon us, like a mother [bird] sheltering her fledglings.

For discussion of this source, see SCK: 131. On the protective, enveloping quality of *Shekhinah*/Mother/Shabbat on Friday nights, see Ibid.: 128–31 passim and 243.

120. This reading is based on the double-meaning of the root QDSH, indicating both sanctification and betrothal.

121. On the image strictly monogamous *Shekhinah* see SCK: 116. Also see *Sod ha-Shabbat* Section 12, above.

122. This interpretation of *'Attah Qiddashta* first appeared in Judah ben Yaqar's *Perush ha-Tefillot* 1:89, then in de Leon's *Rimmon* 29b and shortly thereafter, in *Sefer Ṭaᶜamei ha-Miẓvot* [SṬM] of Joseph of Hamadan and the OZ of David ben Judah he-Ḥasid. For the germane *Rimmon* and OZ passages see SCK: 171–72 (n211) and pp. 118 and 120. For a possible precursor see the *Roqeaḥ* source cited in SCK: 176 n231. The SṬM passage briefly states:

> For this reason we recite *'Attah Qiddashta,* viz., to betroth *Ẓaddiq* and *Malkhut* . . . the Groom and the Bride, the Community of Israel. This is alluded to by our Rabbis of blessed memory, [in the teaching] "the prescribed time [for marital intercourse] for scholars is on Sabbath nights." (Meier ed.: 297)

Similar interpretations passed into the exoteric literature relatively quickly, as evinced by *Abud.* (ca. 1340):

'Attah Qiddashta should be recited because the Sabbath is called "Bride" and the Holy One, blessed be He, is called "Groom." This prayer was established on account of the betrothal [*qiddushin*] of Groom and Bride. (p. 147)

123. As he subsequently notes, ibn Gabbai is here quoting from *Abud.*: 147.

124. That is, Jacob ben Asher, ca. 1270–1340, author of the authoritative halakhic code, *'Arbaʿah Ṭurim* [Ṭur]. The germane passage is from OḤ 268. See there!

125. The TY's claim here recalls Z 2:90a.

126. See M. Sanh. 4:1 and esp. MT "Sanhedrin" 3:3–5.

127. Once again ibn Gabbai rejects an exoteric rationale for the performance of a prayer. It should be noted, however, that some Kabbalists accepted the notion of *Va-Yekhullu* as testimony, even though they presented deeper esoteric rationales, as well. See, e.g., OZ 40a (cited in SCK: 118–19).

128. From *Abud.*: 147.

129. Cf. Z 2:207b:

> This day [Shabbat/*Shekhinah*] is wreathed with seventy crowns and the supernal holy Name [*Shekhinah*] is completed on all sides.

On the motif of sefirotic adornment, see SCK: 200.

The *Zohar* does not mention the mystical significance of the seventy words in the doubled *Va-Yekhullu*, however. (This interpretation is Meir ibn Gabbai's own, as telegraphed by the introductory phrase, *li nir'eh ha-ṭaʿam*—"it seems to me".) More specifically, the *Zohar* attributes this seventy-fold adornment to the seventy words in the *Qiddush* over the wine (35 in *Va-Yekhullu* and 35 in the closing blessing). For details see 1:5b and 2:207b. Also see *Sod ha-Shabbat* Section 10, and n150 below.

130. ***"Ẓaddiq* and *Ẓedeq."*** See, e.g., the word-play in *Zohar* 1:49a:

> When She is united with Her husband [here, *Yesod*] She is called by His name: *'ish, 'ishah* [man, woman]: *Ẓaddiq, Ẓedeq*.

Also see Moses Cordovero, PR: Gate 23, s.v. "Ẓedeq":

> Since *Malkhut* and *Yesod* are unified on Shabbat, there are six, rather than seven Sabbaths: *Ḥesed, Gevurah, Tif'eret, Neẓaḥ, Hod,* and *Yesod/Malkhut*.

131. By standing the devotee points or alludes to the divine world. On ritual gestures as a means of evoking the celestial realm in Zoharic Kabbalah, see the symbolism of the raised and lowered fingers, discussed in SCK: 273–75.

132. This interpretation is a virtual quotation from OK to TB Shab. 119b. After citing the germane Gemara', Ṭodros Abulafia wrote:

> Through the merit of Israel, when they keep the Sabbath and scrupulously observe its miẓvot . . . the supernal entities are gladdened, and the Spirit of Knowledge and the Fear of the Lord [*Tif'eret* and *Malkhut*] unite, as in Primordial Creation. Hence, [whoever recites *Va-Yekhullu* becomes a partner in that which constitutes the Work of Creation.

Note how both ibn Gabbai and Abulafia subtly recast the meaning of the divine-human partnership mentioned in the Talmud. The Rabbinic caveat "as though" disappears; metaphor gives way to a kind of mystical reality. By dint of his theurgic power, the Kabbalist actually becomes God's partner in the ongoing "Work of Creation": here understood as the process of divine restoration.

133. According to TB Pes. 112b, no one should walk alone at night, particularly in non-settled areas on Wednesday and Friday nights, when demons were held to be the most menacing. (This may be related to certain astrological associations; see my Ph.D. dissertation, "The Sabbath in Classical Kabbalah" [Univ. of Pennsylvania, 1984] p. 533 for details.) Medieval authorities explained that recitation of "Shield of Our Fathers" lessened the danger because it gave late arrivals opportunity to finish the service together with the rest of the congregation; consequently, no one would have to walk home alone. See RaSHI ad TB Shab. 24b, *Viṭri*: 83, *Manhig*: 138, *Abud.*: 149, etc.

The notion that Friday evening was a particularly dangerous time was at loggerheads with the midrashic/Kabbalistic view that Sabbath was a pre-eminetly safe time, in which there was no need to ask for protection, "because the Sabbath itself protects." This clashing of viewpoints is acknowledged and (to a degree) harmonized in *Zohar* 2:205a. As shall be seen, Meir ibn Gabbai stopped short of formally rejecting the Rabbinic rationale for reciting "Shield of Our Fathers"; however, he is clearly more enthusiastic about the mystical rationale.

134. This phrase is taken verbatim from *Abud.* 149, where the author betrayed a dissatisfaction with the Rabbinic rationale. Abudraham commented: "We who are not confronted with such danger recite this [prayer] only because of the custom of our ancestors."

135. Lit., "the daughter of seven," referring to *Shekhinah*'s absorption of the seven *sefirot* above Her. Cf. Z 3:266b: "The maiden Israel inherits seven blessings; thus She is called *Bat-Sheva*ᶜ."

136. See n118.

137. **"heresy."** Heb., *qiẓẓuẓ*; lit., a severing [of the shoots], ff. TB Ḥag. 14b and Gen. R 19:4. According to Z 1:53b, the Primordial Sin was that of qiẓẓuẓ. Adam worshipped and partook of *Shekhinah* alone, severing Her from the higher *sefirot* and "divorcing" Her from Her husband, *Tif'eret*. He thereby disrupted the unity of the cosmos. For discussion see G. Scholem,

Major Trends in Jewish Mysticism (New York, 1967) [hereafter, *Major Trends:*]: 221–23, 236, and 404–05; and D. Matt, *Zohar*: 215.

The focus on *Shekhinah* in this prayer does not cause a similar *qizzuz* because at this juncture She and *Tif'eret* are inextricably bound, *du-parzufin*, one entity. See pp. 13–14 above.

138. Meir ibn Gabbai is here referring to the prayer, *Rezeh Na' vi-Mnuhatenu*, which follows "Shield of Our Fathers."

"You shall rest in Her." The TY is here offering a mystical rationale for the use of the feminine form *BaH* instead of the masculine *BO:* in Him. Because of the grammatical androgyny of Shabbat both forms are equally viable; indeed, both forms are found in the Spanish liturgy. For example, *Abud.* utilized the masculine form, *bo*, whereas the OZ utilizes the feminine form for Friday evening, and the masculine form for Sabbath morning. R. David ben Judah he-Hasid provided a mystical rationale for so doing: the first refers to the eschatological Shabbat, *Binah*, whereas the second refers to the male Sabbath, *Yesod*. See OZ 55a and 61b for details. Also see Joshua ibn Shu^cayb's *Derashot* (Krakow, 1596) fol. 27c, where the rationale provided coheres with ibn Gabbai's. Ibn Shuᶜayb explained that *bah* is to be recited on Sabbath night and *bo* during the day, for "the day belongs to *Zakhor (Yesod)* and the night to *Shamor (Malkhut)* [ff. *Bahir* 182]."

Later adepts took this one step further, adopting—for patently mystical reasons—the RaMBaM's version of this prayer for *Minhah:*

> "And you shall rest *BaH*" is recited on Friday night to correspond to *Malkhut*, the Bride; "And you shall rest *BO*" is recited on Saturday morning to correspond to *Tif'eret*, the Groom, while "And you shall rest *BaM* [in them]" is recited at *Minhah*, corresponding to their union. (cited in *Magen 'Avraham* to ShA OH 268)

139. In preparation for marital intercourse later that night.

140. ZH " 'Aharei Mot' " 48d (*Sitrei Torah* [ST]). The TY text contains slight variations from the printed version of ZH here, primarily in the form of omissions. On several occasions I have included the omitted ZH phrase [in brackets] for the sake of clarification. Compare!

141. Ps. continues: "He will order His angels to guard you wherever you go."

142. Included in ZH text.

143. Due to their profanation of Shabbat, God's Name, *YaH* (Kabbalistically, *Shekhinah*) leaves them. Stripped of this divine aura, they are reduced to defiled beings, representatives of the "destructive Fire," *Sitra' 'Ahra'*. For another Kabbalistic usage of this image, see *'Iggeret ha-Qodesh* in Cheval ed., *Kitvei RaMBaN* 2:234. This imagery is based on TB *Sotah* 17a:

> When a man and a woman are worthy, the *Shekhinah* abides in their midst; when they are not worthy, fire consumes them.

RaSHI (ad loc.) explains:

> "When a man . . . worthy, etc.": For *Shekhinah* bestowed His Name upon them and was in their midst. *Yod* was given to the man and *He'* to the woman.
> "Fire consumes them": The Holy One removes His name from their midst and they are left as "fire" and "fire."

144. Heb., *ma'akhalo.* E.p. and Warsaw ed. inadvertently omit the *khaf.*

145. Meir ibn Gabbai has altered the actual *Mekhilta'* text which reads: "From this I know only about the *Qiddush* for the day. Whence do we know that the night [also requires a *Qiddush*]?" Apparently ibn Gabbai has based his reading on RaSHI's comments to TB Pes. 106a:

> "I know only about the *Qiddush* for the day. Whence do we know that the night [also requires a *Qiddush*]?": Quite the contary, the essence of the sanctification is at night.

(Note that Meir ibn Gabbai cites this TB source immediately thereafter, further proof that he has been influenced by RaSHI's interpretation.)

146. This argument is based on the hermeneutical principle of *ribbui,* "inclusion" or "expansion." The particle *'et* indicates that the entire Sabbath is to be properly kept. Since keeping the entire Sabbath necessitates sanctifying it throughout, one is obligated to recite *Qiddush* at day, as well as at night.

147. **"Bridal Canopy."** A multivocal symbol. On one level, the Jew's newly adorned home is the *ḥuppah,* set to receive the Bride. On the another level, it is the sefirotic world that becomes *Shekhinah*'s *ḥuppah,* arching over Her in anticipation of Her sacred marriage. For illustrations of both images, see SCK: 218–19 and 116. On the *Qiddush* as the wedding ceremony itself, see Ibid.: 113–14 and 118–19.

148. That is, the red *Qiddush* wine symbolizes *Gevurah* whose *shefa*ᶜ flows into *Shekhinah* at this hour, strengthening Her and giving Her cheer. On Wine/*Gevurah*'s invigorating power, also see *Sod ha-Shabbat,* p. 68 above.

149. In the Talmudic context, the singing refers to the chanting of the Levites in the Temple as they poured the libations. This Gemara' suggests that the Sabbath *Qiddush* retained a certain priestly quality in the Rabbinic period. Also see BB 97a–b where it is stated that "one may only recite *Qiddush* over wine that is fit for libation on the altar."

Kabbalistically, the singing Levites connote the forces of *Gevurah* which cheer *Malkhut* and kindle Her love before She unites with the Holy One. Cf., e.g., *Rimmon* 30a; also see fol. 29b on the power of wine during Friday night *Qiddush.* Ibn Gabbai does not make any of these associations explicit here, however.

150. In other words, the *Qiddush* is simultaneously a marriage ceremony and an act of divine coronation. The TY's image is drawn from Z

2:207b. For discussion see n129. Also see TZ 47 (84a) where each of the seven lower *sefirot* is said to contain the full complement of ten *sefirot*. Each of the seventy words in the *Qiddush*, therefore, corresponds to a different divine aspect.

"Thirty-five words in *Va-Yekhullu* and thirty-five in 'Who has sanctified us. . . .'" The intervening blessing over the wine *(bore' peri ha-gefen)* is halakhically distinct from *Qiddush ha-Yom* and is not in part of the mystical word count. Like the introductory phrase *Yom ha-shishi* (recited just before the word *Va-Yekhullu*), the blessing over the wine is ritually "invisible" here.

The word-count in "Who has sanctified us" merits closer scrutiny. Although the text of the *Va-Yekhullu* was obviously fixed, the content of the closing benediction varied from locale to locale. Most versions contained between forty-one words (e.g., SRA and *Abud.*) and forty-five (*Viṭri*). Apparently, Moshe de Leon opted for an abbreviated version due to the mystical significance of seventy. He never supplied an exact text for this benediction, however; nor is it known precisely which words Meir ibn Gabbai is using here. For more on the Zoharic *Qiddush* and rationales for its omissions, see Joseph ibn Shraga, *Sod Qiddush le-Maᶜalei Shabbeta'* (ca. 1500), printed in Abraham Elmalik, ed., *Liqquṭei Shikheḥah u-Fe'ah* (Ferrara, 1556) fol. 39a-b; and Ḥayyim Viṭal, Shaᶜ*ar ha-Kavvanot* 2:79, which provides a complete text of the seventy word *Qiddush*. On the esoteric significance of word-counting during the Friday night prayers and *Qiddush*, see also Eleazar of Worms, *Perush ha-Tefillot*, MS Paris 772, fol. 113b and 118a-b.

151. Ff. Z Ibid. In the *Zohar*, this probably means that *Shekhinah* is perfected by an influx of energy from *Ḥokhmah* (the 32 paths of Wisdom) and the Patriarchs (the Three Rungs of Holy Apples). See I. Tishby, MZ 2:504.

152. **"the totality of Creation."** The sefirotic pleroma, which now flows into *Shekhinah* as the *Qiddush* of Creation, the *Va-Yekhullu*, is recited. Kabbalistically, heaven here connotes the upper sefirotic world (until *Tif'eret*) whereas earth refers to the lowermost rungs, eventuating in *Shekhinah*.

153. *'Elohim* commonly connotes three rungs, *Binah*, *Gevurah* and *Shekhinah*: it thereby includes all three sefirotic triads. Its three-fold repetition symbolizes the downward flow of *shefa*ᶜ from the upper triad unto the final rung. As noted, the Zoharic source for this paragraph is 2:207b, from which ibn Gabbai diverges in minor ways alone. For parallels, see 1:249b and 3:273a (RM).

154. Cf. *Abud.*: 160:

R. Tam [Tos. to TB Pes. 106b] writes that bread cannot be used for *Qiddush*, but RaSHBaM [ad loc.] permits it, as does R. Amram [SRA: 28].

Also see the discussion in *Kol-Bo:* 34bff. The predominant Spanish position was to permit bread.

155. **Discussion.** Meir ibn Gabbai's previous treatment of the *Qiddush* stressed the theurgic and symbolic importance of using wine. This would appear to challenge the legally established option of using bread. But, in fact, it is the halakhah that takes precedent over, and moderates, the seemingly absolute nature of the Kabbalistic mythic ideal. Indeed, the halakhah seems to guard against a certain absolutism that might otherwise ensue. To put it in another way: the esoteric interpretation follows rather than determines the halakhah. Ibn Gabbai finds a hidden meaning in the established ruling: Because *Malkhut* has already attained a secure position in the divine realm, the need to cheer Her through wine has become less urgent. Hence, bread may be used, even though it is not optimal. (By way of contrast, cf. *Shoshan Sodot* 77a, where the use of bread is flatly rejected on theurgic grounds.)

Earlier it was seen how Kabbalistic considerations dictated the rejection of the Spanish custom of reciting *Ve-Hu' Raḥum* on Shabbat. There, however, ibn Gabbai was following a Zoharic precedent which had already attained a certain halakhic status. (See J. Katz, n104 above.) Almost without exception, Meir ibn Gabbai's rationales are of a highly conservative nature, buttressing—rather than posing a challenge to—the nomic structure.

156. From *Midrash Va-Yekhullu* which adds that the three recitations correspond to the three mentions of *'asher* therein. This midrash is cited in *Haggahot Maimuniyyot* chap. 29, *Roqeaḥ* sec. 49, and is alluded to in *Abud.*: 147.

157. Meir ibn Gabbai's correlates the earthly sacramental meal with the Sabbath-feast in celestial Eden. See below.

"The fourth Palace." Using the terminology of Merkavah-Heikhalot Mysticism, the *Zohar* speaks of seven celestial palaces which now comprise the realm between the sefirotic world above and the material world below. According to I. Tishby (MZ 1:419–420):

> These *heikhalot* [palaces] are populated by ranks of spirits, lights *ḥayyot*, *'ofannim*, seraphs, and other angelic creatures, each sparkling and completing each other. They serve and adorn the divine powers and seek to unite with their Master. In each Palace one celestial spirit stands as officer-in-charge. . . . In each palace there are passageways over which guards are appointed. . . . These palaces are stages of Celestial Eden, a place of rest for souls after death. . . . They are stations through which souls pass pass [in their descent into the body]. . . . Prayers and souls ascending in *devequt* [communion] rise through the stages of the palaces on their journey to the World of Emanation.

Each of these palaces is nourished by a particular *sefirah* (ranging from *Binah* to *Malkhut*); in some of the more dualistic accounts, each exists over against a parallel "Palace of Defilement," issuing from *Sitra' 'Aḥra'*. The palace mentioned in the TY, *Zekhut* (Merit), is linked with *Gevurah* and stands over against the fourth Palace of Defilement called *Ḥovah* (Demerit). *Zekhut* is generally imaged as a celestial court, where each soul is judged after death. On Shabbat, however, its harsher aspects are generally "sweetened" and great joy reigns. See Z 1:43bff., 2:251–53b and 265a for details.

"Ḥayyah." Ff. Z 2:252b, the presiding deputy is called Tumiel, while the seraphim are named Seraphiel, Baraqiel, Qarashiel, and Qedumiel. The ensuing TY passage is a paraphrase of this Zohar text.

158. This Zohar passage builds on the famous Talmudic image (Shab. 119b) of the two ministering angels who accompany one on Shabbat. Also see *Sod ha-Shabbat,* p. 30 above.

159. The preceding Scriptural verse, well-known to the *Zohar*'s readers, sets the condition for these rewards: "If . . . you call the Sabbath a delight, then . . ."

160. *NeGa*ᶜ, of course, is a re-ordering of the letters in *ᶜoNeG*, thereby dramatizing the radical shift from Cosmos to Chaos, from Good to Evil. Although the TY is here following Z 2:252b, the origin of this word-play is in *Sefer Yeẓirah* 2:4. For discussion, see G. Scholem, *Kabbalah:* 25–26. For other examples of its Zoharic usage, see 2:265b; 3:273a (RM); and TZ Intro (12a) and 21 (58a).

161. Here I am following the *Zohar*'s usage of the third person plural rather than the awkward *'omer* used in the TY.

162. At this point Meir ibn Gabbai ends his paraphrase of Z 2:252b.

"River of Fire." This image derives from Dan. 7:10. In Kabbalah, the *nehar di-nur* is the stream that flows through Supernal Eden. It is said to contain both restorative and destructive properties. For example, it is in this stream that souls are ritually immersed and cleansed. All impurities are burned up therein, whereas all that is pure passes through unscathed. (See *Zohar* 1:20la, 3: 211b; 3:16b (RM); and TZ Intro [4a].) In the text utilized by Meir ibn Gabbai here, the destructive qualities of the river are highlighted: The seraphim stand guard over it so that no worthy soul will be burned by it. This account differs from the one presented earlier in Z 2:252b, wherein the river—like a supernal Sambatyon—rests on Shabbat:

> Every day of the week the River of Fire flows, singeing some seraphim and officials. When Sabbath arrives, a tribunal goes forth and the river of fire quiets, its storms and sparks cease.

163. The term *Supernal Eden* may refer to either the divine world or to the Heikhalot. Here, it clearly connotes the sefirotic totality, ibn Gabbai's new, more sublime focus. Also cf. the widespread Kabbalistic notion that during the sacramental meals "a river goes forth from [divine] Eden to water the Garden [*Shekhinah*]." (Gen. 2:10) See Z 2:63b, 3:273a (RM); TZ 24 (69b);

J. Giqatilia, *Sha'arei 'Orah* 1:113 and *Sodot* sec. 4; Baḥyya ben Asher to Ex. 20:8; *Sefer ha-Yiḥud* (from Joseph of Hamadan's circle) s.v. "Sod Shalosh Se'udot be-Shabbat"; et al.

164. That is, by tasting the full array of foods prepared for the festive Meal, the devotee directs his attention to, and participates in, *Shekhinah*'s perfected condition. Cf. Z 1:48b and TZ 24 (69b). The former reads:

> During the nightime feast one should taste everything to indicate that the *Sukkah* of Peace is encompassed by All [nourished by the divine totality]; one should, however, leave one delicacy [untasted] for the daytime feast.

165. **"Remember and Keep."** Symbolizing the union of *Tif'eret* and *Malkhut*. Cf. OK to Ber. 39b:

> "R. Abba said: On Shabbat one should break bread over two loaves." What is the reason? Scripture speaks of "double bread, two omers for each." [Ex. 16:22] The extra loaf alludes to the added [spirituality] of Shabbat exemplified by the *neshamah yeterah*. But why two omers? An omer is 1/10 of an ephah, [ff. Ex. 16:36] making 2/10's of an ephah for each loaf. But since the two "tenths" [*Shekhinah* and *Tif'eret*] unite on Shabbat, the [Children of Israel] gathered "two omers for *one*." [re-reading Ex. 16:22] For this reason, we break over two loaves on Shabbat indicating that they are really one entity, one essence.

Also see *Qanah* 65b:

> The two *ḥallot* should be joined together . . . No dualism is indicated here, as it is written: "You shall keep my Sabbaths": two Sabbaths, viz., *'Aṭeret Tif'eret* [*Malkhut* and *Tif'eret*]; and the two are one. . . . The two loaves should be held by the ten fingers to unite all ten *sefirot*.

166. **"Bottom loaf."** Authorities differed as to which loaf was was to be broken. Cf. *Kol-Bo* sec. 24:

> There are those whose custom is to break over the bottom loaf; but our custom is to break over the top one.

Kabbalists differed in similar fashion. Grounding their rulings in mystical rationales, OZ (52b/67b) claimed that the top loaf should be broken, whereas the OK held that the bottom one should be consumed. The OK source appears to be the "tradition received" by ibn Gabbai. See below for details.

"R. Ṭodros ha-Levi, etc.": OK to Ber. 39b. Here Ṭodros Abulafia offered a second explanation, differing somewhat from the one presented in n165 above. The top and bottom loaves are said to represent *Binah* and *Malkhut*, respectively. One is to consume only the bottom loaf, thereby indicating that *Binah* and the uppermost rungs are beyond direct experience. Although Abulafia's first explanation was focused on the specific drama of Shabbat—the mystery of *hieros gamos*—here he was making a general theological statement:

> "R. Ashi said: I saw that R. Kahana held two [loaves] but broke bread over one." So it is fitting because the one [left unbroken] is the "Eye" [*ᶜAyin*] of which it is said: "No one has seen the Eye, O God, but You," [re-reading Isa. 64:3] for even the greatest of all the prophets did not merit this, as Scripture says: "No one can see My face [*panai,* the innermost aspect]; for no man may see Me and live." [Ex. 33:20]

On the two loaves as *Binah* and *Shekhinah* see Z 3:98a (RM) and the *SHeLaH*'s interpretation of this OK passage ("Massekhet Shabbat"). Also see the aforementioned OZ passage (52b/67b):

> The Mystery of the two loaves. One should break over two because there is to be a "double portion" on Shabbat. This is well and good because the double portion of bread alludes to supernal wisdom called "Bread" [*Ḥokhmah/Binah*], as it is written: "Asher's bread shall be rich;" [Gen. 49:20] and to the Diadem as well, to wit: "for bread is Elohim's" [Lev. 21:22]. . . . The first is called *leḥem ᶜashir,* enriched bread, while the second is called *leḥem ᶜoni,* the bread of poverty. . . . Since we are enjoined to bring together the Upper and Lower Wisdom, we break over the two loaves. . . . One should actually break the top loaf . . . because the bread [i.e., the blessings] of Shabbat issue from the upper one.

167. Heb., *ᶜonat talmidei ḥakhamim.* Parts of this section were analyzed in Appendix II to SCK. See there for broader discussion.

168. This prescription attests to a mildly ascetic ideal for the Rabbinic virtuosi. According to the Talmud, the frequency of marital intercourse was to vary according to occupation and ability; common laborers, e.g., were to have intercourse with greater regularity than scholars. See Ket. 61bff. On the distinguishing function of *ᶜonat talmidei ḥakhamim,* see J. Neusner, *There We Sat Down* (2nd ed., NY, 1978): 92f.

On the Sabbath as the preferred time for marital intercourse, also see the R'oSH's gloss to TB BQ 82a:

> Scripture hints that Shabbat is the appropriate time, as it says: "ve-shameru *B*enei *Y*isra'el *'*et *H*a-shabbat." [Ex. 31:16] This may be read as an acronym for *BiY'aH,* intercourse.

169. In offering this mystical rationale, ibn Gabbai is following *Zohar* 1:75a–b. During the week, when *Shekhinah* is among the *qelippot* of *Siṭra' 'Aḥra',* She closes Herself off lest She be sullied. But on Shabbat, as She returns to Her Husband, She opens up and receives His love. In the words of Moshe de Leon "on Shabbat all the gates are open." This theme is further developed in the TZ, as noted by I. Tishby (MZ 2:495). During the week, She is called "the virgin whom no man had known," [Gen. 24:16] "the locked garden," the "sealed spring," [Cant. 4:12] and even, "Fear" [*yir'ah.*] But on Shabbat, the garden opens, the spring flows, *Yir'ah* gives way to *'Ahavah,* Love. In the evocative imagery of TZ 6 (22a):

> During the six days of the week *Shekhinah* is a folded rose, but on Shabbat and holy days, She opens to receive fragrance and spices [from Her husband] and to give souls and joy to Her children [below].
> For discussion see SCK: 115–16 and 292–93.

170. **"man . . . house."** That is, *Tif'eret* is not in union with *Shekhinah*. On *Shekhinah* as the divine home, see SCK: 223 and 292. Also see TB *Yoma'* 13a and Shab. 118b: "His house—that means his wife."

The TY's point is that the adept and his wife should be perfectly synchronized with the supernal rhythms, for they are the earthly symbols of the divine Pair. For discussion, see SCK: 192–94, 197 and Appendix II.

171. **"Throne."** a common term for *Shekhinah*. Meir ibn Gabbai's conflation of "royal" and sexual imagery in this passage recalls Z 2:135a–b, "Raza' de-Shabbat":

> The holy Throne of Glory is united in the Secret of One, prepared for the High Holy King to rest upon Her. . . .

"days of impurity and separation." Heb., *yemei niddah,* referring to the period of menstrual 'impurity' in which a woman is "forbidden to her husband."

172. Here ibn Gabbai is quoting from TZ 56 (90b). The term *ẓaddiq ve-raᶜ lo* is from TB Ber. 7a: "The righteous man who is in adversity is a righteous man who is the son of a wicked man."

173. The souls of the offspring which hopefully will be conceived.

174. By engaging in intercourse on Friday nights, the adept is aligning himself with the divine model. As noted earlier, the Kabbalist is the one who is most finely attuned to the supernal rhythms.

175. Ff. *Zohar* 3:82a. Also see 2:89a.

176. **"from midnight onwards."** According to TB Ned. 20b, midnight is an ideal time for intercourse. The *Zohar* gives this notion an explicit mythic underpinning. According to 3:167a: "Midnight is the ideal time for marital coupling [for ordinary Jews] because it is the time of coupling on high." Also see 3:81a:

> The Companions indicated the proper time for marital intercourse: He who wishes to sanctify himself in accord with the will of his Master should only have intercourse from midnight onwards . . . for at that time the Holy One is in the Garden of Eden [*Shekhinah*] and a great holiness is aroused. Thus, this is the time for ordinary persons to sanctify themselves.

Although ibn Gabbai does not discuss this rationale here, he did so earlier in the TY (43bff.) This second view obviously clashes with the one under discussion until now; it is useful to distinguish between them more clearly. In our TY text, the adept is bidden to wait until Shabbat because *Shekhinah* is in *niddah* during the week; the mythic rationale for abstinence could not be more clear-cut. In the other schema, the motivations for waiting are less dramatic, being a matter of degree: 1) Although supernal coupling takes place nightly, Shabbat is the time of the most profound divine union, resulting in the birth of particularly high souls. Moreover, 2) the presence of the Sabbath-soul lifts the adept onto a higher spiritual rung and helps him draw down one of these choice souls. Hence, waiting is a desideratum. (The presence of the *neshamah yeterah* can, of course, be used to buttress the other argument, as well; see the ensuing TY for a case in point.)

"but scholars . . . Torah study." According to Rabbinic tradition, it was David who first established this precedent, rising at midnight to study and pray. See TB Ber. 3b, PRK Chap. 7, et al. In the *Zohar*, midnight was held to be a time of cosmic grace, marking the waning of *Din's* power and the inception of divine union. It was therefore considered to be a propitious time for sacred study. Cf. Z 1:206b, 136a–b; 2:57a; 3: 68a, 22a, 156b, 175b, etc. For discussion, see *Sod ha-Shabbat* Section 18.

177. Paraphrased from Z 3:81a. The *Zohar* continues:

> But scholars who know the ways of Torah arise at midnight to study and to join themselves to the Community of Israel [*Malkhut*] in praising the holy Name and holy King. . . . Their time for intercourse is on the [most favorable] night, Shabbat . . . when the Will of All abounds.

178. **"For then they are crowned, etc."** As noted in n176, the presence of the *neshamah yeterah* enables the adept to draw forth a singulary high soul into conception. Cf., e.g., Z 2:204b–05a:

> When scholars bask in this holy and sublime spirit [the Sabbath-soul] . . . they must engage in marital intercourse, for this spirit draws down all these holy souls to the bed, and through this spirit, the holy people transmit sacred souls to their offspring.

On the supernal source for the Sabbath-soul, see SCK: 124–25 and 126; on its descent through the Garden of Eden, see Z 2:204b (the passage quoted here) and the discussion in SCK: 132–33 and 135.

179. ***SHaMaR*.** Here Meir ibn Gabbai begins a paraphrase of *Zohar* 2:89a–b (presented in n182); echoes of 3:82a may be heard as well. The definition of *SHaMaR* as "waiting" is based on RaSHI ad Gen. 37:11:

> "His father *SHaMaR* the matter": He waited and looked forward to the time of [the dream's] fulfillment.

Also cf. Israel Al-Naqawa, *Menorat ha-Ma'or* 3:575:

> "Keep [*SHaMoR*] the Sabbath day." [Dt. 5:12] Remember it always; i.e., eagerly await its arrival . . . like one who looks forward to meeting a person he loves.

The root *SHMR* has an additional sexual connotation in the *Zohar* and TY. Hence, the phrase *'asher yiSHMeRu 'et shabbetotai* may best be rendered:

those who anxiously await the Sabbath and conserve their seed until that time.

180. This phrase recalls Isa. 56:4: ["As regards the eunuchs who keep my Sabbaths] and who have chosen what I desire."

181. This section is marked by rather obvious phallic imagery.

"strengthen His covenant." Ff. Z 2:89a. Kabbalistically, a reference to the divine "phallus," *Yesod,* by means of which *Tif'eret* and *Malkhut* unite.

"Seed of peace and truth." Ff. Jer. 2:21. Kabbalistically, Peace and Truth connote *Tif'eret,* from whom these holy children derive.

182. As noted, Meir ibn Gabbai has been drawing on Z 2: 89a–b. Because it frequently clarifies the TY text, it is worth reprinting here:

> Those companions who know the mystery [of the divine coupling which takes place on Shabbat] direct their hearts to their Creator and are blessed with fruit on that night. Hence, Scripture states: "who keep it," [Isa. 56:4] as in "his father kept the matter in his heart."[Gen. 37:11] For this reason exactly they are called "eunuchs"! For they wait until Shabbat, when it is the desire of their Creator, as it is written: **"who have chosen that which I desire . . ."** [Isa. 56:4] What is "that which I desire"? The *Maṭronita'.*
>
> **"and who uphold My covenant"** so that all may be one. **"My covenant,"** i.e., the one needing no specification [*Yesod*].
>
> Come and see! "Six days shall you labor and do all your work, but the seventh day is a Sabbath unto the Lord." [Ex. 20: 9–10] **"All your work"** i.e., the work of human beings. For this reason the companions only couple when it "the work of the Lord," not that of persons. What is His work? Coupling with *Maṭronita* to draw forth holy souls into the world.
>
> Hence, the companions are consecrated unto their Creator on Friday nights, directing their hearts to Him, that they might bring forth sublime children, holy children, who do not stray to the right or to the left, truly children of the King and Queen. Of these ones it is said, "You are children to the Lord, your God." [Dt. 14:1]. "To the Lord" indeed! For they are called His children, children to the King and Queen. . . . The world is sustained for the sake of these children. When the world is on trial, the Holy One looks upon them and has compassion on the world.

The rest of the TY's discussion is closely modelled on the continuation of this passage. Compare.

183. Kabbalistically, "House" connotes *Shekhinah* whereas Moses refers to *Tif'eret.*

184. **"celestial sphere."** Cf. Z 2:174a: "That celestial place from which souls come is called *Yad:* Portion [i.e., *Shekhinah*]."

"is full of sons and daughters." Following Z 2:89b, ibn Gabbai is rereading *ṭov mi-banim u-mi-banot* (conventionally, "better than sons and daughters") to signify a plenitude of souls. The Zohar passage reads: "And this portion is complete [*be-'ishlemuta'*], 'good' [*ṭov*]: filled with sons and daughters."

According to *Zohar* 3:7a and 91b, the perfected mystic (*shalem*) is one who has coupled with his wife and given birth to both a son and a daughter.

185. Note the shift from the plural form ("*they* will bring forth holy souls") to the singular: "I will give *him* a memorial." I. Tishby (MZ 2:740) suggests that *him* refers to that small elite initiated in Kabbalistic wisdom, whereas *they* refers to scholars in the more general, exoteric sense.

186. **Discussion.** The ensuing section is the longest in *Sod ha-Shabbat.* Prayer takes on a dazzling variety of significations here. As interpeted by Meir ibn Gabbai, most have a theosophical-theurgic valence, intended strictly for *ẓorekh gavoha.* The basic categories include:

(1) Apotropaic prayers which symbolize and/or effect *Shekhinah's* separation from *Siṭra' 'Aḥra'.* (In the Sabbath setting, these prayers tend to be *confirmatory* rather than transformative in thrust: they rehearse *Shekhinah*'s successful escape from Evil.)

(2) Prayers that rehearse and/or effect *Shekhinah*'s ascent unto Her home in the sefirotic pleroma. Having been liberated from the clutches of Evil, She is borne aloft by the angelic Chariot.

(3) Prayers which dramatize, promote and/or confirm intradivine union, most prominently between *Shekhinah* and *Tif'eret/Yesod* or

(4) between the seven active *sefirot* and the three recondite rungs. Union may be effected by descent, i.e., the downward the flow of *shefa*ᶜ from on high, or by ascent, the absorption of the active *sefirot*—singly or in aggregate—in the uppermost reaches of the Godhead.

(5) Prayers that adorn or coronate divinity. Each word is imaged as a blossom of supernal light, woven via recitation into a garland or crown for the Godhead. Borne aloft by the devotee's contemplation and angelic praise alike, these luminous crowns wend their way through the angelic worlds and return to their Source, to restore and augment divinity. Closely related are those

(6) Prayers whose words from a Chariot upon which the divine world rests.

As it transforms divinity, prayer also transforms the devotee:

(7) As prayers articulate events unfolding in the angelic and divine realms, they enable the adept to participate in their mysteries in the proper

way. The adept becomes "like a holy ministering angel" (see n242), a participant in the celestial chorus of praise and exaltation. Further, the adept experiences divine gnosis, able—through the mystical imagination—"to gaze upon the beauty of the Lord and frequent His palace." (ff. Ps. 27:4)

(8) Prayer is also a ladder for actual pneumatic ascent and mystical communion, *devequt*. For one who knows the mystical intentions or *kavvanot*, the words of prayer serve as two-fold symbols: not only reflecting the life within the upper worlds but also providing markers or blazes for the adept on his otherwise uncharted ascent to the divine. Through such contemplation, the soul of the "seeker may [mount up and] cleave unto the Sought" (ff. TY 7a). As Meir ibn Gabbai noted, "through the mystery of . . . prayer the Bride's children are included in Her."

(9) As an epiphenomenon of his attempts to restore and augment divinity, the adept may help bring down its blessing or *shefa*ᶜ. If adornment-prayer (category 5) returns the divine flow to its source, prayer may also help bring it down, nourishing the adept and his world, making the divine immanent. (See Meir ibn Gabbai's description in my Introduction, p. 78 n17 above.)

Other prayers in this section stretch beyond the current mythic moment and point to other critical junctures in time:

(10) Some prayers attest to and rehearse the miracles of Creation and the Exodus from Egypt, e.g., two historical moments traditionally associated with the Sabbath.

(11) Others attest to, and afford a taste of, the *future Sabbath*, the post-Messianic era, wherin "all shall be Shabbat."

(12) As an epiphenomenon, some prayers help one obtain favor in the World-to-Come.

(13) Finally, Meir ibn Gabbai reserves a limited place for "pedestrian" prayer, *ᶜavodah le-zorekh hedyoṭ*, petitions to satisfy basic human needs. One example of this will be seen in this section (s.v. "Reẓeh na' vi-mnuḥatenu," n306).

These *yod gimmel middot*, these 13 aspects of prayer, are not intended to be exhaustive, but rather, suggestive. Surely, they are not self-contained; frequently several categories interweave in a single prayer. I shall elaborate and illustrate as the discussion proceeds.

187. These are discussed in TY: 18a–20b.

188. This section is a paraphrase of *Zohar* 2:205b. See there. Also see 2:131b and *'Or ha-Ḥammah* ad loc.:

> It is permissable to engage in the needs of the congregation during this week, even during prayer; but this cannot be done on the Sabbath.

189. On **"the two angels"** see n158.
"in songs and praises of one's Master." E. p. and Warsaw ed. omit this phrase. Z 2:205b adds: "and immerse oneself in the study of Torah."

190. At this point Meir ibn Gabbai begins his interpretation of *Pesuqei de-Zimra'*, "The Verses of Praise," which constitute the opening section of the *Shaḥarit* service. The prayer referred to here is from I Chr. 16:8–36. It is presented as a poem of thanksgiving, offered at King David's behest by the Levite Assaf, to celebrate the recapture of the Ark of the Covenant from the Phillistines.

191. **"It recites this song in a lovely . . . voice."** Here Meir ibn Gabbai is relying on a passage in Z 2:196a (cited below). The *Zohar* identifies the "song of the sun" with Ps. 105, which opens with the same phrase as the Chronicles text!

The notion that the sun offers praises to God is already expressed in Biblical poetry; cf., e.g., Ps. 148. This image was extended in the works of Merkavah mystics who envisioned all of creation as a chorus offering songs of praise, each creature in its own fashion. The musical nature of the sun's praise is underscored in two of the better-known Merkavah works: *Pereq Shirah,* which derives from the Talmudic era, and *'El 'Adon,* now thought to be of Amoraic origin. For details see n284 and M. Beit-Arie, "Pereq Shirah: mova'ot u-mahadurah biqoṛtit" (Ph.D. diss., Hebrew Univ., 1967; 2 vols.). References to the song or praise of the sun are found in the more exoteric literature, as well. Cf. TB *Yoma'* 20b, which refers to the voice of the sun; and *Tanḥuma',* " 'Aḥarei Mot" (9) which states, "from the time when the sun begins to shine until the moment it sets, it never ceases uttering praise to the Holy One."

192. Conventionally, "let them fear you as long as the sun shines." Meir ibn Gabbai's re-reading of the verse is based on *Zohar* 2:196a. The germane passage reads;

> When the sun emerges in the morning, Israel below takes up the song together with the sun above, as it is written: "Let them revere You together with the sun." When the sun proceeds in its orbit, it breaks forth in sweet melody and chants a song. What song does it chant? "Give thanks to the Lord; Call upn His name. . . . Sing praise unto Him." [Ps. 105:1–2] And Israel praises the Holy One throughout the day, together with the sun.

The *Zohar* proceeds to speak of the awesome power of the sun's song:

> R. Eleazar said: If humankind did not have sealed hearts and closed eyes, they would not be able to withstand the sweet voice of that

orb, the sun, as it traveled its course, uttering praises before the Holy One, blessed be He.

193. I Chron. 16:4 relates that David "appointed certain of the Levites to minister before the Ark of the Lord and to celebrate and give thanks and praise to the Lord, the God of Israel." Although 16:37 makes clear that such ministrations were to take place daily, there is no evidence that *Assaf's Psalm* was to be recited regularly. This notion is articulated only in later sources. Cf., e.g., RaSHI and I Chron. 16:4 and YS 2:188.

194. **"Levites."** Here the *Ḥayyot* or "Holy Living Creatures" which minister to *Malkhut* (the Ark). For details see n210–11.

"all is symbolic." Heb., *ha-kol dugma'*. For the lower world is the reflection of the one on high. Prayer is the means—par excellence—of aligning oneself with the celestial paradigms. For discussion, see SCK: chap. 2, passim.

195. **"illumine."** A play on words: the root *SPR* can also be construed as *SaPpiR*, a radiant sapphire.

196. Meir ibn Gabbai's interpretation of Ps. 19:1 is closely modelled after *Zohar* 2:136b:

> When the Day [*Tif'eret*] shines forth, as it does each Shabbat, joy pervades the cosmos. This is: "The heavens proclaim [*meSaPpeRim*] the glory of God, and the firmaments declare His handiwork." What is meant by "heavens"? It signifies that heaven [*Tif'eret*] in which the Supernal Name and the Holy Name [*Binah* and *Ḥokhmah*] are made visible. . . . "proclaims" [*meSaPpeRim*]: What is meant by it? Not the mere telling of a tale [*SiPpuR*]. . . . Rather it signifies that [the heavens] are illumined and flash with the sparkling of supernal light . . . which comes from the Supernal Book [*SeFeR ʿIla'ah*], the Father of All [*Ḥokhmah*], and from that Book which is the Mother of All [*Binah*].

"With this light the moon shines forth." Ibn Gabbai thereby completes the sentence, as it were, extending the *Zohar*'s interpretation to the term, *kevod 'el*. Hence, "The heavens proclaim the glory of God" may be read: As *Tif'eret* receives the supernal light from on high, He illumines "the glory of God," *Shekhinah*.

At this point ibn Gabbai begins his interpretation of verses 8–10, which form a distinct literary unit. Again, his reading closely follows the *Zohar* text (2:137b).

197. **"the fifty Gates."** The fifty aspects through which *Binah* is manifest. See *Zohar* 1:3b–4a for details. The origin of the phrase is Talmudic (TB Ned. 38a): "Rav and Samuel said: Fifty Gates [conventionally, degrees] of Understanding were created in the world, and all but one were given to Moses . . ."

"five lights." The five rungs—*Ḥesed, Gevurah, Tif'eret, Neẓaḥ,* and *Hod*—directly responsible for conveying *Binah*'s light. Each light shines forth through ten channels, yielding the "fifty gates." Cf. Z 2:206a.

198. **"Six Points" [*shesh qeẓavot*].** *Tif'eret*—the Great Name—and the five *sefirot* which are clustered around it.

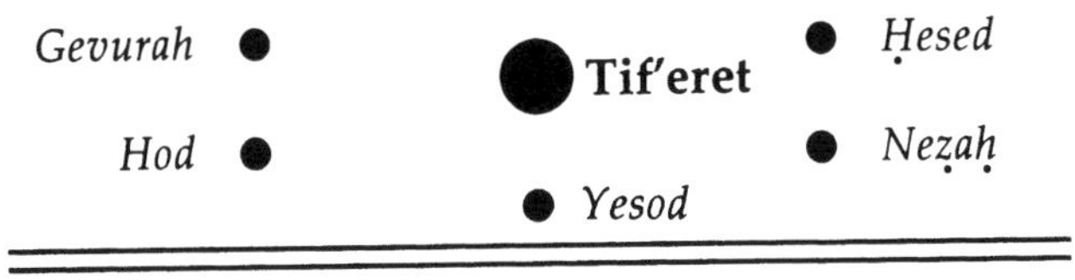

199. This interpretation is also a paraphrase of Z 2:137b.

200. That is, *Yesod* serves as the conduit linking *Tif'eret* with *Shekhinah*.

201. **"drove him away."** *va-yegareshehu*; i.e., caused a separation, or to use a more daring phrase, "divorced" him. Extrapolating from Z 2:137b, ibn Gabbai interpreted this verse in rather remarkable fashion. A more conventional translation might read: "A song of David when he changed his demeanor [i.e., feigned madness] in the presence of Avimelekh, who drove him out, and he left." The more extended Biblical account in I Sam. 21:11–16 makes it clear that it is the Philistine king, Akhish (in Ps 34. misnamed Avimelekh) who is doing the turning out. In the TY something quite different is occurring: it is David (sefirotically, *Shekhinah*) who is forcing the separation. Each Sabbath eve, *Shekhinah*'s demeanor changes; to use a Zoharic image, the mask of fear gives way to the countenance of love. She is accordingly empowered to leave behind the oppressive Avimelekh (Kabbalistically, *Siṭra 'Aḥra'*) and return to Her true husband, *Tif'eret*. This prayer rehearses "last night's" drama.

202. **"dross."** *Siṭra' 'Aḥra'*. That is, the cosmic refuse that lies outside the sefirotic pale which is likened to gold. In this schema, Evil is the byproduct of divinity's self-purification. For discussion, see I. Tishby, MZ 1:297–98.

203. The core of this psalm is an acrostic, each of its twenty-two verses beginning with the appropriate letter in the Hebrew alphabet.

"twenty-two letters . . . Moon." This passage freely combines cosmological, sexual, and linguistic imagery. The twenty-two archetypal letters—containing the totality of divine energy—are said to derive from *Binah*. They coalesce into a kind of sacred language at *Tif'eret*, the "Written Torah." (See *Zohar* 1:156b [ST] and 2:206a for details.) The emergence—or here, the renewal—of the Oral Torah is portrayed as the illumination/impregnation of *Shekhinah* with these sacred letters. The twenty-two verses of this Psalm symbolize the completion of *Shekhinah* that occurs on Shabbat.

204. We may now compare the TY with *Zohar* 2:137b. Note the absence of Torah imagery in the latter:

> On this day the Moon separates from the Other Side in order to be illumined by the Sun. This is referred to in [Ps. 34:1]: "A song of David, when he changed his demeanor, etc." After [the moon] separated from [the Other Side] it joined with the sun. This song of praise is composed of the 22 letters that the sun brought into the moon . . ."

205. The right hand connotes *Ḥesed* whereas the left one refers to *Gevurah*. Cf. *Zohar* 2:137b:

> Then follows the union of the *Maṭronita'* with Her husband. This is alluded to in the [psalm], "The prayer of Moses [sefirotically, *Tif'eret*], the man of *'Elohim* [*Shekhinah*]." [Ps. 90] He spread out both his right hand and his left to receive her and to be one with her . . .

206. **"Na^comi."** I.e., *Binah*, the source of *No^cam*. On *No^cam* and *Na^comi*, see *Sod ha-Shabbat*, Section 22, s.v. "Vi-hi No^cam" [May the Pleasantness].

207. An example of an apotropaic prayer. See pp. 67–68 above. At this point ibn Gabbai turns to Ps. 98 which—in his reading—dramatizes the ascent of *Shekhinah* into the sefirotic pleroma. Having been liberated from her captivity in Philistine *(Siṭra' 'Aḥra')*, She is now borne aloft by the angelic forces unto the "Land of Israel."

208. Referring to the two milk-cows, who unguided, transported the Ark of the Covenenant from Philistine to Israelite territory.

209. TB AZ 24b. The extended passage reads:

> "And the cows *YeSHaRna* [took the straight way] to the way of Bet-Shemesh." What is meant by *YeSHaRna*? R. Johanan said in the name of R. Meir: They rendered song. R. Zuṭra ben Ṭobiah said in the name of Rav: They directed their faces towards the Ark and rendered song. And what did they sing . . . ?
>
> R. Simeon ben Laqish said: [They sang] the "Orphaned" [i.e., anonymous] Psalm . . . O sing unto the Lord a new song . . . [Ps. 98]
>
> R. Isaac Nafḥa said: Rejoice, rejoice acacia[-shrine]/Stretch forth in the fullness of your majesty/Girdled in golden embroidery/ Praised in the recesses of the palace/Resplendent in the finest of ornaments.

The motif of the singing kine is also found in Gen. R 54 and in *'Eliyahu Rabbah*, chap. 12.

210. Kabbalistically, the Throne (i.e., the Ark) connotes *Shekhinah*.

"According to the path of truth, etc." As G. Scholem has shown (*Jewish Gnosticism, Merkabah Mysticism and Talmudic Tradition* [NY, 1965]: 24ff.), the identification of the singing kine with the *Ḥayyot* who bore aloft the Throne derives from the early Amoraic period, long predating its Kabbalistic usage. Indeed, the TB passage cited above cannot be understood apart from its uncited link with the Heikhalot literature, which frequently spoke of the singing *Ḥayyot*. Commenting on Isaac Nafḥa's majestic hymn, Scholem wrote: "Just as the Holy Living Creatures, bearing the throne, sing hymns to the throne, so do these kine, bearing the Ark, sings hymns, to the Ark [where *Shekhinah* resides]." The supernal *Ḥayyot*, in other words, serve as explicit models for the kine below.

This link between the kine and the *Ḥayyot* remained significant in such Kabbalistic works as the *Zohar*. See, e.g., Z 1:123a, 2:137b–138a, 3:201a and esp. 2:13a, the source that ibn Gabbai seems to be drawing upon here. It reads:

> The cows . . . when they carried the Ark . . . chanted this praise: "A Psalm. O sing unto the Lord a new song." [Ps. 98] . . . When these *Ḥayyot* carried the Throne [another version: the Ark] to bear it aloft they chanted this song . . .

211. **"twelve cattle."** It may seem curious that the two kine of I Sam. 16 are here suddenly transformed into twelve cattle or oxen *(baqqar)*. Nonetheless, from a symbolic point of view, these mixed metaphors make sense. For both the kine and the molten cattle symbolize the *Ḥayyot*, as they bear aloft *Shekhinah*. This relationship is made clearer in the ensuing phrases: *Shekhinah* is the perfect red heifer whereas the "cows of the Bashan" (ff. Amos 4:1) are Her offspring, the *Ḥayyot*. On the former, see Z 3:76b: "The red heifer is called *Bat-Shevaᶜ*, the perfect mother." Also see 3:243b:

> Lower *Shekhinah* is "the perfect red heifer." [Num. 19:2] "Red" from the side of *Gevurah*, "perfect" from *Ḥesed*, the rung of Abraham, "without a blemish" from the aspect of the Middle Column [*Tif'eret*].

Even more telling is the allusion to the "Sea of Bronze"—kabbalistically, *Shekhinah*—ff. II Kings 16: 15, 17 and 25:13; Jer. 52:50, 52:17; I Chr. 18:8; et al. This Sea, off course, refers to the bronze tank or reservoir in the Temple courtyard that was supported by twelve molten cattle. In the *Zohar* this passage was re-read as an allusion to *Shekhinah* and the twelve angels or *Ḥayyot* that minister to her. Cf. 1:241a, e.g.:

> R. Abba said: "He made the sea of cast-metal" and it is written: "It stood upon the twelve cattle, three facing north, three facing west, three facing south and three facing east." [I Kings 7:23–25] Surely it is so for this Sea is restored through the twelve in two worlds, the upper world and the lower one. Through twelve above: the chariots appointed on high [*Ḥesed, Gevurah, Tif'eret, Yesod*]; and twelve below: the twelve tribes [the *Ḥayyot*]. When Jacob [*Tif'eret*] saw this supernal restoration and realized that *Shekhinah* was standing by his side, he sought to complete this [act]. He called to his twelve sons and told them to gather and prepare themselves to complete the Faith [*Shekhinah*].
>
> Come and see. The twelve tribes are in four camps, in four directions: three facing north, etc. with the Sea above them. . . .

> The body of *Shekhinah* is above them, as it is written: "And the Sea resting upon them."

Also see 2:164b:

> *Shekhinah* is not in the quorum [of angelic beings] for She stands above them, as it is written: 'And the Sea rested upon them."

For further discussion of the twelve cattle as angelic creatures, cf. 1:157b–58a, 235a, 240b, 246a and *'Or ha-Ḥammah* ad loc.; and *ZḤ Va-Yeẓe'* 35b and Ruth 93b. Our TY passage is quoted in *Yalqut Re'uveni* ad Num. 19:1, where it is attributed to the much later *Kavvanat ha-'ARI.*

212. **"illumined":** *me'irah.* E.p. and Warsaw ed. misprint, *metirah.* Here Meir ibn Gabbai looks at Ps. 98:1 in a new light. In the preceding paragraph it was the *Ḥayyot* who sang unto *Shekhinah.* Now it is *Shekhinah* who is singing unto Her Lover, rejoicing as Her light is restored. Apparently, this is the preferrable reading. See the following note for explication.

213. "Eagle" is a common appellation for *Shekhinah.* Cf. PR: Gate 23 "Nesher" for examples. In this section the TY has been recasting Z 2:138a:

> You may ask why it is written, "a new song," if they [i.e., the *Ḥayyot*] perpetually chant it? But surely it is new, for it is called new in connection with the renewal of the Moon. When it receives light from the sun, then it is a "new moon"; thus it is said: "a new song."

214. **Bet-Shemesh,** Lit., the house of the sun [= *Tif'eret*]. To restate this passage in sefirotic terms: *Ḥesed* and *Gevurah,* the right and left hands, lift up *Shekhinah* from above, just as the *Ḥayyot* do from below. She is thereby borne aloft to Bet-Shemesh/*Tif'eret* in two-fold fashion. Also cf. Z Ibid. and 2:241a.

"Lord . . . sun and shield." A paraphrase of Ps. 84:12. Cf. Z 2:224b wherein both sun and shield are identified with *Tif'eret.*

215. Cf. the Zohar source—2:138a—which utilizes royal rather than cosmological imagery to indicate *hieros gamos:*

> Because on the Sabbath the Throne ascends on high, it was established that this praise be recited on the Sabbath.

216. Cf. Ex. R 15:4:

> Through the merit of the Patriarchs [*zekhut 'avot*] I will redeem them. As it is written: "Leaping upon the mountains" [Cant. 2:8]: The mountains are the patriarchs.

And compare Gen. R 68:2: " 'I lift my eyes to the mountains [*HaRiM*]': i.e., I lift my eyes to the Fathers [*HoRiM*]." Kabbalistically, of course, the Patriarchs connote *Ḥesed, Gevurah,* and *Tif'eret.*

217. In good Kabbalistic fashion, the questions of the Psalmist and Job are turned into theosophical affirmations. *Shekhinah*'s restoration is shown

to ultimately come from *'Ayin* [*Keter:* the mystical Nothing], whence all existence springs. Cf. TZ 70 (127a); and *Zohar* 2:83a:

> " 'Whence [*Me-'ayin*] comes my help?' *Me-'ayin* should be read as in the verse, 'He came even to the Ancient of Days [i.e., *Keter*]." [Dan. 7:13]

There are Rabbinic precedents for turning *me-'ayin* from a question into a positive statement. See, e.g., TB *Soṭah* 21b on Job 28:20: "Wisdom will come from humility"—the *'ayin* that entails the restraining of ego.

218. In Ps. 121:3: He that guards you will not slumber
v. 4: He that guards Israel
v. 5: The Lord is your guardian
v. 7: The Lord shall guard you from all evil
He shall guard your soul
v. 8: The Lord will guard your going and coming now and forever

219. Heb., *ᶜOlam ha-Raḥamim: Keter* or more generally, the upper Triad which is without any trace of *Din.*

220. This passage recalls *Zohar* 1:172b. Compare!

221. The terms *Jerusalem* and *Kingdom* refer to both the heavenly Jerusalem *(Shekhinah)* and the earthly city which is Her symbol. See Z 3:118a and 3:78a for illustration.

222. Ff. *Zohar* 2:229b, 3:78a and 118b, the twelve tribes connote the twelve conduits linking the seven bottom *sefirot;* their primary function is to convey the *shefaᶜ* from on high. *YaH* connotes *Ḥokhmah* [*Yod*] and *Binah* [*He*], whence the *shefaᶜ* derives. Z 3:78a explains:

> "The tribes of *YaH*": What are these twelve tribes? Twelve lines that spread forth from this great and mighty Tree [the sefirotic corpus], which they inherit from the aspect of the Father and the Mother.

223. **"twelve springs of water."** Cf. Z 2:64b:

> The Holy One has a Tree, a great and mighty Tree which contains nourishment for the entire cosmos. This tree is encompassed by twelve lines. . . . So it is written, "And they came to 'Elim, where there were twelve springs of water." [Ex. 15:27]

This first Kabbalistic usage of this image is in the *Bahir* (161 and 165); ultimately it derives from *Sefer Yeẓirah*'s notion of the twelve cosmic radii, the so-called *gevulot 'alakhson* (5:2). For discussion, see G. Scholem, *Re'shit ha-Qabbalah ve-Sefer ha-Bahir* (Jerusalem, 1961/62): 171–72 and 312.

"Spring of Justice." *Ḥokhmah* and *Binah* are the Spring, the source of Justice *(mishpaṭ)*, generally an appellation for *Tif'eret. Mishpaṭ* here is a shorthand for all twelve conduits whose lines converge at *Tif'eret,* See I. Tishby, MZ 2:224 for discussion.

On the **twelve cattle,** see n209–11.

224. The former refers to *Tif'eret/Yesod*, and the latter to *Malkhut*.

225. Two allusions to the union of the divine Male and Female. "Walls" and Righteousness *(Ẓedeq)* connote *Malkhut* whereas Peace *(Shalom)* connotes *Yesod*.

226. **"rest."** Heb., *MaNoaḤ*, closely related to *MeNuḤah* which (like *Ṭov*) is a more common name for *Yesod*. Kabbalistically, this verse takes on added resonance since the "you" referred to here is Ruth, a mystical name for *Malkhut*.

227. Heb., *shalom ba-kol*, lit., peace in all. Generally speaking, an indication of cosmic well-being. In its more specific sense, it signifies the union of *Yesod* and *Malkhut*, the divine All.

228. That is, *Malkhut* who is now dwelling "in the heavens," in union with *Tif'eret*.

229. Heb., *'adam;* conventionally, translated as a collective plural, "men" or "persons."

230. A reference to *Sitra' 'Aḥra'*. Cf. *Zohar* 2:272b: " 'When the man rose up against us.' [Ps. 124:2]: This man is Pharaoh [the human symbol of *Sitra' 'Aḥra'*]."

Ibn Gabbai uses even stronger language than the *Zohar*, employing the term *'Adam ha-Beliyyaᶜal* (Eng., Belial). Kabbalistically, *'Adam ha-Beliyyaᶜal* is the personification of Cosmic Evil, equated with Sammael or one of his four principal charges. Cf., eg., TZ 69 (118b) and 67 (98a–b) and Z 2:118a–b (RM). On the term *'Adam ha-Beliyyaᶜal* see G. Scholem, "Bil'ar, Melekh ha-Shedim" in *Maddaᶜei ha-Yahadut* 1 (1925/26): 112–27; idem, *Kabbalah*: 385–88; and the discussion in my thesis "The Sabbath in the Classical Kabbalah": 494–95.

231. Kabbalistically, the waters of impurity beneath the sefirotic Tree; the *qelippot* under Belial's jurisdiction. Cf. *Zohar* 2:264b.

232. In the Biblical verse the word *SHiYNaYiM* is written in defective form *(ketiv ḥaser)*, i.e., without the first *Yod;* it is therefore identical in spelling with the Hebrew word for "two": *SHeNaYiM*.

It is my surmise that ibn Gabbai has interpreted the unusual spelling of SHi[Y]NaYiM in terms of the "*two* wicked persons" referred to in I Kings 21:10, 13: *shenayim 'anashim benei veliyyaᶜal*—in other words, as a reference to Sammael and his nation: the demonic *qelippot*.

233. **"men."** Here, in a positive sense, as in "truly human" [sic!].

234. Cf. TB BM 114b:

For it has been taught: R. Shimon bar Yoḥai said: The graves of the Gentiles do not defile, for it is written: "And you my flock,

> flock that I tend, are men." [Ezek. 34:31]: Only you [Israel] are designated "men."

What is meant only in ritual terms in the TB is mythicized and generalized in Zoharic Kabbalah. Cf. Z 2:21a:

> "You are men." [Ezek. 34:31] You are called 'man' but not the rest of the nations who are idolators . . . [But] all Israel are called "men" [i.e., truly human].

This distinction is repeated many times in connection with Ezek. 34:31. Cf., e.g., Z 1:86a, 20a; 2:121a, 221a, 265b; and 3:219a.

235. Death here refers to Cosmic Evil, or to use another image, *'Adam ha-Beliyyaᶜal.* Cf. *Zohar* 1:29a:

> In the time-to-come God will sweep away all evil from the world, as it is written: "He has swallowed up death forever;" [Isa. 34:8] and everything shall be restored to its rightful place, as it is written: "On that day the Lord shall be one and His name one." [Zech. 14:9]

236. This is excerpted from TB Ber. 62b, where, following Rabbinic convention, *'Edom* is taken to signify Rome:

> R. Eleazar once entered a privy, and a Roman came and thrust him away. R. Eleazar got up and went out, and a serpent came and tore out the other's gut. R. Eleazar applied to him the verse, "Therefore will I give a man for you." [Isa. 43:4] Read not *'aDaM* [a man] but *'eDoM* [a Roman].

In the Kabbalah, as well, Edom refers to Rome or more generally, to the Christian or Gentile oppressors of the Jews, who according to certain classical sources (e.g., Jer. 30:11, PRK 30a, Z 2:53a) must be severely punished before the advent of the Messiah. In the Zoharic tradition, human Edom is often hypostatized and aligned with Sammael and the potencies of the demonic. For example, in ZḤ "Yitro" 44b, Edom is a synonym for the *qelippah* called *'esh mitlaqqaḥat* (a flashing Fire), whereas in 3:29a it more generally connotes the celestial home for the demonic forces. In our TY passage, Edom signifies Sammael/*'Adam ha-Beliyyᶜal.*

237. That is, from divinity; sefirotically, most closely associated with *Tif'eret.*

238. **Discussion.** Meir ibn Gabbai thereby finds two levels of meaning in this prayer. On the one hand, it symbolizes the drama that unfolds on each Shabbat, viz., *Shekhinah*'s escape from *Siṭra' 'Aḥra'*; on the other hand, it adumbrates the complete Redemption that will unfold in the eschaton, "the world that is entirely Shabbat"—when Evil itself will be destroyed. Recitation of this Psalm is thereby seen as a dress rehearsal of the praise people will offer in that age.

239. This passage is based on *Zohar* 1:232b:

> What is the meaning of YaH [in "Halleluyah"]? It is the supernal Name [*Ḥokhmah* and *Binah*] that is supreme above all. Therefore, [Ps. 135 begins with] "Halleluyah": a word in which both the praise and the Name are combined.

Also cf. 1:16b and 1:178b.

240. Heb., *SeTaM*. Cf. *Zohar* 1:232b, Meir ibn Gabbai's source here: Just as the name YaH is not disclosed [SaTiM: hidden, anonymous], so those who offer the praise [i.e., "the authors"] are not disclosed. It is thus fitting that all should be hidden [SaTiM] in the realm of this sublime mystery [amidst *Ḥokhmah* and *Binah*].

241. **"Great Name,"** That is, the more accessible rung of *Tif'eret*.
"Those who know this mystery." The Kabbalists.
"in the House of the Lord." At the rung of *Shekhinah*.

This is a good example of the way in which Kabbalistic prayer affords the adept *entrée* into the supernal mysteries. The TY is here following the aforementioned *Zohar* passage:

> But thereafter, there is a disclosure, as it says: "Praise the name of the Lord; give praise, you servants of the Lord." [Ps. 135:2] Because this is a realm that is not hidden as is that supernal realm [YaH]. . . . This realm is called Name [*Shem:* here, *Tif'eret*] as it is written, "whereupon is called the Name, the Name of YHWH" [II Sam. 6:12].

242. As ibn Gabbai noted in the beginning of Section Thirteen "on Shabbat one must engage only in songs of praise, in [non-petitionary] prayer and in words of Torah." By doing so, the adept is consciously emulating the activity of those ministering angels whose sole task is to praise God. The notion that prayer is angelic activity par excellence derives from Apocalyptic and Merkavah circles, and is reflected in the exoteric tradition in such prayers as *Qedushat Yoẓer,* where the angels are said to continously recite the *trishagion*. For other germane sources, see EJ 2:974 (s.v. "Angels").

For further discussion of the adept's angelic transformation during Shabbat, see *Sod ha-Shabbat* Section 18 ("Torah Study"); and SCK: Appendix II.

243. Cf. the famous Aggadah in TB *Beiẓah* 16a:

> R. Yoḥanan said in the name of R. Ṣhimon bar Yoḥai: Every miẓvah which the Holy One gave to Israel, He gave to them in public, except the Sabbath which was given in privacy, as it is said: "It is a sign between Me and the Children and the Children of Israel forever." [Ex. 31:17]

As A.J. Heschel pointed out:

> the phrase "Between . . . and" is a Hebrew expression for intimacy between husband and wife [cf. Ned. 79b]. The word forever, *le-ʿolam* is written in such a way that it may be read as if it were

vocalized *le-ᶜaLeM*: to be kept a secret [TB Beiẓ. 16a]. (*The Sabbath* [NY, 1951]: 109)

244. *Ḥiddush* is the technical term utilized by the medieval philosophers—Judah and Samuel ibn Tibbon, Al-Ḥarizi, etc.—to denote the doctrine of Creation *ex nihilo*. Meir ibn Gabbai is here alluding to Ps. 135:6–7, which underscores the ongoing nature of this *ḥiddush*, God's willful Creation:

> The Lord does as He pleases, in heaven and earth, in the seas and all the depths; He makes clouds rise from the ends of the earth; He makes lightening for the rain and brings forth the wind from His storehouse.

245. A reference to Ibid.: 8–9: "It was He who smote the first born of Egypt, both man and beast. He sent signs and wonders into the midst of Egypt, on Pharaoh and all his servants."

On the Exodus attesting to Creation: The roots of this notion appear to be Biblical. For example, both Isa. 51:9–11 and Ps. 89:10–11, depict God's Redemption of Israel in terms of His defeat of the primordial forces of Chaos. As He liberates Israel, He once again utterly vanquishes Rahab, the monster of the deep and symbol for Egypt:

> It was You who hacked Rahab in pieces, that pierced the dragon;
> It was you who dried up the Sea, the water of the Great Deep;
> That made abysses of the Sea, a road the redeemed might walk.
> (Isa. 51:9–11)

For discussion of this motif, see John Day, *God's Conflict with the Dragon and the Sea* (Cambridge, 1985), esp. pp 25–27 and 91–93.

This notion was cast in propositional form by such thinkers as Philo and the medieval Jewish philosophers. Philo held that the miracles recorded in the Scripture, among them those that occurred in Egypt and in the Wilderness, are evidence of God's power to change the order of nature. (Cf. Moses 1:12, 65ff.; Migr. 15, 83ff.) This change in order is the essence of Creation which he considered the greatest of all such miracles. The medievals argued in yet more rigorous fashion. Miracles, divinely intended anomalies within the natural order, provide empirical evidence of God's willful Creation of the Universe out of nothingness. (For details, see Saadiah, *Book of Beliefs and Opinions:* [Rosenblatt ed.]: 48; Judah ha-Levi, *Kuzari*: 1:91; RaMBaM, *Guide for the Perplexed*, 2:22, 25; et al.) The most profound miracle was the Exodus from Egypt, with its variety of astonishing signs and supernatural wonders. See, e.g., RaMBaN ad Ex. 13:16 and Dt. 5:15; and Joseph Albo *ᶜIqqarim:*

> "'Remember" and "Keep" were uttered as one.' [TB Shev. 20b]: "Remember" refers to the existence of an agent who created the world [i.e., *zekher le-maᶜaseh bere'shit*] and "Keep" to the ongoing Creation exemplified by the Exodus from Egypt. . . . And not only at the time of the Creation of the world, but even after the world has come into being, He exercises his Providence and changes nature,

> compelling it to perform His will and desire at all times, as He did in delivering Israel from Egypt . . . (Husik ed., vol. 3: chap. 26)

246. That is, Shabbat is both *zekher le-maʿaseh bere'shit,* in commemoration of Creation, and *zekher li-yẓi'at miẓrayim,* in commemoration of the Exodus. For discussion, see I. Heinemann, *Ṭaʿamei ha-Miẓvot* (Jerusalem, 1959) 1:56, 66, 73, 84, and 90 and the sources therein.

Moreover, as indicated in the preceding paragraph of the TY, Shabbat is *'ot le-ʿolam,* a perpetual sign of intimacy between God and Israel. Hence, Psalm 135 alludes to all three Biblical rationales for Sabbath observance. To recapitulate: Shabbat is a sign of intimacy (verse 4); and a symbol of God's Creation of the World (verses 6–7); and a symbol of the Exodus from Egypt (v. 8–9). Thus far, Meir ibn Gabbai's interpretation of Ps. 135 is not specifically Kabbalistic; rather, it affirms Rabbinic and philosophical commonplaces.

247. A reference to Ps. 135:10–12.

248. In its plain sense, a reference to 'Ereẓ Israel; Kabbalistically, *Malkhut.*

249. On the symbolic nexus between celestial and earthly Jerusalem, cf. OK to Shab. 119b; *Zohar* 1:80b–81a, 183b; ZḤ "Noaḥ" 26b; and *Sod ha-Shabbat* p. 72 above.

250. **"cleave to the Lord, etc."** A paraphrase of Deut. 4:4.

"He will make a full end, etc." A paraphrase of Jer. 30:11.

"For I will make a full end of all the nations where I have scattered you." See n236.

251. Y[od] =10; the two H[e']=2(5)=10; the W[aw]=6. Cf. this numerological interpretation with the one given in TB Pes. 118a.

252. Cf. TB Ber. 4b and especially, Pes. 118a:

> What comprises the Great *Hallel?* R. Judah says: From "O give thanks" [Ps. 136:1] until "By the rivers of Babylon." [Ps. 137]

253. The Creation is the subject matter of verses 5–9 and the Exodus, verses 10–16.

254. The subject matter of v. 17–22.

255. **"Perhaps."** Heb., *'ulai.* This caveat indicates that ibn Gabbai is presenting an original rationale here.

256. **"intimate knowledge."** Heb., *daʿat:* i.e., experiential knowledge. The TY echoes the Messianic promise of Isa. 11:9: "For the land shall be filled with knowledge [*deʿah*] of the Lord as water covers the sea."

"For then I will make, etc." In *Zohar* 1:118a, this Biblical verse is understood as promising the universal assimilation of Kabbalistic wisdom.

257. Heb., *'El ha-Shamayim:* a reference to the supernal *'El, Binah.*

258. A series of allusions to the ultimate *hitballe^cul* (cosmic "swallowing") or apokatastasis, whereby all of Creation, including the seven lower *sefirot* will be reabsorbed in *Binah*, the Cosmic Sheath *(nartiq)* or Womb. In that era, all shall be divinity: "the Lord alone shall reign." For discussion of this phenomenon, see SCK: 32 and 98–100; and *Sod ha-Shabbat*, n335–36.

259. From the Sefardic Grace after Meals on the Sabbath. The first part of the phrase is originally found in Mekh. "Beshallaḥ," chap. 7; the second part is from M. *Tamid* 7:4. Sefirotically, the term "life everlasting" connotes *Binah*.

260. **"sublime and lofty God":** Heb., *romemut ve-ᶜillui*. Kabbalistically, a reference to *Binah*.

Discussion. Meir ibn Gabbai constructed a sort of meta-history based on this Psalm. Through the clues therein, he delineated six critical junctures in Time:

(1) Creation

(2) The Exodus from Egypt and the inheritance of the Land: the "first Redemption."

(3) The "Second Redemption" inaugurating the period of the Second Temple

(4) (The current Exile and the coming) Messianic Redemption

(5) Resurrection

(6) Reabsorption into divinity via mystical "swallowing"; cosmic *unio mystica*

261 This prayer was discussed previously in TY, p. 21b.

262. Heb., *mizmor shir le-yom ha-Shabbat*. The preposition *le-* can mean either "of" or "for." Here, the latter meaning is stressed.

263. Despite Meir ibn Gabbai's attribution of this Midrash to PRE 19, it is actually a conflation of that source and Mid. Ps. 92, as noted by R. David Luria in his commentary to PRE. Compare!

264. **"the king whose is the peace."** Heb., *melekh she-ha-shalom shelo*, a word play on Shelomo (Solomon). Cf. TB Shev. 35b and *Mishnat Shir ha-Shirim*, ed. S. Lieberman, in G. Scholem, *Jewish Gnosticism*: 126. Kabbalistically, the Song of Songs is the duet chanted by *Malkhut*, the divine bride, and *Tif'eret*, the supernal Solomon, "king of peace."

In the TY here, *Malkhut*—the divine Sabbath—offers Ps. 92 to *Tif'eret*, Her beloved. Also cf. Z 2:138a:

> [Ps. 92] is a song of praise sung by the world below [*Malkhut*] to the world above [*Tif'eret*], to a day which is entirely Sabbath, that is, "the king whose is the peace."

265. In ibn Gabbai's reading *le-* clearly means "of."

266. I have been unable to locate the source.

267. Cf. *Zohar* 3:56b:

> What is the meaning of "A song; a Psalm . . ." [Ps. 48:1]?. . . . It is a doubled song; i.e., a song that is more sublime than all the others. Since it is as sublime as the Song of Songs, a word connoting 'song' is mentioned twice. And so too, with "A Psalm; a song of the Sabbath day." [92:1]

268. **"anonymously . . . author."** Mystically, a reference to *Malkhut*. The Biblical proof-texts presented here contain phrases in which the understood subject, God, is omitted. Ibn Gabbai's interpretation here recalls *Zohar* 2:138a:

> And this is "A psalm; a song" [Ps. 92:1]: whose author is not mentioned, as explained above. "For the Sabbath day": a supernal day, the supernal Sabbath [*Tif'eret*]. . . . [The anonymous author] is the anonymous Sabbath, Sabbath eve [*Malkhut*]; and the phrase "the Sabbath day" refers to the supernal Sabbath . . . the mystery of the Male.

269. **"for a day that is . . . everlasting."** Only the first part of the phrase is found in the TB. On the second phrase, see n259.

270. See n258.

271. This prayer dramatizes the mystical adorning of *Shekhinah* each Shabbat. Cf. Z 2:138a, upon which ibn Gabbai draws here. Note the absence of *Ẓaddiq* imagery in the original:

> "The soul of every living creature": . . . This soul comes forth [on Sabbath eve] from this Eternal Life [*Yesod*] whence all blessings derive. . . . [Eternal Life] showers blessings on [*Shekhinah*] below. This soul which derives from [*Yesod*] has permission to bless the Place [*Shekhinah*]. . . . And the locus from which the souls derive blesses Her from above. Thus, this Name receives blessing from below and from on high; it is encompassed on all sides.

For more on the Sabbath-soul, see SCK: 121–38.

272. **"All."** In its more general sense, this term denotes the entirety of blessings, both from on high and below, that surround *Malkhut*. In its more precise Kabbalistic sense, 'All' signifies *Yesod* and the totality of divine blessings which it has absorbed.

273. *MaH*, which means 'What?' or 'Quiddity', is numerically equivalent to 45: M[em]=40 and H[e']=5. The number 45 is a mystically significant number, the numerical equivalent of the *ketiv male'* (plene form) of the Tetragrammaton. *MaH*, therefore may indicate the sefirotic totality. (See the ensuing TY passage and n276.) Ibn Gabbai is basing his interpretation on *Zohar* 2:138a:

> During the week, She receives blessings from the rest of the souls below. On the Sabbath She [also] receives blessings from the su-

pernal souls that bless her with *MaH:* 45 words . . . as we indicated in the mystery of *MaH* . . . which is the lower World [*Shekhinah*].

274. Why did ibn Gabbai find it necessary to list all the words here? It seems that he did so to solve a textual problem. It is held in *Zohar:* Ibid. that there are 45 words in the first paragraph, 50 in the second, and 100 in the third. Yet, a survey of *siddurim* extant in ibn Gabbai's time reveals a variety of wordings for this prayer. (Recall that he lived in Ottoman Turkey, where a variety of liturgical traditions co-existed) Apparently, ibn Gabbai is trying to establish a text that harmonized with the reckoning of the *Zohar.*

275. ***'aT-BaSH,*** a form of gematria wherein the first letter of the alphabet is replaced with the final letter, the second letter with the penultimate one, etc.

"YeẒ": Y[od]=10; Ẓ[addi]=90.

276. That is, all ten rungs with all ten of their inner aspects. Note that this interpretation is not based on *Zohar* 2:138a, which never overtly links the 45 words with the sefirotic totality. In all likelihood, Meir ibn Gabbai has been drawing on a different Zohar source, 2:17a, here:

> The last rung is the mystery of the Lower World [*Shekhinah*] that is called *MaH.* It is taught [TB Men. 43b]: "Do not read *MaH,* but *Me'aH,* 100." For then, all the supernal rungs are completed.

277. ***MiY.*** M[em]=40 and Y[od]=10; *MiY* means "who," a common appellation for *Binah.* See Z 1:1b and 2:138a; and G. Scholem, *Major Trends:* 221.

"Primordial Sea." This reference to *YaM/Binah* is not found in *Zohar* 2:138a; in all likelihood ibn Gabbai is using the term as an allusion to the water imagery found in the second paragraph of the prayer.

278. Here ibn Gabbai is again following *Zohar* 2:138a:

> From here follows other praises. They are composed of 100 words that are the completion of All [i.e., of *Shekhinah* and consequently, the sefirotic Gestalt.]

This Kabbalistic interpretation may be contrasted with the exoteric rationale found in *Abud:* 165–66, et al.: "This [paragraph] contains one hundred words, alluding to the one hundred blessings that are to be recited each day."

279. **"remaining words."** That is, through *Yishtabbaḥ.* These words serve as a "Chariot" supporting the sefirotic world. (See n186, point 6 above.)

Despite ibn Gabbai's attribution, the printed version of the *Zohar* (2:138a) does not make this claim. Rather, it states that the hundred words in the final paragraph "form a Chariot on which the Supernal Wholeness rests." See there.

280. Heb., *pores ᶜal ha-Shemaᶜ*: An idiom of Rabbinic origin, meaning to proclaim or recite aloud the four benedictions of the *Shemaᶜ*. Also, *pores 'et ha-Shemaᶜ* (cf. M. Meg. 4:3, Lev. R 23, etc.). RaMBaM, MT "Tefillah" 8:5,

uses the phrase to specify the prayer leader's audible chanting of these blessings.

281. **"this section is lengthier."** A reference to the greater restorative powers elicited through recitation of *Ha-Kol Yodukha* and *'El 'Adon* as opposed to their weekday counterparts, *Ha-Me'ir la-'Areẓ* and *'El Barukh.* On this mystical rationale, see *Zohar* 2:132a:

> "Who forms light . . . and creates all things." Both I and my friends have commented that these [the Sabbath *Yoẓer* prayers] are acts of restitution upon the upper world [*Tif'eret* and above], while *'El Barukh* ["The Blessed God"] are words of restitution for the lower world [*Shekhinah*].

282. *Tif'eret.*

283. **"Chariots."** The angelic world; **"cosmic forces":** Heb., *manhigei ha-ᶜolam.*

284. This prayer, attributed to Merkavah mystics of the Amoraic period, is an acrostic hymn of praise to God, the Creator of the luminaries. It poetically describes the activity of those celestial spheres just mentioned in the TY, including the Chariots, the stars, and the sun. For discussion, see Meir Bar-Ilan, *Sitrei Tefillah ve-Heikhalot* (Ramat Gan, 1987).

285. Here Meir ibn Gabbai is following *Zohar* 2:205b which contrasts the structure of *'El 'Adon* with that of *'El Barukh.* In the former, each verset begins with a new letter, whereas in the latter, each successive word begins with the next letter. Therefore, *'El 'Adon* has a greater interval between each alphabetical unit, and in the mystical hermeneutic, a greater sefirotic value. The Zohar source reads:

> *'El 'Adon.* This song of praise is composed of twenty-two supernal holy letters that are crowned with the Patriarchs [*Ḥesed, Gevurah,* and *Tif'eret*] and the supernal Holy Chariot [*Binah*]. Opposite them are twenty-two "small" letters of the lower world [*Shekhinah*] which enter *'El Barukh.* There the only interval between the [alphabetical] letters is the one between each word. But in the supernal world [*Binah*] there is ample interval, with holy mysteries between each letter.

On the twenty-two small letters, see Z 1:3b and n288. For another Kabbalistic interpretation contrasting these two prayers, see OZ 39b quoted in SCK: 120; and cf. SCK: 177 n241.

286. This paragraph is a close paraphrase of Z 2:132a. Compare.
"Six Entities." Same as the "Six Points." See n198.
"Mother of the Cosmos." *Binah.*

287. **"Chariot."** A reference to the four *sefirot* (the *Patriarchs* and *Shekhinah*) which together form the Supernal *Merkavah.* See *Zohar* 1:211a and 242a and the discussion in I. Tishby, MZ 1:416.

"the One who rides in the . . . heavens." A reference to *Binah,* which is sometimes called *rokhev shamayim,* the rider of the heavens, i.e., the Patriarchs.

288. **"Great Alphabet."** Aramaic, *'alfa-beita' rabbati;* Kabbalistically, *Binah,* which is said to be pregnant with twenty-two "Great Letters" (*'otiot gedolot* or *'atvvan ᶜila'in ravrevin*) which, when emanated, form the divine building blocks for Torah and Creation. The Great Alphabet is contrasted with the twenty-two Small Letters (Ara., *'atvvan zeᶜirin*) found in *Shekhinah.* Cf. n285. For further discussion on these two mystical alphabets, see Z 1:3b, 228b, 3:2a and TZ Add. 9 (116a).

"twenty-two . . . Great Letters." Corresponding to the twenty-two words in these verses. Cf. Z 2:132a:

> The [verses containing] the first two and last two letters together form the full complement of 22 letters, for they contain 22 words parallel to the 22 letters.

289. Lit., letters.

290. Seventy-two is the numerical value of *Y, YH, YHW* and *YHWH* (10+15+21+26). The sacred 72-letter Name derives from the mystical literature of the Geonic period; kabbalistically, it is generally associated with the Patriarchs. For details, see G. Scholem, *Kabbalah:* 52.

291. On this mystical coronation of divinity, cf. *Zohar* 2:132b:

> The seventy-two-letter Name is encompassed in the hidden meaning of the *Patriarchs,* Right, Left and Center; She [*Shekhinah*] is crowned with them so as to become the Holy Name.

Also cf. Z 2:132a:

> There remain eighteen other letters which rise to their Chariot in groups of four, and so there are seventy-two words, the mystery of this Great Name, a holy engraving of seventy-two letters with which the Holy One [*Tif'eret*] is crowned. And this Name is a crown for the Community of Israel [sefirotically, *Shekhinah*].

292. This section is a paraphrase of *Zohar* 2:205b. See n295 for details.

"sixty Chariots." Each Sabbath eve sixty Chariots are said to descend into the *Heikhalot,* the celestial Garden of Eden. Cf. Z 2:240a:

> On [Sabbath eve] when this spirit [the Sabbath soul] descends, the sixty Chariots that crown the "Six Points" descend with it into the Garden of Eden.

293. The Zohar source specifies that both the Chariots and the souls of the righteous bear this praise aloft. See n295.

294. **"There all remains."** Lit., "stands." TY uses the plural *ᶜomedim* which could be construed as a reference to both the praise and those that bear it aloft. The *Zohar,* however, uses the singular *qayyema',* indicating that

it is the praise that remains there until the *Qedushah* of *Musaf* (the Additional Service).

This *Qedushah,* of course, is the so-called "Crown" Sanctus, *Qedushat Keter,* which begins: "A crown of glory, Lord our God, is given You by the countless angels on high together with Your people Israel assembled beneath. . ."

295. **"supernal splendor."** Sefirotically, a reference to *Binah.*

In the preceding passage we see a classic example of how prayer may serve as a means of adorning or coronating divinity. Meir ibn Gabbai's source, Z 2:205b, describes this process in striking fashion:

> When this song of praise ascends on high, the sixty supernal Chariots mentioned above join together and take it from the holy People. They ascend with it to where it is [woven into] a crown for [the decoration of] many heavenly Chariots and for all the righteous in the Garden of Eden. All these Chariots and all these souls of the righteous, all ascend with this praise unto the Throne of Glory. When this praise of all Israel reaches the holy Throne, it halts there until the supernal *Qedushah* of *Musaf* [is recited]. Then, the lower aspects rise up to the ones above, and all is united in the uppermost reaches: All is one. This is the praise that rises above all others.

296. Heb., *'Avot, Gevurot, Qedushot:* the first three benedictions of the *ʿAmidah.* Having explained the *Yoẓer, Ga'al Yisra'el* and the beginning of the *ʿAmidah* in Part One of the TY, ibn Gabbai glosses over them here. See TY: 25a–34b for details.

297. *Qedushat ha-Yom,* the fourth of the seven benedictions, consists of a series of prayers specifically concerned with Shabbat. They are: "Moses Rejoiced," "The Children of Israel Shall Keep the Sabbath," "You, Lord our God, Have Not Given the Sabbath Day to the Nations," "Those Who Rejoice in Your Kingdom" and "Be Pleased with Our Rest."

298. A reference to *Tif'eret,* which is at the heart of the sefirotic world.

299. A quotation from the prayer. Kabbalistically, *Shekhinah.*

300. *Neẓaḥ and Hod.* By dint of their union, *Tif'eret* and *Shekhinah* remove the Tablets' "stoniness" or harsh qualities. The ensuing quotation is also taken from the prayer.

301. From the prayer, "The Children of Israel Shall Keep the Sabbath." (Ex. 31:17ff.)

302. Printed TB text actually reads: "R. Yoḥanan said in the name of R. Shimon bar Yoḥai."

303. See n243.

304. Biblically, a sin offering of one male goat *(se^cir ḥaṭṭa't)* was required at each of the sacred festivals: on the New Moon (Num. 28:15), Passover (28:22), Shavuᶜot (25:30), the New Year (29:5), the Day of Atonement (29:11) and on each day of Sukkot (29:16, 19, etc.). However nothing was required for the Sabbath. Not surprisingly, this anamoly captured the Kabbalistic imagination.

As I have noted, most sacrificial offerings *(QoRBanot)* fulfilled two major functions: 1) *Piyyus ha-Din:* the warding off of cosmic Evil by appeasing and (so, neutralizing) it; and 2) *Yiḥud:* the subsequent drawing near *(QeRuB)* of the forces of holiness, the effecting of sefirotic harmony. (Cf. *Zohar* 3:224a). However, one *qorban,* the *seᶜir ḥaṭṭa't* was seen in a different light. Like the hair in the tefillin (n45) it was offered purely as a bribe to Satan, a way of keeping the darker forces at bay. Such neutralization of Satan's power was deemed unnecessary on the Sabbath, when the demonic forces lay dormant and cosmic well-being was basically assured. For germane Zoharic sources, see Z 1:64b, 138b; 2:269a and 3:258b; for related discussion, see MZ 2:194ff. and 209. Also cf. the parallels in *Sefer Sod ha-Shem* fol. 171c and *Sod 'Ilan ha-'Aẓilut,* p. 85, two works from the *Temunah* circle.

305. Heb., *ᶜet raẓon:* a time of sefirotic harmony.

306. Here Meir ibn Gabbai reserves a role for prayer that addresses purely human needs, *ᶜavodah le-ẓorekh hedyoṭ.* Such moments are exceedingly rare in the TY, where service "for the sake of divinity," *le-ẓorekh gavoha,* is described as the central human task. This petitionary prayer can only be entertained because sefirotic unity is so secure and powerful at this hour. For further discussion see n478.

307. Heb., *yemot ᶜolam:* the seven lower *sefirot.*

308. On this tradition, see TB Shab. 86b. Ibn Gabbai here seems to be quoting from *Abud.:* 171.

309. **"eight verses."** It is difficult to determine the exact content of the TY's version of this prayer for two reasons:

1) In most Sefardic *siddurim* the prayer consists of nine rather than eight verses. Cf., e.g., *Abud.:* 171. Moreover, the order of the nine verses frequently varies.

2) Ibn Gabbai directly quotes only the first verse, and gives only sketchy information regarding the other verses; e.g., he notes from which of the three major divisions of Scripture the first three verses derive.

However, based on that evidence, the version found in *Sefer Moᶜed ha-Shem* most likely reflects ibn Gabbai's ordering:

(1) Dt. 4:35
(2) Ps. 86:8
(3) I Kings 8: 57
(4) Ps. 28:9
(5) Num. 10:35

(6) Ps. 132:8
(7) Ibid.:9
(8) Ibid.:10

"seven qolot." The seven voices (or, in some interpretations, thunderbolts or tones) with which God spoke to Israel at Sinai. The origin of this notion is Rabbinic, based on the seven mentions of the term *qol* in the Revelation narrative (Ex. 19–20). Cf., e.g., Ex. R 28:6; Mid. Ps. 68 and 92; Tanḥ. "Shemot" 25; and the *Yelammedenu* source preserved in YS ad Ps. 29. These seven revelatory voices became the subject of mystical speculation among Ḥasidei Ashkenaz and were correlated with the seven lower *sefirot* as early as the *Bahir*. According to the latter (sec. 45), Israel perceived only the seven active *sefirot* at Sinai; the three upper voices remained unheard. Also see OK to Ber. 29a and TZ 30 (74b). For discussion, see L. Ginzberg, *Legends* 6:39, G. Scholem *Das Buch Bahir*: 33; and n330 below.

"maftir." Kabbalistically, *Shekhinah*.

310. That is, the first three verses come from all three sections of the Hebrew Bible. See the list above. Kabbalistically, the Torah connotes *Tif'eret;* the Prophets, *Neẓaḥ* and *Hod;* and the Writings or Hagiographa, *Shekhinah*. On Shabbat *Shekhinah* is nestled securely within the divine pleroma.

311. **"YHWH."** *Tif'eret* and its five contiguous *sefirot*, which form a protective circle around the "Glory," *Shekhinah*.

312. **"ten divine utterances"** According to M. *'Avot* 5:1, the world was created with ten *logoi*, hypostases of the ten utterances mentioned in Gen. 1:3–29 and 2:18. Kabbalistically, the Ten Utterances and the Decalogue connote the sefirotic totality. Cf. *Zohar* 2:93b, 156a–b and 176a–b.

"contained in the two Names." On YHWH containing the sefirotic totality, see SCK: 30. On YHWH/*Tif'eret* + *'Elohim/Shekhinah* embodying the supernal Decalogue, see *Sod ha-Shabbat*, p. 13 and n4, above.

Discussion. While at Sinai, all Israel immediately understood the mystery of the unified Godhead. Each Shabbat during the Torah service, this Sinaitic insight is experienced anew.

313. See p. 19 above.

314. Meir ibn Gabbai is here following Z 2:205b–06a:

> "And they read in the book of the Torah of God with an interpretation, and they gave the sense and caused them to understand the reading." [Neh. 8:8] We have already explained this [in TB Meg. 3a]. The esoteric meaning of these verse stops, accentuation and Masoretic notes, and of all punctuation and supernal mysteries, was transmitted to Moses at Sinai. But if the Torah were given to Moses with all this punctuation, why is the Torah-scroll, which is filled with all this sanctity devoid of these mysteries?. . . . The hidden meaning is [as follows]: When the holy Throne [*Shekhinah*] is crowned and encompassed by the Written Torah [*Tif'eret*], then all these

> forms, accentuations and Masoretic notes secretly enter the Holy Throne. They are recorded in the Oral Torah, which becomes impregnated with them as a woman is by a male. Then the supernal letters [of the written Torah] remain alone, as is fit [i.e., in accordance with *Tif'eret* more recondite nature]. . . . The Throne is blessed and crowned through the mystery of the Written Torah.

315. **"Uphold . . . hold up."** This word-play is based on the dual meaning of the Hebrew *meqim*. Cf. TJ *Soṭah* 7:4:

> "he who will not uphold . . ." [Dt. 27:26]: This is the prayer-leader who does not raise the Torah scroll and show the script to the congregation."

"faith of Israel." Heb., *sod 'emunat Yisra'el.* Kabbalistically, an allusion to *Shekhinah*'s completion as She receives the Masoretic notes and accents—the supernal energy—from *Tif'eret.*

316. See n309. Here a clearly kabbalistic rationale is intended. Cf. Z 2:206a:

> On this day seven men must go up [to the Torah], corresponding to the seven Voices [the seven lower *sefirot*] which comprise the mystery of Faith.

Representatives of the congregation thus become the earthly symbols of—and participants in—the divine mystery.

317. Kabbalistically, the Kohen becomes the symbol of *Ḥesed;* the Levite, of *Gevurah;* and the *Yisra'el, Tif'eret.*

318. **"sixth . . . Ẓaddiq."** *Yesod* is the sixth of the active *sefirot.*

"and is set up on high." This phrase is omitted in the e.p. and Warsaw edition.

On the word-play concerning *yaRUẒ:* Although this word generally means "runs," ibn Gabbai follows Z 3:164b and employs a much rarer meaning: to "read or declaim fluently." This usage is found in Hab. 2:2: "Write the vision and make it plain upon the tablets, that a man may *yaruẓ:* read it quickly."

Ibn Gabbai's point is that only a meritorious person should be given the sixth *ᶜaliyah,* for he must symbolize the supernal *Ẓaddiq,* "the Pillar of the Cosmos." He thereby gives a Kabbalistic rationale for the medieval custom of reserving the sixth *ᶜaliyah* for a scholar. On this custom see EJ 15:1254. On its Zoharic interpretation, see 3:164b:

> Whoever is called up to the Torah must be righteous. Who is called righteous? The sixth person of the seven. . . . He should be the most righteous of all.

319. The sixth *ᶜaliyah,* in other words, contains apotropaic powers. The preceding passage is a close paraphrase of *Zohar* 3:164b. Compare!

320. **"all streams,"** i.e., the *shefaᶜ* from the (six) *sefirot* above Her. Cf. *Zohar* 2:234b.

321. Referring to Ezra's public recitation of the Torah.

322. **Discussion.** In this section, Meir ibn Gabbai makes explicit that which was hinted at before: the reading of the Torah is considered a dramatic re-enactment of the theophany at Sinai. The reader on the *bimah* (pulpit) parallels "God speaking above," while the congregation attending to the Torah-reading in rapt silence parallels the People at Sinai "standing below." On the theme of silence at Sinai, also see Ex. R 29:9.

For further discussion, see the Zohar source (2:206a–b) cited in n327 and my comments in SCK: 166 n174.

323. The single voice mystically denotes the sefirotic unity (the mystery of Faith) that reigned during the theophany, and which recurs each Sabbath as the Torah is again "received."

324. Heb., *sarsur*. Both representative and emissary.

325. Cf. *Tanḥuma'* "Yitro" (15):

> "And the Lord spoke" [Ex. 20:1]: Scripture says: "Then did He see it and declare it; He prepared it, yea, and searched it out." [Job 28:27] Only afterwards does it say: "And He spoke unto man." [Ibid.:28] This teaches you the way of Torah. If you are called up to the Torah you should not be so presumptuous as to speak before the community until you have rehearsed the [portion] several times to yourself.

326. **"Yofiel."** In late Geonic magical traditions and classical Kabbalah, Yofiel was the angel presiding over the "secrets of Torah." According to *Shimmusha' Rabba'* (mentioned in n45), whoever received wisdom from Yofiel was granted special theurgic powers. In the *Zohar,* Yofiel was also portrayed as the personal teacher of children who died young. See Z 2:206b, 274a; 3:177b; and especially, 2:147b. For discussion, see G. Scholem, "Sidrei de-Shimmusha' Rabba' " in *Tarbiẓ (16) 1945: 196–209 and Kabbalah:* 30–31.

"fifty-three holy Chariots." corresponding to the fifty-three weekly Lessons as reckoned by *Zohar* 2:206b. As Jacob Katz has noted (*Halakhah ve-Qabbalah:* 46), this Zoharic myth implicitly undermines the validity of the Palestinian triennial cycle, according to which the Torah was divided into some 154–175 weekly portions. (See TB Meg. 29b and Sof. 16:10.)

"minister to . . . Torah." Heb., *shimmush ha-Torah. Shimmush* is a technical term indicating magical or theurgic power (in this case, deriving from esoteric knowledge of Torah).

327. Throughout this last section the TY has been relying on Z 2:206a–b. Because this source clarifies certain ambiguities in the TY and makes more apparent the *Sinaitic* quality of Torah-reading, it merits full citation here:

> Only one person may recite from the Torah [at a time]. The rest must attend to the reader's words in silence, *as though they were receiving the words this very moment from Mt. Sinai.* [emph.

mine] Another person should stand next to the Torah, but in silence, lest two Words be heard. . . . For if two voices are heard [simultaneously] reading the Torah, it is a lessening of the mystery of Faith and a lessening of the glory of the Torah.

The people must be silent, with [only] one reading, as it is written: "God spoke all these words, saying," [Ex. 20:1] He being above and all the people below, as it is written, "and they stood at the foot of the mountain." [Ex. 19:17] And it is further written, "And Moses [here paralleled by the person called up to the Torah] went up to God." [Ibid.:3]

The reader must direct his heart and will to that which he says, for he is a representative of his Creator, charged with the responsibility of communicating [these words] to the entire community. He is the symbol of the supernal One [*ke-dugma' ʿila'ah*]. Thus, whoever goes up to read the Torah should prepare beforehand at home, or else he ought not read from the Torah. From where do we learn this? From Scripture [concerning what God did] before He gave the Torah to Israel: It is written first "Then did He see it and declare it; He prepared it, yea, and searched it out" [Job 28:27] and only thereafter, "He spoke unto man." [Ibid.:28]

It is forbidden for the reader to break off anywhere save where Moses indicated. Nor may he conflate one week's portion with that of another. The inner reason is as follows: When each weekly portion is completed, it is adorned with a crown and presented before the Holy One, blessed be He. At the conclusion of the yearly cycle they all present themselves before the Holy One, thus crowned, each one announcing, "I am from Sabbath X"; I am from Sabbath Y."

At that moment, the Holy One calls to Yofiel, the celestial chief, and to the 53 holy Chariots under his charge who minister to the secrets of the Torah-reading, each one ministering to its own Lesson and Sabbath. It is forbidden to confound the weekly portions, disarranging so much as a word or letter, thereby causing the Chariots to overlap. Rather, each [Lesson] should be read in accord with the limits set by the Holy One and each [Chariot] should stand guard over its appointed Lesson.

When the portion is adorned with a crown, i.e., when it is completed by the congregation, the words ascend. They are gathered up by their appointed Chariot which lifts them up before the Holy One. These words actually stand before Him and proclaim: "I am Portion X that has been completed by congregation Y." If the Lesson has been properly completed, these words ascend and are formed into a crown for the Throne of Glory, while its ministering Chariot stands over it. So it proceeds each week until they are all fashioned into a crown for the Throne of Glory. The Throne ascends with

> the crown into the uppermost reaches, and all becomes one totality. And so, happy is the portion of whoever completes the weekly Lesson in the proper manner, in accordance with the divisions fixed on high.

328. **"reflects the Torah portion."** Most *haftarot* were selected because they were felt to bear some relationship to the Torah portion.

329. **"Bride reflects the Written Torah."** Through this analogy, ibn Gabbai is correlating the Haftarah with the *Shekhinah*.

"Everything is included in Her." Ibn Gabbai conveys the perfected quality of *Shekhinah* via a traditional Kabbalistic word-play, linking *KaLlaH* (Bride), *Ha-KoL* (everything), and *KaLuL* (is included): *ki khen ha-kallah . . . ve-ha-kol kalul bah.*

330. **"for it contains seven *qolot*, 'Voices.'"** The phrase "the Lord's voice" [*qol YHWH*] appears in Ps. 29 seven times. Hence, this Psalm was linked with the theophany at Sinai. This connection was first implied in Mekh. "Ba-Ḥodesh"; it was stated more explicitly in *Midrash Yelammedenu* [in YS ad Ps. 29] which held that "the seven mentions of *qol YHWH* . . . correspond to the seven *qolot* in the Giving of the Torah." For Kabbalistic treatment, see *Bahir* 48; Z 1:23b–24a; and TZ 30 (74b).

Recitation of Ps. 29 here dramatizes the original theophany and its recurrence each Shabbat, as the seven Voices or active *sefirot* again become one. It is possible that ibn Gabbai is also alluding to a more esoteric teaching here. See n335–36.

331. The notion of 18,000 worlds or *ᶜolamot* is first mentioned in TB AZ 3a, the source quoted here. The Gemara' begins:

> Or it may be said that He rides a light cherub and courses through 18,000 worlds; for it is said, "The chariots of God are myriads, etc."

The number 18,000 is derived as follows: "The Chariots of God are *ribbotayim*": two myriads or twice 10,000, "less *'alfei*": 2,000—"*she-'einan*": that are lacking.

This concept of 18,000 worlds, suggesting that God was too great to confine to one Creation, was understandably attractive to the Kabbalists, and terse references to it are found in RaMBaN's *Commentary to Sefer Yeẓirah;* R. Baḥyya ben Asher ad Num. 10:35; Zohar 1:23b–24a; and 3:23b (RM). RaMBAN, e.g., alludes to eighteen sefirotic aspects—parallel to the TY's "18 citations of the Divine Name"—which suffuse the 18,000 cosmic entities or "worlds." He maintained that each of the nine *sefirot* below *Keter* has two polar aspects; one in which *Din* predominates and another in which *Raḥamim* does. Although each aspect brings forth 1,000 worlds, the entire eighteen-fold emanation is subsequently crystallized in all 18,000 *ᶜolamot.* For further discussion, see G. Scholem's *Ha-Qabbalah be-Gerona* (Jerusalem, 1963/64): 300–01; and *Ursprung und Anfange der Kabbale* (Berlin, 1962): 399ff.

The explicit linking of this cosmological speculation with the "eighteen citations" of Psalm 29 first appears in *Zohar* 1:23b–24a, which Meir ibn Gabbai paraphrases here. The source reads:

> There are seven Palaces of Light below, corresponding to the seven voices in [Ps. 29]: "Ascribe unto the Lord." There are eighteen citations of the divine Name therein, by means of which the Holy One courses through 18,000 worlds: "The Chariots of God, etc." [AZ 3a]

332. **"enlightened."** Heb., *maskil*. Connoting an initiated Kabbalist. The boldly speculative nature of this teaching prevents its explication. (See the warning in n336!) As I will soon demonstrate, Meir ibn Gabbai has circumspectly alluded to the doctrine of *shemiṭṭot* or Cosmic Cycles developed in Gerona Kabbalah. (For general discussion, see G. Scholem, *Kabbalah:* 116–22 and E. Gottlieb, *Meḥqarim be-Sifrut ha-Qabbalah* [Tel Aviv, 1976; hereafter, *Meḥqarim*]: 332–39.) The 18,000 *ᶜolamot* (worlds) referred to here are actually the 18,000 Ages or Creation-Cycles—i.e., aeons—to which certain Kabbalists limited the cosmic-process.

333. Cf. TB Shab. 30a and MQ 9a. Meir ibn Gabbai's wording seems to be a paraphrase of *Abud.*: 174. See there.

The remainder of this passage (through n336) refers to the drama of *hitballeᶜut* or *apokatastasis;* it has been analyzed in SCK: 196–97. The discussion will be limited to new information here.

334. Cf. TZ 57 (91b): "All angels are called by the name YHWH." Also cf. *Zohar* 1:23b upon which ibn Gabbai seems to be drawing:

> On Sabbath . . . the supernal *Ḥayyot* who are called exclaim "Lift up your heads, O Gates . . . ," etc.

335. **"reabsorption of the Holy." Heb.,** *hitballeᶜut ha-qodesh,* the technical term for mystical "swallowing" or reincorporation of the seven active *sefirot* in *Binah* at the end of a Cosmic Cycle. See SCK: 98–100 for discussion.

"ascension of the Glory." Heb., *histallequt ha-kavod.*

"world that is entirely Shabbat." Another reference to this *hitballeᶜut,* ff. the Kabbalists' re-reading of TB Sanh. 97a. The Gemara' reads:

> Six thousand years shall the world [kabbalistically, "aeon"] exist and 1,000 shall it be desolate. . . . Just as the seventh year is one year of release in seven, so in the world, 1,000 years out of seven shall be fallow, as it is written: "And the Lord alone [kabbalistically, the upper Triad] shall be exalted on that day"; [Isa. 2:11] and it is further said: "A Psalm, a song for the Sabbath day" [Ps. 92:1], meaning a day [kabbalistically, an aeon] that is entirely Shabbat.

336. Heb., *ve-ha-devarim ᶜattiqim. ᶜAttiq* here means esoteric, or veiled. Cf. 1 Chr. 4:22 and Ruth R 1:1. Also see Z 1:135b (MN):

> "The wine preserved in its grape from the six days of Creation. [TB Ber. 34b]": *'Ellu devarim ᶜattiqim.* These are veiled words, whose

meaning shall never be revealed to humankind from the day of Creation; they will be disclosed to the righteous in the time to come.

Discussion. As noted above (n332), ibn Gabbai does not feel at liberty to explicate this passage because it alludes to the process of "periodic creation": the secret doctrine of *shemiṭṭot.* This may become clearer by comparing the TY with the more expansive account found in R. Baḥyya ben Asher ad Num. 10:35. As G. Scholem has noted (*Kabbalah:* 121), Baḥyya was the first known Kabbalist to explicitly correlate the 18,000 *ᶜolamot* of AZ 3a with cosmic aeons. Analysis suggests that R. Baḥyya served as the ultimate—and quite likely, the direct—inspiration for ibn Gabbai here. Some points of comparison:

(1) Prooftexts used. Both authors relied on Ps. 24 and TB AZ 3a to portray the process of periodic creation.

(2) Terminology. Both use *histallequt* and the root *BLᶜ*, technical nomenclature for apokatastasis.

(3) Caveats against explication. Both Baḥyya and Meir ibn Gabbai abbreviated discussion, maintaining that the doctrine of the 18,000 aeons cannot be publicly taught.

Still, there is one possible difference which should be pointed out. Ibn Gabbai seems to associate Psalm 24 with the mystical absorption of Being into *Binah,* the "supernal Ark." However, Baḥyya clearly spoke of a more radical regression of the cosmos into *'Ein Sof:* Although the incorporation of all Being into *Binah* occurs at the end of each *shemiṭṭah* or seven millenium cycle, the ascension into *'Ein Sof* occurs only during the cosmic Jubilee, at the end of the full cycle of seven *shemiṭṭot.* To facilitate comparison, an excerpt from Baḥyya's discussion is printed below:

> For all seven [*sefirot*] return and ascend unto *Binah* . . .
> This is the destruction of the cosmos [ff. TB Sanh. 97a] . . . the cessation of the downward flow of *shefaᶜ* . . . But there will not be utter chaos here.

Baḥyya was registering his disagreement with those Kabbalists—e.g., Joseph ben Samuel of Catalonia—who held that the world returns to utter chaos at the end of each *shemiṭṭah* but that reabsorption into the upper triad occurs only during the Jubilee. (See G. Scholem, *Kabbalah:* 120 and Gottlieb, *Meḥqarim:* 335ff.) Baḥyya ben Asher continued:

> Rather, all will return as in the beginning; the *sefirot* will bring down that which they received from above and the cosmos will then be renewed. So it will be from one seven [millenium cycle] to the next, until the Great Jubilee . . . whereupon all ten *sefirot* will return to their source in *'Ein Sof.* For this reason, the world will necessarily be in primordial chaos, for "the heavens shall be

rolled up as a scroll" [Isa. 34:4] and the "earth wear out like a garment" [Isa. 51:6; cf. PRE 51] for *Tif'eret* and the Glory [*Malkhut*] and their analogues, the sun and the moon, skies and earth, shall be swallowed up into the Holy [*niBLe*ᶜ*u 'el ha-qodesh*] and return to their foundation. *This process is explained by King David in Ps. 24* [emph. mine], "The earth is the Lord's and all the fullness therof," for the return of the upper and lower worlds to their primal source is mentioned there: it begins with the lower worlds and concludes with the upper. This Psalm speaks of the withdrawl [*histallequt*] of the holy potencies . . . of their ascent and return to *'Ein Sof*: "Lift up your heads, O Gates, up high, you cosmic Doors!" *The enlightened will understand these verses, for I am not at liberty to say more in broad daylight.* [emph. mine]

So it follows that all that exists will be null and void, but after the Jubilee it will be renewed, for the ten rungs once again will unfold from *'Ein Sof;* then the *shefa*ᶜ will flow in the upper and lower worlds, as of yore. So it happens from Jubilee to Jubilee until 18,000th, for each *sefirah* will serve as the activating mode for 1,000 Jubilees: the ten *sefirot* above and the ten below.

Lest one think that these Jubilees are infinite, Scripture reminds us: "Return, O Lord, the myriads" [Num. 10:36] to show that God will establish for the world two myriads. This would [normally] constitute 20,000 Jubilees, but Scripture adds "Israel's thousands" [Ibid.] to indicate that He substracts 2,000 from these myriads. This is the meaning of "The Chariots of God are myriads, even thousands *shin'an.*" [Ps. 68:18] Do not read *SHiN'aN,* but *SHe'eiNaN:* that are not . . ." [TB AZ 3a] One must not include 2,000 and so, there are 18,000 Jubilees. This is the hidden meaning of the verse: "Its circumference shall be 18,000." [Ezek. 48:34] Thus, it is maintained in chapter 1 of AZ [3a] "Or it might be said that He rides a light cherub and courses through His 18,000 worlds, as it is said: 'The chariots of God are myriads, etc. . . .' "

Therefore, know that this matter cannot be reflected upon [openly] for it is included among those topics which one should refrain from discussing, as it is said: "What lies above, what lies below; what lies ahead and what lies behind." [TB Ḥag. 11a].

337. ***"Musaf."*** From the mystical nullity or "emptying" of *hitballe*ᶜ*ut,* ibn Gabbai returns to the fullness of the current Shabbat. The *Musaf* service corresponds to *Yesod,* which is now filled with the added blessings of Shabbat. Cf. *Zohar* 3:302b:

> On the Sabbath, the Additional Service corresponds to "Ẓaddiq, the foundation of the world," [Pr. 10:25] called All [*kol*] and called *Musaf*. For [*Ẓaddiq*] bestows upon the Sabbath additional pleasure.

The correlation between *Musaf* and *Yesod* is sometimes amplified through a word-play based on the root *WSF,* indicating surfeit. The *MuWSaF* service is said to correspond to *yoWSeF* (Joseph), the *Zaddiq* who, on Shabbat, brings forth a surfeit [*toWSeFet*] of blessings and additional souls. On this theme, cf. Z 1:259b: "During *Musaf* an abundance of divine light from the Holy Ancient One [*Keter*] collects in *Yesod*." Also see TZH 99c:

> An additional portion issues forth from the aspect of *Zaddiq* who is the crown of all *musafin* . . . In it is the surfeit of *Hokhmah, Binah, Da^cat* and all the aspects of the Holy One [*Tif'eret*] . . . [which it imparts unto *Shekhinah*] as it says, "One that scatters, yet increases" [Prv. 11:24] . . . From it [*Yesod*] comes to abundance of extra-souls that accrues to each person on the Sabbath.

338. **"remember and keep."** The fourth benediction of the Sefardic *Musaf*, which begins: "On Mt. Sinai You commanded Moses concerning the mizvah of remembering [*zakhor*] and keeping [*shamor*] the Sabbath . . ."

"united in the additional service." *she-mityahadim bi-tfillat Musaf*. The preposition *bi-* can also signify "through." It is conceivable that ibn Gabbai has this meaning in the back of his mind here. To re-read the phrase in this light: Through *Musaf* (i.e., *Yesod*) *Tif'eret* and *Shekhinah* are brought together. Cf., e.g., OK to Ber. 6a and TZ 6 (20a):

> "Remember" and "Keep" are the Holy One and *Shekhinah*. Happy is he who unites them *be*-—through—the Sabbath day, which is *Yesod*.

339. **"Qedushah Rabbah,"** meaning the Great or Enlarged Sanctus. The second meaning seems to have been the original one, stemming from the addition of the *Shema^c* to this *Qedushah* in the fifth century. The other meaning became primary in later medieval times. For details, see *Manhig* 1:171; *Abud.*: 171 and the discussion in I. Elbogen, *Ha-Tefillah be-Yisra'el* (Tel Aviv, 1972): 49 and 400.

For the Kabbalists, the greatness of this *Qedushah* is correlated with the supernal drama it narrates: the supreme coronation of divinity.

"Rabbis of blessed memory have long expounded, etc." As noted, the image of prayer as a coronation ceremony derives from Merkavah mysticism. Prayer is a conceived as a cooperative venture between Israel below and the angels on high. An angel is said to receive Israel's prayers, proceeding to weave a glorious crown from them. As it utters the Name, this crown ascends to the divine palace and adorns the Holy King. This Merkavah imagery entered into the exoteric Rabbinic tradition by the Amoraic period. Cf., e.g., the famous Gemara' (TB Hag. 13b) wherein the *'ofan* Sandalfon weaves a crown for God's majesty. Also see the more extended description in Ex. R 21:4:

> After all the individual congregations have completed their prayers, the angel ministering to them gathers all the prayers offered in all the congregations and weaves from them a crown to adorn the head of the Holy One, blessed be He. As it says, "unto You [*^caDeYkha*] who hears prayers, all flesh shall come." [Ps. 65:3].

> *ᶜaDeYkha* means "crown," as it says: "You shall clothe yourself with them all as an ornament [ᶜaDY].
>
> Further it says: "Israel in whom I will be glorified [etPa'eR]." [Isa. 49:3] for the Holy One is crowned with the prayers of Israel, as it says, "And [I put] a beautiful crown [*ᶜaṭeret tiF'eRet*] upon your head." [Ezek. 16:12]

To facilitate understanding of the TY's interpretation, the complete text of *Qedushat Keter* is appended here. The version utilized follows *Abud.*: 171:

> A crown [of glory], Lord our God, is given You by the countless angels on high, together with Your People Israel assembled beneath. In unison, all of them thrice acclaimed Your holiness, as it is written by the prophet:
>
> "They keep calling to one another: Holy, holy, holy is the Lord of Hosts; the whole earth is full of His glory." [Isa. 6:3]
>
> His Glory fills the cosmos; His ministering angels ask: "Where is his glorious place, to revere Him?" [Angels] respond with praise and say: "Blessed be the glory of the Lord from His place." [Ezek. 3:12]
>
> From His place may He turn with compassion to His people, who acclaim His oneness evening and morning twice every day, and with tender love recite: "Hear O Israel, the Lord is our God, the Lord is One." [Dt. 6:4]
>
> The One is our God; He is our Father; He is our King; He is our Deliverer. He will again save and redeem us; He will again in His compassion proclaim to us in the presence of all the living: Behold, I will redeem you in the future as I did in the past, "to be your God; I am the Lord your God." [Num. 15:41], etc.

340. **"source."** Heb., *maqor.* Warsaw ed. misprints *maqom.*

"Lord our God." *Ḥokhmah* and *Binah* which convey the *shefaᶜ* to the **"Middle Column,"** *Tif'eret/Yesod.* Here Meir ibn Gabbai is paraphrasing TZḤ 100c:

> This is the supernal Crown [*Keter*] referred to in the Sabbath *Qedushah:* "A crown [of glory] is given to you, Lord our God." What is "Lord our God"? The Father and the Mother, who crown the Middle Column and *Shekhinah* with it.

341. "The fine oil" refers to the *shefaᶜ* emanating from *Keter* which descends "onto the head," i.e., *Ḥokhmah,* "and from there to the rest of the aspects [*middot*]": the seven lower *sefirot.* Consequently, the divine Glory (*Shekhinah,* or more generally, the sefirotic totality) is perfected.

The imagery used here recalls Z 3:7b:

> "How good and pleasant it is that brothers [i.e., the *sefirot*] dwell in unity. It is like fine oil upon the head, running down the beard and over the collar of his robe." [Ps. 133:1–2]
>
> What is this oil? It is the oil, the liniment of holiness that issues forth from the Holy Ancient One [*Keter*], gathering in the

> celestial River [*Binah*] which suckles Her children, [bringing forth oil] to kindle the lamps [the seven lower *sefirot*]. This oil is drawn down to the King's head and then upon His beard [*Binah!*] and therafter, upon all the garments of glory that adorn Him. As it is written, "that comes down . . . over the collar of his robe [*ᶜal pi middotav*]": That is, over His *middot* exactly, [those divine aspects] which are the King's crowns.

342. In this passage the downward flow of *shefaᶜ* is recounted."Disciples of the Lord" and "Hosts" both refer to *Neẓaḥ* and *Hod*. "Land of Israel," connotes *Shekhinah*, whereas "Lord's Glory" refers to the *shefaᶜ* She receives from the six *sefirot* above Her. For Zoharic parallels cf. ZḤ 100d and esp. TZ 18 (34b).

343. Kabbalistically, the acronym 'aYeH refers to the upper Triad. The letter *Alef* ['] signifies *Keter*, *'alufo shel ha-ᶜolam* (the Chieftain of the Cosmos), the letters *Yod* [Y] and *He'* [H] refer to *Ḥokhmah* and *Binah*. In typical Kabbalistic fashion, Meir ibn Gabbai has transformed the question: "Where ['*ayeh*] is the Place of His Glory?" into a theosophical teaching: " *'aYeH*—the upper triad—is the source for the Glory, the seven *sefirot* below.

344. **"home on high."** Heb., *ha-ramatah 'el beitah*. That is, the upper triad. The Hebrew phrase recalls I Sam. 1:19.

Discussion. This passage marks a turning point in the supernal drama of *Qedushah*. Until this point, the movement has been downward, as the lower *sefirot* are imbued with sacred energy from on high. Here, the lower *sefirot* begin their ascent, signalling the onset of a more profound, primal union.

345. **"Glory of God's Name."** Kabbalistically, the divine effulgence that collects in *Shekhinah*, and by association, *Shekhinah* Herself.

"Wisdom." Refers to the lower *Ḥokhmah*, or *Shekhinah*. The *Bahir* distinguishes between supernal Wisdom (the second *sefirah*) and his Daughter, the lower Wisdom, often called "the Wisdom of Solomon" or the "Wisdom of 'Elohim." This distinction between the two Wisdoms is one of the Gnostic elements in the *Bahir*, paralleling the Sophia imagery found in the Valentinian tradition. For discussion, see G. Scholem, *Das Buch Bahir*, pars. 44 and 90a; and *Re'shit ha-Qabbalah ve-Sefer ha-Bahir*: 205 ff.

The ensuing two paragraphs seem to be a mystical midrash on the Gemara' (TB Ḥag. 13b) mentioned in n339.

> Sandalfon . . . fashions crowns [out of Israel's prayers] and recites "Blessed be the glory of the Lord from His Place." [Ezek. 3:12] *But there is no one who knows His Place . . . [emph. mine]*

346. This parable alludes to *Shekhinah*'s mysterious, utterly transcendent nature. She is the regal Queen, the distant Mother, hidden within the king's chamber. The sons—the heavenly retinue, and by extension, Israel

below—can only know that She exists and is worthy of blessing; face-to-face knowledge cannot be attained.

347. **"[the people from] her place."** *mi-meqomah.* R. Margaliot and G. Scholem eds., and Meir ibn Gabbai's AQ (3:32) all read: *"mi-meqomekh"*—from your place—thereby directing the conversation to the Princess.

Discussion. Although the preceding parable depicted the transcendence of *Shekhinah,* here Her radical immanence—Her active presence in the lower world—is underscored. The maternal, queenly imagery gives way to the more accessible "princess" *(bat melekh).* The passage has a distinctly Gnostic flavor, recalling myths of the fallen Sophia, Wisdom's Daughter. The allusion to *Shekhinah*'s origin in the sefirotic world, the "Realm of Light," specifically calls to mind descriptions of the Gnostic pleroma. The image of *Shekhinah* as source of light is highly suggestive, as well. As Scholem has pointed out, Syrian Gnostics frequently referred to the fallen Sophia as a "fragment of light." In the *Bahir* passage *Shekhinah* is depicted as a stranger in a strange land, exiled to this world so as to bring Redemption: "through Her deeds she illumines the world." Here, too, Scholem sees Gnostic influence. He draws parallels to the "Hymn of the Daughter" in the *Gospel of Thomas,* where it is the Daughter's aim to return Creation to its Source and to bring about Redemption through re-uniting with her Mate.

Ibn Gabbai does not comment directly on these *Bahir* parables here. However, evidence of this mature understanding of the last parable is found in AQ 3:32. Upon quoting the *Bahir,* he explained:

> "She is taken from the Realm of Light": That is, from God's Wisdom, for Wisdom comes from Wisdom [*Malkhut* derives from *Ḥokhmah*]. And this is a distant place from which She issues forth. For "the Lord is seen from afar [*me-RaḤoQ;* i.e., from *Ḥokhmah*]." [Jer. 31:13] She is blessed from this Place and this is the hidden meaning of "Blessed be the Glory of the Lord from His Place." (Ezek. 3:12) . . . The intended meaning [of the Glory] is the final *He'* of the Divine Name . . . *Shekhinah;* and the Abode [*BaYiT*] of *Shekhinah* is the letter *BeYT* [B] of *Bere'shit* [i.e., *Ḥokhmah;* ff. Z 1:15a, et al.]

This passage is also discussed in AQ 2:43. See there.

348. At this point ibn Gabbai returns to his interpretation of the *Qedushah* proper. He correlates the prayer with the two religious moments alluded to in the *Bahir:* the experience of God's utter transcendence and hiddenness; and the experience of divine immanence, of communion with God.

349. **"So too . . . home on high."** Through recitation of the *Qedushah* the adept lifts up the lower seven rungs—most pointedly symbolized by *Shekhinah,* the Glory par excellence—unto the upper triad. In a very real sense, this is the moment of mystical homecoming.

"compassion will well up." Heb., *yitmalle' raḥamim;* in Rabbinic Hebrew, an idiom meaning, "He will be compassionate" (see Gen. R 33:2).

Here a more literal translation seems preferable to preserve the sefirotic allusion to *Raḥamim Gemurim,* Total Compassion: *Keter,* the *sefirah* without a trace of *Din.*

"love will be bestowed, etc." Heb., *le-RaḤeM,* indicating the downward flow of love from *Keter.* The reference to the cleaving children is intriguingly ambiguous, connoting the lower rungs on a primary level, and the devotees, on a secondary one.

350. A close paraphrase of *Zohar* 2:138b.

351. **"You."** Heb. *'Attah.* A reference to the union of *Malkhut* and *Tif'eret.* Apparently, ibn Gabbai is reading *'Attah* [אתה] as a compound word. MS Adrianople reads: את י״ה , whereas e.p. reads: א׳ת ה׳. את sometimes indicates the masculine potency (cf. PR: Gate 23 " 'Et") whereas the letter ה commonly signifies *Shekhinah.*

352. This verse is not found in printed versions of *Zohar* 2:138b; apparently, it is ibn Gabbai's insertion. *Raḥoq* is here an apellation for *'Ein Sof.* According to Moses Cordovero (PR:23), *Raḥoq* is used when *Shekhinah* and *Tif'eret* ascend into highest divine reaches. This most profound of all sefirotic unions also implies lessening of Divine Providence, *mi'uṭ ha-hashgaḥah.* I shall address the theological implications of this below.

353. **Discussion.** This is a striking passage theologically. It underscores both the primal integration that occurs each Shabbat during *Qedushah* and the dangers that longed-for divine ascent poses to the devotee. As *Shekhinah* unites with Her Lover, She ascends to the primordial Source, the Root of All Roots, the mystical Nihil. The Jew is thus in danger of losing contact with Her, of being left behind, bereft and without anchor: with "nothing." He must redouble his contemplative efforts and cleave unto Her, "holding onto Her to not let Her grow distant." In other words, through *devequt* he forces Her to remain immanent.

The *Qedushah* thereby serves two potentially conflicting tasks; one "for the sake of divinity," helping to effect the most transcendent union, and a second task "for the sake of humanity," lest divinity vanish into *'Ein Sof.* The urgency of the second task is captured in vivid fashion by the Zohar source, 2:138b:

> "Be not far off" [Ps. 22:20]: for She ascends to be crowned by Her husband and all is in the upper world. Then He [*Tif'eret*] wishes to ascend to *'Ein Sof,* so that all be bound together in the uppermost reaches. And so it is said, "Be not far off": Do not withdraw and leave us. Thus, while offering up praise [here referring to the Sabbath morning prayers] Israel must include themselves [within the Divine Glory] and cleave to [*Shekhinah* and *Tif'eret*] from below. For should this Glory [the two rungs in union] wish to rise aloft and so withdraw from them, behold, Israel below holds fast to it, not letting it grow distant.

354. **"My Gazelle."** *'eyaluti*. On the image of the beloved as a gazelle in Hebrew literature, see R. Scheindlin, "Medieval Hebrew Love Poems" in *Prooftexts* 5:2 (1985): 105–35, passim, and sources therein. Also see Prv. 5: 18–19 and Cant. 2:17.

Discussion. Divine Providence resumes, born of the Holy One's abiding love for Israel and Israel's abiding communion *(devequt)* with the Holy One. Supernal blessing can again stream into the world.

355. Heb., *baqqashat raḥamim*. Lit., to ask for mercy; in the Rabbinic idiom, "to pray." Kabbalistically, *Raḥamim* alludes to *Keter*.

356. **"time of grace."** Heb., *ᶜet raẓon;* referring to the mainfestation of the "Compassionate One," *Keter*, who remains hidden throughout the week. His emergence—after the drama of the Lovers' ascent/withdrawl—is clearly one of the peak moments in the experience of Shabbat. On *ᶜet raẓon*, also see *Sod ha-Shabbat*, p. 61.

"the wide streams, etc." A picturesque description of the downward flow of *shefaᶜ*. Aroused from on high, it streams down from the River *(Binah)* to nourish the saplings (the lower *sefirot*) that are planted in the Garden *(Shekhinah)*. Cf. *Zohar* 1:141b. This image of abundant sefirotic nurturing attests to the fullness of this moment, the flowing quality of the Time of Grace.

357. A reference to the martyr's *Shemaᶜ*, which is recited twice daily to "proclaim divine unity." For details see Seligmann Baer, *Seder ᶜAvodat Yisra'el*. (Roedelheim, 1868): 237 and the sources therein. The *Shemaᶜ* is one of the quintessential prayers of sefirotic unification in Zoharic Kabbalah. For discussion, see I. Tishby, MZ 2:277–80 and 312–18; and cf. SCK: 213 n41.

358. **"Section 14."** The next three sections of *Sod ha-Shabbat* (as well as Section 18) are focused on miẓvot that are not time-specific but rather apply throughout Shabbat.

"To cease from labor. . . ." Ibn Gabbai provides several mystical rationales for this miẓvah. He begins by focusing on the intradivine events of primordial Creation.

"Know that. . . ." As Scholem has noted, the ensuing discussion (through n370) is an uncited adaptation of R. Joseph Alcastiel's tenth *teshuvah* (responsum) to R. Judah Ḥayyaṭ. See G. Scholem, "Li-Ydiᶜat ha-Qabbalah bi-Sfarad ᶜErev ha-Gerush," *Tarbiẓ* 24 (1954): 191–93, esp. n125–26.

"through Faithfulness." *be-'Emunah*. Conventionally, "in faithfulness." Kabbalistically, a reference to *Shekhinah*. On *Shekhinah*'s role as emissary and actualizer of divine power, cf. Z 1:5a:

> [*Shekhinah*] brought forth all of their workings and energy . . . Their workings were revealed only through the "Earth." All these workings, both for the first days and the last, depended on the Sabbath day. Thus, it is written, "And God completed His work through

the seventh Day," [Gen. 2:2] i.e., through Shabbat, the fourth leg of the Throne [*Shekhinah*].

359. **"Right Crown."** *Ḥesed,* the first of the supernal Days of Creation. **"in accord with the other rungs."** In other words, although a specific *sefirah* or Day set the tone, this in no way compromised sefirotic unity. Cf. *Zohar* 2: 149b and especially, Joseph Alcastiel's responsum (cited above). As shall be seen, Meir ibn Gabbai has here considerably streamlined Alcastiel's text. The latter included linguistic and mathematical components missing in ibn Gabbai's schema. Alcastiel wrote:

> The first day originated in the Right Rung [*Ḥesed*] and was composed of all the Crowns [*sefirot*] and letters [through which the world was created, ff. *Sefer Yeẓirah*]. . . . All [the divine] letters and the ten Crowns were permutated and a creation was activated which was specially concentrated in the Right Crown. It engraved its pattern in the tenth Crown [*Malkhut*]. As *Malkhut* actualized its pattern in the corporeal world [through the mediation of the ten spheres (or angelic worlds) below], it became Sunday, a day composed of all ten divine rungs. . . . as specially concentrated in the Right Rung.
>
> [Thereafter], another permutation of letters and Crowns was [effected], now correlated with the Left Arm [*Gevurah*]. This rung too contained all the Crowns [and letters], and engraved its pattern in the Tenth Crown. As She [*Malkhut*] actualized this pattern, it became Monday in the corporeal world [etc.] . . . In this fashion Creation proceeded through the sixth day, [attaining spiritual perfection only on Shabbat, as shall be seen shortly].

In this schema, a given *sefirah* set the tone for each day of the primordial week. Divine unity, however, was in no way compromised; for each rung contained the structure of all ten *sefirot* and worked in consort with the divine totality.

According to Joseph Alcastiel, this seven-fold schema has defined the basic rhythmic structure of "weekly time" ever since Creation. Still, this schema has not rendered absurd the concept of unilinear time, wherein each successive day has a unique character. For the divine elements are permutated daily; and, Alcastiel explained, they include not only the *sefirot* and the twenty-two basic letters of the supernal alphabet but three versions of that alphabet (each with different sefirotic correlates) as well as the full complement of archetypal vowel-points and cantillation notes. Together these comprise a divine language or archetypal Torah, a variegated cosmic code. Because there are "thousands of myriads" of possible permutations of Crowns, letters, vowels and notes, no two Sundays, e.g., are precisely the same. Each one has its unique configuration or *parẓuf.*

It is this complex schema that ibn Gabbai is drawing on and simplifying here.

360. See *Sod ha-Shabbat* p. 13 and n9.

361. **"Work of Creation."** Here, the *sefirot* from *Ḥesed* to *Yesod* which are brought forth by *Binah* (the Lord). See the discussion in SCK: 32.

"For the Lord made six days." The preposition *be-* (in) is understood in Ex. 31:17, but not written. Its omission gave rise to a series of mystical interpretations, beginning with the *Bahir* (57):

> "For the Lord made six days" [Ex. 31:17] . . . As you said, the Holy One made six beautiful vessels [the six *sefirot* above *Malkhut*].

The absence of the preposition *be-* was noted more explicity in such later sources as RamBaN ad Ex. 20:11; the *Responsa* of R. Solomon b. Adret, Vol. 1 #423; and Joseph Giqatilia's *Sha^carei 'Orah* 2:46:

> This is an esoteric reference to the *sefirot* . . . from *Binah* to *Yesod,* as it is said: "For the Lord [*Binah*] made six days." "Six," not "in six."

Also cf. the numerous Zoharic sources employing this symbolism, including 1:36a, 2:89b, 3: 257a; ZḤ "Lekh Lekha" 26c (MN); and TZḤ 147b.

362. *Shekhinah* is here depicted as a receptive female *sefirah,* collecting and transmitting the *shefa*ᶜ that descended from the six active, or male forces. On the one hand, only She can complete the process of supernal creation, yet She lacks the power to independently bring forth a "viable creation." See below for further explanation.

363. An allusion to the angelic worlds created by *Shekhinah.*

364. **"now, however . . . "** Meir ibn Gabbai ff. Joseph Alcastiel, smoothly shifts the focus from the primordial Sabbath to the current one, which is seen as a reflection of *illius temporis.*

"two authorities." Heb., *shettei rashuyyot.* A Rabbinic term connoting Dualism. Cf. TB Ḥag. 15a, Ber. 33b; Gen. R. 1:1; Tanḥ. "Qedoshim" 3, et al.

"Her external agencies." The angelic worlds.

"authority of Her husband." *Tif'eret.* The imagery used here is a good example of how certain sacralized conventions (ff. Gen. 3:16) are given cosmic status in the Kabbalah.

Discussion. On Shabbat, with the weekly Work of Creation completed, *Malkhut* is no longer an emissary, but reigning Queen. She is no longer dependent on the efflux above Her and functions independently, in a certain sense. Were there to be profane activity while She reigns, *shefa*ᶜ would be brought down that originated in *Malkhut.* Hence, two realms would be created, one under the authority of the supernal *sefirot* and another under *Malkhut*'s sway. This disruption of supernal unity—the separation of *Shekhinah* from Her Husband—is considered the archetypal sin in Kabbalah. See n137.

365. **"therefore . . . swelling its influence."** Heb., *kol ha-po*ᶜ*el shum pe*ᶜ*ulah le-hakhin she-yitpasheṭ ve-yif*ᶜ*al* ᶜ*olam ha-ṭiv*ᶜ*i* ᶜ*al derekh ḥol.* Warsaw

ed. misprints: *le-heikhan*. On a profane act increasing the influences of *Sitra' 'Ahra'*, see SCK: 210–11 n35.

"cuts off the shoots." Heb., *meqazzez ba-netiᶜot;* i.e., commits a heretical act by disrupting divine unity. See n137 and the note below.

366. As the liminal *sefirah*, poised between worlds, *Malkhut* has a volatile nature. While *Tif'eret* is an unchanging "Tree of Life,"

> *Malkhut* is the Tree of Knowledge of Good and Evil . . . that ever changes, oscillating from one coloration to another, from evil to good. (*Zohar* 1:221b)

Her status depends on the identity of Her contiguous partner: when united with the sefirotic world above, the Good within Her predominates; when severed from it, Evil is allowed to surface. According to a line of thought first expressed in the *Bahir* and developed in Gerona, the Tree of Knowledge actually contains a latent aspect of Death, which emerges when the Tree is wholly weighted to the side of Evil. To express this in other words: when She is separated from the Tree of Life She becomes susceptible to certain life-denying forces, most purely expressed in *Sitra' 'Ahra'*.

Therefore, one should understand the human consequences of profaning Shabbat/*Malkhut* (viz., the offender's susceptibility to death) not as a willed act of divine punishment, but rather as the necessary outcome of one's behavior. Having separated *Malkhut* from *Tif'eret*—having "cut the shoots"—one has awakened Death within Her and cut off one's own source of Life.

Concerning this radical *Shekhinah* imagery, see *Bahir* 161 and "Sod ᶜEz ha-Daᶜat" attributed to R. Ezra, and analyzed in G. Scholem's article "Sitra' 'Ahra' (*Pirqei Yesod:* 194ff.). Also see Z 1:35b, Joseph Alcastiel's direct (and hence, ibn Gabbai's ultimate) inspiration here.

367. **"appease Her."** Heb., *le-fayyes daᶜatah;* also, to "please Her." *Malkhut*, left alone, would constitute a dark, lonely, dead world. To guard against this situation, She is united with *Yesod*.

"sixth . . . seventh." Reflecting the confusion regarding the sefirotic order found in the *Bahir*. E.g., *Tif'eret*, the sixth rung, and *Yesod*, the seventh, are both called *Shamayim* [heavens]; moreover, both function as a divine Throne. This blurring of identity is stated most pointedly in sec. 154: "Is the seventh perhaps none other than the sixth?" For details, see *Re'shit ha-Qabbalah ve-Sefer ha-Bahir:* Lecture 21.

In Gerona and Zoharic Kabbalah, *Yesod* became crystallized as the ninth *sefirah*, or as the sixth of the active *sefirot* (starting from *Hesed*, the "Right Arm"). Yet, the *Bahir* tradition associating *Yesod* with seventhness/Shabbat was also preserved, often by identifying *Yesod* as the seventh of the active *sefirot* starting from *Binah*. For explanation see SCK: 70; and Joseph Giqatilia's *Shaᶜarei 'Orah* 1:106.

368. **"spiritual world."** Lit., formal world (*ᶜolam ha-zuriyyi*).

"physical world." Lit., corporeal world (*ᶜolam ha-gufiyyi*). Common philosophical nomenclature, here ff. Joseph Alcastiel.

Through the union of the two sevenths or cosmic Sabbaths, the natural world—*ᶜolam ha-tivᶜi*—is spiritualized, imbued with divine blessing. By contrast, the profane modality grows impoverished, unable to sustain its influence on the lower world. Hence, its "rungs shrink and shut down," grow silent. The Sabbath-cosmos reigns.

369. **"unbounded inheritance."** *naḥalah beli meẓarim.* Ff. TB Shab. 118a: "He who delights in the Sabbath is given an unbounded inheritance." Kabbalistically, this term connotes the unimpeded flow of *shefaᶜ*, emblem of the Sabbath-cosmos.

"two cherubim." *Neẓaḥ* and *Hod, sefirot* that are often associated with the generation of power. On their identity as Cherubs, cf. *Zohar,* 3:236a; 302a; and ZH 26d and 31d (both MN).

"days of rest." Kabbalistically, *Yesod* and *Malkhut,* the two Sabbaths.

370. The "Wings" are the *qelippot,* the profane forces that obscure and hem in the seven lower *sefirot* and prevent full experience of the divine. The phrase "constricting boundaries" (Heb., *sod ha-meẓarim*) contrasts with *naḥalah beli meẓarim,* the Unbounded Inheritance, mentioned above. Herein ends ibn Gabbai's paraphrase of Joseph Alcastiel (see n358).

371. In the ensuing passage Meir ibn Gabbai provides a Zoharic rationale to account for a halakhic paradox: the fact that the Torah mandated the kindling of fire in the Temple, while proscribing it elsewhere.

"Sanctuary . . . provinces." A word-pair used by the Rabbis to distinguish between ritual behavior appropriate in the Temple and all outlying areas. Cf. TB Ket. 24b and Suk. 43a.

372. Ibn Gabbai's explanation is based on the homology between the Temple and *Malkhut,* and the provinces or settlements and *Siṭra' 'Aḥra'.*

On the proscription of fire in the settlements, cf. *Zohar* 2:89b:

> It is written "You shall kindle no fire in your settlements on the Sabbath day." [Ex. 35.3] Why so? Lest *Din* be seen on this day. Were you to object: What of the fire on the altar that ascends [even on Sabbath]? The verse specifies: "in your settlements" and not "on high [the altar]."

Discussion: Concerning the sacrificial fire in the Temple. Ibn Gabbai here implies what the *Zohar* states more clearly: The sacrifical fire in the Temple is permissable because it symbolizes that holy supernal fire—burning within *Malkhut* each Shabbat—that destroys *Din.* However, any fire kindled outside the Temple, in the provinces calls forth the strange fire of the external forces and profanes the Sabbath-cosmos. Cf. *Zohar* 2:203b and 89b, which reads:

> The [sacrificial] fire that ascends on high rises to subjugate *Din.* As we have learned [in TB *Yoma'* 21b] there is a fire that consumes fire; and the fire of the altar consumes the other fire [*Din*].

Also see Z 2:208a:

> On Sabbath all fires except one are hidden for the duration of the Sabbath. Only the holy supernal fire that is revealed and included in the holiness of Shabbat may burn. When this fire is manifest all other fires remain hidden. This is the fire of the Binding of Isaac [*Malkhut* in union with *Gevurah*] which burns on the alter on Sabbath . . . This is the fire that consumes fire [here, *Malkhut* seemingly consumes or sweetness *Gevurah*'s harshness].

In other words, there is but one proper fire in the celestial cosmos on Sabbath, and that is the fire of the supernal altar, *Malkhut*. Furthermore, only the sacrificial fire in the Temple, *Malkhut*'s earthly reflection, can properly symbolize this divine burning.

A final germane source is Z 3:254b (RM) which claims that a profane fire is not permissable on the Sabbath because it engenders *kil'ayim ṭov ve-ra*ᶜ, an improper fusion of good and evil. However,

> A sacrificial fire may be kindled on the Sabbath because it is a holy fire. Its holiness fuses with the holiness of the Sabbath, but it is forbidden to mix a profane fire with the Holy. Thus Israel is told: "You shall kindle no fire in your settlement on the Sabbath day." [Ex. 35:3] For this entails an improper fusion of good and evil.

For further discussion, see the analysis in SCK: 210–11 n35.

373. "heretics." Heb., *meqaẓẓeẓim ba-neṭiᶜot.*

374. Kabbalistically, a reference to the ultimate Sabbath, at the end of the Cosmic *Shemiṭṭah*. Cf. n335 and see G. Scholem, *Kabbalah:* 120: "In the seventh millenium . . . the Sabbath day of the cycle, the sefirotic forces cease to function and the world returns to chaos."

Our TB, RH 31a, begins:

> R. Qaṭṭina said: The world is to last 6,000 years and 1,000 it will be desolate, as it says: "And the Lord alone shall be exalted on that day." [Isa. 2:11]

"a cosmos that is entirely, etc." A textual variant also found in Ṭodros Abulafia's *'Oẓar ha-Kavod* and other Sefardic sources. The printed edition of the TB reads "days."

375. Heb., *ᶜolam ha-neshamot.* Generally, a reference to the World-to-Come. In the Kabbalah, the resting place for the souls of the righteous located in the celestial Garden of Eden. Cf. *Zohar* 2:246a, 253a, 259a, and MZ 1:419.

376. "Sabbath eve" connotes this world, whereas the Sabbath signifies the World-to-Come. See *Sod ha-Shabbat* p. 17.

Discussion. According to the TY, resting (or refraining from profane labor) serves three critical functions: 1) In its theurgic valence, it enables the aspect of Good within *Shekhinah* to flourish, even as the forces of Evil are rendered dysfunctional. As a result, the natural world is richly blessed, spiritualized. This rationale is focused on the current Shabbat, even as it recalls the primordial drama. 2) It is a means of purification, subtly transforming the devotee and enabling him to attain the World of Souls upon his death. This rationale is focused on the adept's future fate. 3) It symbolizes—and partakes of—the final Sabbath, the seventh millenium. Here the universe/aeon's ultimate fate is acknowledged. On this last point, see SCK: 97–100.

377. The Gemara' continues:

> For it is written: "Then shall you take delight in the Lord and I will set you astride the heights of the earth; I will feed you with the heritage [*naḥalah*] of Jacob your father, etc." [Isa. 58:14].

378. **"Saturn."** In medieval Jewish thought, popularly viewed as the star of evil that brings misfortune to Israel. In the Zoharic tradition, Saturn (Heb., *Shabbeta'i*) is personified and feminized, equated with Lilith. Standing over against *Malkhut*, the divine Sabbath, Saturn constitutes the quintessential anti-Sabbath force. Thus, the word-play in TZ 21 (56b): "*SHaBbeTa'I* contains the words *'I SHaBbaT*, meaning 'no Sabbath'."

"on Saturday Saturn holds sway." The correlation of the seventh day with Saturn (the seventh planet) was initially recorded in the first century B.C.E. by Tibullus (Works I, 3:18) and soon became a commonplace in the Greco-Roman world. However, it is found in Rabbinic literature only in *Sefer Yeẓirah* 5:5. According to one version of this text. "The letter *beit* . . . is correlated with Saturn in the cosmos and with the Sabbath in the temporal realm." The links between Saturn and Saturday were elaborated in medieval Muslim and Christian astrology (see R. Klibansky, F. Saxl, and E. Panofsky, *Saturn and Melancholy* [London, 1964]) and became more or less fixed in Jewish sources by the ninth century, with the rise of astrologically influenced works.

In the Geonic *Baraita' de-R. Samuel* (Ch. 9), melancholy Saturn is held to be "in charge of famine, tragedy, poverty, destruction and illness, bodily injury, death, and sin." Similar descriptions are also found in the anonymous *Baraita' de-Mazzalot* and in Shabbetai Donnolo's tenth century commentary to *Sefer Yeẓirah*, the *Ḥakhmoni* (Castelli ed., 71–72):

> Saturn is extremely cold and dry; it is in charge of death and torture . . . and evil. It holds sway on the Sabbath day.

From this medieval commonplace he draws a distinctively Jewish conclusion: "Thus, no work ought to be done on it." Other pre-Zoharic descriptions of Saturn's baneful influence may be found in *Baraita' de-Mazzalot* (A. Wertheimer, *Battei Midrashot:* 35); in Abraham ibn Ezra's astrological works, *Sefer Re'shit Ḥokhmah* (Ch. 4) and *Sefer Ṭeʿamim* (also Ch. 4); and *Sefer Razi'el*. These astrological conceptions were largely absorbed into the Zoharic literature (esp. the TZ/RM) and mythologized, Saturn now becoming the demonic Lilith. See, e.g., 3:34a (RM), 279a (RM), 282a; TZ Intro. (21a), 48 (85a–b) and 70 (124b). Important views concerning Shabbetai and Shabbat are found in post-Zoharic literature, including Baḥyya ben Asher to Dt. 18:11;

R. Joseph ben Shalom Ashkenazi's *Perush le-Sefer Yezirah* (attributed to the RaBaD); *Sod 'Ilan ha-'Azilut*, p. 85 (ed. G. Scholem); the closely related *Sefer Sod ha-Shem* (fol. 171c); and *Sefer ha-Peli'ah*. Also see *Abud.*: 170.

For a more positive view of Shabbetai and its effect on Shabbat, see the early thirteenth century mystic Elhanan ben Yaqar of London's *Perush le-Sefer Yezirah*, discussed in R. Kiener, "The Status of Astrology in the Early Kabbalah," *Mehqerei Yerushalayim be-Mahshevet Yisra'el* 6:3–4 (1987): 28, English section.

379. A reflection of Meir ibn Gabbai's ambivalent attitude towards astrology. Saturn's power over sublunary beings in general is acknowledged, although its influence upon observant Jews is categorically denied (thereby preserving the doctrine of Providence).

There are many precedents for this view. See TB Suk. 29a; R. Samuel's remarks in Shab. 156b; and Ibid. 156a, where it is stated: "There is no constellation for Israel." Also see ibn Ezra to Ex. 23:38; Dt. 4:19; and Lev. 23-24 where he implied that *mizvat Shabbat* and the sacrifices were given to Israel expressly to negate the destructive influence of Shabbetai. (On this, also see I. Heinemann, *Ta'amei ha-Mizvot* [Jerusalem, 1959], 1:68–69).

Another significant source is RaBaD of Posquieres. In a passage reminiscent of Abraham ibn Ezra, he maintained that the Creator had given all events unto the power of the stars, but that one could escape one's astrological fate by choosing good over evil (i.e., by choosing the Torah). I might note that a similar tone of ambivalence regarding astrology may be found in contemporary Christian authors. For details see R. Klibansky, F. Saxl, and E. Panofsky, *Saturn and Melancholy*: 178ff.

Ibn Gabbai's understanding of astrology bears the direct imprint of the Zoharic tradition. The *Zohar*, in general, and the TZ/RM, in particular, shared the by-now familiar ambivalence towards astrology. The TZ/RM took astrology for granted, using its imagery and terminology in several places (most notably RM 3:281b). But as A. Altmann has shown (EJ 3:788ff.), it deprived astrology of most of its influence. Here, too, it is observance of Torah which renders Israel immune to planetary influence. Consider, e.g., Z 3:216b(RM):

> Before the Torah was given all creatures were subject to the power of the constellations. Once Israel was given the Torah they were exempt from the power of stars and constellations. . . . Whoever studies Torah is exempt from this influence.

Also see ZH "Yitro" 37a, the source ibn Gabbai had in mind here:

> This mystery holds sway over Shabbetai's nation [i.e., certain Gentiles] but not over the Holy People. For the Holy People have no portion or inheritance in stars or constellations, only in the Holy One, blessed be He.

For further discussion of this motif, see my thesis, pp. 532–33.

380. All children of Saturn observe a sort of anti-Shabbat, a day devoid of joy. Such people both emulate and are influenced by Saturn's dominant

characteristic, melancholia. The TY here echoes several Zoharic passages. Cf. Z 3:272b (RM):

> Those who serve her [Lilith/Shabbetai] wear black garments on Sabbath night. They extinguish lamps and break into lamentation and mourning.

and ZḤ "Yitro" 37a (TZ?):

> Those who are in the clutches of Shabbetai . . . must fast and exhibit sorrow and woe; wearing black garments . . . eating neither meat nor wine nor oil. They delight not in the delicacies of the world, but sit in the houses of sorrow, set apart from their fellows.

Most of these attributes presented in the TY and Zoharic corpus—Saturn's melancholia, the notion that her children wear black, that they extinguish lamps and are misanthropic—have their roots in the Greco-Roman and Arabic astrological traditions, where they were frequently associated with Jewish Sabbath observance. Parallels can also be found in medieval Christian sources. On the Jewish debt to and polemical reshaping of these ideas, see my thesis, "The Sabbath in the Classical Kabbalah": 534–35 and 538.

381. **"snakes and scorpions."** This interpretation is found in TB Shab. 22a. Also see TB Ḥag. 3a, Tanḥ. 1:20, 2:13; Gen R 84:16 and RaSHI ad Gen. 37:24.

"exile of Israel." Kabbalistically, an allusion to the demonic Shabbetai, the "snake-filled pit" into which Joseph (Israel/*Shekhinah*) was cast. Each Sabbath this Exile must be left behind through Sabbath-observance and joy. The TY is here quoting from TZ 48 (85a–b). The extended passage reads:

> Shabbetai is the Splenetic One [Lilith], Wrath, an Evil Woman, a bitter darkness [melancholy]. Of Shabbetai it is said: "'The pit was empty, there was no water in it." [Gen. 37:24] Rather, it contains snakes and scorpions." That is, hunger and thirst, lamentation and wailing, darkness and woe [her demonic forces]. This pit is the Exile of Israel.

Also cf. ZḤ "Yitro" 33d (TZ?):

> For Lilith is a bitter darkness [melancholy], a drought without water, which is " 'the pit [that] was empty, with no water in it' but rather, containing snakes and scorpions," referring to her mixed multitudes [demonic forces]. But Joseph was within, referring to Israel who is exiled within her, within this pit.

See Z 3:279a (RM) and TZ Intro (6a) for further details. For further analysis of the imagery and cross-cultural parallels, see my dissertation, p. 536.

382. **"it behooves Israel to make certain changes, etc."** Here ibn Gabbai provides a Kabbalistic rational for the Talmudic tradition that "one's Sabbath garments should not be like one's weekday garb" (TB Shab. 113a); that one should partake of special feasts and delight in the Sabbath (Ibid. 118a–119b; Beiẓ. 16a); and that the home and festive table be properly ordered (TB Shab. 119). His point: *ʿOneg Shabbat* has apotropaic significance.

By making these changes, the melancholic forces of Shabbetai are warded off and *Shekhinah*/Jew/Cosmos protected. Saturday is turned into Shabbat. This notion is richly attested in the TZ/RM. E.g.:

> Whoever wishes to be protected from Shabbetai must change his name, his place and his deeds [confusing Shabbetai]. (TZ 70 [124b])

> *SHaBbeTa'I* is composed of the letters, *'I SHaBBaT*, meaning No Shabbat. Thus, Israel must change its place, its name and its deeds [on the Sabbath]. . . . One must act differently than on weekdays, changing his dress and his meals, so that he [partake of] the Sabbath delight. (TZ 21 [56b–57a])

> Through delighting in the Sabbath the Maidservant [Lilith] is negated. She is forced to remain in darkness . . . Wearing black garments like a widow. . . . "As the one [Kabbalistically, Shabbat/*Shekhinah*] is flourishing, the other [Shabbetai/Lilith] is laid waste." [TB Meg. 6a] (Z 3: 272b [RM])

Another significant source is ZḤ "Yitro" 33d–34a [TZ?], wherein Sabbath-delight is said to redeem Israel (and by implication, *Shekhinah*) from the travails of Exile:

> On the Sabbath one must exhibit joy, in contrast to the maid-servant Lilith. Wherever Shabbetai dwells in sadness, one must exhibit joy. In a place of darkness, light. In a place of travail, joy. In order to transform all things. For Lilith is melancholia [a bitter darkness] . . . the pit . . . of snakes and scorpions . . . Israel's exile.
>
> But whoever honors the Sabbath escapes from this pit. Whoever, sins, remains ensnared. . . . He who observes the Sabbath ascends unto *Malkhut*, who is the Sabbath. . . . On the Sabbath one must adorn oneself in nice clothing. For he is the child of Shabbat, the child of the Queen. But if not, he is the child of Lilith . . .

Clothing, in short, reveals one's spiritual parentage, indicating just "who" one is.

The two Zoharic sources that ibn Gabbai seems to have consulted most closely in this section are TZ 48 (85a–b) and ZḤ Yitro 37a. The former source provides a supernal paradigm for donning fresh clothes each Shabbat:

> Because of Shabbetai, the Exile of Israel. . . . Israel must make a complete change, as we have previously stated [TZ 21, (56b)]. . . . Regarding this Splenetic One, it is written: "Take that which imprisons you [*ne'alekha*] off of your feet" [Ex. 3: 5] the soiled shoe, the fetid drop, "for the ground on which you stand is holy ground," namely, Shabbat. Concerning Lilith, *Shekhinah* says: "I had taken off my robe—was I to don it again? I had bathed my feet—was I to soil them again?" [Cant. 5:3] For this reason [to symbolize *Shekhinah*'s liberation and to ward off Shabbetai], one must make changes in one's clothing, in lighting, and in the food one eats.

The more spare ZḤ passage, which the TY follows more closely here, reads:

> This [planetary] mystery holds sway over Shabbetai's nation, but not over the Holy People. On this day Israel must exhibit joy, partaking of food and drink, wearing gaily-colored garments, and preparing the home and festive table. But such is not the case for those who are in the clutches of Shabbetai, who must fast, etc.

The Kabbalistic rationale for the custom of changing garb for Shabbat may reflect the TZ/RM's acquaintance with certain astrological views current in Spain and Western Europe. I have found several thirteenth century Christian sources that ascribe to Saturn's children loathsome dressing habits. Consider, e.g., Michael Scot, the astrologer and philosopher who flourished in Toledo and Cordova in the early thirteenth century and interacted extensively with the Jewish intelligentsia. He wrote: "Children born under Saturn are the poorest and most despicable of men . . . negligent in dress and misanthropic." Also suggestive is Bartholomew Anglicus' description in *De Proprietatibus Rerum,* Ch. 8: "Subjects of Saturn . . . are not loathe to wear foul and stinking clothing." (cited in R. Klibansky et al., *Saturn and Melacholia:* 191 and 187.)

For further discussion of the significance of Shabbat-dress, see SCK: 231–32 and 237–42.

383. Through *ᶜOneg Shabbat, Shekhinah*—and by extension, the Jew—is purified from Her entanglement in the demonic. "I am fleeing" refers to the actions of Hagar, a Kabbalistic appellation for Lilith, whereas Sarai connotes *Shekhinah.* On Lilith as *Shekhinah's* maidservant, see Z 3:277b (RM).

384. Here Meir ibn Gabbai turns from the apotropaic significance of *ᶜOneg Shabbat* to its more purely positive functions: its ability to regale the Sabbath-Soul and to invest *Shekhinah* and the lower worlds with divine blessing. The ensuing section is a paraphrase of Z 2:204b, a source analyzed in SCK: 135–36. Discussion will be restricted to new material here.

385. The "End Point" connotes *Malkhut* whereas "Supernal Thought" refers to the sefirotic emanation in general.

386. Here ibn Gabbai returns to the Talmudic source with which he opened this section. See n377.

"Wide Streams," "Jacob's heritage," "unbounded heritage." These terms are best read generally, to connote the downward flow of blessing from the sefirotic world unto the Sabbath-observers.

387. **"measure for measure."** Heb., *middah ke-neged middah;* a reflection of the conditional nature of the promise in Isa. 58:13–14. The TY here recalls OK to Shab. 118. See there for details.

The correlation between this downward flow of blessing and *ᶜoNeG Shabbat* is perhaps best stated in the word-play found in Z 3:272a (RM) and other sources:

> The inner meaning of Sabbath-delight, ᶜ*oNeG,* is "And the River, *N*ahar [the *shefa*ᶜ], went forth from ᶜeden [*Binah*] to water the Garden, *G*an [*Shekhinah* and the worlds below]." [Gen. 2:10] . . . As it is said: "He who delights in the Sabbath is given an Unbounded Heritage." [TB Shab. 118a]

388. This section is analyzed in SCK: 203–05. Again, only new comments will be added here. Throughout this discussion, ibn Gabbai's major source of influence is Z 3:105a. Also see the parallel references in 1:32a, 2:47b, 3:21a, 94b and 105a; and TZ 48 (85b).

389. **"separates friends."** *mafrid 'alluf.* This proof-text is Meir ibn Gabbai's own addition. The point is that profane speech fractures sefirotic unity, driving a wedge between *Shekhinah* and the Holy One. The phrase *mafrid 'alluf* can also be rendered "caused the Chieftain [of the world] to withdraw," thereby alluding to the second consequence of profane speech: the withdrawal of *Keter*—"the supernal Holy One," the "Cosmic Chieftain"—from the lower *sefirot.* This ambiguity stems from the fact that *mafrid 'alluf* has two distinct meanings in the midrashic tradition. Cf., e.g., Gen. R 20:2:

> "A deceitful man sows strife and a whisperer separates familiar friends [*mafrid 'alluf*]." [Prv. 16:28] "A deceitful man" refers to the Serpent, who spoke perversely of the Creator. "And a whisperer": he is so called because he whispered words against the Creator, namely, "You shall not die." [Gen. 3:4] "And separates familiar friends": *mafrid 'allufo shel* ᶜ*olam.*

This last line is generally rendered, "he caused divinity to depart," ff. the midrash in Gen. R 19:7. See there.

> The Zohar source, 3:105a, supports both readings of *mafrid 'alluf:* The Holy One and the Community of Israel ask: "Who is this one who seeks to break up our union and sends the profane here?" The Ancient Holy One [*Keter*] does not manifest himself here or dwell amidst the profane.

However, the first option reads more smoothly in the TY text, and seems preferable here.

390. **"It defiles the sanctuary of the Lord,"** Refers to the sullying of *Shekhinah.* Cf. Z 3:47a for a parallel source.

"Now if this occurs . . . and lower worlds." This *a fortiori* claim seems to be ibn Gabbai's own.

391. **"rouses the holy entities."** Herein ends ibn Gabbai's paraphrase of Z 3:105a.

"daughters of Zion, etc." The verse continues: "and gaze upon King Solomon, even upon the crown with which his mother adorned him on his wedding day." Ibn Gabbai's use of the verse goes unexplained, and since no precise Zoharic parallels exist here, any decoding must remain tentative. The most plausible reading is that the "daughters of Zion" refers to the holy words uttered by Israel. They rise to adorn Solomon [*Tif'eret*] from below, even as the Mother [*Binah*], "the deepest of all streams" (Z 3:98a) adorns him above. All this takes place on "his wedding day," the Sabbath, the day when *Tif'eret* and *Malkhut* are joined.

For a slightly different reading, cf. the *Zohar*'s use of this Canticles verse in 2:22a, 3:61a–b and 98a. There the daughters of Zion connotes the *shefa*ᶜ brought down by *Binah*. 2:22a reads:

> It is the Jubilee's desire to crown the Witness [*Tif'eret*] and shower him with blessing, to cause the sweet springs to flow over him, as it is written, "Go forth, daughters of Zion, and gaze upon King Solomon, upon the crown with which his mother adorned him on his wedding day."

392. Although the three previous sections of *Sod ha-Shabbat* treat *miẓvot Shabbat* that are always timely, here ibn Gabbai focuses on a rite that can be applied only rarely.

"a dream-fast." A fast observed after experiencing an ominous dream for the purposes of neutralizing it. For general discussion of this ritual in Rabbinic and Medieval Judaism, see J. Trachtenberg, *Jewish Magic and Superstition*: 245 ff.

"And even on the Sabbath." R. Joseph claimed that the miẓvah of the dream-fast takes precedence over the miẓvah of partaking in the three festive meals (TB Shab. 118a). Despite R. Joseph's injunction, there were some Medieval authorities who questioned the advisability of keeping a dream-fast on the Sabbath and prescribed its postponement. See J. Trachtenberg, Ibid. and Meir Baqal (ed.), *Sefer Pitron ha-Ḥalomot ha-Shalem* (Jerusalem, n.d.): 122–23 for these minority opinions. As shall be seen, the TY offers a distinctively Kabbalistic rationale for keeping dream-fasts on the Sabbath.

393. **"a fast on the Sabbath."** Ibn Gabbai clearly understands this to connote a dream-fast, though classical commentators were divided as to whether the text refers to a dream-fast or to special cases where fasting is permitted for the sake of *teshuvah* (Repentance). (The first interpretation was the more common one.) For details, see Tos.; *Ḥiddushei ha-RaSHBa'*; and A. Steinsaltz ad loc.; also BY to Ṭur OḤ 288:4.

There is some evidence, however, that the second interpretation was closer to the original meaning. Y. Gilat has shown that there was a long-standing minority tradition, attested in Greco-Roman sources, and found in a few Amoraic and medieval texts, permitting fasting on Shabbat. He writes: "One school of thought considered the Sabbath totally dedicated to God, and thus felt it should be devoted entirely to prayer, study and the cleansing of the soul. This approach was accompanied by asceticism, fasting and general denial of pleasure." Or more precisely, this ascetic devotion was deemed a form of *ᶜOneg Shabbat*. The tradition of Sabbath-fasts persisted among certain *ḥasidim* even unto the twelfth and thirteenth centuries, "either as a manifestation of piety or as a means of repentance and atonement for sins." This practice was also common in sixteenth century Safed. See Ḥ. Viṭal, *Sefer Ḥezionot* (ed. A.Z. Aeshcoli, Jerusalem, 1954): 42. For further discussion, see Y. Gilat's article "Taᶜanit Shabbat," *Tarbiẓ* 51 (1982/83): 1–15. Also see R. Goldenberg "The Jewish Sabbath in the Roman World" in W. Haase and N. Temporini, eds. *Aufstieq und Niedergang der Rominschen Welt* II.19.1 (Berlin, 1979): 440 n109; and S. Baron, *A Religious and Social History of the Jews* (NY, 1952–) 5:245 and 6:330 n24.

"seventy years standing." An obscure phrase, understood by RaSHI et al., to mean a decree binding from one's youth; a long-standing edict.

A textual note. The TY's version of this Gemara' differs somewhat from the printed edition, but corresponds to the *girsa'* preserved in such works as *'Aggadot ha-Talmud* and *Menorat ha-Ma'or*. For details see *Diqduqei Sofrim* 1:166 and *Divrei Sofrim* ad loc.

394. Heb., *ve-saveᶜa yalin bal yippaqed raᶜ* conventionally read, "He shall be satisfied and shall not be visited with evil." Here, the TY is following the interpretation of *Zohar* 3:105b:

> One is never warned in a dream without a reason. Rather, he is warned so that he may ask for compassion. Woe to the person who is not warned in a dream, for he is called "evil," as it is written: "One who rests satisfied and is not visited [in a dream] is evil." [Prv. 19:23]

Both the *Zohar* and the TY reflect the notion that the ominous dream itself—and not only the ensuing fast—contains a positive aspect. The nocturnal warning is a sign of God's caring and an impetus to *teshuvah*.

395. **Discussion.** The TY suggests that it is for metaphysical reasons that a dream-fast may not be postponed. This argument is based on the Zoharic assumption that a) each of the seven temporal days is a reflection of its correponding supernal Day or angelic rung, and b) that each Day has (or should have) authority over its temporal symbol alone. See Z 2: 204a–b, 3:85a, 92a and 105b for details. The problems caused by postponing a dream-fast are two-fold: First, the person loses his right to angelic counsel, for "a Day can only request compassion [before the sefirotic court] on behalf of that which occured on it." Moreover, the negligent person dis-orders Time itself. For a Day does not complete its jurisdiction over Time until all is set in proper order. To postpone fasting (even for the sake of *ᶜOneg Shabbat*) causes the Day to remain in power beyond its appointed tenure. The supernal Day is thereby linked with an improper temporal symbol; Time becomes "confused."

The two most influential sources for the TY here are 3:92a–b and 105b. The former reads:

> We have learned that "fasting is as potent against an [ominous] dream as fire against straw." [TB Shab. 11a] But the dream-fast must occur on the same day as the dream and not on a day

> thereafter. Why? Because every day below is controlled by a corresponding Day above. . . . This Day does not pass until the [dream's] decree has been annulled . . . through fasting.

The *Zohar* then offers another—seemingly contradictory—explanation; however this rationale also underscores the confusion of Time caused by postponing the fast:

> Should one postpone the dream-fast until another day, it would be subject to the control of another Day. . . . Thus, over each day below is appointed a Day above. One should take care not to impair that Day and blemish it [by not fasting thereon.]

3: 105b reads:

> Each day has its power. If one fasts on account of a dream, his sentence is annulled before the day ends . . . Thus, one must fast on that day and not thereafter. For one Day holds power only over what happens on it . . . Therefore, one must not postpone his fast from one day to another. As we have learned, *davar yom be-yomo* [Ex. 5:13, 19; an idiom generally rendered, "each day, in a fixed way," but here read quite literally:], "that day's occurence belongs to its Day" and never to another.

These Kabbalistic rationales may be compared with the non-sefirotic explanations for Sabbath dream-fasts recounted in M. Baqal (ed.), *Sefer Pitron ha-Ḥalomot:* 121.

1) One who postpones his fast runs the risk of having the dream come true, before it could be neutralized.
2) As a matter of conduct, one should always attempt to thwart an evil decree without delay.

396. Kabbalistically, "a decree of seventy years" refers to a negative "edict" agreed upon by the seven lower *sefirot,* which form the celestial Sanhedrin or high court. This edict can only be overruled by its "President," the Holy Ancient One *(Keter),* who enters the court on Sabbaths alone. See n398 below (Z 3:105a–b) for details. For an alternate explanation, see 3:89a.

397. On Sabbath as a day of special Providence, see the discussion in MZ 2: 294f.

"for on Sabbath rest and joy." Here ibn Gabbai begin his paraphrase of Z 3:105b. On Shabbat as a day of rest in Gehinnom, see Z 3:94a–b; 288b (IZ); et al. For the Rabbinic basis for this teaching, see TB Sanh. 65b.

398. TY's source, Z 3:105a–b, reads:

> [The Sabbath] is a time of joy above and below . . . the Joy of Complete Faith. . . . On this day even the sinners in Gehinnom rest. Now when the [celestial beings] see this person without joy or rest, so unlike all those above and below, they all ask: "Why is this one grieving?"
>
> On this day the Holy Ancient One is revealed. The prayer of the grieving man ascends unto Him and all harsh decrees against

> him are annulled. Even if the King's Court had agreed upon the judgment, it is rendered null and void. Because when the Holy Ancient One is revealed, complete freedom and joy are present . . .
>
> Thus we learn: "the decree of 'seventy years' is annulled." [Ber. 31b] What is meant by "seventy years"? Even though all seventy regal crowns agreed with this sentence . . . it is annulled. For the Ancient Holy One shelters this person.

Lest one engage in a Sabbath-fast for another reason, the *Zohar* cautions:

> This applies only if one is alerted in a dream on the night of Shabbat.

399. Cf. *Zohar* 1:75b.

400. **"everyone."** Heb., *kol ha-ᶜolam.*

"sad-faced." Heb., *u-fanav zoᶜafim.* Here, a rare meaning of the root *ZᶜF* is intended, connoting pain or sadness. Cf. Gen. 40:6 and Dan. 1:10 for parallel usages.

401. **Discussion.** The anomolous act of Sabbath dream-fasting boldly grabs the King's attention. For it runs counter to both the joyous nature of the day (represented as the rejoicing son) and the miẓvah of Sabbath-Delight (here depicted as the wedding feast). The fast is an appeal, made over the heads of the supernal Sanhedrin, unto its President, the Holy Ancient One. The dream-fast attests to the penitent's remorse, even as it rouses the Ancient One's compassion. Moved, He frees the suffering subject from the iron-bound decree, depicted in the parable as chains. Cf. *Zohar* 3:105a–b, the TY's source here. It appends the following explanation *(nimshal)* to the parable:

> So it is with one who fasts on the Sabbath. The rest of the world rejoices while this one is sorrowful and bound in chains. When the Ancient Holy One appears and sees this man is fettered, even though all "Seventy Years" . . . have concurred in his sentence, it is annulled.

Also see Z 2:207a–b.

402. Concerning the divided Sabbath-spirit and the benefit it derives from *ᶜOneg Shabbat,* see SCK: 135–36 and the sources therein.

Discussion. In this passage, ibn Gabbai gives a distinctively Kabbalistic rationale for the Rabbinic dictum, "Yet all the same he should be punished, etc." Because *ᶜOneg Shabbat* has cosmic repercussions, failure to partake of it cannot be dismissed in the fashion of certain exoteric authorities. Cf., e.g., Ṭur (OḤ 288:4) which held: "This fast is as a delight unto him," i.e, his form of *ᶜOneg Shabbat.* (On this tradition, see n393 above.) For the Kabbalist, by contrast, fasting causes "a diminution on high." This derogation can only be repaired by another ritual act, viz., a fast of atonement to be observed immediately thereafter. Thus, ibn Gabbai reflects the traditional ambivalence towards the practice of Sabbath dream-fasts: It is an imperfect solution, itself in need of resolution.

The *Zohar* records a lively internal debate that reflects conflicting medieval opinions of the practice. It strongly questions the value of these fasts before finally legitimating the practice. 3:105a reads:

> R. Yose said: does one who fasts on the Sabbath denigrate it or not? Should you say he does not, realize that he neglects the Meal of Faith. His punishment must be great since he has done away with Sabbath-delight. [R. Isaac] replied: On the contrary, I have heard that this person is regarded above all others by those on high . . .

Also cf. *Zohar* 2:207a–b, upon which Meir ibn Gabbai selectively draws:

> Whoever keeps a fast on Sabbath, arouses two Accusers who indict him before the Holy King. One is the celestial holy spirit that is deprived of the Sabbath-delight which it deserves. The other, Sanagariah by name, presides over those who keep a fast. These two rise up before the King and accuse him. The spirit [sojourning with the Jew] is deprived of its earthly delight. When it is incomplete below, its supernal portion cannot be completed either. Since the spirit is not perfected above or below, this person is deserving of curses.

In contrast to the TY's view, the *"decree of seventy years"* is not removed by the Sabbath dream-fast alone. Here, annullment is a two-step process, requiring the completion of a second fast, to atone for the negative effects of the first:

> However, if he makes good on another occasion . . . the punishment decreed by the seventy supernal [Years] is annulled.

403. See, e.g., the opinion brought in RaVYaH's name in *Haggahot 'Ashiri* to TB *Taanit* (chap. 1). Also see Ṭur OḤ 288:4, which states:

> One is permitted to fast on Shabbat because his soul is anguished over the dream he beheld . . . [However,] he must fast on another day to atone for having neglected the principle of Sabbath-Delight. But there is no need to observe this fast immediately, on Sunday, but rather, when he so wishes.

Many exegetes, however, disagreed with this ruling and held that—barring health problems—Sunday was the proper choice. Cf., e.g., RaSHI and RaSHBa' ad TB Ber. 31b.

404. A reference to R. Shimon bar Yoḥai and the Comrades, heroes of the *Zohar.*

405. **"violates the territory."** Heb., *hissig gevul,* ff. Dt. 19:14, where it literally means to move a boundary stone. See p. 22 and n68 above.

Fasting on the Sabbath redraws the cosmic boundaries, taking away from the domain of *Shekhinah* and sullying Her.

406. **"that which he took away."** From the Sabbath-soul and divinity, "by robbery": i.e., by fasting instead of partaking in Sabbath-Delight. The Zoharic source for this last section is 2:207a–b:

> "What is the remedy?" Let him keep another fast to atone for this one." Why? As he did away with Sabbath-delight, let him do away with the pleasure of the week-days. But should he neglect Sabbath-delight while rejoicing on the weekdays, he is like one who thinks more of [profane] matters than of the Holy One. For he has neglected the supernal spirit; he has not regaled the Holy of Holies that rests upon him [each Sabbath]. Yet he entertains that other profane spirit which rests on the world after Sabbath. *It* he regales! Thus, punishment must be exacted in this world and in the next.
>
> For this reason, a second fast is required on Sunday, when the Profane Spirit first comes to rest on the world. This [second] fast provides healing because the profane spirit is not given more weight [than the Sabbath]. Your mnemonic is: "He shall restore that which he took away by robbery." [Lev. 5:23]

407. At first blush, this last sentence seems most puzzling; it seems to undermine the whole kabbalistic rationale for keeping a second fast and negates the claim that an ominous dream has a positive aspect. However, this bewilderment dissolves when one realizes that there is a lacuna in the TY text here. Comparison with the TY's source, *Zohar* 2:207b, reveals that the *him* referred to in the last sentence is not the so-called *robber (gazlan)* of the previous sentence, viz., he who keeps a second fast on Sunday and "restores what he took away." Rather, it denotes one who omits the Sunday fast. Such a person is called a *ganav*, an impenitent thief. This distinction between robber and thief is based on a well-know Talmudic passage, BQ 79b:

> The robber [*gazlan*] puts the honor of the slave [i.e., human society; kabbalistically, the profane realm] on the same level as the honor of his owner [God], whereas the thief [*ganav*] does not put the honor of the slave on the same level as the master, [but higher].

Bearing these categories in mind, Moshe de Leon explained:

> For a "robber" does not discriminate between the Holy One and people [kabbalistically, does not accord higher honor to either the holy or profane realms]. Therefore, his punishment is less than that of a "thief" who thinks more of humankind than of God. This thief receives punishment in this world and in the next.

The copyists of the three TY MSS under study here seemed unaware of the textual ellipsis and assumed that only the robber was being spoken of in this passage. Therefore, they tried to emend the text to render it more plausible. JTSA Mic. 1646, JTSA Mic. 1553 and MS Adrianople all emend the Zoharic phrase *ne*ᶜ*enashin*—they are punished—to *ma*ᶜ*anishin*, they punish. JTSA 1553 and Adrian. read:

ואין בני אדם מענישין יותר מזה אבל הקב"ה מעניש אותו בעוה"ז ובעוה"ב

JTSA 1646 has the variant phrase:

. . . אבל הקב"ה מעניש אותו יותר מזה . . .

In translation:

Human beings may not punish [*maʿanishin*] him further; only the Holy One may punish him.

They thereby avoided the confusing assertion that:

No person may be punished [*neʿenashin*] further; but the Holy One may punish him.

However, as soon as the missing Zohar source is consulted, it is clear that *neʿenashin* is, in fact, the correct reading. This wording, albeit with the ellipsis, was recorded in the Istanbul e.p.

408. **"Torah . . . Truth . . . Jacob."** common appellations for *Tif'eret*. On the equation of Truth and *Tif'eret*, cf. *Zohar* 2:267a; on the equation of Truth and Jacob cf. 1:161a and 2:162a.

On the more unusual correlation of "Mouth" with *Tif'eret*, see Z 2: 123a and TZ 21 (50a): "Truth is none other than Torah, as it is written: 'The Torah of Truth was in his mouth.' " (Mal. 2:6) Also see AQ 1:22, which is basically an expanded treatment of *Sod ha-Shabbat* Section 18. In AQ Meir ibn Gabbai clearly stated, "the Written Torah is the Mouth that actualizes [i.e., articulates] the potential thought . . . found in *Ḥokhmah* and *Binah*."

409. The ensuing passage is a reworking of *Zohar* 2: 200a. This paraphrase is briefly interrupted by an interpolation of 3:40b. Also see n416 and n419 below.

410. **"Writing . . . Celestial Palace."** Designations for *Binah*. Cf. *Zohar* 2:200a; AQ 1:22; as well as TZ 59 (89a): *KeTaB*, Writing . . . refers to the Supernal Mother." This latter image constitutes a Kabbalistic version of the Islamic notion of the eternal Scriptures as *Umm al-kitāb* [*'Em ha-ketav!*].

In classical Kabbalah, the *sefirot* are often likened to elements of language and emanation to the process of articulation. *Binah* is called "Writing" because it is more exoteric than *Ḥokhmah* (called Thought), yet more hidden than *Tif'eret* (Voice) or *Malkhuṭ* (Speech). For discussion, see SCK: 8, 11, and 34.

411. The Torah and its Palace (*Tif'eret* and *Binah*).

412. Here ibn Gabbai temporarily leaves his paraphrase of *Zohar* 2:200a and draws upon 3:40b.

413. **"le-HWRTM."** In the Masoretic text, the term is written in abbreviated orthography, without the second *WaW*. This unusual spelling provides the basis for the Kabbalistic vocalization, le-HoWR*a*TaM rather than the conventional, le-HoWR*o*Tam.

Textual variants: The two JTSA MSS and e.p. misspell the term le-HWRWTM. By adding the second *Waw* they miss the point of the Kabbalistic interpretation. MS Adrianople correctly reads: le-HWRTM.

"Torah . . . mizvah." *Torah* here denotes *Tif'eret*/Written Torah; *mizvah* signifies *Malkhut*/Oral Torah. This interpretation has its roots in Rabbinic hermeneutics. Cf. TB Ber. 5a: *"Torah* refers to the Biblical text [i.e., the Written Torah]"; and TB Yev. 20a: *"Mizvah* signifies the words of the Sages [the Oral Torah]."

414. **"chamber."** An allusion to the enveloping, womb-like quality of *Binah.*

415. **"Wine . . . grapes."** A reference to *Binah* and Her *shefa*[c]. This image stems from the Rabbinic legend (TB Ber. 34b and Sanh. 99a) that God is storing the Wine of Paradise, "the wine preserved in its grapes," for the righteous in the World-to-Come. L. Ginzberg (*Legends* 5:98) speculates that this legend is based on early midrashic traditions that the forbidden fruit was a grape. Thus, the fruit that brought sin into the world will bring healing in the future age. In the Kabbalah, this Wine becomes a symbol of the hidden essence of the supernal Eden, *Binah,* which is "preserved," or protected from all external contact at present. This Wine, or concentration of divinity, can only be experienced in the eschaton. The relevant Zoharic sources include 3:40b (cf. n416); ZH "Ruth" 76a which reads: "The preserved wine issues forth from the World-to-Come [i.e., *Binah.*]" Also cf. 1:135b:

> It is the veiled essence never revealed to humanity from the day of Creation, but which will be disclosed to the righteous in the future.

"Supernal Book." This may plausibly refer to either *Hokhmah* or *Tif'eret.* The Zoharic source here (3:40b) leaves open both options (though the first seems smoother), while the parallel sources provide contradictory evidence. In Z 2:200a, a source used by ibn Gabbai elsewhere in this section, the Supernal Book is clearly *Tif'eret:* "The Supernal Book is the Written Torah, for it is closed and exists only in Writing." However, the evidence in 2:137b points to *Hokhmah:* "The mystery of the Supernal Book, the Father of All." It is clear that in his later years ibn Gabbai subscribed to this second reading. In AQ 1:22 he quoted Z 3: 40b and commented:

> "The Book and the Writing" refers to *Hokhmah* and *Binah,* the origin of the Written Torah which is the Mouth that actualizes what exists only potentially in Thought.

Because AQ 1:22 is generally an elaboration of ideas already present in the TY rather than a wholly new reading, I am inclined to weigh the AQ's evidence most heavily here; *Hokhmah* would seem to be the probable referent.

416. So ends Meir ibn Gabbai's close paraphrase of Z 3: 40b. Compare!

417. **"upon the Mouth."** Following *Zohar* 2:200a (cited in n419), there are two basic ways of reading this phrase: with respect to *Malkhut* and with respect to the Chariots. For both are called "Mouth" in this section.

Interpretation A: The Oral Torah exists at the edge of the sefirotic world, or to use the Kabbalistic imagery, *upon* the Mouth *(Malkhut).* As such, it is poised to project beyond the enclosed (esoteric) divine realm, much like Speech about to be uttered and made "public." In this reading, the Oral Torah (and its key-word," *upon*) contrasts with the Written Torah which remains fully within the sefirotic world, "*within* Writing."

Interpretation B: The Oral Torah may be viewed from another vantage point. For it *rests upon* the Celestial Chariots, which exist just below the sefirotic world. Here these Chariots are the Mouth.

The second reading seems the smoothest here. For further discussion, see my disseration, pp. 549–50.

418. **"there is separation."** The beginning of the sub-sefirotic world, called the World of Separation or Multiplicity *(ᶜalma' de-peruda')*. This Biblical phrase is conventionally rendered: "from thence, it was parted [*yiPpaReD*]." A consideration of the entire verse is helpful here:

"A river went out of Eden to water the Garden": Kabbalistically, referring to the descent of the *shefaᶜ* from *Binah* unto the lowest rung, *Malkhut*.

"and from thence it was parted": As the *shefaᶜ* leaves the sefirotic world, it enters the World of Multiplicity.

"and became four heads": refers either to the four lower Chariots [cf. *Zohar* 2:15b (MN); 1:158a, 248b; MZ 1:445–46], or more generally, to the lower world as a whole, as in: "This river [leaves the Garden] . . . and thence is scattered to the four corners of the world." (Z 1:208a) Theologically, it seems fitting that the Oral Torah rest upon the World of Separation or Multiplicity. For unlike the Written Torah, the Oral Torah contains seemingly multiple and contradictory teachings. For a fuller treatment of this topic, see ibn Gabbai, AQ 1:21–22 and 3:20–24; as well as G. Scholem's extended discussion in "Revelation and Tradition as Religious Categories" in *The Messianic Idea in Judaism* (NY, 1971): 290ff. (esp. 298–303).

"Sphere of Unity." Heb., *kelal ha-yiḥud*: the sefirotic world.

"Palace." Unlike *Binah*, which envelops or shelters the Written Torah, the sub-sefirotic Chariots can only serve as a pedestal for the Oral Torah.

419. Here ibn Gabbai ends his paraphrase of *Zohar* 2:200a. Note de Leon's two-fold use of the term *she-be-ᶜal peh:*

> The Supernal Book is the Written Torah, literally, the Torah that is *in* writing. For it is hidden and exists only within Writing. What is this place? The World-to-Come [*Binah*]. The Lower Book is called the Oral Torah, *Torah she-be-ᶜal peh,* literally, the Torah that is upon *ᶜal peh*. What does *ᶜal peh* connote? The lower Chariots upon which this Torah rests. Because they are not included within the Supernal writing [*bi-khlala' di-khtiva'*, i.e., the sefirotic realm], they are called *ᶜal peh,* "beyond the Mouth" [below *Malkhut*].
>
> This Torah rests *ᶜal peh,* "upon the Mouth" [here meaning, upon the Chariots], as it is written: "From this point on, there is Separation." [Gen. 2:10] Even though the supernal Torah exists on

> high, it is not called *ʿal ha-ketav,* "upon the writing" but *she-bi-khtav,* "in writing." For this Torah exists within Writing [*Binah*]. Writing forms a Palace for the Torah; it is concealed within. And so it is called the "Torah; it is concealed within. And so it is called the "Torah that is in Writing." . . . . But the lower Torah rests upon her Chariots and so is called *ʿal peh,* "upon the Mouth." Because the [Chariots] remain outside the realm of Supernal Writing, they cannot form a Palace [sheltering] this point . . .

420. On the two *torot* as twins, cf. Z 2:78b:

> As regards the Torah it is written: "And you shall meditate upon it, day and night." [Hos. 1:8] "Day" corresponds to the Tongue [Written Torah/*Tif'eret*] and "night" to the Mouth [Oral Torah/*Malkhut*]. And these two are one, twins.

Closely related is a teaching that depicts their sefirotic correlates, *Tif'eret* and *Malkhut,* as mirror images:

> *Shekhinah* is His actual image, the image of the Holy One. She equals His measure and stature, without addition or diminution. (TZ 62 [94b])

For ibn Gabbai's treatment of these twin *torot/sefirot,* cf. TY p. 93a, "The Mystery of the Nuptial Blessing" on *Ẓaddiq* and *Ẓedeq;* and AQ 1:22, where the two *torot* are imaged as a series of dyads: *du-parẓufin,* two lovers, two friends, two brothers, two siblings, and most significantly here, as twins. An excerpt:

> These two *Torot* were intended to be as one, bound together, each influencing the other. Their existence depends on the other. They are brother and sister, twins. Thus, one must study both of them and unite them. As it says, "You shall meditate upon it, day and night. . . ." "Night" is the Oral Torah and "day" connotes the Written Torah. The inner meaning of these two is *YHWH 'Elohim,* the complete divine Name, the mystery of true union.

421. Cf. Cant. R 5:2 and *Pesiqta' Rabbati* 15:6. The former was often called *Midrash Ḥazita* in Geonic and Medieval literature, its name deriving from the opening passage: "Should you see [*ḥazita*] a man diligent in his business." (Prv. 22:9) The source quoted by ibn Gabbai is actually from Cant. R; the *Pesiqta'* text is a close parallel. Note that in the *midrashim* the twins are God and Israel.

422. On the supernal Oral Torah as the symbol and expositor of the Written Torah above, see G. Scholem, *On the Kabbalah and its Symbolism:* 49–50. On *Shekhinah* as actualizer of divinity's "potential power," see n358 above.

423. **"Sage."** Solomon. **"Through the gates."** Heb., *ba-sheʿarim.* Conventionally, "in the gates." Kabbalistically, *Shekhinah* is the "Gate of Righteousness," the entry to the supernal mysteries. Cf. Z 1: 103a–b: "She is

the gate through whom the Blessed Holy One . . . who is hidden and concealed becomes known." In other words, only through the prism of Oral Torah may the recondite Written Torah be apprehended.

424. Cf. n413 above and Abraham ibn Ezra to Ex. 24:12: " 'Torah' refers to the Written Torah and 'the miẓvah' to the Oral Torah, for all the miẓvot were given to Moses at Sinai." Also cf. *Perush ha-'Aggadot le-R. ʿAzri'el* to Ber. 5a.

425. **"So it is in the case . . . the Written Torah needs it."** Both the G. Scholem and R. Margaliot versions read: *Kakh torah she-be-ʿal peh; 'af ʿal pi she-hi' ner, ẓerikhah torah she-bi-khtav le-fareq qushioteha.* ("So it is with the Oral Torah; even though it is a Lamp, it needs the Written Torah to solve its problems.") However, this assertion stands contrary to reason, for it is the Written Torah that stands in need of the Oral Torah's elucidation! Ibn Gabbai has emended this confused wording by adding the particle *lah* [*ẓerikhah lah torah she-bi-khtav*], thus reversing the subject and object and transforming the meaning. In *Das Buch Bahir*: 108, Scholem notes the absurdity of the *Bahir* text and emends his translation in accordance with the TY's solution. He states:

> The closing phrase, as it stands, is contrary to common sense, asserting the converse of that which is to be expected. . . . Quite naturally, it is the Oral Tradition and not the Written one which should be the proper object of the [sentence]. Should one merely exchange the phrases *Written Torah* and *Oral Torah*, as is found in a few instances, a meaningful reading is not obtained either. Here the Written Torah is precisely not a Lamp, but on the contrary, a mysterious Light, as it were, dense and dark. . . . [He follows the emendation of the TY and adds:] The version in the TY may be adapted . . . so that we can make sense of this absurd passage.

In AQ 1:22, ibn Gabbai emended the *Bahir* more drastically, leaving no doubt as to how he reads the text:

> So it is in the case of the Written [!] Torah. Even though it is a Light [!], it stands in need of the Oral Torah to resolve its problems and explain its mysteries.

Discussion. This parable is built on paradoxical uses of light imagery. From one perspective, the Written Torah is "lighter" than the Oral Torah (i.e., closer to the luminous divine Source), yet it is also "darker" (more mysterious and hidden; less accessible to human understanding). The "dark light" of the Written Torah, i.e., its mysterious nature, is imaged as "a room hidden away at the end of a house." For ibn Gabbai—if not for the *Bahir*'s author—this image likely recalls that of the Written Torah hidden within the recesses of its Palace, *Binah*. Even though it is day outside—even though the Written Torah is a radiant source of divine truth—its mysterious contents cannot be disclosed without employing the less powerful but paradoxically brighter—more exoteric—Lamp, the Oral Torah.

426. **"celestial counterparts."** Heb., *dugmatan le-ma^clah.*

"They are joined . . . a kiss." The allusion here is to the union of the two divine cherubs, *Tif'eret* and *Shekhinah*. See the interpretation of Job 41:9 in *Sod ha-Shabbat* p. 14 and n20, above. On kissing as a symbol for divine coupling, see n431, below.

"the Tabernacle becomes one." Through the union of *Tif'eret* and *Shekhinah*, the divine structure is unified. This image is employed in Z 3:229a (RM), where the author is commenting on mystical prayer:

> "And make one cherub at one end and one cherub at the other end." [Ex. 25:19] [I.e., before the *ᶜAmidah, Tif'eret* and *Shekhinah* are still separated.] But when the prayer-leader repeats the Prayer and concludes "Amen" there is another bonding. The two Names [*YHWH* and *'Adonai*] unite. . . . As "Amen" is recited "the Tabernacle becomes one" [Ex. 26:6], for the one [cherub] is united with the other.

427. Heb., *shalom ba-kol.* Lit., "peace is in all." Kabbalistically, a reference to the union of Peace [*Tif'eret/Yesod*] with the divine All, *Shekhinah.*

428. **"Torah on high."** *Shekhinah.* See n430. The TY here recalls OK to Shab. 114a:

> "What are *banna'im,* builders? . . . scholars who are engaged all their days in building up the world." Verily, when scholars engage in Torah-study for its own sake they bind Torah to Torah. The structure of the world is sustained through this.

Also see Z 1:4a and 47a.

429. Cf. TB Shab. 30a. That study entails sublimation of the sexual drive is implied here and elsewhere in *Sod ha-Shabbat*. See pp. 34–35 above and n439 below.

430. The *Bahir* adds:

> What is this Torah [on high] that you are discussing? It is the Bride who is adorned and crowned . . . It is the betrothed of the Holy One, blessed be He.

431. **"Now, when Israel . . ."** The remainder of this section is analyzed in SCK: Appendix II. See there for additional points.

"Mother on high." *Shekhinah*. Throughout this section ibn Gabbai seems to have derived inspiration from two Zoharic sources:

> It is the Community of Israel who said: "Let him kiss me" [Cant. 1:2] rather than "let him love me." Because . . . kissing is the cleaving of spirit to spirit. The mouth is the medium for kissing, the organ and origin of the spirit [i.e., breath]. . . . Thus, kisses come from the mouth, expressing love, the cleaving of spirit to spirit in inseparable union. [2:124b]

And:

> Why did Solomon, in his description of the love between the upper and lower worlds [*Tif'eret* and *Shekhinah*], begin praising their love by using the phrase: "Let him kiss me"? Because . . . that deep love, wherein spirit is bound to spirit cannot be expressed save through a kiss. A kiss comes from the mouth, the source of *ruaḥ:* spirit, breath. When two kiss, their spirits join and become one; their love becomes one.

The passion of divine kissing is perhaps best portrayed in *Zohar* 1:70a–b:

> The *yannuqa'* [wunderkind] began speaking: "Let him kiss me with the kisses of his mouth." [Cant. 1:2] This refers to that supernal desire in which affection issues from the mouth like fire. . . . For when a mouth is joined with another mouth in a kiss, a fire issues forth out of affection; one's face shines. There is mutual rejoicing and joyous union . . .

Throughout this section kissing and kissing mouth-to-mouth may be read as simultaneously oral and sexual (genital) imagery. In Rabbinic literature, e.g., the terms *kisses* and *kisses of the mouth (neshiqot ha-peh)* are sometimes used to indicate sexual union. Cf. TB Yev. 55b: *haʿara'ah zo' neshiqah* ("sexual intercourse is *kissing*") and RaSHI to *Soṭah* 4a: *neshiqat 'ever* ("the 'kissing' of the phallus"). On *peh* as sexual organ, see TB Sanh. 100a and Men. 98a, s.v. *peh shel maṭah.*

It should be noted that the sexual connotation of the lovers' kisses is still a subtext in the TY at this point; it becomes the primary meaning in the ensuing passage.

432. **"Thus [the Bride] says."** Heb., *ke-'illu to'mar*. This is a specifically medieval usage. See *Millon Ben-Yehudah* (Jerusalem, 1959) 1:234.

"If only." Ibn Gabbai's wording recalls RaSHI to Cant. 1:2:

> This is the song chanted by [the Community of Israel] in her exile . . ." If only King Solomon would kiss me with the kisses of his mouth . . . as a groom before a bride, mouth to mouth.

433. **"man . . . home."** The sexual imagery of the kissing becomes clearer here; *home* simultaneously connotes *Shekhinah* and the vagina. On this symbolism, see p. 34 and n170, above.

434. In other words, Torah-study becomes a sort of divine "aphrodisiac." It promotes the most intimate union of *Tif'eret* and *Shekhinah,* or to use the grammatical metaphor, it enables *Shekhinah* to address Her lover as *You* instead of the more distant *He (derekh nistar).*

"How good is your love *mi-yayin:* through wine." Here ibn Gabbai diverges from the conventional reading: "Your love is better than wine."

On the likening of Torah to wine, cf. TB *Taʿanit* 7a where pure Torah-study is compared to an elixir of life *(sam ha-ḥayyim).* Also cf. *Zohar* 2:124b, which probably served as the TY's primary source here:

> The Community of Israel said: "Let him kiss me with the kisses of his mouth," that his spirit be joined to mine, that we may never

> grow apart. For "how good is your love through wine"! Why is wine mentioned here? . . . R. Ḥiyya said: "Because 'wine' refers to Torah."

Also see the parallel passage in AQ 2:24.

435. **"the divine structure in completed."** Ff. MS Adrianople which reads: *mashlimim BiNYYaNO*. The other MSS and e.p. all read: *mashlimim BeYNeNu* (peace is fulfilled between us)—another logical alternative.

"the Holy One and the Community of Israel." Although the primary meaning is sefirotic here, this phrase also evokes the love between God and the People Israel as subtext.

436. Ibn Gabbai here reframes the mythic focus for Torah-study, shifting from divinity to the:

"Adept." Heb., *shalem*, referring to the Kabbalist. This term is borrowed from medieval philosophy, and literally means, "the perfected" or "complete one." Cf., e.q., *Kuzari* 1:1:

> In the perfect person [*shalem*] . . . the Active Intellect is with him . . . he is the Active Intellect itself and . . . there is no difference between them.

In both the philosophical literature and the TY, *shalem* implies a purely spiritual state of existence. To quote *Kuzari* 5:12: "As soon as the soul is separated from [the body] it becomes *shalem*, perfect." For a contrasting view of *shelemut*, see the Zohar passage in n184, above. For broader discussion, see R. Kiener's treatment of "Perfect Man" traditions in "Ibn al-ᶜArabi and the Qabbalah," *Studies in Mystical Literature* Vol. 2 (1982): 26–52.

"like an angel." This notion is found in numerous Talmudic sources, including TB Ned. 20b, Giṭ. 62a, Pes. 33a and Qid. 72a which states: "The scholars of Babylonia are like the ministering angels." Also see the philosophical sources cited in n437. In the Zoharic literature, cf. 1:12b:

> "Bless the Lord, you angels of his." [Ps. 103:20] Those who engage in Torah-study are called his angels on earth."

437. As with *shalem*, the TY appropriates philosophical terminology here and gives it a distinctively Kabbalistic coloration.

(a) **"In his comtemplation."** Heb., *be-ᶜiyyun*. Although, in philosophical usage, *ᶜiyyun* generally connotes philosophical speculation or intellection, here it signifies mystical contemplation or meditation.

(b) **"Their activity is purely contemplative."** The JTSA MSS and e.p. all read: *Ki sekhel kol ᶜisqeihem*, a rather awkard phrasing. MS Adrianople reads more smoothly: *Ki be-sekhel kol ᶜisqeihem*. This line is a paraphrase of Ps. 111:10.

Discussion. The notion that angelic activity is that of pure *sekhel*, i.e., "purely contemplative," is first recorded in the philosophical sources. Such disparate thinkers as Judah ha-Levi (*Kuzari* 5:10, 12, 21), Abraham ibn Ezra, and RaMBaM (*Guide* 1:49; 2:6, etc.) used *sekhel* doubly, as a synonym for "angel" and to indicate their defining activity: a self-contemplation wholly divorced from corporeality. People who engage in contemplation may themselves become angelic. Cf. *Kuzari* 5:10:

> Thus, man may reach the rung of the angels who have no need of natural [i.e., physical] powers, because they are *sekhalim,* divine Intellects.

The angelic quality of contemplation is widely discussed in the Medieval Christian tradition, as well. Thomas Aquinas, e.g., distinguished between *ratio,* discursive knowledge which was distinctively human activity (i.e., work), and more passive contemplation, *intellectus,* which was seen as a superhuman or angelic attainment, an inspired state of "non-work." Hence, contemplation was the process whereby one overcame one's humanity and paradoxically fulfilled its highest promise: becoming "more than human," "like the angels." For details see Thomas Aquinas' *Quaestiones disputatae de veritae* 15:1 and Josef Pieper's discussion in *Leisure: The Basis of Culture* (NY, 1952), chap. 2.

438. From TB Ber. 17a:

> In the World-to-Come there is neither feasting nor drinking . . . but the righteous sit with crowns on their heads feasting on [variant: basking in] the splendor of the *Shekhinah.*

See the earlier allusion in *Sod ha-Shabbat,* p. 53. Also see the Zoharic treatment in 1:135b (MN), 2:116a–b, ZḤ "Noaḥ" 21a, etc.

439. **"It is devoid of bodily concerns." Discussion.** The TY, like the *Zohar,* oscillates between two models for spirituality. Although one model underscores the Kabbalist's sacred physicality and even sexuality on the Sabbath, the other stresses his pure, angelic qualities. Which model is summoned depends largely on the ritual context—the activity to be performed—and its attendant mythos.

For examples of the first model, see *Sod ha-Shabbat* Sections 12 and 15 ("Marital Sex" and "Sabbath-Delight"); also see *Zohar* 2:47a (on Isa. 58:13) and 204b where bodily pleasure is deemed essential for the well-being of one's Sabbath-soul. It is, of course, the second model which is highlighted in the TY here. The Sabbath is portrayed as a day so utterly transforming that bodily concerns are superceded and the future—non-corporeal—world, glimpsed. To wit: "[The Sabbath] is the World of Souls." Also in this vein, cf. *Sod ha-Shabbat*: 53 above: "On the Sabbath . . . the spiritual world flourishes, while the physical world lies dormant"; and *Zohar* 1:1b and 2:205a–b:

> The Sabbath is the day of souls and not of the body. It is under the dominion of the "Bundle of Souls" [*Binah*]; on it the upper and lower [realms] are united.

Not surprisingly, prayer and study are the activities thought to best reflect this purely spiritual cosmos:

> Sabbath is the day of the soul; hence, one should concern oneself only with songs of praise, prayer and Torah-study. (Z 2:205b)

The TY's current depiction of Torah-study as purely spiritual is psychologically striking, since it follows a highly erotic description of its effect on the celestial world. The sexually charged language of divine eros gives way to the portrayal of the disembodied scholar.

440. Thereby aligning oneself with the "World of Souls." *Zohar* 2:88b implies that it is the presence of the Sabbath-soul which makes possible this alignment. For it is:

> the soul containing the totality of perfection, a model of the World-to-Come . . . this soul is called "Shabbat."

441. In other words, *li-shmah* may also be read: " for her sake," for the sake of one's Sabbath-soul. In the *Zohar,* one is enjoined to regale one's Sabbath-soul not only through "food, drink and fine garments" (2:204a) but also through Torah-learning. The Sabbath-soul is said to take special delight in each new meaning *(ḥiddush)* the adept uncovers. As it is regaled, it ascends on high to join with its "other half," thereby "becoming whole." See SCK: 135–36 and *Sod ha-Shabbat,* pp. 54 and 57 for details. Also see Z 3:173a–174a, passim.

442. **"in the light of Life."** To bask in the divine splendor; to have intimate knowledge of God.

"I am glorified." A reference to the Sabbath-soul, which can only be perfected by Israel.

Discussion. Torah-study on/Shabbat therefore services four major purposes in the TY:

(a) a theurgic one, promoting the union of *Shekhinah* and *Tif'eret,* the Oral and Written *Torot.*

(b) a reflexive one, whereby the devotee is transformed into an "angel." Through sacred learning, he is transported beyond his bodily self, becoming "purely spiritual." In this sense, Torah-study is an ec-static experience.

(c) Moreover, this Sabbath-transformation has a prospective meaning, affording the adept with a foretaste of his ultimate reward in the World-to-Come, the realm of perpetual Shabbat. Through Sabbath Torah-study he glimpses the splendor of *Shekhinah.* And finally,

(d) Through sacred learning he regales his Sabbath-soul, and perfects it.

443. Generally, these prayers are recited in the later afternoon, in the waning hours of Shabbat. See n444 and 453.

444. "order [of Biblical verses]." Heb., *seder.* Apparently a Hebraization of [Qedushah de-] *Sidra'* (lit., the Sanctus of the Biblical Portion) as this prayer is commonly called. Or more simply, *seder* may be rendered as "prayer" or "liturgical unit." *U-va' le-Ẓion* is generally recited during the Morning Service, but on Shabbat its recitation is postponed until *Minḥah.*

For further discussion see J. Heinemann, *Ha-Tefillah bi-Tqufat ha-Tanna'im ve-ha-'Amora'im* (2nd ed., Jerusalem, 1966): 166–68 and L. J. Leibreich, "An Analysis of U-Ba Le-Ziyyon" in HUCA 21 (1948): 175–209.

"Din is aroused." According to Z 2:63a, *Minḥah* marks the beginning of *Din*'s ascendance:

> At the time called "dusk" [i.e., late afternoon, the traditional time for *Minḥah*], *Din* begins to hold sway. For this reason it was Isaac [symbol of *Gevurah* or *Din*] who established the *Minḥah* prayer.

Also cf. Z 1:92a, 132b (cited in n452); and 2:21a:

> From the first glimmering of light until its waning, it is called "Day," which is the aspect of *Ḥesed*, Love. Thereafter, it is called "Evening," the aspect of *Din*.

445. **"Compassion."** Here a reference to *Ḥesed* or possibly to *Keter*, which is drawn forth at this hour. See n449. The TY accords this prayer a special significance not found in the *Zohar*. As shall be seen, ibn Gabbai's emphasis on the power of the *Qedushah de-Sidra'* derives from his reading of TB *Soṭah* 49a.

446. Here ibn Gabbai seems to conflate TB *Soṭah* 48a and 49a. The printed edition of the Talmud reads:

> R. Shimon ben Gamliel said in the name of R. Joshua: "Since the day the Temple was destroyed there is no day without a curse." [48a]

It is Rabba who adds the Amoraic gloss, found on 49a:

> And the curse of each day is more severe than that of the preceding.

Manhig: 106 also attributes this gloss to "R. Shimon ben Gamliel in the name of R. Joshua." This is possibly ibn Gabbai's source.

447. **"for the Temple sustained the world."** See ARN (A) 35:1; Tanḥ. (Buber) "Bere'shit": 43 and "Terumah": 94; PRK (Buber): 56 ff.; and the discussion below.

"Service is one of the pillars," Ff. *'Avot* 1:2:

> The world rests upon three things: upon the Torah, upon [divine] Service [*ᶜavodah*]; and upon the practice of charity.

Discussion. In the Aggadic literature, the Temple was widely portrayed as the *axis mundi:* an earthly conduit for all blessing, both natural and spiritual. (For details, see R. Patai, *Man and Temple:* 84–139 and R. Goldenberg, "The Broken Axis" in JAAR 45 [1977]: 869ff.) According to several Rabbinic accounts, the world was incomplete until the Temple was erected. Cf., e.g., Tanh. (Buber) "Terumah": 94:

> Before the Temple was built the world rested upon a two-legged throne. [ff 'Avot 1:2] Once it was built, the world was firmly established and stood aright.

Although the Rabbis imputed cosmic significance to the Temple's structure and even to its furnishings (cf. *Tadshe'* in *Beit ha-Midrash* 3:164 ff. and YS to I K *siman* 185), the Temple *cult* was most frequently viewed as the primary means of drawing down divine blessing. See ARN (B) 4 and 5 which notes: "When the Temple Service exists, the world is full of blessing . . . When it does not exist, the world is devoid of blessing."

These themes are extended in the Zoharic tradition and given a more obviously theosophic coloration. On the Temple as a source of blessing, cf. Z 1:203a; as source of the world's restoration, see 1: 209b; on the Holy of Holies as a source of blessing, see 1:84a, 2:157a, and 3:161b. On the Temple as an apotropaic warding off *Siṭra' 'Aḥra'*, cf. 2:190a and 239a. On the Temple as reflection of the divine order, see ZḤ Cant. 77a.

448. In short, the *Qedushah de-Sidra'* functions as partial replacement for the Temple, helping to sustain the world and invest it with sweet blessing. Its recitation at *Minḥah* specifically helps sustain the Sabbath-cosmos, warding off the rising forces of *Din*. For a comparison with non-mystical rationales for reciting this prayer at *Minḥah* on Shabbat, see *Manhig*: 184–85; *Kol Bo* sec. 40; *Abud.*: 122; as well as my dissertation: 561–62.

449. **"a time of Grace"; "Compassion."** See n356 above.

"the King's fury" connotes the forces of *Din*, which are pacified, or neutralized, by *Keter*'s "sweet light."

There are numerous Zoharic parallels to the TY here. Cf., e.g., 2:88b which shares the same symbolism as the TY. Also see 3: 129a (IR) and 3: 288b (IZ) where the revelation of *Keter* is described in highly anthropomorphic imagery. During the week, the glistening "forehead" of the short-tempered *Ze*ʿ*ir 'Anpin* (corresponding to the six lower *sefirot* from *Ḥesed* to *Yesod*) is disclosed at *Minḥah* and sinners subjected to punishment. But on the Sabbath, the forehead of the compassionate *'Arikh 'Anpin (Keter)* is revealed, and the forces of *Din* swept away. According to the IR source:

> When is the Forehead [of *Keter*] revealed . . .? At Sabbath *Minḥah*. . . . Now, at this time during the week, *Din* rules through the Small Face. But on Shabbat, that glistening Forehead called Grace [*ra*ʿ*ava'*] is revealed. At that hour, [divine] anger is forgotten, Grace is present and prayers are accepted; as it is written, "I offer my prayer to You, O Lord, at a time of Grace." [Ps. 69: 14]

Discussion. For Meir ibn Gabbai Sabbath *Minḥah* is typified by two opposing rhythms, like tide and undertow. In the waning light of day, *Din* begins to rouse itself, and the end of Shabbat is intimated. But at precisely this moment, the Sabbath-cosmos is reinforced and deepened, as *Keter* emerges from the hidden recesses and bathes the divine world in light. The distinction between the weekday cosmos and that of Shabbat is underscored. *Din* is neutralized: "the King's fury abates."

In many ways, *Minḥah* is the high point of Shabbat in the TY. If Friday night is most closely aligned with *Malkhut*, and Sabbath morning with *Tif'eret*, *Minḥah* is the time of *Keter*, of *supreme* Grace, *ra*ʿ*ava' de-ra*ʿ*avin*. See *Sod ha-Shabbat*: 65 and n514. For opposing views, cf. n467 and n508–09 below.

450. **"peace . . . pervades the cosmos."** Heb., *shalom ba-kol;* lit., peace is in all. As I have noted, this is a multivocal phrase. In a general kabbalistic sense, it refers to the pacification of the entire divine world, including the aspect of *Din* (Fury). More narrowly, it connotes the union of *Tif'eret/Yesod (Shalom)* with *Malkhut (Kol).* Both connotations are found in the Zoharic sources cited below.

On Ps. 69:14 as an attestation of divine unity, see Z 2:156a:

> At Sabbath-*Minḥah* . . . all [celestial] anger is removed, and all polarities are integrated, becoming one. Even though *Din* is roused [at this hour], it is sweetened. Thus, a verse of unification is needed to unite all the rungs. For when there is union, *Din* is integrated with Compassion and all is sweetened. . . . Concerning this hour, it is written, "[This is] a time of Grace," [Ps. 69:14] when all is One.

Also see 1:116b; and 2:253b:

> "And Jacob [*Tif'eret*] kissed Rachel [*Malkhut*]." [Gen. 29:11] When they kiss one another, it is called *ʿet raẓon,* the time of Grace [here: time of Desire]. For now there is wholeness and all faces shine. At this moment, all prayers ascend, for it is a time of *Raẓon,* Grace. As it is written: "I offer my prayer to You, O Lord, at a time of *Raẓon*" [Ibid.], which is their moment of union.

451. **"I offer my prayer."** Heb., *va-'ani tefillati;* here read hyperliterally as: "I [with] my Prayer," referring to the union of *Malkhut* and *Tif'eret.* On *Malkhut* as the divine "I," see G. Scholem, *Major Trends*: 218. On "Prayer of Moses" as an appellation for *Tif'eret,* cf. Moses Cordovero, PR: Gate 23, "Tefillah."

"a time of Grace." *ʿet raẓon.* Also read hyperliterally as: Time (with) Grace. Referring to *Malkhut* as the "Time of Peace" *(ʿet shalom)* is rather unusual. Evidently, She is so-called because She is now complete, *shalem,* united with the supernal *Shalom (Tif'eret).* This unified entity joins with *Keter.* In other words, this prayer dramatizes two stages of divine union: first, the relatively common coupling of *Malkhut* and *Tif'eret* and thereafter, the much rarer union of the divine totality, symbolized by the *yiḥud* of the lowest and highest rungs.

Discussion. The key phrase in this prayer is *ʿet raẓon.* It takes on at least three shades of meaning in the TY:

1) Sabbath-*Minḥah* is a "favorable time" for prayer, because

2) the Supernal *Raẓon, Keter,* is disclosed at this hour. As a result *Din* is quieted and re-integrated into divinity, and

3) the entire sefirotic world, from lowest to highest, is one. A joyous sense of grace pervades the cosmos.

452. This passage is briefly discussed in SCK: 201. Only additional comments will be included here.

"love." That is *Ḥesed,* which holds sway in the morning hours. Because *Ḥesed* signifies divine wholeness, the whole Torah reading is read during its reign.

According to Z 1:132b, the "entire day" refers to the morning hours only!

> The time for *Minḥah* begins as the sun declines towards the West; before that hour it is called "Day." From dawn onward it is Day to wit: "*Ḥesed* persists the entire day." [Ps. 52:3] You might think that the entire day lasts till darkness has set in. But it is written: "Alas for us! for day has departed. The shadows of evening grow long." [Jer. 6:4] This shows that Day corresponds to the time for receiving the Morning Prayer; for "*Ḥesed* persists when it is entirely day," when the sun is in the East. . . . But when it declines in the West . . . it is the time of *Minḥah*: for Day has departed and *Din* is roused.

453. **"But at . . . ."** Here ibn Gabbai begins his close paraphrase of Z 2:206b. Compare.

"dusk." Heb., *ᶜerev;* i.e., late afternoon.

"ten verses . . . more." Generally, the first *ᶜaliyah* of the next Shabbat is divided into three portions. According to TB Meg. 21b, at least 10 verses must be read.

454. **"[the Torah] proceeded from the fusion of these two."** Compare Z 2:84a-b. At Sinai,

> "All the people saw the voices." [Ex. 20:15]. There were five voices [ff. TB Ber. 6b] and the people saw with them. . . . There were actually five voices belonging to the Right and five voices belonging to the Left. But those belonging to the Left were included in the Right.

Also cf. TB Ber. 62a s.v. Dt. 33:2.

"Fire." Kabbalistically, ... *Din,* the Left. This obscure verse is traditionally rendered: "At his right hand was a fiery law [*'eshdat*] unto them."

Here ibn Gabbai concludes his paraphrase of Z 2:206b.

455. **"consummation."** Heb., *tashlum;* indictating both completion and perfection.

"Sabbath liturgy." Heb., *ha-tefillot;* the specific focus is on the intermediate blessings of the *ᶜAmidot,* each of which sets the tone for its Service. Cf. AQ 2:10:

> The middle blessings [of the Sabbath *ᶜAmidot*] . . . all allude to the supernal union . . . And we wrote in the TY that . . . "You are One" is the consummation of the *middle blessings* [emph. mine].

456. In the ensuing passage ibn Gabbai focuses on the Kabbalistic meaning of the intermediate blessings of the four Sabbath services. Because the middle benedictions vary from service to service, they are interpreted as setting the tone for it; each blessing discloses the particular sefirotic drama

unfolding at that time, providing a kind of phenomenology of Shabbat. This passage has been discussed in SCK: 201–02. See there for interpretation.

On the intermediate blessings setting the tone, cf. Eleazar ben Judah of Worms' interpretation (cited in R. Jacob of Kiev's *Shoshan Sodot:* 79a); Ṭur OḤ 292; TZ 18 (34a); Israel Al-Naqawa's *Menorat ha-Ma'or* 2:191 (reprinted in A. J. Heschel's *The Sabbath:* 54–55); *Abud.:* 147–48; and esp. OZ 39b/54b, translated in SCK: 120–21. For a modern variant upon this tradition, see F. Rosenzweig's *Star of Redemption* (Boston, 1972): 311–13.

457. On Yakhin and Boaz as pillars of the Temple, see I Kings 7:21. Kabbalistically, they connote *Neẓaḥ* and *Hod,* respectively. Cf. *Zohar* 3:58a, 282a; and TZ Intro (12b).

458. **"in intimate union."** Hebrew idiom: *mamtiqim sod.* Cf. Ps. 55: 14–15.

459. **"He".** the seven lower rungs. **"His Name."** *Keter.* See, e.g., *Bahir* 141:

> *Keter ᶜElyon,* blessed and praised be "His Name". . . . [He is] the Unity of Unities, one in all His names [the lower *sefirot*].

460. TZ 18 (34a). The text is left in the original Aramaic. Ibn Gabbai presents only portions of the TZ text here, thereby creating a certain amount of confusion. Making matters more difficult, he seems to be quoting the passage almost as an afterthought. It is not especially well-integrated into the TY: It breaks the flow of ibn Gabbai's own narrative (see n471) and several of its explanations contradict points made in the TY. I surmise that ibn Gabbai discovered this passage only after completing his book, and felt obligated to include it as an alternate reading.

461. The TY and TZ both correlate the Friday night benediction with *Malkhut,* but give Her a different "partner." Here She is linked with "the Levites," the Left Side of divinity. On this association see Z 1:143b; 3:155b and 179a–b; TZ 21 (55b), 47 (84b), et al.

Discussion. The key term here is "sanctified." Apparently "You sanctified the seventh day" is taken to mean: "The Left Side [*Gevurah* and *Hod*] gave strength to *Malkhut.*" The association of *sanctify* [*QDSH*] with the Left is commonly found in Zoharic sources, especially in the *Tiqqunim*. Cf., e.g.,TZ 47 (84b):

> "Purify and Sanctify" [Lev. 17:19] "Purify" is from the Side of the Priests [the Right] . . . and "Sanctify" is from the Left, as it is written: "You shall sanctify the Levites." [ff. Num. 8:17 and Neh. 12:47]

On the Sabbath-union of *Malkhut* and the Left, also see OZ 45a/60a which speaks of the sacred marriage of Rebecca and Isaac.

462. In other words, *Binah* is *Tif'eret*'s portion *(ḥelqo).* The TY, it will be recalled, identified *ḥelqo* with *Malkhut.* For parallels to this TZ, see Ibid.

21 (45b and 59a). On *Binah* as the "Soul of every living thing" see I. Tishby, MZ 2:501, n181.

Based purely on the image of Moses receiving the Torah, the TZ's interpretation would seem preferrable to Meir ibn Gabbai's for Moses ascended—not decended—to receive "his portion."

463. **"Lips."** Conventionally vocallized *SheFaTtaYiM:* sheepfolds, but here read as *SeFaTaYiM.* Cf. TZ 21 (45a–b) for a more explicit usage. In this context, the Lips connote the lower *sefirot.*

464. The text continues:

> Concerning Her it is said: "and he lighted [*YiSHKaB*] upon that place," [Gen. 28:11] meaning that place where the twenty-two letters of the Torah abide [i.e., *Binah*].

The author arrives at this interpretation by reading *YiSHKaB* as *YeSH K"B:* there are twenty-two (in that place)! This pun is repeated in TZ 70 (132b) and Z 1: 156b (ST). On the mystical alphabet within *Binah,* see *Sod ha-Shabbat,* p. 45 and n288 above; and I. Tishby's discussion in MZ 1:153.

465. **"brings together."** Aram., *'aḥid.* Lit., grasps or holds fast.

Although ibn Gabbai interprets this prayer as the *tashlum* (consummation) of all four Prayers, the TZ accords it somewhat more limited significance. "You are One" corresponds to YHWH, i.e., *Tif'eret,* that central rung linking the "two others": *Binah* above and *Malkhut* below. Also see TZ 69 (99a):

> The Central Column is the link between Mother and Daughter, as in הוה [HWH] of the Divine Name.

This is an apt image, for the column-shaped *Waw*—symbol of *Tif'eret*—is located between the two *He*"s (kabbalistically, *Binah* and *Malkhut*) in the Tetragrammaton, while grammatically, the *Waw* is a copulative!

466. Here the TY breaks off abruptly, omitting a passage that does much to clarify the TZ. The TZ proceeds to correlate the three Services with the three aspects of the extra-soul received on Shabbat:

> These [three] correspond to the additional *neshamah,* the additional *ruaḥ,* and the additional *nefesh.*

This tripartite division of the Sabbath-soul is peculiar to the TZ and RM. *Neshamah yeterah* originates from and hence, denotes *Binah,* whereas *ruaḥ yeterah* represents *Tif'eret,* and *nefesh yeterah, Malkhut.* See SCK: 126. The omitted TZ passage continues:

> [*Nefesh yeterah*] corresponds to the Sabbath eve and the prayer "You sanctified."

At this point, ibn Gabbai resumes his quotation.

467. In other words, the TZ suggests that the climax of Shabbat is reached during the Morning service:

**MORNING: *Binah/ Neshamah Yeterah*

**AFTERNOON: *Tif'eret/Ruaḥ Yeterah*

**EVENING: *Malkhut/ Nefesh Yeterah*

The TZ is here following the sefirotic order of the three Festive Meals as presented in *Zohar* 2:88a: the first meal corresponding to *Malkhut,* the second to *Keter* or the upper triad, and the Third Meal to *Tif'eret.* For ibn Gabbai, however, the sefirotic climax of both the Prayers and the Meals occurs at *Minḥah.* Concerning the latter, see *Sod ha-Shabbat* p. 65 above and n514 below.

468. **"They symbolize [all] this."** Aram., *le-qivla' lon.* Warsaw ed. emends to: *la-qovel,* also connoting "correspondence."

469. R. Margaliot's ed. of TZ reads: *de-kalil kolhu ẓelotin,* "which encompasses all the *prayers.*"

470. Here the focus is on the *Musaf Qedushah,* rather than its intermediate blessing. The TZ continues:

> This crown is none other than the supernal Crown, *Keter.*
> **"Lord our God"** refers to Father and Mother.
> **"Holy, holy, holy":** to the Patriarchs.
> **"Lord of Hosts"** refers to the Covenant of Circumcision [*Yesod*] and the two Thighs of Truth [*Neẓaḥ* and *Hod,* commonly called *ẓeva'ot,* Hosts].
> **"The earth is full of His Glory"** denotes *Shekhinah.* [*Shekhinah* is the earth, now filled with the sefirotic totality or "Glory."]

In short, the *Musaf* prayer—not "You are One"—is the consummation of the Sabbath prayers in the TZ. Note that all ten *sefirot* are brought together here.

471. Here Meir ibn Gabbai abruptly returns to his discussion of the prayer "You are One," picking up where he left off prior to the TZ interpolation.

472. Ibn Gabbai interprets the phrase *Tif'eret Gedullah* both hyperliterally and mystically. *Tif'eret,* usually rendered "crown" or "ornament," here is read as a reference to the sixth *sefirah,* whereas *Gedullah* quite obviously connotes the fourth rung, *Ḥesed. 'Emet* (Truth) is another appellation for *Tif'eret.*

473. **"A Diadem of Salvation."** Heb., *ʿaṭeret yeshuʿah;* here read: "A Diadem that is saved" a reference to the redemption of *Malkhut* via *Ḥesed/ Tif'eret.*

"is perfected." Heb., *tukhlal,* ff. MS Adrianople. E.p. contains the equally plausible: *li-khlol.*

474. **"On high."** Apparently including the upper triad. A sefirotic reading of the verse can only inferred from the larger context:

"rest and holiness." *Binah* and *Ḥokhmah,* soon to be in union with:

"Your People." The seven lower *sefirot.* (On Rest connoting *Binah,* see Moses Cordovero, PR: Gate 23 "Menuḥah"; on the correlation between *Ḥokhmah* and "holiness" [*qedushah*] cf. Z 2:43b.)

475. **"the . . . oil."** Heb., *ha-shemen.* Warsaw ed. misprints: *Ka-shemen.* The prayer now proceeds to symbolize the descent of the *shefa*ᶜ the "fragrant oil," from the hidden recesses of *Keter* onto the Head, *Ḥokhmah,* and thereafter, onto the lower rungs, here called "the supernal Chariot." To these lower *sefirot,* Meir ibn Gabbai now turns his attention.

476. *Abraham* refers to *Ḥesed, Isaac to Gevurah.* Each rejoices as it receives the divine flow. On the correlation of the "Levites" with *Gevurah,* cf. n461.

477. The entire divine world is filled with vitality and attains equipoise: Blessing comes to *Tif'eret* [Jacob], and then to *Neẓah and Hod,* his "children." Finally it reaches "Truth and Faith" [*'Emet ve-'Emunah*], *Yesod and Malkhut.* The perfect union of these two, the quintessential male and female entities, indicates the perfection of the sefirotic whole.

478. Although ibn Gabbai reserves a role for *ᶜavodah le-zorekh hedyoṭ,* prayer for human needs, it can only be entertained after fulfilling *ẓorekh gavoha,* service for the sake of divinity. See the discussion in n306 above. In permitting even a secondary role for *ẓorekh hedyoṭ,* young ibn Gabbai was more moderate than in his mature period. Consider the radical view of prayer expressed in AQ 2:6:

> The faithful servant of God, the whole one who loves Him with an undying love, strives to unite His Great Name with His Glory in his every act. . . . As he does so, he must not inject so much as a trace of his own needs, be they bodily or spiritual. . . . For all these requests and needs are from the aspect of the Profane. . . . Whoever thinks of them or injects them into his prayer . . . brings the profane into the Temple Court and defiles the holy Sanctuary.

Concerning Meir ibn Gabbai's mature position, see E. Gottlieb, "Mashmaᶜutah shel ha-Tefillah ba-Qabbalah" in *Meḥqarim:* 50–55, and R. Goetschel, "Le Service Divin" in his *Meir ibn Gabbai:* 273–344.

479. Here Meir ibn Gabbai gives the prayer a second, distinctly eschatological reading. Apparently, he was inspired by Z 1:164a, cited below.

480. **"A singular People."** Heb., *goi 'eḥad.* Or more baldly: the sole People; humanity will be Jewish. Cf. *Sod ha-Shabbat* pp. 39–40 above.

Conventionally, this phrase means "a unique People." The *Zohar* source for this section, 1:164a, reads:

> At the end of days "there will be one King on high and below, and one People to serve Him, as it is written: "and who is like Your People, Israel, a singular nation on earth." [I Chr. 17:21]

481. The three verbs—*yagel, yerannen,* and *yanuḥu*—are now read in the future tense to indicate the final Redemption of earthly Israel, symbolized by the Patriarchs and their children. A sefirotic reading may also be implied here.

482. This prayer follows the reader's repetition of the *ᶜAmidah.* It consists of three verses from Psalms, all beginning with the word, *Ẓidqatekha,* "Your righteousness." In the Sefardic rite they are ordered as follows: a) 36:7, b) 71:19, and c) 119:42.

On this prayer, see B. Lewin, *'Oẓar ha-Ge'onim* (Haifa-Jerusalem, 1928–42) 2:103; SRA: 80; Tos. to Men. 30a: *Manhig:* 186–87; Ṭur OḤ: 292; *Abud.:* 179; and I.Z. Idelsohn, *Jewish Liturgy and its Development* (NY, 1960): 146.

483. The ninth century Gaon of Sura', generally called Rav Sar Shalom. According to EJ 14: 888, he has 100 extant responsa, mostly concerning prayers, benedictions and Torah-reading. This particular opinion can be found in Lewin's *'Oẓar ha-Ge'onim* secs. 315 and 317, and in the many sources cited there.

484. Analysis of the pertinent sources suggests that Sar Shalom's ruling ends here; it seems that ibn Gabbai mistakenly attributed the next two sentences to him, as well. See n485 for further discussion.

"Acknowledgement of the divine justice." Heb., *ẓidduq ha-din,* the idiomatic term for the Jewish burial service, of which this prayer is reminiscent. Cf. EJ 16: 1017–18.

On the death of Moses at Sabbath-*Minḥah:* There is a rich literature that attempts to pinpoint the hour of Moses' death, mostly by extrapolating from clues in Josh. 1:1 and 6:15. Although most classical sources hold that Moses died on the 7th of 'Adar, authorities differed as to the day of week. Sunday, Monday, Friday, and Saturday compete for this distinction. The prevalent opinion among post-Talmudic authorities is that Moses died on Shabbat afternoon. See L. Ginzberg, *Legends* 6: 167–68 for details. The *Zohar* subscribes to this position, as well. See 2: 89a and 156a–b.

485. The TY has apparently taken this quotation from *Abud.:* 179, from which it differs only incidentally. Particularly revealing is ibn Gabbai's use of the honorific *Mar* [Sar Shalom] rather than the usual *Rav.* As B. Lewin notes (Ibid., n10), this apellation is peculiar to Abudraham. Further evidence is presented in n486.

"to refrain from public study." Heb., *she-lo' li-qboᶜa midrash;* an ambiguous phrase. This translation is defended in the extended discussion below.

"for when a scholar dies . . . activity." Cf. TB MQ 22b:

> When a scholar dies his House of Study suspends activity. When the presiding judge dies all the Academies in the city do so. . . . When a *nasi'* dies all the Houses of Study suspend their activity and the assembled people enter the synagogue. Seven persons read from the Torah and thereafter, they depart . . . For neither a halakhic nor an aggadic theme should be discussed in a house of mourning.

"Our ancestors' custom . . . for us". Contrast this quotation from *Abud.* with *Manhig: 187:*

> It is customary not to study Torah. This is not strictly prohibited, though, but a custom and a way of paying tribute [to Moses].

(For a latter-day reflection of this custom, see S.Y Agnon's "A Whole Loaf," Part 4.)

Discussion. Precisely what is to be refrained from at this hour? Due to the ambiguity of the directive *she-lo' li-qboᶜa midrash* and the multiplicity of medieval interpretations, it is hard to determine what course of action ibn Gabbai is advocating.

For example, one tradition (cited in B. Lewin, *Ibid:* sec. 315) prohibits activity in the *beit ha-midrash* (as opposed to the synagogue) at this time. Others discourage sacred study in any setting. Still other traditions simply limit what may be studied or how something may be learned.

Several of the earliest—Geonic—traditions are recorded in B. Lewin. Although the passages seem confused at times, three basic approaches may be derived. The first approach, recorded in *SRA,* apparently does not limit what may be studied, but simply requires that Torah-study be conducted "in a low voice," i.e., privately.

The second approach permits the study of M. *'Avot* and *Qinyan Torah* (Ibid., Chap. 6) but not the Mosaic book par excellence, Scriptures. E.g.,

> R. Paltai said: *'Avot* yes, Scriptures, no—for Moses our teacher perished at this hour.

(A similar tradition, recorded in the later *Roqeaḥ,* allows for reading *midrashim* and legends, but presumably not Scripture.)

The third approach suggests refraining from all study at this time, and counsels one

> to sit quietly between *Minḥah* and *Maᶜariv* . . . to honor Moses our Teacher who died at this hour, and to uphold the Gemara': "When a Nasi dies, etc."

These conflicting patterns may be found in later Provençal and Spanish sources, as well. For example, the *Manhig* records the second and third customs, noting that the second predominates in "Spain, Provence, and Babylonia." Moses Maimonides (MT "Shabbat" 30:10), however, implied that the third custom is preferred. (Indeed, the dominant Spanish custom was to study *'Avot* after *Shaḥarit* rather than at *Minḥah.* See Ṭur OḤ: 292.) *Kol-Bo* goes against the grain and claims that one may study both *'Avot* and Torah in the House of Study, only that

> the *beit midrash* should open a bit later to honor the Teacher and Father of Torah who perished at this hour.

However, this interpretation appears to be an anamoly, without much halakhic influence.

In light of the piecemeal and conflicting evidence, how is one to read the TY here? What does the phrase *she-lo' li-qboᶜa midrash* mean and how should it be translated? Minimally, it would mean to refrain from public study of Scriptures (Approach #1); maximally, to refrain from any form of Torah-study (Approach #3). There is cirumstantial evidence that ibn Gabbai subscribed to a relatively maximal approach on Kabbalistic grounds (see n487 and n494).

However, when translating *she-lo' li-qboᶜa midrash* caution necessitates that one adopt a vague expression, e.g., "to refrain from public study." Such vagueness has the merit of reflecting the ambiguity of the Hebrew original, as well.

486. As previously noted, some authorities do not accept the notion that Moses died at this hour. Here ibn Gabbai appears to be offering a rejoinder to Abudraham (*Abud.*: 179-80), who wrote:

> Objections may be raised to this opinion, for apparently Moses died on Sabbath eve, as stated in *Seder ᶜOlam* [Rabba'],

the midrashic chronology mentioned in the TB and ascribed to a third century Amora'. Abudraham found other reasons for reciting "Your Righteousness" at *Minḥah*:

> (1) As an acknowledgement of divine justice (*Ẓidduq ha-Din*: here meaning, "punishment") for those sinners who will be returned to Gehinnom upon the conclusion of this Service. (Cf. *Sod ha-Shabbat* pp. 67–68, and n541.)
>
> (2) As a warning against the three evil decrees that may befall those who do not partake in the Third Meal following the Service (ff. TB Shab. 119a). Each *Ẓidduq* corresponds to a punishment.

487. Cf. *Zohar* 2:88b–89a [=MZ 2:533]; and esp. 2:156a–b:

> Moses departed from the world during the Sabbath-*Minḥah* prayers, during the "Time of Grace." At that moment there was Grace on high, but sorrow below.

This *Zohar* clearly mandates that Houses of Study be closed:

> Hence, the gates are closed on Shabbat from *Minḥah* onwards.
>
> Which gates? The gates of the House of Study, to remind us that with the death of Moses, the Faithful Shepherd, the study of Torah [temporarily] ceased. Moses' House of Study was closed then, and needless to say, all the others . . .
>
> If Moses' own Torah grieved, who would not grieve? And so, all the gates of the Houses of Study are closed at this hour, and everyone must acknowledge the Holy One's [Justice] by praising

Him, saying: "Your righteousness is like the mountains of God, etc."

488. Here ibn Gabbai continues his paraphrase of Z 2: 156a–b. Compare!

On the death of David on Sabbath afternoon, cf. TB Shab. 30a–b. The notion that Joseph, too, died at Sabbath-*Minḥah* is first recorded in the *Zohar* (Ibid.). As I suggest in my dissertation (pp. 573–75 and 579), certain Messianic considerations may have led Moshe de Leon to group these three virtuosi and assign them a common time of death. See there for fuller discussion.

"all were included in Moses." Discussion. The inclusion of David and Joseph within Moses may be related to three interwined factors:

(1) The esoteric Medieval traditions which granted Moses cosmic status as a quasi-divine figure with an all-encompassing or universal soul *(neshamah kelalit).* (See, e.g., Z 2: 47a, 191b; 3:9a; and Z 3: 223a, 260b, 279b, and 282b [all from RM]; and TZ 61 [94a], etc.) For discussion, see my dissertation (Ibid.) and Y. Liebes, "Ha-Mashiaḥ shel ha-Zohar": 87 ff. and 105–107 in *Ha-Raʿyon ha-Meshiḥi be-Yisra'el* (Jerusalem, 1982).

(2) Specific sefirotic associations that build on #1: The *Zohar* and TZ/RM correlate Moses with *Binah* and *Tif'eret,* two inclusive *sefirot.* In the TZ/RM esp., Moses often serves as the symbol of *Binah,* the supernal *neshamah kelalit.* He/It contains the full sefirotic complement, including Joseph (*Ẓaddiq/Yesod)* and David *(Malkhut).* For sources, see Z 3:223a (RM), 247a (RM), 274a (RM) and TZ 70 (138a). The inclusive nature of the divine Moses is also highlighted in the *Zohar* proper. In one famous passage, it is said that Moses embodied all ten *sefirot:*

> R. Yoḥanan said: Moses was arrayed in all ten spheres, as it is written: "He is trusted throughout My household." [Num. 12:7] (2:21b–22a [MN])

More frequently, the divine Moses is linked with the *Tif'eret,* which—like the higher *Binah*—is an inclusive *sefirah,* one subsuming the supernal Joseph and David. See n492–94 for examples. Ibn Gabbai links Moses with both *Binah* and *Tif'eret* in the ensuing passage, moving between the two referents as the sefirotic drama dictates.

(3) Specific eschatological associations made in the *Zohar,* whereby all three are seen as Messianic prototypes, with Moses the culminating or supreme Messianic figure. This will be discussed at n497, below.

489. **"Your righteousness."** Heb., *ẒiDQatekha;* here suggesting Joseph, who is called the *ẒaDdiQ.* Kabbalistically, *Joseph* connotes *Yesod* in union with *ḤaGaT,* the "supernal mountains" or "Patriarchs," above. Cf., e.g., Z 1:247b (ff. Gen. 49:26?):

> Jacob [*Tif'eret*] gave unto Joseph the praise [i.e., *shefaʿ*] of all the Patriarchs.

"the mountains are the Patriarchs." See n216 above. This gloss is supplied by ibn Gabbai. The *Zohar* source, 2:156a reads:

"For Joseph is singly comparable to the Mountains of God [*ḤaGaT*], to all the supernal mountains.

490. Although *Zohar* 2: 156a passes over this phrase without comment, ibn Gabbai amplifies: "the place where the infinite waters abide" *(she-sham ha-mayim she-'ein la-hem sof)*. Kabbalistically, this probably connotes *Binah*/ Moses, whose waters irrigate the *sefirot* below.

491. The TY continues its paraphrase of Z 2:156a. Cf. n493.

"The heights." Kabbalistically, *Binah,* the rung attained by Moses. Also see Z 2:88b–89a.

"You are the heights." Heb., *ve-'attah marom;* meaning: You, Moses, are the symbol of *Binah.*

492. **"great and wondrous things."** Heb., ff. Dt. 10:21, *ha-gedolot ve-ha-nora'ot.* Kabbalistically, they connote the Right and Left sides, esp. *Ḥesed (gedullah)* and *Gevurah (nora')* which are contained within the sefirotic Moses. Should one maintain a consistent or static reading here, Moses would denote *Binah.*

An alternate possibility, however, is to read this phrase more dynamically. If the first clause depicts Moses' ascent unto the divine heights, this one depicts his descent unto *Tif'eret,* which embraces Right and Left, including *Neẓaḥ* and *Hod.* Such an interpretation would mean that all seven lower *sefirot* are alluded to in the three verses and would dramatize Moses' inclusive nature. See the Zohar source in n493 which seems to support this reading.

493. **"everlasting."** On the eternity of David's station, see 2 Sam. 7: 16. *Ẓedeq,* King David and *'Emet* (Truth) all connote *Malkhut.* The Zoharic source for this section, 2:156a, reads:

> The second verse is directed to Moses, the faithful prophet. And so it is written, "Your righteousness, O God, reaches the heights; You have done great things." [Ps. 71:19] for [Moses] absorbs from all sides, from Right and from Left.
>
> The third verse is directed to King David, as it is written, "Your righteousness is *ẓedeq le-ᶜolam,* eternal, and Your Torah is Truth. The "Eternal" [*le-ᶜolam*] esoterically refers to David [*Malkhut*].

494. **"Written . . . Torah."** Moses is clearly aligned with *Tif'eret* here; David, of course, represents the Oral Torah, *Malkhut.*

"the houses of Study suspend their activity." The mention of both Oral and Written Torot here suggest that all formal study ceases, not just Scriptural learning. See n485.

495. In the Midrash (Ex. R 1:8) it was the generation of Joseph that warded off Exile:

> "Joseph died, and all his brothers, and all the generation." [Ex. 1:6] This verse teaches you that so long as one person who went down to Egypt was alive, the Egyptians could not subjugate Israel.

The *Zohar*, by contrast, emphasizes the protective role of Joseph, who alone is the *Ẓaddiq* who sustains Israel, i.e., *Ẓaddiq Yesod ʿOlam*, the Axis Mundi. In addition to the TY's source, Z 2: 156a, see Z 1: 180a and 193b. The former reads:

> As long as Joseph was alive, the Exile could not prevail; he warded it off. As soon as he died, the Exile began.

On the sefirotic implications of Joseph's death, see below.

496. **"When Joseph died . . . When Moses died . . . When David died."** Heb., *ke-she-met*, etc. The TY/*Zohar* echoes the formula found in the famous Mishnah "Mi-she-met" (TB *Soṭah*, end). In both cases the death of the virtuoso marked the onset of a spiritual decline.

"the sun faded." Or grew dark *(ḥashakh)*.

"[the Oral Torah] lost its normal lustre." Heb., *shavah me-'eitanah*, an idiom indicating that something has left its normal state. Cf. TB *Soṭah* 36b, s.v. "shavah le-'eitanah."

"the moon no longer caused its light to shine." Isa. 13:10 is written in the future tense, but read by the *Zohar*/TY in the past tense.

Discussion. Kabbalistically, the death of each of the three great souls creates a diminution within both the human and sefirotic realms. The human loss is both cause and emblem of the cosmic one.

The death of Joseph not only ushers in the era of earthly Exile but of divine alienation. Upon his death, *Yesod*, the "well-springs" of the supernal *Yosef* (lit., abundance) run dry, and *Shekhinah*, the Community of Israel, is deprived of nourishment. Her Exile amidst the hostile cosmic forces begins.

As Moses dies, the loss is registered within his sefirotic paradigm, *Tif'eret* and its web of symbols. The sun fades, the Written Torah loses its lustre, the luminous glass *('ispaqlaria' she-me'irah)* darkens. The cosmos has become a colder place.

When David dies, it is *Malkhut*'s diminution that is emphasized; to use the *Zohar*'s images, the Oral Torah and moon grow dim. For further discussion of this passage see the following note.

497. The Zohar source which the TY is paraphrasing, 2: 156a–b, reads:

> Thus, everything is gathered up at this time, both the Written Torah [Moses] and the Oral Torah [David]. The gates of the Torah, indeed the gates of the entire world, are closed at this time.
>
> When Joseph the *Ẓaddiq* died, the wells and springs dried up and the Tribes began their descent into Exile. The celestial beings recited the verse: "Your righteousness is like the mountains of God; your judgments like the endless Deep." When Moses died, the sun in its splendor was darkened; the Written Torah was locked up, that light of the luminous glass. When King David died, the moon gathered up its light and the Oral Torah followed suit.
>
> From that time on, the lights of the Torah have remained hidden. Divergent interpretations of the Mishnah have increased,

> Sages dispute and the great minds are fraught with confusion, so that to succeeding generations the [full] joy of Torah has been lost. . . . When a [great] man dies, the Sages proclaim a fast. Since the greatest joy of the Written and Oral *Torot* was gathered up at this hour, is it not fitting that the gates of Torah not be closed up then?
>
> For these reasons we recite the *Ẓidduqei ha-Din*, "Your Righteousness."

Discussion. There are certain undercurrents in the TY's Zohar passage that merit spelling out.

(1) The death of each virtuoso is expressed in specifically anti-eschatological imagery; that is, traditional Messianic imagery has been turned on its head. Exile supplants Redemption; the hiding of Torah replaces the Revelation of new mysteries; the sun and moon diminish, instead of reaching full empowerment. (cf. Isa. 30:26) Through these metaphors, the impact of the virtuosos' demise is heightened.

(2) It is no accident that the *Zohar* correlates these anti-eschatological images with these three figures, for they are all Messianic ciphers in the *Zohar*. If their death brings about cosmic tragedy, their future incarnation *(gilgul)* will bring about *tiqqun*, full healing.

(Messiah ben) David and (ben) Joseph are Messianic figures of long-standing and require no elaboration here. More striking is the status of Moses. The *Zohar* intimates that this "faithful shepherd," the archetype of RaSHBI (and according to Y. Liebes' skillful reading, of Moshe de Leon himself) is *the* quintessential Messianic figure. He is the one who subsumes and succeeds the two others. On Moses as the ultimate Messiah, see Z 3:260b:

> Moses is the consummation of the King Messiah. When he will be present, the world will be complete. . . .

Also see ZḤ 8d (MN):

> Why has the day of the Messiah been postponed through this [last] Exile . . . ? Israel will return from this . . . Exile through the Merit of Moses.

For other examples, see Y. Liebes, "Mashiaḥ shel ha-Zohar": 105–07.

In many ways, the recitation of *Your Righteousness* underscores the unredeemed nature of the world. It is an elegiac pause in the Sabbath-cosmos. For at this moment during the *Minḥah* service the focus is not on the Messianic dénouement, but on its postponement; on the death of three redeemers, not on their future manifestation.

498. Late afternoon, time for the third sacramental meal. Meir ibn Gabbai here broadens his discussion to include all three feasts. The three prescribed Sabbath meals (discussed in TB Shab. 117b ff.) become sacramental meals, or in the *Zohar*'s words, "meals of mystery," in which the secrets of the pneumatic world are disclosed. For previous treatment, see *Sod ha-Shabbat* Sections 11 and 15 and the corresponding notes.

499. Here ibn Gabbai is paraphrasing *Zohar* 2: 88a. Compare!

500. **"it is taught."** In *Zohar* 2:63b; see n501.

"All blessings depend on the seventh day." Kabbalistically, the seventh day is *Binah,* the Great Sabbath, who imparts blessing or "manna" to the six Days or *sefirot* below Her. In a secondary sense, the seventh day may also connote *Shekhinah,* sustainer of the angelic Days.

On the overflow of blessing into the world each Shabbat see SCK: 79–85 and 87–88. Also see A. Steinsaltz's lovely "A Note on the Kiddush Ritual" in his *Thirteen-Petalled Rose* (NY, 1980).

501. **"it is further taught."** Again in *Zohar* 2:63b. The cited passage reads:

> R. Judah said: Every day the world is blessed through that supernal Day, the seventh. For the six Days receive blessing from the Seventh, and each gives of its blessing on its appointed day. . . .

Kabbalistically, the fact that no manna was given on the seventh day symbolizes a divine mystery, intimating that *Binah,* the Sabbath's archetype, does not receive manna or divine blessing but rather, bestows it.

502. **"on the seventh [day]."** Heb., *ba-yom ha-shevi^c^i;* here ibn Gabbai returns to his close paraphrase of Z 2:88a. Compare!

503. Z 2:88a, reads: *ma'in de-'ihu be-darga' di-mheimanuta'*: whoever is on the rung of Faith; i.e., participating in the divine mysteries.

504. **"the Sabbath day as well."** To insure the unimpeded flow of blessing throughout the day. (For another mystical rationale, see *'Or ha-Ḥammah* ad loc.)

On the symbolic significance of setting the Sabbath-table, see Z 2:63b and below.

505. **"no blessing . . . empty table."** As cited in the Zohar source, 2:88a, ff. TB Ber. 40a. Also see Z 2:63b.

For the mystic, physical nourishment symbolizes and calls forth spiritual blessing. A full table represents the fullness of blessing in the sefirotic and lower worlds, while an empty table intimates its absence. On the symbolic significance of having abundant and various food on Shabbat, see *Sod ha-Shabbat* p. 33 above. On the import of preparing a festive table, see p. 54.

Discussion. The pleroma of weekly blessing contained in the Sabbath and its sefirotic counterpart, *Binah,* is prepared during these Sacred Meals. Participation in the festivities simultaneously brings down the *shefa^c^* to the lower rungs and provides the means whereby Israel may be sustained during the six days of the week. To forgo a Sabbath meal, in short, is to risk spiritual "malnutrition."

506. **"supernal dew and great Light."** referring to the divine energy emanating from *Keter* (the Holy One). It fills the entire shimmering pleroma,

down to *Shekhinah*, the "Field of Apples." *Dew* and *light* evoke images of fertilization, illumination, vivification. See the discussion in SCK: 81–82.

On *Shekhinah* as the fragrant Field of Apples, cf. TB *Taᶜanit* 29a and G. Scholem's comments in *On the Kabbalah and its Symbolism:* 140:

> In this metaphor the field is the feminine principle of the cosmos, while the apple trees define *Shekhinah* as the expression of all the other *sefirot*, which flow into Her and exert their influence through Her.

"thrice each Sabbath." Each meal, in other words, is a symbol of and mysterious link to the drama of Shabbat. The meals correspond to the "three rungs of Faith" (Z 2:204)—i.e., to the three *sefirot* of the Middle Column: *Keter, Tif'eret,* and *Malkhut*—a kind of shorthand for the sefirotic totality. Each meal highlights a different sefirotic aspect, and has its unique mood. See n508–14 below.

The Zohar source for the TY, 2:88a, reads:

> On this day, the Small Face is filled with the dew which descends from the Holy Ancient One, the Most Hidden. He brings it into the Field of Holy Apples thrice each Shabbat, so that all may be blessed as one.

The *'Or ha-Ḥammah* ad loc. adds:

> The Table is set thrice to correspond to the three kinds of blessing which well up from three supernal sources . . . Three times these sources well up and flow into each other . . . so that all is blessed as one. . . . The festive table becomes a vessel in which to receive this blessing and the rest of the days are nourished by this overflow of Sabbath bounty.

Zohar 2: 61b depicts this flow of blessing occuring on a reduced scale during the week. For further discussion on the descent of blessing during the sacramental meals, see I. Tishby's remarks in MZ 2:503.

"the King's feasts." Again alluding to the Zohar source (2:88a), which reads:

> Prepare the meal of perfect faith
> To rejoice the heart of the Holy King
> Prepare the meal of the King. . . .

In the Lurianic ritual this invocation opened all three Sacred Meals.

507. **"[symbolic] structure."** Heb., *seder;* "order." Here ibn Gabbai attempts to sort out two of the several *sedarim* mentioned in the *Zohar;* he first considers 2:88a and thereafter, 3: 288b (IZ). For a third interpretation see 2: 88a–b and n514 below.

508. **"daytime feast."** Heb., *seᶜudat ha-boqer;* i.e., the late morning or noon repast.

"above the Lord." Heb., *ᶜal YHWH.* Conventionally rendered: in the Lord. It seems that the *Zohar* is, at once, reading the phrase hyperliterally—*above* YHWH—and sefirotically, to allude to *Keter*, the "Ancient of Days," who is "above YHWH," i.e., the array stretching from *Ḥokhmah* to *Malkhut*. See n509 and *'Or ha-Ḥammah* to Z 2:88b.

509. Here Meir ibn Gabbai has compressed the discussion in the *Zohar*. It reads:

> R. Shimon said: Whenever one completes the three festive meals on the Sabbath, a voice proclaims: "Then shall you delight yourself in the Lord." This signifies one meal, corresponding to the Ancient, most Holy One [*Keter*]. "I will cause you to ride upon the high places of the earth." This denotes a second meal, corresponding to the Field of Holy Apples [*Malkhut*]. "And I will feed you with the heritage of Jacob." [Isa. 58:14] This signifies completeness, for the cycle is completed with a reference to the Small Face [*Tif'eret*/Jacob].
>
> Accordingly, one should complete the cycle of feasts, delighting and rejoicing in each meal, for together they constitute the Complete Faith [the sefirotic totality]. . . .
>
> R. Eleazar asked his father: "How are these festive meals ordered?" He replied: "Of the nighttime feast it is written: 'I will cause you to ride upon the high places of the earth.' On this night the *Maṭronita'* and the whole Field of Holy Apples are blessed [uniting with *Tif'eret*]. Correspondingly, a person's table is blessed and he is granted an additional soul. This night is the time of the *Maṭronita*'s joy. One must participate in Her joy and partake in Her meal.
>
> Concerning the second meal, on the Sabbath day, it is written: "Then shall you delight yourself *ᶜal YHWH*": above the Lord, exactly! For at this hour the Holy Ancient One is disclosed and all the worlds rejoice and are complete. We contribute to this joy, partaking in His meal.
>
> Concerning the Third Meal it is written: "I will feed you with the heritage of Jacob." This is the meal of the Small Face [the array of the eight middle *sefirot* with *Tif'eret* at its center] which is now in complete harmony. From this perfection, the six days of the week are blessed. One must rejoice at His meal and so complete the cycle of meals, for they are the Perfect Faith of the holy seed of Israel.

On the third meal connoting completeness also see Z 3: 273a (RM):

> The three meals complement and complete the seven blessings of the Sabbath *ᶜAmidah*, bringing the number of blessings to ten, the full sefirotic array.

510. **"in another fashion."** In the IZ (3: 288b) which ibn Gabbai quotes in the Aramaic. As I. Tishby has noted, "these contradictory accounts attest that the author of the *Zohar* never reached a definitive position on this matter."

511. **"I never neglected."** Cf. R. Shimon's speech in Z 3:95a (n524, below).

512. **"I had no need to fast on Shabbat."** R. Margaliot (*Nizozei Zohar* to 3:288b, n10) suggests that the meals may have served as an antidote to "troubling dreams." See below for a refinement.

"I had no need to do so on weekdays." It is likely that never having to fast means that R. Shimon bar Yohai never had a nocturnal emission *(qeri)*. On R. Shimon's singular qualities, also see *Zohar* 2:15a:

> R. Shimon ben Gamliel . . . said: "R. Shimon bar Yohai is indeed a lion. . . . He is different from all the others. . . . a man who has never to fast when beseeching God, since he decides and the Holy One confirms his decision. . . ."

513. Kabbalistically, the sefirotic totality.

514. **"Central Column."** Heb., *qav ha-'emza'i*. A reference to *Tif'eret*.

"at Minhah." On the revelation of *Keter* during *Minhah*, see p. 61 above.

"This order is the better one . . ., etc." Meir ibn Gabbai uses a kabbalistic rationale to resolve the contradictory orders within the *Zohar*. In his schema, the consecutive meals point to ever-higher mysteries, moving from the divine All *(Shekhinah)* to the divine Nothing (*Keter*; cf. Bahyya ben Asher, *Shulhan shel 'Arba'*, in *Kitvei Rabbenu Bahyya ben 'Asher*: 482.)

Discussion. Prior to the rise of Lurianic Kabbalah, no consensus was reached regarding the proper symbolic order of the meals. As noted, Moshe de Leon listed no fewer than three orders in the *Zohar*. In addition to the two already cited, see Z 2:88a–b where R. Hamnuna Sava (another version: R. Abba) implies that the meals point to ever more fully realized (progressively immanent) blessing: beginning with *Keter*, then proceeding to *Tif'eret*, etc. A variant on this third order is found in *Sefer ha-Yihud* (JTSA MS 1737; from the circle of Joseph of Hamadan) where blessing descends from *Hokhmah*, the recondite Source, to *Binah*, the Edenic river, and finally, at the third meal unto *Shekhinah*, the Garden. A fifth order is recorded in the OZ (53a/68a) of David b. Judah he-Hasid:

> The evening meal corresponds to the Diadem [*Malkhut*] which holds sway at night; the second meal corresponds to *Hesed* which is sovereign during the day; and the Third Meal corresponds to *Gevurah* which holds sway at twilight.

Finally, the anonymous author of MS Paris Hebr. 596 (fifteenth century, Italy) reports a Nahmanidean tradition that correlated the three meals with *Malkhut*, *Tif'eret* and *Yesod*, respectively. However, the most common pattern was probably the one accepted by Meir ibn Gabbai (i.e., IZ 3:288b). This order was employed by Joseph Giqatilia (*Sha'arei 'Orah* 1:113 and with a slight variation in *Sodot* sec. 4); Menahem Recanati (ad Gen. 2:10); R. Bahyya ben Asher, ad loc., and in *Shulhan shel 'Arba'*: 482; the *Qanah* 66a–b; Judah Hayyat (*Minhat Yehudah* 73b); and R. Moshe ben Jacob of Kiev, *Shoshan Sodot* 79a.

It was only in the later sixteenth century that the tables were turned, so to speak: the Zoharic order (2:88a) rejected by ibn Gabbai became dominant, and soon thereafter, universally accepted. See Isaiah Horowitz's SHeLaH, "Massekhet Shabbat" for a pointed example.

515. By restricting the Third Meal to the late afternoon, ibn Gabbai is providing a *kabbalistic* rationale for a firmly rooted Sefardic tradition. See, e.g., *Manhig*: 179–80, Ṭur OḤ 291, and esp. *Abud.*: 181–82, whose language ibn Gabbai seems to be echoing here and throughout this section. Also see Baḥyya ben Asher, *Shulḥan*: 483 and OZ for kabbalistically inclined rationales.

"as some do." *Manhig* indicates that although the Spanish and Provencal Jews make the Third Meal at *Minḥah* only, the French custom is to eat it in the morning, immediately after the second meal. He added:

> The French custom . . . simply is not viable. It is as if they divide the Sabbath morning meal into two.

The French custom is generally attributed to R. Tam and is recorded in many Ashkenazic sources. Cf. e.g., *Sefer ha-Yashar* (Rozenthal ed., secs. 69 and 70) and *Shibbolei ha-Leqeṭ* sec. 93 (Mirsky ed.: 329). Various rationales are given for this custom. The kabbalistic OZ (Ibid.) rejects the Ashkenazic custom for mystical reasons but not unsympathetically adds:

> In Ashkenaz and France they divide the meal into two in the winter because the days are short and because they leave the synagogues near noon [i.e., late!]. However, they do not follow this custom in the summertime.

However, less pragmatic reasons are more commonly found for eating the third meal before *Minḥah*. They seem to be relatively late, i.e., cited to explain an already existing custom:

(1) *Kol Bo* ("Hilkhot Minḥah") reports that many do not eat after *Minḥah* to honor Moses who "died in the late afternoon."

(2) More widely cited is a prohibition against eating after *Minḥah* because such an activity "steals from the nourishment of the dead" who, according to legend, eat at twilight. See R'oSH to TB Pes. 105a; Tos. ad loc.; the *Sefer Mordechai* (late thirteenth century, Ashk.), and R. Baḥyya ben Asher to Ex. 20: 8. (For an explanation of this practice, see J. Trachtenberg, *Jewish Magic:* 67–68 and now I. Ta-Shma, "Be'erah shel Miriam—Gilgulei Minhag Ẓarfat bi-Sᶜudah Shelishit shel Shabbat," *Meḥqerei Yerushalayim be-Maḥshevet Yisra'el* 4 [1985]: 251–70.)

By the late Middle Ages, the Third Meal was firmly associated with the waning hours of Shabbat in most Ashkenazic communities. It would be worthwhile assessing the impact that the spread of Kabbalah might have had on this development.

516. The somewhat convoluted Hebrew reads: *ve-'ein ka'n hakkira' bi-sᶜudat shabbat she-naᶜaseit la-ḥaẓa'in, ve-lo' bi-sᶜudah shelishit*, etc. The *Abud.* text (181) on which ibn Gabbai seems to have relied is clearer: *she-ᶜosin*

se'udat shabbat la-ḥaẓa'in ve-'ein ka'n hakkira' ba-se'udah ha-shelishit, ki zeman ha-se'udah hi' be-minḥah. In translation:

> For they divide a Sabbath meal into two. This in no way affords honor *to the Third Meal* [emph. mine], for the Third Meal should take place in the late afternoon.

Also see Baḥyya ben Asher (*Shulḥan shel 'Arba'*: Ibid.):

> Such a division affords no honor to the splendid and sublime [*ha-nifla'ah ha-'elyonah*] Third Meal, which should take place in the late afternoon.

517. This proof is supplied in the aforementioned *Manhig*, Baḥyya ben Asher and *Abud.* sources, as well.

518. Generally, the ritual burning of the last leaven *(bi'ur ḥameẓ)* is to be done by 10 a.m. on the day before Passover. When Pesaḥ begins on a Saturday night, however, the burning must take place on Friday, and sufficient food is to be reserved for the first two Sabbath meals.

In this passage the Third Meal is assumed to take place in the afternoon, i.e., after "the fourth hour."

519. This ruling is cited in many Medieval sources, among them: the *Manhig;* Baḥyya; and *Abud.* which Meir ibn Gabbai seems to have quoted verbatim. Compare!

On the discrepancy between the fourth hour (approx. 10 a.m.) and the "sixth hour" (approx. noon), see the *Manhig*'s solution. After citing the TB passage, he glossed:

> There is no reason to leave [leavened] food for the third meal at *Minḥah*. For the prohibition against leaven is already stated in the Torah [ff. Ex. 12:15!], effective from the sixth hour on, and according to the Rabbis, from the fourth hour.

Like *Abud.* and the *Zohar* (cf. n524), ibn Gabbai accepted the later hour; this serves to emphasize that the Third Meal must take place after noon.

520. Ibn Gabbai now turns to the problem of the Third Meal on the eve of Pesaḥ. On the one hand, no leavened food is permitted in the afternoon and on the other, one is enjoined not to partake of *maẓẓah* until the Seder (see RaSHI to TB Pes. 13a, et al.). One possible solution—eating the Meal before noon—is impossible on Kabbalistic grounds, as is the option of forgoing the Third Meal this one time (see n524). A third option, the Ashkenazic custom of eating fruit or fish for *se'udah shelishit,* is unacceptable in Sefardic circles. (See See BḤ to Ṭur OH 444 and ReMA' to ShA OH 444; also, n524 below.) Hence, the TY's dilemma: How to fulfill the miẓvah of the Third Meal (so crucial for mystical reasons) while upholding the dietary restrictions of the hour. For fuller discussion of the halakhic issues, see M. Kasher and Sh. Ashkenazi, eds., *Haggadah Shelemah* (Jerusalem, 1967): 179–96.

521. One solution to the dilemma is to eat enriched maẓẓah *(leḥem 'ashirah),* for it is neither unleavened nor, strictly speaking, maẓẓah *(leḥem 'oni),* which cannot be eaten before the *Seder.* See n522 for clarification.

"Whoever eats . . . father-in-law's house." That is, he is jumping the gun! Cf. RaSHI ad loc:

> One should not eat mazzah before the Seder in order to eat it with great appetite.

In this passage the TY is again following *Abud.*: 181. Also see the aforementioned Bahyya ben Asher and Tur OH citations. By contrast, some communities prohibited use of enriched mazzah before Pesah. See ReMa' to ShA OH 444.

522. According to TB Pes. 36a only *lehem ʿoni* fulfills the mizvah of eating mazzah on the first night. Also see Tur OH 462. However, as noted above, it must not be eaten before the Seder.

523. Ff. *Zohar* 3:94b–95a, quoted in n524.

Discussion. Under these extraordinary circumstances, the mizvah of the third Meal can be fulfilled by mystical study and contemplation, so long as it is done at a properly set table. If R. Tam has provided an exoteric solution to the problem, the *Zohar* has provided a recondite one. The feast has become a purely spiritual meal, a mystery feast without food—truly a meal directed towards the *Keter*, the divine Nothing.

On the mystical import of setting the Sabbath table, as distinct from the act of eating, see *'Or ha-Hammah* to 2: 88b. Also cf. TB Shab. 119b:

> R. Hanina said: one should always set his table on the termination of Shabbat even though he need eat only an olive's bulk.

On the choice of *maʿaseh merkavah*, "the Construction of the Chariot," as the object of contemplation, see below.

524. Ibn Gabbai speaks of this spiritual banquet in circumspect fashion.

Discussion. In Z 3: 94b–95a, Moshe de Leon grappled with the question of whether one should forgo the third Sabbath meal and blemish the Sabbath, or eat the Third Meal and detract from the festive meal on Saturday night. (Consideration is not limited to Passover here.) Both options are carefully weighed by the Comrades. Then R. Shimon bar Yohai responds: if the first day of a festival occurs on Shabbat, one may forgo the Third Meal for the sake of the second night of a festival. (Note that the Diaspora observance is being discussed—an historical anachronism, betraying the *Zohar*'s medieval Spanish origin!) But if the holiday begins on Saturday night, one must partake in the third meal, even if this detracts from the festival.

R. Shimon then adresses the specific dilemmas of the first night of Passover:

> One might think that the case of a Sabbath immediately preceding Pesah is different and that the Third Meal, the Meal of the King [*Tif'eret*] should be waived for [two] reasons:
>
> (1) because of the mizvah of mazzah and *maror*, which one must eat with hunger (cf. n521), and
>
> (2) because of the prohibition of leaven; for one may not eat bread after the sixth hour, and a repast [lit., set table] without bread does not constitute a meal. . . .

Although it is halakhically permissible to waive the Third Meal, he elects not to do so for *mystical reasons:*

> However, all my days I have endeavored to avoid forgoing the Third Meal, even on those *Shabbatot* which coincided with a festival. For on the Sabbath day, the field of holy Apples is blessed [fertilized] and the upper and lower worlds are vitalized; the Torah [*Malkhut*, the Oral Torah and *Tif'eret* the written Torah] is bound into one.
>
> R. Abba said: This is what R. Shimon used to do. When the time to partake in the Third Meal arrived, he would arrange the table and contemplate the Construction of the Chariot. He would proclaim: "This is the Banquet of the King who is coming to eat with me." For the Sabbath is, in every way, more important than the other holidays and seasons.

N.B. Although ibn Gabbai interprets this last passage as referring to the eve of Passover only, the *Zohar* seems to be referring to any conflict between Shabbat and a festival! Although ibn Gabbai made clear that RaSHBI did not eat at the Meal preceding Pesaḥ, the *Zohar* only implies this.

Perhaps the most intriguing—and ambiguous—reference in the passage is to the contemplation of Chariot. Generally, this connotes mystical meditation on the inner workings of divinity. One can only infer its specific meaning here, for, as Meir ibn Gabbai noted, this ritual is "a *veiled* mystery." The wording seems to suggest an ascent of the adept to the sefirotic realm, or viewed from another perspective, the descent of the King [*Tif'eret;* for ibn Gabbai: *Keter*] to the realm of the devotee:

> R. Shimon . . . would contemplate the Construction of the Chariot and proclaim: "This is the Banquet of the King who is *coming to eat with me.*" [emph. mine]

This experience seems to be one of mystical communion whereby person and God meet. Sefirotically, the descent of the King unto *Malkhut*, the Field of Holy Apples is symbolized by the presence of God at the festive Table, here a metonym for the divine Female. (For an example of this metonymy, see Z 2:88b cited in n509 above.)

The *'Or ha-Ḥammah* to this *Zohar* (3:94b–95a) more simply suggests that Torah study, in general is mandated here. Contemplation of the Chariot is only one such example.

> Without a Third Meal, the Sabbath, in the final account, is incomplete [*ḥaser ha-shelemut*]. . . . One can fulfill it through Torah learning. As R. Shimon says: "I can complete it through *divrei Torah.*" . . . even through contemplation of *maaseh merkavah*, which surely attests to the divine unity . . .

According to Abraham Azulai, Torah study is an appropriate substitute because during the Third Meal "the Holy Apple Orchard is encompassed within *Tif'eret.*" Torah study, like the sacramental meal, effects this very union:

> R. Shimon says: I would complete the Sabbath through words of Torah. I would prepare a banquet with it, for through such activity

> . . . the Torah which is *Tif'eret* is bound to the Oral Torah which is *Malkhut,* and all becomes one, even unto *Ḥokhmah.* Through Torah-study, the Meal is completed, what would otherwise be impossible.

On the sacramental value of Torah learning, also see *Sod ha-Shabbat,* Section 18, above.

525. Cf. Z 3: 273a (RM) (also cited in n387):

> May my lot be with those who complete three meals on the Sabbath. . . . The mystery of Sabbath-delight [*ʿoNeG*] is "A River went forth from Eden to water the Garden." [Gen. 2:10]

In the TY here, the Garden corresponds to *Keter* or more generally, the upper triad.

On *ʿoNeG* as a mystical acronym, see also Joseph Giqatilia, *Shaʿarei 'Orah* 1:45 and Baḥyya ben Asher to Ex. 20:8.

526. The adept's spiritual ascent from *Malkhut* to *Keter* may be seen as a paradisical journey: moving upstream from the lush garden into celestial Eden itself.

527. **"To add . . . profane."** Heb., *le-hosif me-ḥol ʿal ha-qodesh:* idom indicating the prolonging of a holiday, whether by beginning it early or by extending it into a portion of the next day. On beginning Sabbath early, see *Sod ha-Shabbat,* Section 7. On prolonging the Sabbath on Saturday night, see *Manhig:* 198; *Shibbolei ha-Leqeṭ:* 429–30; Ṭur OḤ 293; and *Abud.:* 182.

On the symmetrical nature of extending Shabbat, both before and after, see n67 above. Also see the opinion of Jacob ben Asher, cited in SHeLaH "Massekhet Shabbat":

> Why is it written both *shabbat shabbaton* [Ex. 31:15] and *shabbaton shabbat* [Ex. 16:23]? To show that there should be a *shabbaton,* a surplus of Shabbat, before the Sabbath must officially begin, and a *shabbaton* after the Sabbath may be ended.

528. Meir ibn Gabbai's Zoharic source for this paragraph, 2:207a, ends here. It reads:

> When the Sabbath is about to depart, Israel below must prolong it, for it is a great and exalted day. On it, a great and much beloved Guest visits us. So we must detain Her, making every effort to prevent Her premature departure.

529. A paraphrase of Gen. 31:27: "I would have sent you off with joyous song." The TY here recalls the *Shibbolei ha-Leqeṭ* passage cited above. Also see BY to Ṭur OḤ 300.

530. This midrash was first recorded in the *Manhig:* 198 and was widely cited thereafter. The halakhic work, *'Or Zaruʿa* (early thirteenth century) 2:95, cited it in the name of R. Tam "who found this midrash in the

'Aggadah." As I. Rafael noted (*Manhig* ad loc.) "this midrash does not appear to be extant." On ibn Gabbai's source, see n532.

531. **"already alluded."** See p. 23 above.

"High mystery." E.p. reads: *maᶜalat sod,* indicating a sublime mystery. This reading seems preferrable to *maᶜalah sod,* the version found in the MSS.

532. TB Shab. 119a. Here Meir ibn Gabbai has been paraphrasing *Abud:* 182. Compare!

> On Saturday night, before the evening prayer, it is customary to chant verses from psalms. The reason is given in the Midrash: "It [The Sabbath] may be compared to a Bride or Queen who is escorted with song and words of praise." The Sabbath is the Queen [one version adds: and Bride], as is stated in the chapter "All Sacred Writings" [TB Shab. 119a]: "Come let us go forth to greet the Sabbath Queen . . . Come O Bride, come O Bride!" So we escort the Sabbath in purity, with songs and words of praise.

533. **"Genesis Rabbah."** This midrash is not found in any extant collections. It was first cited as an anonymous tradition in *Viṭri:* 591 and was discussed as an Aggadah in Tos. to Ket. 7b. For details of its medieval transmission, see my thesis: p. 590 n534.

"a new guest has arrived." Lit., a new face—*panim ḥadashot.* This idiom is used in TB Ket. 7b (end) wherein R. Judah maintains that *panim ḥadashot,* i.e., a new guest, must be present each night in order to recite the special nuptial blessings during the week following a wedding. *Tosafot* (ad loc.) cites the missing *Genesis Rabbah* passage, and claims that the Sabbath constitutes a new guest. For further discussion of this phrase see Sh. Lieberman, *Tosefta' ki-Fshuṭa',* "Megillah": 1184.

534. MS Adrianople varies slightly: *ke-she-hakhnasat[!] shabbat she-ba'ah kallah me-ḥadash.*

Again ibn Gabbai's reliance on *Abud.* Ibid. is evident. Compare!

535. Cf. *Shibbolei ha-Leqeṭ* 429–30: "Just as one accompanies a king when he arrives, so one accompanies him as he departs."

536. **"Havdalah."** The ritual distinguishing the holy Sabbath from the profane week. The reference here is to the private *Havdalah,* included in the fourth blessing of the *ᶜAmidah.* For discussion see TB Ber. 33a; Pes 103b–04a; Ṭur OḤ 294, and I. Z. Idelsohn's synopsis in *Jewish Liturgy:* 148.

537. In ibn Gabbai's discussion of the public *Havdalah,* the so-called "*Havdalah* over wine," which follows the evening service. See there.

538. Significant portions of this final section of *Sod ha-Shabbat* have been analyzed in SCK: Chap. 4. I shall therefore focus on new information here.

539. "May the Pleasantness" was briefly discussed in the Morning Service, p. 37 above. Here it connotes not only Ps. 90:17 but the series of prayers preceding the public *Havdalah*. See I. Rafael's comments to *Manhig*: 192, line 24.

540. **"As we have explained"** See pp. 26–27 and 30 above.

"For Shabbat protects the cosmos." See p. 27 and n112 above. For discussion see SCK: 131, 182–83 n282, and 242–43.

541. Here Meir ibn Gabbai is probably following 2: 207a:

> When Israel breaks forth into "May the Lord's Pleasantness" . . . all the wicked in Gehinnom break forth into a chorus. . . . At this moment Dumah [see n107] comes forward and a herald proclaims: "Return, O wicked unto She'ol, all peoples who forget God!"[Ps. 9:18]

Also see Z 1:14b, 17b, 48a, 237b; 2:207a; TZ 6 (24a), and many others.

The notion that an angel summons the wicked back to Hell on Saturday night is midrashic. It is alluded to in Gen. R 11:5 and explicitly stated in Tanḥ. "Tissa" sec. 33:

> During the week, we [sinners in Gehinnom, who profaned the Sabbath] are punished, but on Sabbath we rest until the [final] prayers are concluded. Thereupon the presiding angel, Dumah, arrives . . . and casts our souls back to the [nether] world, as it is written, "A land whose light is darkness, the shadow of death and disarray [*lo' sedarim*]." [Job 10:22] What is meant by "the shadow of death"? Go back to the place of Death for *lo' sedarim*, there are no more prayers; the service has been concluded!

Other midrashic recastings are found in *Pesiqta' Rabbati* 23:3, YS Job sec. 906 and in *Mid. 'Aseret ha-Dibberot* sec. 4 (A. Jellinek, *Beit ha-Midrash* I: 74). This unhappy return is first associated with "May the Pleasantness"in SRA (Goldschmidt ed.: 81) and thereafter, in *Viṭri* sec. 147 and *Manhig:* 189:

> On Sabbath eve, the angel Dumah (who presides over the demons) proclaims: "Go forth sinners, and leave Gehinnom and rest, as Israel does each Sabbath." As Sabbath departs he proclaims: "Return, O sinners, unto Gehinnom, for Israel has concluded its prayers." This refers to the recitation of "May the Pleasantness" on Saturday night . . .

542. Kabbalistically, *Noʿam* is the divine energy radiating from *Naʿomi/YHWH (Binah).* See p. 37 and n206 above.

"Pleasing [radiance]." Heb., *sod noʿam ʿelyon:* literally, "the mystery of the supernal Pleasantness." As Moses Cordovero noted (PR: Gate 23), *Noʿam* is generally imaged in terms of light. Accordingly, one might translate Ps. 90:17: "May the Lord's pleasing radiance shine on us."

543. **"delivers us."** "On the protective qualities of this verse, see SCK: 257–58. For Zoharic parallels see Z 1:17b and esp. 1:97b:

> This Pleasantness issues from the World-that-is-Coming [*Binah*], from which all light streams forth, radiating in every direction. That beneficent light which our patriarchs [sefirotically, the middle triad] inherited is the light of the World-that-is-Coming, that light called *No^cam*, Pleasantness.
>
> Another interpretation: The World-that-is-Coming itself is called Pleasantness because as it is quickened, all joy and goodness, light and freedom are bestirred . . .
>
> Thus we learn that when the Sabbath arrives the wicked in Gehinnom gain respite, enjoying comfort and ease. But when the Sabbath departs, we must beckon the supernal Joy unto us, and be delivered from the punishment that the wicked undergo from that hour forward. We do this by reciting "May the Lord's Pleasantness [shine] on us," referring to that Pleasant Radiance which brings us pervasive joy.

544. **"Gaze upon . . . Sanctuary."** Lit., "To gaze upon . . . and to frequent." Meir ibn Gabbai read the verse as if there were a causal connection between its two phrases. Recitation of this prayer enables one to remain amidst the divine mysteries. On beholding *Noᶜam*, also see Z 3:171b ("Rav Metivta' "):

> In every cosmic cycle, a herald gathers the inhabitants of the Garden of Eden, the men and women, all those children of the Faith . . . and brings them to the Yeshiva of the Firmament [Meṭaṭron's Yeshiva]. . . . All enter inside, passing through hidden veils and secret chambers which shimmer with the Pleasant Aura [*Noᶜam*] of YHWH. They come into the Palace [*heikal*] of YHWH's Love. Thus, it is said: "To gaze upon YHWH's Pleasantness and to frequent His sanctuary [*heikhalo*]." [Ps. 27:4]

545. The apotropaic Ps. 91 is recited immediately after "May the Pleasantness." The name "Song against demons" (*shir shel pegaᶜim*) is first recorded in TJ ᶜEruv. 26c and TB Shev. 15b. On the magical import of this psalm, see also G. Scholem, "Havdalah de-Rabbi Aqiva," *Tarbiẓ* 50 (1982): 248 and 251.

546. Heb., *ḥuẓ la-yishuv*. The Zoharic source for this passage (1:14b) has it *le-gow midbera'*: into the wilderness, i.e., the realm of *Siṭra' 'Aḥra'*. The source reads:

> When the Sabbath enters, holiness reigns over the cosmos. *Siṭra' 'Aḥra'* is weakened and goes into hiding for the rest of Sabbath. . . . When the Sabbath departs, innumerable bands of [evil spirits] roam the world. The recitation of the Song against *pegaᶜim* was instituted to ward them off, lest Israel come under their control. Where do these spirits roam on Saturday night? They set out hastily, intending to gain rule over the holy People. But when they see [Israel] immersed in prayer, reciting this Song and making *Havdalah*,

> first in the *Tefillah* and again over the wine, these spirits flee. They wander to and fro till they reach the wilderness. May the Compassionate One deliver us from their ilk and from the Evil Side!

Also see 1:17b.

547. On the *Seder Qedushah* (also *Qedushah de-Sidra'*) see pp. 60–61 and n444–48 above.

548. **"Completes . . . the prayers."** Rabbinic idiom, *mashlimin sidreihem. Sidreihem* here refers to "May the Pleasantness," "You are Holy," etc. See its usage in n541 above.

The Zoharic source for this section, as in n541, is 2: 207a. Compare with the TY!

549. **"May the Pleasantness."** Meaning the entire *seder* or series of prayers preceding *Havdalah*. See n539.

> On reciting these prayers slowly, cf. p. 66 above. Also cf. *Abud.*: 184: It is customary to chant "May the Pleasantness" in a melodious voice and at a measured pace, in order to lengthen the respite of the wicked; for their return to Gehinnom is delayed till the prayers are completed.

550. Here Meir ibn Gabbai is paraphrasing *Zohar* 1:14b. See the end of n551 for the text.

"such an act causes the flames of Hell to be kindled prematurely." Here the Kabbalistic tradition is drawing on two Aggadic notions:

(1) that the fires of Hell abate on Sabbath (TB Sanh. 65b and RaSHI, ad loc.) and

(2) that the wicked return to Hell as soon as Sabbath ends.

By kindling a fire, one profanes or ends the Sabbath, and causes corresponding action on high: the rekindling of Gehinnom's Profane Fire and the premature return of the wicked. Lest this occur, the *Havdalah* flame must be lit well after sunset. (See Ṭur OḤ 293, 299 for halakhic details.)

For further discussion see my dissertation: 594 and now, I. Ta-Shma, "Be'erah shel Miriam" (cited in n515): 251–76.

551. **"blessings recited."** A reference to the series of Biblical verses which immediately precede the *Havdalah*. These verses were included to confer blessings upon the congregation as they left the sanctity of the Sabbath and entered a new week. See *Viṭri* sec. 201; *Manhig*: 200; Ṭur OḤ 295 and *Zohar* 1:14b below.

"Blessed . . . comings and . . . goings." For Meir ibn Gabbai perhaps an allusion to the protection conferred by the Sabbath as one goes out into the profane—and dangerous—week. Cf. *Zohar* 2:137b:

> When the Sabbath departs a herald proclaims . . . "Return, O wicked, to She'ol!" Come and see. God protects the souls of the righteous, delivering them from the clutches of Dumah . . . for it is written: "the Lord will guard your coming and your going, now

> and forever" [Ps. 121:8]; "the Lord will guard your very being." [Ibid.:7]

The primary Zoharic source for this section of TY is 1:14b. It reads:

> Our Rabbis of blessed memory said: Three sorts of people bring evil upon themselves. He who curses himself; he who throws away a loaf of bread or even crumbs amounting to an olive's bulk; and he who lights his candle on Saturday night before Israel has recited the *Qedushah* of the Biblical Portion.
>
> For he causes the flames of Gehinnom to be kindled prematurely. There is a place in Gehinnom assigned to those who profane the Sabbath. They . . . curse the one who prematurely lit the candle, saying "The Lord is about to shake you severely, fellow! Indeed, He will wind you about Him as a headdress, a turban. Off to a broad land [here, a euphemism for Gehinnom]!"[Isa. 22:17–18] For it is not fitting to light a candle on Saturday night until Israel makes *Havdalah* in the *Tefillah*. [Only] then may one recite the *Havdalah* over the wine for until that [last] moment it is still Shabbat; its holiness is sovereign. But when the *Havdalah* is pronounced over the wine all the armies and camps which have charge over the weekdays return to their stations and to their appointed tasks . . .

The *Zohar* then clarifies that the armies actually return to their station at the private *Havdalah*, but do not resume dominion till the candlelighting. By lighting the candles early one causes an improper, ill-timed changing of the Cosmic Guards. (See SCK: 259–60, 268 and 278 n8). The *Zohar* continues:

> All the aforementioned cursing occurs only if one lights a candle prematurely, before completing the final *Qedushah*. But when one waits until it is completed, the wicked in Gehinnom acknowledge the justice of the Holy One. They confirm for that person all the blessings recited by the congregation: "May God give you of the dew of heaven." [Gen. 27:28] "Blessed shall you be in the city and blessed shall you be in the country." [Dt. 28:3] "Happy is he who is considerate of the wretched [i.e., in Gehinnom]; in bad times may the Lord keep him from harm." [Ps. 41:2]

552. On the necessity of reciting a second public *Havdalah*, see TB Ber. 33a–b and Tos. ad loc. *Abud.*: 190–91 summarized the medieval position:

> Whoever makes *Havdalah* in the *Tefillah* must also do so over wine. . . . One may begin work after the *Tefillah*, but it is forbidden to eat until one makes the *Havdalah* over wine.

"must be made over wine." According to some authorities in TB Ber. Ibid. Also see TB Pes. 113a:

> R. Yoḥanan said: Three types will inherit the World-to-Come . . . including he who recites the *Havdalah* over wine on Saturday night . . . reserving wine for it.

On the consequences of using and not using wine, see PRE 20; SRA: 84; *Viṭri* 102 and *Manhig:* 195. Many of the medieval authorities took a more lenient position. Tosafot to Ber. (ad loc.) allows the use of any liquor for *Havdalah*. BY to Ṭur OḤ 296 permits any beverage except water. The TY subscribes to the more stringent position, discovering in it a Kabbalistic *sod*.

553. As the ordinary soul is enlarged and exhilarated upon reception of the Sabbath soul, so is it weakened and bereft upon its departure. This notion is widely expressed in Kabbalistic sources. For an early source, see Jacob Nazir's comments as quoted in I. Tishby, MZ 2:498, n67. Also cf. *Zohar* 3:35b:

> When the Sabbath departs the bond [uniting the three aspects of soul] is severed; the *neshamah* ascends and the *nefesh* and *ruaḥ* [the lower two parts of the soul] are left estranged and saddened.

554. On the connection between wine and *Gevurah*, see pp. 31–32 and n148. On the significance of this TY passage see SCK: 261. Also cf. Moshe de Leon's interpretation in *Sefer ha-Rimmon* (MS Brit. Mus.) 32b, discussed in SCK: 279 n11.

555. **"fragrant herbs."** Heb., *besamim;* also including any aromatic spice. In the Sefardic rite, herbs were generally used. The blessing reads: *Bore' ᶜaẓei vesamim*, Creator of fragrant trees.

"To regain serenity of spirit." *Besamim* serve as "smelling salts" for the soul. On the special link between sweet scents and the soul see TB Ber. 43b; also see the sources quoted in S.Y. Agnon, *Yamim Nora'im* (Tel Aviv, 1973): 279–80. For extended discussion on the spiritual healing afforded by the *Havdalah* herbs, see SCK: 262–67.

"for the Sabbath-soul has left him." Cf. Tos. to TB Beiẓ. 33b:

> We recite a blessing over spices on Saturday night to comfort ourselves over the loss of the additional soul.

However, most pre-Kabbalistic sources omit mention of the *neshamah yeterah* entirely. Consider, e.g., Moses Maimonides' well-known statement (MT "Shabbat" 29:29):

> Why is a blessing said over fragrant spices at the conclusion of the Sabbath? It is to cheer the soul which is saddened at the *departure of the Sabbath* [emph. mine].

For further discussion see I. Tishby, MZ 2: 482, 485–86 (on the pre-Kabbalistic sources); and 498–502 (on the mystical tradition).

556. This is the classic—and sole—Talmudic source on the Sabbath-soul. (It is repeated verbatim in *Taᶜanit* 27b.) Apparently, Resh Laqish is reading *shabbat* to mean: once it—the Rest—has ceased. Moreover, he is dividing *VaYiNnaFaSH* into two particles: *VaY:* woe! and *NeFeSH:* soul. He concludes with the gloss: *she-'avdah nefesh*, an ambiguous phrase (see n558) generally rendered: that soul is gone!

557. **"An objection."** Indicating an *apparent* textual problem.

"Midrash of R. Shimon bar Yoḥai." Z 2: 204b, printed below (n561).

558. R. Shimon asks: Whose is the woe? That is, which experiences the primary loss at Sabbath's end, the body or the soul? The question points out the ambiguity in the Talmudic phrase, *she-'avdah nefesh,* wherein *nefesh* may be either subject:

Woe! For the soul has lost X

or object: Woe! For X has lost the soul.

Should one opt for the second reading, X would necessarily refer to the body. R. Shimon's argument is a rhetorical ploy, introduced to be refuted; for the diminution at Sabbath's end is a spiritual one.

559. *moshekhet 'eleha:* or, draws unto itself.

560. **"crowned . . . indwelling spirit."** The *neshamah yeterah* is imaged both as a crown of glory resting upon the Jew and as a presence abiding within his soul. On the Sabbath-soul as a crown for the Jew and his ordinary soul, see Z 3:242b (RM); Z 2: 135b–36a, 205a, and 3: 173a. On the soul as the abode *(dirah)* of the Sabbath-soul, see Z 2:204b. For general discussion, see SCK: 126, 129 and 260.

561. **"vay la-nefesh."** By adding the preposition *la* (to) to Resh Laqish's statement "vay nefesh," the ambiguity mentioned in n557 is dissolved.

"it has lost its crown." And become, relatively speaking, ordinary.

562. The Zoharic source, 2: 204b, reads:

> It is written: *Va-yinnafash* [Ex. 31:17]. It is explained: "Woe to the forlorn soul" [ff. TB *Beiẓah* 16a and *Taʿanit* 27b.] A fine interpretation of the Biblical verse! But one might think that it ought to read *vay guf,* woe to the body, for *it* has lost the soul! But this is the heart of the mystery: Each person has a soul which takes in a spirit on Sabbath eve. This spirit resides within one's soul all Sabbath long and the soul is enlarged, with greater power than before.
>
> Thus we learn: The souls of all Israel are crowned on the Sabbath, crowned by this indwelling spirit. As soon as the Sabbath departs and the spirit ascends, *vay la-nefesh:* woe to the soul that has experienced such a loss! For it has lost its supernal crown and its holy power.

563. See, e.g., pp. 17, 40, 53, and 60 above.

564. **"with which He will adorn us. . . ."** A reference to the ultimate pneuma which is said to be composed of an effulgence of divine light. Cf., e.g., Z 208b–09a:

> The supernal spirit joyously descends unto a person on Shabbat and fills his soul with joy. His soul is lifted onto the same rung it will be on in the World-that-is-Coming. . . . That spirit will give him delight in that future World. As it is written: "Then shall you delight yourself in the Lord" [Isa. 58:14] and "The Lord will . . . satisfy your soul with sparkling flashes [*ẓahẓaḥot*]. [Ibid.: 11]

which, according to the *Zohar*, enlighten the soul in that world.

"But I cannot speak." "Meir ibn Gabbai's reticence suggests an eschatological mystery which cannot be taught in public. For previous examples of this reticence, see pp. 49–50 and notes 332 and 336, above.

In the absence of explicit discussion, one can only surmise how ibn Gabbai was reading the Gemara'. Kabbalistically, it may be an allusion to a) the ultimate divine union and/or b) the full integration of righteous humanity into this unified realm. A sefirotic reading of the Gemara' yields: On "that day" *Tif'eret* ("the Holy One," the "Lord of Hosts") will become one with *Shekhinah* (the "diadem of *Tif'eret*"). This unified sefirotic world will directly adorn and by implication, transform, those who uphold *Tif'eret* and the sefirotic world and who properly contemplate its mysterious beauty *(meẓappin le-tif'arto)*. For a variation on this reading see OK to TB Meg. 15b.

565. **"the choicest way of fulfilling this miẓvah."** Heb., *miẓvah min ha-muvḥar.*

Discussion. On myrtle [Heb., *hadas*] as the choicest aromatic, see *Manhig:* 195; Ṭur OḤ 297; and *Abud.:* 188. For conflicting views see *Roqeaḥ* 356 and Ephraim of Bonn's explicit rejection of myrtle, cited in *Abud.:* Ibid. Only two pre-Zoharic sources provide rationales for using myrtle. The first is *Sefer Ḥasidim*, Wist. ed., sec. 522. Its argument is exegetical in nature, based on the principle of *semukhin:*

> "A myrtle shall rise as a testimony to the Lord, and everlasting sign [Isa. 55: end]. . . . Those who hold fast to it, who keep the Sabbath and do not profane it, etc." [Ibid. 56: 1–4] All this proves that the Sabbath needs myrtle.

However, it is likely that there was an underlying esoteric or magical rationale for using myrtle not stated here. For its importance in the *Havdalah* ceremony was not conditional upon its fragrance:

> Even if one has myrtle that is dry and without fragrance he should wrap it around fragrant spices and bless them [together].

A more explicit rationale is found in R. Eleazar of Worms *Perush ha-Tefillot* (MS Oxf., Bodl. 1204) fol. 135b:

> We smell myrtle sprigs in order to restore the soul. For the soul smells all, including the stench of sulfur from Gehinnom with which sinners of Israel are punished when the Sabbath departs. For this reason, the soul smells myrtle.

The Zoharic tradition develops highly elaborate, theosophic-theurgic rationales for using *hadas*. The sefirotic triad *Ḥesed, Gevurah*, and *Tif'eret* are symbolised as three sprigs of myrtle, whereas their *shefa*[c] is called "the myrtle's scent." See, e.g., *Zohar* 3:35a which reads:

> As [Eleazar, Yose and Ḥizqiah] walked along they came upon a man carrying three branches of myrtle [recalling TB Shab. 33a!]. As he drew near, they inquired: What is this for? He replied: To revive the fainting one [the soul]. R. Eleazar said: You have spoken well. But why three? The man said: One for Abraham [*Ḥesed*,] a second

> for Isaac [*Gevurah*] and a third for Jacob [*Tif'eret*]. I bind them together and smell them . . . because this scent refreshes the weakened soul. By this act of faith, blessings are sustained and drawn from above.

Also consider TZ Add. 6, 143b:

> All sorts of spices may be used in the blessing, though I use myrtle. For each sprig has three leaves . . . which are the three Patriarchs.

For additional examples, see the notes below and esp. the extended analysis in SCK Chap. 4.

566. **"For myrtle brings to mind the souls' abode."** Heb., *li-rmoz 'el maqom ha-neshamot.* The scent of myrtle is crucial for the enactment of the mythic drama. The myrtle leaves are redolent of the Supernal Myrtle *(Tif'eret)* from which the souls derive. Cf. ZḤ Cant. 64d (MN):

> The scent of myrtle is a fragrance wafting down from the Supernal Myrtle. It is a divine point which goes forth into the world . . . to strengthen [the ordinary soul].

For further discussion see SCK: 264–67.

567. Although the identity of *it* is not explained, it probably connotes the soul. On a sefirotic level, it may also connote *Malkhut,* the supernal Soul, who is alluded to in the next sentence.

568. A reference to Esth. 2:7. Kabbalistically, Queen Esther is the symbol of *Malkhut*. Cf. TY p. 81b; Z 1:183b; 3:275b–76a.

"in its honor." That is, after *Hadas. Malkhut* is called Hadassah because it unfolds from the *HaDaS (Ḥesed, Gevurah, Tif'eret).* See Moses Cordovero, PR: Gate 23 "Hadas":

> The three sprigs of *hadas* refer to the three Patriarchs, while *HaDaSsaH* is *Malkhut,* composed of *HaDaS* and the final *He'* [H] of the Divine Name.

Discussion. Although Meir ibn Gabbai treats the blessing over spices in rather summary fashion here, he analyzed the symbolism of fragrant smells elsewhere in the TY (p. 89b). After an extended discussion of the mystical significance of incense offerings, he turned to the mystery of *besamim.* Drawing on Z 3:105a and 35b, he wrote:

> From the earthly fragrance we come to fathom the heavenly Covenant. On Saturday night when the Sabbath-soul [*neshamah*] departs, one is diminished; his *nefesh* and *ruaḥ* grieve over their loss. The [devotee] smells the fragrant spices to gladden and strengthen [these two] and to draw them together. Through this fragrance the [departed] *neshamah* is strengthened in the supernal Faith [the sefirotic world]. She is energized in the presence of these supernal spirits [lit., intellects: *devarim sikhliyyim*].

For extended analysis of the ritual blessing over spices in the Zoharic tradition, see SCK: 262–67.

569. Amid the numinous darkness of *Havdalah*, attention is now focused on the flickering flame, on the dramatic interplay of light and dark, and on the myth this play symbolizes.

For Rabbinic discussion of this blessing, cf. M. Ber. 8:4; TB Ber. 33a, 53b; and Pes. 8a, 54a. Also cf. Ṭur OḤ 296 and 298 for a synopsis of Medieval legal discussion.

570. **"the Fire of the North."** That is, the forces of harsh *Din*. On the North symbolizing evil cf. Ezek. 1:4 and Jer. 1:4, and their midrashic and mystical re-readings. Of special interest here are *Zohar* 2: 130a, 203a–b (upon which ibn Gabbai seems to drawing), and ZḤ Cant. 74b, which reads: "The North Wind . . . is the evil Fire where cosmic evil abides."

571. In other words, in the post-Sabbath world, *Din* has a legitimate place and function. The purpose of the ritual is to ensure that this restoration take place within proper limits, in orderly and timely fashion. For details see SCK: 260 and 268; for the contrasting view that *Din* must be ritually suppressed, see Ibid. pp. 268–70 and Z 1:17b where the *Havdalah* ceremony as a whole wards off *Siṭra' 'Aḥra'*:

> The *Havdalah* is directed against the Left . . . When Israel performs the ritual with the myrtle and wine and recites the *Havdalah*, the Left Side withdraws from them and goes down to its place in She'ol.

A textual note. The language of the TY in this paragraph is almost identical with that of the *Ketem Paz* to *Zohar* 1:20b (fol. 75b). It is conceivable that the *Ketem Paz* is relying on the TY here. Compare.

572. **"Four Camps."** The angelic powers just below the sefirotic world. Cf. *Zohar* 2:208a and I. Tishby's interpretation in MZ 2:507–08.

"candlelight." Any lamp may be used, so long as it has multiple wicks (TB Ber. 52b). A torch *('avuqa')* is considered to be particularly appropriate (TB Pes. 8a).

"lights of the Fire." Heb., *me'orei ha-'esh;* from the *Havdalah* blessing: "Blessed are You . . . Creator of the lights of fire." Kabbalistically, these angelic powers are so called because, as the candles are lit, they are illumined—or vitalized—by the divine Fire, *Shekhinah*. Cf. *Zohar* Ibid. (analyzed in SCK: 273–74).

Discussion. In the Zoharic tradition the blessing over the fire most commonly symbolizes two simultaneous processes: the re-emergence of the powers of *Din* and the transfer of Providential authority from *Shekhinah*/divinity to the angelic realm, the so-called "Changing of the Cosmic Guard." Although ibn Gabbai opened this section by highlighting the first process, he now unself-consciously moves to the second.

573. **"bend."** Heb., *kofin*. Warsaw ed. reads: *kofefin*. That is, the fingers are curled into the palm. On the evolution (and non-Kabbalistic significance) of this custom, cf. n582 below.

"right hand." Thereby dramatizing (manually "signing") that the Four Camps are intimately related to the beneficient divine realm. For discussion, see SCK: 273 and n582 below.

574. **"Lower Chariots."** The four Camps are so-called because they bear aloft and protect divinity, specifically *Malkhut.* Cf. p. 20 above where the *Din*-like character of these Chariots was emphasized.

On "Candle" or "Lamp" *(ner)* as a symbol for *Shekhinah* see p. 23 and n74 above.

For interpretation of this TY passage, see SCK: 273. On the mystical significance of bending down *(kofin)* the fingers, see SCK: 274–75; and this study, n577–78 below.

575. Here Meir ibn Gabbai is drawing on two word-plays and a proof-text (Ex. 33:23) found in *Zohar* 1:20a and 2:207b ff.

(1) The backs of *('aḥorei)* the fingers are implicitly linked with the *'aḥorayim,* or the divine "backside" as the angelic Camps are often called.

(2) The inner side *(penimi)* of the fingers is homologized to the *panim,* the divine Face or Countenance, i.e., the sefirotic world.

Although in the non-mystical tradition, it is customary to gaze at the palms, as well, the TY and *Zohar* specify: the nails only. The rationale is mystical. As the Sabbath departs, only the angelic presence can be perceived; the divine Face is beyond one's lowered ken. Like Moses at Sinai (Ex. 33:23), "face-to-Face" revelation cannot be had.

576. Because the inner part of the fingers represent the now-imperceptible *sefirot,* they remain unseen, in darkness. For the *sefirot* are illumined only by the *concealed* light of *Keter* (the "Supernal Lamp," the "Black Fire").

577. The symbolism of bending down the four fingers is stated more explicitly in *Zohar* 2:208a. See n578 below.

578. As noted, ibn Gabbai has been echoing ideas found in Z 1:20b–21a and 2:208a–b, drawing on the latter, in particular; it reads:

> When we recite the blessing over the fire, four Chariots—four [angelic] legions called *me'orei ha-'esh,* "the lights of the fire"—descend to be illumined by this blessed fire. Thus, we must bend the fingers of our right hand so that they catch the light of the blessed candle. The fingers symbolize those "lights of the fire" that are illumined by, and derive power from, that blessed Candle.
>
> These [legions] are lower rungs and so, we bend our fingers before the candle to show that they are illumined by and subject to a [higher] light. Normally, when we offer blessings we raise our [ten] fingers [cf. Z 2:67a and 76a,] thereby showing the high sanctity of the supernal rungs [the ten *sefirot*] which rule over all. All these rungs are blessed together and illumined by the Supreme Lamp [*Keter*.] But [at *Havdalah*] we bend our fingers down as we catch the light, alluding to those lower rungs that are illumined by the

> Light on high [*Malkhut*]. Thus, they are called "the lights of the Fire."

The *sefirot*, by contrast, are called *me'orei 'or*, the luminaries of *Light*. Cf. 1:20b–21a. The text continues:

> Fingers lie at the heart of the mystery, for they symbolize both the upper and the lower grades. The upper grades are indicated when the fingers are raised on high. When they are raised, both upper and lower realms are blessed. But when the fingers are inclined downwards only the lower rungs receive light [the *shefa*ᶜ extends from *Shekhinah* below]. This second mystery is [symbolized by] the fingernails.
>
> They are on the backs of the fingers while the fingers themselves constitute the inner side. The nails . . . are *panim 'aḥerot*, "Other Faces," belonging to those who must derive light from the Candle. These faces are called *'Aḥorayim*, the Rear Ones.

That is, they are liminal: faces with respect to the lower worlds and the backside for the world above. Cf. MZ 1: 293 n1. To use another image, they are the *qelippot*—or shells—for the world above but the inner kernel or essence *(moḥa')* with respect to the world below. The *Zohar* passage continues:

> The inner nail-less side symbolizes the Inner Face [*sefirot*] which remains hidden. This mystery is indicated in the verse: "You shall see My back," referring to the outer side of the fingers and the nails; "But My face shall not be seen," [Ex. 33:23] referring to the inner side . . . the Inner Face. So when we recite the blessing over the candlelight, we must show the outer side of the fingers, letting the nails catch the light. But the inner side need not face the candle . . . for it is illumined by none other than the Supernal Lamp [*Keter*] which is utterly concealed and hidden, on high, on high. . . . Hence, the nails and outer part of the fingers should be held up to the light, but the inner parts not. For they are hidden and illumined by the hidden; innermost and illumined by the innermost; exalted and illumined by the most high. Happy is Israel in this world and in the World-to-Come!

For further discussion, see SCK: 273–75.

579. See p. 20 above. The *Havdalah* symbolizes two simultaneous processes: the re-emergence of *Din*, and the transfer of power to the angelic authorities. The nail symbolism is similarly dual, evoking the benevolent angelic forces (as above), but also the harsh forces of "Another Causality," *Siṭra' 'Aḥra'*. On the ambivalent symbolism of nails elsewhere in *Sod ha-Shabbat* see Ibid. and the discussion in SCK: 224–27.

580. "Wicked" refers to *Siṭra' 'Aḥra'* which forms a *qelippah* for the Righteous, *Malkhut*, or more generally, divinity. This proof-text is used in *Zohar* 2:233b where the forces of *Din* have a more obviously positive function:

"I went down to the nut garden" [Cant. 6:11] As a nut has a shell that surrounds and protects the kernel within, so it is with everything holy. Holiness is within and the "Other Side" without. This is esoterically alluded to in Scripture: "The wicked encircles the righteous."

581. **"to sap its strength."** Heb., *le-hatish koḥah.* The act of gazing upon the nails and specifically, of seeing them illumined, is a way of "sweetening" or neutralizing *Din.* The act of symbolically filling them with divine light robs them of their ruinous power. See SCK: 271.

This rationale for gazing upon the nails is not found in the *Zohar* which links the suppression of *Siṭra' 'Aḥra'* to the recitation of the blessing over the fire. See SCK: 268–69. Such a rationale is found, however, in Moshe de Leon's Hebrew work, *Sodot,* MS Schocken 14 (fol. 90b). There is no evidence that Meir ibn Gabbai knew this source directly. In all likelihood, he learned of this tradition through the mediation of David ben Judah he-Ḥasid's OZ, a work quoted elsewhere in the TY. OZ 53b contains the following uncited quotation from the de Leon's *Sodot:*

> Whoever gazes upon his nails in the candlelight, as the Sabbath departs, saps the strength [*matish koaḥ*] of Another Causality which expands throughout the cosmos on Saturday night. [Whoever does so] will be spared harm during the coming week.

This anti-demonic function seems influenced by popular understandings of *Havdalah.* On the magical procedures associated with *Havdalah,* see J. Trachtenberg, *Jewish Magic:* 114 and G. Scholem, "Havdalah de-R. Aqiva," *Tarbiẓ* 50 (1982): 243–81.

The OZ (again ff. *Sodot*) serves as the TY's source for the next few sentences, as well. It continues:

> One should make sure, however, that use is made of the candle's light. When he has done this, let him bless the One who created the light, that he may be delivered from all distress, as in the case of Adam. Our Rabbis of blessed memory [spoke of this]: . . .

At this point the TY and OZ diverge. Compare!

582. **"use is made of the candle's light."** Heb., *ye'otu le-'oro,* following the halakhah [M. Ber. 8:6] that one must derive benefit from the *Havdalah* lamp (lest it be a wasted blessing: *berakhah le-vaṭṭalah).* There is an implicit Kabbalistic rationale in the TY here. The light of the *Shekhinah* should be bright enough and assimilated sufficently so as to weaken *Din.* By holding one's nails up to the flame and using the light, this weakening is symbolically effected.

Discussion. The question may now be raised: How does the Zoharic fulfillment of *ye'otu le-'oro* differ from that found in the elite non-mystical tradition? How do the ritual gestures differ, as well as the accompanying rationales?

The gestures:

(1) The non-kabbalistic literature does not distinguish between use of the right and left hands (cf. Ṭur OḤ 298; *Manhig*: 196; *Abud.*: 189–90, and many others). However, for symbolic reasons, the *Zohar* and TY specify use of the right hand: to indicate that the newly empowered angelic forces are intimately tied to the beneficent divine realm.

(2) The non-kabbalistic tradition never proscribes gazing upon the palm. Indeed, several authorities, e.g., Natronai Gaon, seemingly consider the palm as preferrable to the nails (which were popularly associated with divination practices; see SRA for details). More typical is the view of Spanish scholar David Abudraham (*Abud.*: 189–90):

> It is customary to first look at the nails and thereafter at the palm, as we bless over the light, to show that we derive pleasure from the light and that we can distinguish between the nails . . . and the palm [cf. TB Ber. 53b and TJ Ber. 31c].

Esoteric considerations lead the kabbalist to warn against looking at the palm. Once again, extant custom is modified for patently mythic reasons, to symbolize the now-hidden (transcendent) divinity. Moreover, the emphatic tone of the Zohar's and TY's warnings, and their clever use of proof-texts, suggest a conscious—if restrained—critique of halakhic convention.

There is no such restraint in the pointed words of Moshe de Leon, in his *Sodot* (90a), or in David ben Judah's paraphrase of this text in OZ (54a-b). The latter reads:

> Following the ancient secret teaching [i.e., the *Zohar!*], one should look only upon the nails at *Havdalah* and not upon the inner fingers or palm as many do out of perverse stupidity when they do not grasp the essence . . . I have seen many men stretch out their palms [to the light] and recite the blessing. They do so out of madness [*shiggaᶜon*] and folly [*ṭippeshutam*] . . . The heart of the matter is that we must gaze only upon the nails, for they are the cloak [for divinity].

The non-Kabbalistic *rationales* for looking at the hands seem to be threefold:

(1) Cognitive-halakhic: as a means of establishing a visual distinction, thereby using the light as mandated. Only in *Sefer RaVYaH* (sec. 41) is this visual distinction explicitly related to a broader theme: the separation (or distinction) of the Sabbath from the work week.

(2) Magical: as an omen for good (plenitude) in the coming week or for use in divination. (For sources, see S. Finesinger, "The Custom of Looking at the Fingernails at the Outgoing of Sabbath," HUCA Vol. 12–13 [1937–38]: 354, 364–65.)

Some sources such as the anonymous *Kol Bo* (sec. 41) add a third motive:

(3) Quasi-mythic: to recall the first *Havdalah*. Contemporary legend had it that the first fire issued from Adam's nails, and that Adam discovered

that he was naked—except for his nails—at *Havdalah.* Although this last rationale edges towards one found in Zoharic tradition, these images are not explicity or systematically tied to the devotee's current religious experience.

The Zoharic rationales, by contrast, are explicitly mythic, dramatizing events now unfolding in the supernal realms and enabling the devotee to participate in them. For example, the nails evoke the profane realm; the candle symbolizes *Shekhinah;* and the ritual gesture represents the proper re-ordering of the cosmos after Shabbat.

According to the TY:

(1) Gazing upon the nails symbolizes the re-activation of the angelic powers under *Shekhinah* and effects the separation of the divine world from the lower realms.

(2) It serves as an apotropaic against *Din* and its tribulations. The second rationale implies the transformative nature of the gesture, whereas the first may be seen as either confirmatory or transformative (both opinions are found in the literature).

A third kabbalistic rationale may be found in TZ Intro (10b–11a). There the gesture is not so much transformative as evocative, recalling Adam's first Saturday night. But unlike the *Kol Bo,* the TZ's author explicitly uses the Edenic vignette as a paradigm to explain and enrich the devotee's own experience of leaving Shabbat. To glance at the nails is to recall Adam's loss of his "precious multi-colored garment of nails." This garment was called *me'orei ha-'esh,* and "shone like the Clouds of Glory." Each Sabbath the Jew's soul is garbed in this garment of light (the *neshamah yeterah*) and each Saturday night he is divested of it. This process is evoked by gazing on the very symbol of the "vestigial garment: the nails."

For further discussion of non-Kabbalistic rationales, see my dissertation: 606–07 and D. Noy, "Histakkelut ba-Ẓippornayim bi-Shᶜat ha-Havdalah," *Maḥanayim* 85–86 (1963): 166–73. For comparison with non-Zoharic Kabbalaḥ, see SCK: 281 n29.

583. Halakhically, the blessing can only be recited after use was made of the flame. Cf. M. Ber. 8:6; *Viṭri* 187; MT "Shabbat" 25:29, et al.

584. Here Meir ibn Gabbai provides a paradigm for such a deliverance.

"chapter twenty-one." Chapter 20 in current (RaDaL) editions of PRE. Apparently there were at least two editions known in the later medieval period. *Manhig* and Isaac Aboab *(Menorat ha-Ma'or)* also indicate chapter 21; Israel Al-Naqawa (in his *Menorat ha-Ma'or*) cited chapter 20.

585. That is, after the Sin, so that the Primordial Light was hidden. Adam, newly exiled from the Garden, was now confronted with utter darkness. (On the Primordial Light, see TB Ḥag. 2a, Gen. R 11:2, et al.)

586. Ibn Gabbai uses the midrash, found in a slightly different version in extant editions, to illustrate the two points he has just made: 1) God's saving power and 2) the protective influence of the *Havdalah* fire.

I. Tishby (MZ 2:507) finds this theme, whether stated explicitly or only implied, to be central to the Zoharic understanding of the blessing over the fire:

> The flame of the *Havdalah* candle lights the way for Israel amid the darkness of the week. It helps them escape the terrors of the dark powers that lurk everywhere and seek to lay Israel low. The flame helps the Jews stand firm till the hidden light of the Sabbath returns and shines brightly, again enabling them to enter the divine realm.

587. **"stones."** For example, flint. The point of this ruling is that on Saturday night newly created fire may be used; on Yom Kippur only a pre-existent flame is permissable. Some authorities correlate the Sabbath-tradition with the legend of Adam's creation of fire on the first Saturday night. Cf. TB Pes. 54a, both R. Yose's opinion and the anonymous teaching that:

> We recite a blessing over light . . . at the termination of Sabbath, since it was created then for the first time.

The ruling referred to by ibn Gabbai reads:

> One [*baraita*] taught: We can recite a blessing over light which issues from tinder and stones; while another taught: We cannot recite a blessing over it. There is no difficulty: the first refers to the termination of the Sabbath, and the second to the termination of Yom Kippur.

588. Kabbalistically, the term *binyan,* the Structure or Building, refers to the seven lower *sefirot* as an active unit. Cf. *Sod ha-Shabbat* p. 53 above: "*Yesod* is the sixth in the Structure, counting from the Right Arm [*Ḥesed*] and below . . ."

On *ᶜeẓim* as the seven lower *sefirot,* cf. *Zohar* 1:125a; 3:217b and 58a. The latter reads:

> A river goes out of Eden [*Binah*] to water the Garden [*Malkhut*]." [Gen. 2:10]. . . . The river sends forth deep streams to water the garden and to sate the trees and saplings, as it says: "The trees of the Lord are sated." [Ps. 104:16]

It is difficult to know exactly how Meir ibn Gabbai is reading *yisbeᶜu* here. Were he reading it in a conventional Kabbalistic manner, it would connote satiation, the infusion of divine blessing into the lower *sefirot* on Shabbat. But it is possible that he was vocalizing *YSBᶜU* as *YiShBeᶜU:* "are seven," viz., the seven lower rungs. Such a reading is suggested by *Zohar* 1:125a:

> The trees of the Lord *YSBᶜU:* This refers to the 70 Trees in the Garden of Eden. . . .

589. **"Cornerstone of Israel."** Idiomatically, the "Rock of Israel," following Gen. 49:24. Like Diadem (Heb., *ᶜAṭarah),* this is a common appellation for *Malkhut.* See, e.g., Z 2:146b; and Moses Cordovero, PR: Gate 23 (" 'Even Yisra'el"): "*Malkhut* is the foundation and rock (stone) upon which the upper Structure rests."

The lower seven *sefirot* as a unit are also called *'avanim,* stones. See PR Ibid.

590. **"pre-existent light."** Heb., *'or she-shabat.* Lit., a light that has burned throughout the Sabbath, and by extension, throughout any holiday. As noted, on Yom Kippur the *Havdalah* must be made over a light taken from a source kindled before the holiday commenced. This is contrasted with the newly created light that issued from tinder and stones, appropriate for the Sabbath *Havdalah.* On this contrast see TJ Ber. 8:5; MT "Shabbat" 29:27; and S. Y. Agnon's *Yamim Nora'im:* 378.

Discussion. The TY provides a mystical rationale for this halakhah. Although the Sabbath here connotes the seven lower *sefirot,* Yom Kippur connotes *Binah,* the Supernal Lamp that is above the Structure. (Cf. *Zohar* 3:69b, and MZ 2:517ff. and 554–57.) Hence, the *Havdalah* flame for Shabbat is drawn from its archetype, the supernal tinder and stones, the seven lower rungs. The Yom Kippur flame may be taken only from its paradigm, *Binah,* the pre-existent light. This appellation highlights Her non-created character and Her priority over the seven created *sefirot* below.

The use of newly created light at Sabbath *Havdalah* is given another layer of significance in *Zohar* 1:20a and the *Ketem Paz* ad loc.; and a third meaning in Z 2:208a. For discussion, see my dissertation, p. 611; and SCK: 272–73.

"O House of Jacob, etc." An allusion to the protective—and orienting—power of the divine Lamp and its symbol, the *Havdalah* flame. See I. Tishby's remarks in n586 above.

591. The names of these four *qelippot* are taken from Ezekiel's vision of the Chariot (1:4). In the Zoharic understanding they refer to those sub-divine entities that surround the Throne of divinity. For representative views, see Z 2: 102a; 203a–b; ZḤ "Yitro" 61a–b; and TZ 18 (32b).

Discussion. As I. Tishby points out (MZ 1:289–301 and 321–26), two contrasting views of evil co-exist in the *Zohar.* The first is the dualistic or 'gnostic' one, which portrays *Siṭra' 'Aḥra'*/harsh *Din* as an independent counterforce to divinity. Evil is literally, the Other Side, a pleroma replete with ten *sefirot* of defilement, corresponding to the ten divine ones. The second view is the harmonistic one whose roots are in the Gerona tradition. Here evil is grasped as an essential part of the divine world and plan, an emissary of *Malkhut. Din* administers justice to the wicked, arouses *teshuvah* and serves as *Malkhut's* protector, rather than Her captor or adversary.

Although the dualistic view implies a radical break between the *sefirot* and *Siṭra' 'Aḥra',* the harmonistic view emphasizes the ontological closeness of the *qelippot* to *Shekhinah.* This gradualism is evident in the image of *Siṭra' 'Aḥra',* as a system of four *qelippot* or shells, concentric spheres that surround *Malkhut* as a shell protects the fruit within. The outermost (i.e., most evil) shell is the "Stormy Wind," followed by the "Great Cloud" and the "Flashing Fire," while the innermost shell is "the Encompassing Brightness," a relatively subtle admixture of good and evil, which serves as a kind of buffer between divinity and the lower realms. *Evil* in other words, becomes a relative term, expressed as a matter of degrees along a continuum.

As shall be seen, in the TY, the four *qelippot* serve a more negative role than I. Tishby's neat schema would suggest.

592. Cf. ZH "Yitro" 61a–b:

> "I looked and behold, a stormy wind came out of the North, etc." [Ezek. 1:4] This is the portal to the uncovering of mysteries. They need only be disclosed to the wise of heart, who know to interpret [*li-drosh*] them.

On the ten lower Crowns in which divinity is garbed during the week, cf. SCK: 238–39; and p. 22 above. Here ibn Gabbai freely mixes the dualistic symbol of the ten lower crowns with the harmonistic image of the four shells.

593. **"when sins are committed."** Heb., *ke-she-gormin ha-ᶜavonot,* i.e., by Israel, the proof-text makes clear. The negative or obscuring function of the *qelippot* is emphasized as a result of human sin. See Z 2: 203a:

> When Israel sinned [the Great Cloud] obtained power, as it is said: "He has withdrawn His Right hand in the presence of the foe." [Lam. 2:3] "A Great Cloud" refers to the Cloud of Darkness that eclipsed the whole world.

Cf. *Sod ha-Shabbat* here with Z 2:116a (RM), discussed in SCK: 235–36. Also cf. TZ 56 (90a–b).

Ibn Gabbai's inspiration in this section is TZ 69 (108b–109b). As will be made clear, he abstracts from this source even as he reshapes it. This text is presented in n605 and n636 below.

594. Ff. TZ Ibid. (n605); for interpretation of this passage see SCK: 234–35. Also see I. Tishby, MZ 1:220–21, 224–25 and the sources therein.

595. The Biblical quotations are found in the TZ source, n605. For the Kabbalistic meaning, see there. The last quotation is from TB Meg. 29a, and marks the beginning of a brief digression from the TZ paraphrase. Kabbalistically, "Egypt" connotes *Siṭra' 'Aḥra'.*

Discussion. Here the protective, mothering aspect of *Shekhinah* is stressed, as She takes on Israel's fate as a free expression of Her love and solidarity with them, and as a means of protecting Her children from *Din* and its earthly manifestations.

On the protective quality of *Shekhinah*'s descent into Exile, cf. *Zohar* 1:166a; 3:75a; and 2:216a which reads:

> Should you say: Perhaps She is in Exile and banished from Her people, realize that this is not so. She is in Exile to dwell with Israel and to protect them.

596. That is, they are a punitive instrument used by and subject to *Malkhut,* the woodcutter of this simile. The power of *Din* is channelled,

deprived of independence and arbitrariness. The simile in the TY recalls Isa. 10:15, where the woodcutter is none other than God: "Does an axe boast over him that hews it?" Also cf. YS 1: 170, which likens God's sovereignty over his emissary Moses to the control a woodcutter has over his axe.

In the Zoharic tradition, *Shekhinah* must use *Din* as a lash to dispense justice in the world and to ward off evil. Cf. e.g., *Zohar* 1: 11b, 2: 149b and 172b–173b. Also cf. MZ 1: 283, 293 ff. and 323 ff. This harsh aspect of *Shekhinah,* exhibited during the week, contrasts with Her thoroughly beneficent nature on Shabbat.

597. A manifestation of the *Din*-like aspect of *Malkhut.* Cf. n366 above; and see MZ 1:219 ff. for further discussion.

598. Heb., *ve-ha-devarim ᶜattiqim.* See n336.

599. **"Know that, etc."** Here Meir ibn Gabbai returns to his paraphrase of the TZ source.

"portion of Good, etc." the aspect of *Ḥesed* in the world of *Beri'ah* (the second of the "four worlds," just below divinity). In the TZ they are called "qelippot of light," to be distinguished from the more demonic weekday sort. This contrasts with *Sod ha-Shabbat* (p. 22) where divinity is said to be arrayed in *sefirotic* lights during Shabbat. On the imagery of divinity changing garments for Shabbat, see the detailed discussion in SCK: 231–42. On the doctrine of four worlds, see G. Scholem's brief sketch in *Kabbalah:* 118–19.

600. To rule over the world in profane time, *Shekhinah* needs to make use of *Din* located in *Beri'ah.*

601. Heb., *ve-yekholim le-hitᶜarev ba-hem ha-dalet qelippot..* The term *le-hitᶜarev* here connotes an improper mixing.

602. **"in the mode of Beri'ah."** Heb., *be-derekh Beri'ah,* echoing TZ 69. The point here is that Sabbath garb comes from a realm marked by multiplicity, where Good and Evil co-exist as fully individuated. *Havdalah* insures proper separation of this good and evil, thus maintaining Order, or in Mircea Eliade's term, "Cosmos." The mixing of these two realms is called *tohu va-vohu,* confusion and chaos (TZ 54 [87b]) or *kil'ayim shaᶜaṭnez,* as explained below.

603. On the Biblical injunction against mixed species *(kil'ayim)* see Lev. 19:19 and Dt. 22:9–11. On *shaᶜaṭnez* see Ibid.

These taboos, which so perplexed the Medieval Rationalists, are here given a mystical rationale. Both symbolize the improper fusion of holy and profane, of good and evil. Reciting *Havdalah* guards against *shaᶜaṭnez,* against garbing divinity in a "mixed-up," hence defiling, garment. Mary Douglas has written that "holiness requires that different classes of things should not be confused." (*Purity and Danger:* 53) The Kabbalist is saying much the same here in highly mythological language.

Early Kabbalistic *sodot* on *kil'ayim* and *sha'atnez* are summarized in E. Gottlieb's *Ha-Qabbalah be-Khitvei R. Baḥyya ben 'Asher*: 182–85. Also see *Zohar* 3:86b–87a; the many TZ interpretations, e.g., 66 (97b), 67 (98a), and 69 (109a); and n605.

604. "Sanctuary" generally connotes *Shekhinah*, but here it evidently means Her Sabbath garments; for She cannot be defiled. See n605.

605. **"mode of Emanation."** Heb., *ba-derekh ha-'aẓilut*; ff. the TZ's *be-'oraḥ de-aẓilut*.

The loftiness of divinity is stressed here; it is held to be impervious to pollution by *Siṭra' 'Aḥra'*. On the purity of *Shekhinah* even amidst the Other Side cf. I. Tishby, MZ 1:225 and the sources listed there. Also see TZ 67 (98b) and TZḤ 110b–c.

The purpose of *Havdalah* here is to separate good and evil in the world of *Beri'ah*, to provide a proper garment for *Shekhinah*. This is clarified in TZ 69 (108b–109b). Because of its importance as a source for ibn Gabbai, I shall quote it at length here. The TZ begins in a far more dualistic vein than ibn Gabbai, who spoke of the four *qelippot*:

> As there is a holy Kingdom, so is there a sinful one [*Siṭra' 'Aḥra'*]. [The TZ goes on to list the *sefirot* and their corresponding demonic entities]. . . . These are the ten lower Crowns, which are the *qelippot* or shells for the ten *sefirot*. The *sefirot* are the fruit [*moḥa'*] within. These *qelippot* form a barrier between Israel and their Father in Heaven. The Holy One and *Shekhinah* are cloaked in these *qelippot*, the *Shekhinah* may uphold the dicta, "His Kingdom [*Malkhut*] rules over all." [Ps. 103:19] and "For *'Elohim* is King over all the earth." [Ps. 47:8; ibn Gabbai used 47:9!]. But on high, in His Place [within the sefirotic world], it is said: "Evil cannot abide with you." [Ibid. 5:5]
>
> On high, the Holy One wears *qelippot* as well. But they are cloaks made of many shades of beautiful light. [That is, unlike the weekday *qelippot* they do not filter out the divine light.] In Exile [during the week], He takes these off; He dons other garments so as to protect Israel, who are garbed in *qelippot* below. Hence, the verse: "In all their troubles [kabbalistically, the *qelippot*], He is troubled." [Ps. 91:15]
>
> At first first God gave the *qelippot* over to his emissary, Gavriel. He dispensed [limited] nourishment to Sammael and his legions. But because of Israel's sins, He put on [the *qelippot*]. . . . When Israel walks down the proper path and upholds the Torah and its miẓvot, all works properly. But if, heaven forfend, they do not, the ten Crowns are given over to Sammael, whereupon the *qelippot* no longer need nourishment from the Holy One or even His emissary . . . [That is, the *qelippot* are here depicted as liminal, without an independent identity; they are neither good nor evil in and of themselves.]

In the beginning, when the lower crowns were in the hands of the Holy One, it was said of Israel: "All the peoples of the earth shall see the Lord's name proclaimed over you," [Dt. 28:10] but when Sammael has control of these "foreign crowns," the idolatrous nations show no respect towards Israel. . . . This will persist till the hour Israel's deliverance. Then "I will remove the unclean spirit from the Land," [Zech. 13:2] namely those *qelippot* which cause a separation between the Holy One and Israel. This is the hidden meaning of "But your iniquities have been a barrier between you and your God." [Isa. 59:2]

In the time to come the Holy One will remove these *qelippot* and be disclosed before Israel like the fruit of a nut, as it says: "Then shall your Guide no longer be hidden away, and your eyes shall behold your Guide." [Ibid. 30:20] There will no longer be any barriers between the Holy One and *Shekhinah* and Israel . . .

It is because of these *qelippot* that we must make *Havdalah*. For the Holy One is garbed in them during the week. [Cf. TZ 18, (34a)] But on Shabbat, He is divested of them and arrayed in holy garments, the ten garments of which it is said, "The Lord *BaDaD yanḥennu* [conventionally read: 'alone led him' but here:] wears Ten; no alien god at His side." [Dt. 32:12] For *BaDaD* [*Beit Dalet Dalet*] in gematria is ten, [ten holy garments] corresponding to the ten *qelippot* worn during the week. When He wears the [holy garb], it is said: "*BaDaD*, these other ten, sit outside; they dwell beyond the Camp [in the realm of *Din*]." [Lev. 13:46]

So it was established that [we include] in the *Havdalah*: "who makes a distinction between Sacred and Profane, between light and darkness," lest the profane *qelippot* become bound to the holy ones. There must be no mixing [*taʿarovet*] of the two. This is "You shall not sow your field with two kinds of seed [*kil'ayim*]; you shall not put on cloth from a mixture of two kinds of material [*kil'ayim shaʿaṭnez*]." [Ibid. 19:19] Whoever mixes them, of him it is said: "You have defiled my Sanctuary." [Num. 19.20]

Now on Sabbath, when the Holy One takes off these clothes and dons holy garments, there is no need to intercede before Him concerning the profane garments [text is awk. here] for the fruit [the *sefirot*] cannot be polluted, as it says: "Behold, my Word is like fire, declares the Lord." [Jer. 23:29] [i.e., keeping away evil]

Here the TZ is following TB Ber. 22a, which appends the following to a discussion on *kil'ayim:* "The words of Torah are not susceptible to defilement, as it is said: 'Behold, My Word is like fire.' Just as fire is not susceptible to impurity, so the words of the Torah!" The TZ continues:

For nothing can mix with divinity. However, the garments which He wears on Sabbath and festivals are susceptible to such admixture. *For their sake* [emph. mine], we make *Havdalah*.

> Below [the sefirotic world] there is a Tree composed of a confusion [*kil'ayim*] of good and evil. [Cf. TZ 67 (98a); 53 (87b); and Z 3:283a] Concerning it, Scripture says: "But as for the Tree of Knowledge of good and evil, you must not eat of it." [Gen. 2:17] For its fruit [i.e, the good] is of the [realm of] *Beri'ah* and may be confused with its peel [*qelippah.*] But a "fruit" which is from the light of Emanation cannot be polluted: no admixture may reach it.

Here Meir ibn Gabbai leaves off from his paraphrase of the TZ; he returns to it at the very end of this section. See n636.

606. **"profane."** JTSA MS 1646 reads *bigdei ḥol,* profane garb. In the TZ passage and in *Sod ha-Shabbat* (at n602) the "garments of holiness" clearly connote the "qelippot of light" in *Beri'ah;* here they seem to connote sefirotic entities. Apparently ibn Gabbai has shifted focus and reverted to an earlier rationale for *Havdalah:* to separate the sefirotic world from the profane realms below.

607. **"summit of the Tree."** Heb., *nof ha -'ilan;* the divine world. On the Gentiles claiming the *qelippot,* cf. MZ 1:289 and *Zohar* 1:20b, 75a–b, et al. For an interesting parallel also see Joseph Giqatilia, *Shaᶜarei 'Orah* 2:46–47.

608. Kabbalistically, the seventh day connotes *Malkhut* and the sefirotic world; the six working days, the potencies below Her.

609. Here ibn Gabbai begins a kind of homily on TB Pes. 113a, weaving in various mystical and Talmudic sources.

610. On the rewards for reciting the *Havdalah* over wine cf. *Sod ha-Shabbat* above. For parallels cf. PRE 20; SRA: 84; *Viṭri* sec. 102; *Manhig:* 195; and Ṭur OḤ 296 (end), which cites this Gemara'.

611. That is, all three types attest to and help promote divine unity. Ibn Gabbai now discusses them, case by case. Although the interpretation seems to be largely his own, portions may have been inspired by the *'Oẓar ha-Kavod* to this Gemara'. Compare!

612. Based on TB Ket. 110b. The wording here varies slightly from the printed edition of the Talmud.

613. **"other gods."** Kabbalistically, *Siṭra' 'Aḥra'.*

The second Biblical verse is interpreted via parallel construction *(semukhin)* to mean: only in the land of Israel would He be their God.

614. **"Holy Faith."** The sefirotic realm.

"for the supernal glory rests, etc." For an interesting parallel cf. OK to Ket. ad loc.

Discussion. The inhabitant of the land of Israel partakes of and builds up its archetype, *Malkhut* and the divine world. The one living in Exile partakes of its archetype and controlling force, *Siṭra' 'Aḥra'.*

The belief that *Shekhinah* dwells in the land of Israel commonly co-exists with the belief that She is in Exile, and ibn Gabbai moved unself-consciously between the two. At any event, in this instance the TY seems to be saying: whoever dwells in the Land promotes *Shekhinah*'s presence there and has a more intimate relationship with Her.

For Kabbalistic sources on Her dwelling in the Land, cf. Meir ibn Gabbai's primary source here, OK to Pes. 113a; also see RaMBaN to Gen. 28:18 and Lev. 18:21; and Meir ibn Sahula's comments in *Be'ur Sodot ha-RaMBaN* ad Gen. 28:18:

> "Whoever lives outside the Land of Israel, it is as if he has no God, etc." The chosen Land is under God's dominion alone and when Israel is in the land, the Lord is a God unto them. For then they are under his dominion and providence.

The many Zoharic parallels include: 1:61a, 84b, 108b; 2:33a, 79b, 151b, and 152b. For discussion, see now M. Idel, "The Land of Israel in Medieval Kabbalah" in L. Hoffman, ed., *The Land of Israel* (South Bend, 1986): 170–87.

On Israel's subjection to *Siṭra' 'Aḥra'* when living in Exile, cf. *Zohar* 1:95b, 153b; 2:9a (end), et al.

615. By living in the land of Israel rather than the Exile, the devotee makes a *havdalah* or symbolic separation between Malkhut and *Siṭra' 'Aḥra'*. Hence, he attests to divine unity, as ibn Gabbai noted above (*Sod ha-Shabbat* at n611).

616. That is, whoever dwells in the earthly Israel will be rewarded in the future world by reaching the supernal Israel: the sefirotic realm, the "bond of life." By leaving behind the physical Exile the devotee protects himself from its cosmic correlate, the *Temurot* or "Counter-World." (On the *Temurot*, see p. 21 and n59 above.)

Usually, "bond of life" and "World-to-Come" connote, *Binah* though a more general reading seems preferrable here.

The reception of a commensurate spiritual reward, *middah ke-neged middah*, recalls the language of the OK to Pes. 113a. However, ibn Gabbai's reading is more obviously sefirotic than Ṭodros Abulafia's. Compare! (For a translation of this text, see my dissertation, p. 619.)

617. This verse is used as a proof-text in the OK (quoted in n622 below).

618. See the discussion in *Sod ha-Shabbat*, p. 59.

619. Recalling *Bahir* 196, cited in Ibid.

620. As *Tif'eret* and *Malkhut* unite, *Binah* annoints them with *shefa'*, here called "the fine oil."

621. **"royalty."** Referring to *Malkhut* [lit., the kingdom] and *Tif'eret*, often called *Melekh*, the King.

"outsider." The lower realms or *qelippot*. Also cf. *Zohar* 2:133b–34a.

Discussion. Hence, the one who studies Torah, like the one who lives in Israel, makes a symbolic *havdalah* between sacred and profane, and promotes divine union. Cf. n611 and n615 above.

622. **"from the fruit of his work, etc."** A paraphrase of Ps. 104:13, "The earth is sated from the fruit of your work."

It is useful to compare the TY here with the *'Oẓar ha-Kavod.* Although ibn Gabbai's interpretation is more obviously mystical, there are two points of similarity: the use of 2K 17:26, 27 as a proof-text (cf. n617); and the notion of *middah ke-neged middah,* commensurate reward. Ṭodros Abulafia wrote:

> Whoever brings his children to the study of Torah, is also acknowledged or rewarded [*modeh lo*] as one who has a God. This person knows "the law of the God of the Land" [2K Ibid.] and acknowledges [*modeh be-*] His perfect Torah. Hence, his recompense: that he attain life in the World-to-Come.

623. Heb., *sibbah.* That is, the father is the motive force or prime mover behind this.

624. **"which is immediately followed by."** The speaker is using the hermeneutical principle of *semukhin* here.

Meir ibn Gabbai's text varies somewhat from the printed edition of the TB; it is actually closer to extant versions of TB Ber. 21b. Compare!

625. Perhaps the best source for this view is in PRE 41:

> R. Pinḥas says: The entire generation that heard God's voice at Sinai merited to become accompanying angel. . . . Happy were they in this world and happy are they in the World-to-Come!

Also cf. TB San. 108b where R. Eliezer took issue with the verdict of his colleagues:

> Mishnah: The Generation of the Desert [generally, a more negative term for that generation] has no portion in the World-to-Come.
> Gemara: . . . But R. Eliezer maintained: They will enter the future world, for it is written, "Gather my pious ones unto Me; those that have made a Covenant with Me." [Ps. 50:5]

On the merit of the generation of Sinai in the Zoharic sources cf. Z 3:163a and TZ 69 (111b–112a).

626. For examples of how the public *Havdalah* separates the *sefirot* from the *qelippot* and promotes divine unity, see p. 71 above (on separation); and n565 and n568 (on divine unity).

627. Meir ibn Gabbai now turns to the concluding act of *Havdalah,* the drinking of the sacramental wine.

"The opinion of our Rabbis." See TB Ber. 40a and Sanh. 70a; Gen. R 15:7 and 19:5. Also cf. *Sifrei* "Ha'azinu" 23; Lev. R 12:1; Num. R 10:2 and 8; Esther R 5; PRK 20; and *Pesiqta' Rabbati* 43.

628. Gen. R 19:5.

629. **"fermented juice."** Heb., *surei.* The dregs or the spoiled liquid. **"alien vine."** Here the "Other Side," *Siṭra' 'Aḥra'.* Cf. *Zohar* 1:238b: R. Shimon said: There are vines and there are vines. There is the supernal holy vine and there is the vine called "the vine of Sodom" [Dt. 32:32] and "the alien vine," [Jer. 2:2] the fruit of the "strange god."

"cup of reeling . . . of his wrath." The wine is none other than the venom of the snake, kabbalistically, *Siṭra' 'Aḥra'.* Cf. n631.

Also cf. *Zohar* 2:246b–47a, which distinguishes between the "cup of deliverance" [mentioned in the *Havdalah* ceremony] and the "cup of wrath and reeling":

> There is wine and there is wine. There are cups and there are cups, be they for good or for evil. Concerning wine for good it is written, "Wine that cheers the heart of man" [Ps. 104:15]; concerning wine for evil: "fermented wine, fully mixed." [Ibid. 75:9] Concerning the cup for good, it is written: "I raise the cup of deliverance." [Ibid. 116:13; recited during the *Havdalah!*] Concerning the cup of evil: "the cup of his wrath, the cup of reeling" [Isa. 51:17]. . . . One is from the Side of Purity, the other from the Side of Defilement.

"[In punishment] for this." Heb., *ke-neged zeh,* indicating that a) the punishment was measure for measure and b) that there is a precise correspondence between the spoiled wine of the grapes and the spoiled blood of menstruation. Cf., e.g., Menaḥem Recanati's comments recorded in *Yalqut Re'uveni* 38a:

> "When the woman saw" [Gen. 3:6]: She saw blood. As she squeezed the cluster of grapes, a corresponding action occurred in her: measure for measure [*middah ke-neged middah*].

Discussion. The wine-blood homology is well-known in the history of religions and Jewish Tradition is no exception. (Cf., e.g., the recitation of the Plagues during the Seder and the lesser-known custom of reciting the blessing over wine before reciting the *berakhah* over the virginal blood during the intercourse of bride and groom [SRA 2:406–07].) Here, the wine-blood symbolism carries with it overtones of death. Such associations are explicitly drawn in many Rabbinic and Kabbalistic sources, among them Meir ibn Gabbai's AQ (4:13). The symbol-cluster includes the association of menstrual blood with death (TJ Shab. 2:1; see below), the consumption of the Edenic grapes with the onset of death and human mortality (AQ 4:13 and many other sources), and embraces the notion that Eve's blood was the consequence of the "deadly poison" *(sam ha-mavet)* that the snake injected in her. (Cf. *Yalqut Re'uveni* 37a–38a, etc.)

On menstruation as one of the curses that befell Eve after the Fall, see TJ Shab. 2:1; TB ᶜEruv. 100b; ARN(A), Chap. 1; ARN(B), Chap. 42; Gen R 20:6–7; and Mid. *Tadshe'* 7. Also see L. Ginzberg, *Legends* 5:101 n85. The TJ source reads:

> Adam was the lifeblood of the world and Eve caused death. Therefore, the miẓvah of *niddah* was given to women.

For Zoharic sources see TZ 16 (31a) and 40 (80a).

631. **"residue."** Heb., *sod,* which may also be rendered as "emblem" or "symbol."

"the polluting substance [*zohama'*] that the snake injected in Eve." Although one Rabbinic tradition (recorded in L. Ginzberg, *Legends* 1:96) states that the snake injected his *zohama'* into the fruit, other Rabbinic sources speak of his sexual coupling with Eve. This motif is first found in Hellenistic Jewish sources (see *Legends* 5:123–24 for a list) and is preserved in TB Shab. 146a, Yev. 103b, AZ 22b, et al. In one famous medieval reading, RaSHI (ad Shab. 146a) interprets Eve's plea, "The snake *hishi'ani*—duped me" [Gen 3:13] as "The snake *hissi'ani*—married me"! The Edenic sin, in short, was sexual in nature!

The Zoharic tradition draws upon this theme of improper sexual coupling. The snake's filth is variously symbolized as the deadly poison, Lilith, harsh *Din,* a confused mixture of semen and lead (kabbalistically, the dross of *Gevurah*), and as a substance containing "24 kinds of impurity." Cf. 1:28b, 36b, 122b, 126a, 145b, 253b; 2:168a, 231a; 3: 79a–b, 143a (IR), 161a; TZ 40 (80a), 59 (93a), 69 (99b–100a; 113b), etc.

Kabbalistically, Eve's defilement by the snake represents the fusing (and confusing) of good and evil, both on high and below. A particularly noteworthy source is TZ 40 which provides a mystical rationale for the miẓvah of *niddah:*

> One must separate the pure blood and the menstrual blood. Because of the polluting substance that the snake injected into Eve, the pure waters [esoterically, divinity] became mixed with the polluted waters [*Siṭra' 'Aḥra'*]. For this reason, one [i.e., a woman] is obligated to make a distinction between the two, as it says: "God made the firmament and separated the water which was below the expanse from the water above it." [Gen. 1:7]

632. **"to separate herself from Adam."**

Discussion. Meir ibn Gabbai does not explain this allusion, but AQ 4:13 offers significant clues as to its meaning. Relying on the *Zohar* (3:296a [IZ]), the AQ relates that Adam and Eve were one entity before the Sin. When Eve emerged and separated from Adam's side, they immediately cleaved to each other and entered into a higher union:

> As the *Zohar* states: They joined face to face . . . and became one real body. Thus we learn that when a man is alone he is half a body, and so too, a woman. When they unite, they are whole, one real body. When a man and woman unite, all is one Body: the cosmos rejoices for it becomes one complete Corpus.
>
> Adam and Eve were one complete *'adam,* one person. . . . Through coupling with her, Adam attained fulfillment. When they

> were united face to face they symbolized the completion of the divine Structure [*binyan*] . . . through Eve the *binyan* was completed and the divine union perfected, as in "they became one flesh" [Gen. 2:24] and "The Lord was one and His Name one." [Zech. 14:9]

But by succumbing to the snake's wiles and taking the fruit, Eve sundered the divine unity:

> Through this sin Separation was brought into the world and the Voice [*Tif'eret*] was separated from Speech [*Malkhut*].

This view of the Edenic sin is quite common in Kabbalistic sources and there is every reason to believe that ibn Gabbai was familiar with it as a younger man. We may, therefore, interpret the TY passage as follows: Adam and Eve were one before the Fall. But as she squeezed grapes from the Tree and coupled with the snake, she separated from her true mate, causing Separation within the divine world and the confusion of Sacred and Profane.

633. That is, such an act would recall the initial confusion of sacred and profane which is precisely what the *Havdalah* aims to guard against. This rationale is a good example of how individual men and women are mythicized in the Zoharic tradition—each man becoming Adam and each woman, Eve. Myth is employed to legitimate sex-role or gender differentiation and "explain" women's lesser role.

Ibn Gabbai's rationale also exemplifies how the "Exile from Eden" may serve as subtext and dramatic underpinning for the *Havdalah*. See SCK: Chap. 4 for other examples.

"women customarily . . . wine." I have been unable to locate the origin of this custom. Although its roots may well be popular, it is also conceivable that it stems from halakhic considerations of the elite. In medieval rabbinic circles there was considerable debate as to whether this time-bound miẓvah was Mosaic or Rabbinic, and therefore, whether women were obligated or (even) permitted to make *Havdalah*. The question arose as to whether women's participation should be active (e.g., reciting *Havdalah* themselves) or passive (hearing a man do it). Perhaps the custom of women not partaking of *Havdalah* wine was linked to the second opinion. For a summary of the debate cf. the BḤ to Ṭur OḤ 296.

A number of customs co-existed in mystically informed circles in the sixteenth century. For example, Moshe ibn Makhir reported that in some groups only the person reciting *Havdalah* would drink the wine. He added: "Perhaps there is a mystical meaning for this custom." (*Sefer Seder ha-Yom*, 60a)

In recent centuries the taboo against women drinking *Havdalah* wine spread to Eastern Europe. It is cited in the SHeLaH in the name of Meir ibn Gabbai; from there, it entered the *Be'er Mordekhai* (n20) to the *Matṭeh Mosheh* 4:509. It is preserved in such latter day compendia as A. Sperling's *Ṭa'amei ha-Minhagim:* 188. According to an undated folk-custom, women who drink the wine will develop a mustache! (cited in M. Zborowski and

E. Herzog, *Life is With People:* 58; and in Th. Gaster, *Festivals of the Jewish Year* [NY, 1953]: 276.)

The development of this custom and the TY's role in popularizing it both merit further investigation.

634. In closing, Meir ibn Gabbai echoes some of the eschatological imagery found in TB Pes. 68a (cf. n638) and in TZ 69 (109a–b), the text he relied on earlier in this section.

"In the time to come, etc." All editions except Warsaw read: *ve-ᶜatid ha-qadosh barukh hu' le-hitpasheṭ min ha-qelippah.* Warsaw misprints: *ve-ᶜatid kevod ha-qadosh barukh hu' le-hitpasheṭ:* In the time-to-come the Glory of the Holy One will expand . . .

635. Here ibn Gabbai returns to the issue with which he opened this section, the *qelippot* which divide Israel from "their God in Heaven." The author looks beyond Israel's current plight to the Messianic dénouement. Cf. *Sod ha-Shabbat* with TZ 69 (109a–b):

> In the time to come the Holy One will remove these *qelippot* and be disclosed before Israel like the fruit of a nut, as it says: "Then your Guide will no longer be hidden away, but your eyes shall behold your Guide." [Isa. 30:20] There will no longer be any barriers between the Holy One and *Shekhinah* and Israel.

The TZ concludes:

> In the time of the King Messiah, the Holy One will remove all these *qelippot* from on high, from the middle world and from below. There will no longer be confusion in the heavenly *famila*. At that time, "The Lord *badad yanḥennu* [here read literally!] alone will reign; no alien god at his side." [Dt. 32:12; cf. n606 above and Tar. Onqelos to this verse]. At that time "She will give birth again" [Gen 4:2] so that Israel shall receive a new spirit of holiness, as it is written: "And I will give you a new heart and put a new spirit into you." [Ezek. 36:26]

For discussion see SCK: 238–39.

A textual note. The phrase "will no longer be kept under wraps" (Heb., *ve-lo' yikkanef*) evokes the image of wings *(kenafayim)* currently restraining and concealing divinity. Two Zoharic sources make dramatic use of this image: the lifting of the wings to reveal God. Cf. 2:222b, and 2:116b (RM) which reads:

> Because of the *qelippot* the Holy One is covered over with wings, as it says: "With two He (sic!) covered His face and with two He covered His legs" [Isa. 6:2; kabbalistically, a reference to the four *qelippot.*] But in the time to come "Your Guide will no longer be hidden under wings [*yikkanef*] and your eyes will truly see you Guide." [Ibid. 30:20]

636. **"consumed."** Heb., *billaᶜ*; lit., He will swallow up [death]. Kabbalistically, death connotes *Siṭra' 'Aḥra,'* radical Evil. See p. 40 and n235 above for discussion on this verse.

637. Warsaw ed. inadvertently omits the gloss *sod ha-sar ha-yaduᶜa u-vat zugo*. The meaning of the verse must be inferred from the context. It evidently refers to the renewed meeting and union of the royal pair *Tif'eret* and *Malkhut*. The terms *ashamed* and *abashed* apparently intimate their modesty before coupling. The Scriptural verse continues:

> "For the Lord of Hosts will reign on Mount Zion and in Jerusalem [a reference to the ultimate union of *Tif'eret* and *Malkhut*] and the [unified] Presence will be revealed."

638. The last three proof-texts, Isa. 25:8, 24:3 and 30:6 are all found in TB Pes. 68a in conjunction with the Messianic era.

Kabbalistically, Isa. 30:26 expresses a vision of full restoration, as before the Fall from Edenic perfection and the wearying series of Exiles. *Shekhinah,* the diminished Moon, will regain equality with *Tif'eret,* the Sun. She will shine with Her own light, no longer merely reflecting the light of others. Divinity will regain its primordial power, "the light of the seven days," as the seven active *sefirot* are fully actualized. This process on high will coincide with the full restoration of Israel, below. The cosmos, in short, will be fully healed, or as Meir ibn Gabbai says in closing: in perpetual Shabbat.

On the legend of the moon's diminution and ultimate restoration in Rabbinic literature, cf. TB Ḥul. 60b, Pes. 68a, and Gen. R 6:3. These twin themes are the subject of much mystical speculation in the *Zohar*. Three of the most germane sources are 1:34a, 181a–b, and 2:232a. Also see Shem Ṭov ibn Gaon, *Keter Shem Ṭov,* MS Munich 11 fol. 239b and *Sod ha-Shabbat* p. 14 and n19 above.

On the nexus between the moon's fate and that of Israel, see L. Ginzberg *Legends* 5:34 and *Zohar* 1:192a, 3:181b, etc.

639. See p. 60 and n442 above.

Bibliography

INTRODUCTORY NOTE

The following is a list of selected works used in the preparation of this study. Standard reference works have been omitted from the list, as have basic classics of pre-modern Jewish literature, e.g., the Bible, Mishnah, Babylonian and Palestinian Talmuds, RaSHI's commentaries, etc. These works have been cited according to their standard editions.

This bibliography is divided into two categories: primary sources drawn from the classical (pre-modern) Jewish literature and secondary sources and modern works.

CLASSICAL SOURCES

Aaron ha-Kohen of Lunel. *'Orḥot Ḥayyim* Jerusalem, 1956.

Aboab, Isaac. *Menorat ha-Ma'or.* Jerusalem, 1961.

Abulafia, Ṭodros. *'Oẓar ha-Kavod.* Warsaw, 1879. Reprint. Jerusalem, 1970.

Abudraham, David. *Sefer 'Abudraham* (also: *Abudraham ha-Shalem). Jerusalem, 1963.*

Al-Naqawa, Israel. *Menorat ha-Ma'or.* Edited by Hyman Enelow. 4 vols. New York, 1929–32.

Albo, Joseph. *Sefer ha-ᶜIqqarim.* Edited by I. Husik. 5 vols. Philadelphia, 1929–30.

Alcastiel, Joseph. *Teshuvot la-She'elot ᶜal Derekh ha-Qabbalah she-Sha'al R. Yehudah Ḥayyaṭ.* Printed in G. Scholem, "Li-Ydiᶜat ha-Qabbalah bi-Sfarad ᶜErev ha-Gerush." *Tarbiẓ* 24 (1956): 174–206.

Anav, Ẓedeqiah ben Abraham. *Shibbolei ha-Leqeṭ.* Edited by S. Buber. Vilna, 1886.

Arama, Isaac. *ᶜAqedat Yiẓḥaq.* Venice, 1573.

Asher ben David. *Sefer ha-Yiḥud.* Edited by R. Ḥassidah. *Ha-Segullah* 4 (1937). Also in J. Dan, (ed.). *Ha-Qabbalah shel R. 'Asher ben David.* Jerusalem, 1979.

Ashkenazi, Joseph ben Shalom. *Perush le-Farashat Bere'shit*. Edited by Moshe Ḥallamish. Jerusalem, 1985.

Avraham ben Nathan of Lunel. *Sefer ha-Manhig*. Edited by I. Rafael. 2 vols. Jerusalem, 1978.

Azriel ben Menaḥem of Gerona. *Commentaire sur la liturgie quotidienne*. Translated by G. Sed-Rajna. Leiden, 1974.

———. *Perush ha-'Aggadot le-Rabbi ᶜAzri'el*. Edited by Isaiah Tishby. Jerusalem, 1945.

Azulai, Abraham. *'Or ha-Ḥammah*. 4 vols. Przemysl, 1896–98. Reprint (3 vols.). Benai-Beraq, 1973.

R. Baḥyya ben Asher. *Be'ur ᶜal ha-Torah*. Edited by Ḥ. Cheval. 3 vols. Jerusalem, 1972.

———. *Kitvei Rabbenu Baḥyya ben 'Asher*. Edited by Ḥ. Cheval. Jerusalem, 1970.

Cordovero, Moses. *Pardes Rimmonim*. Munkacz, 1906. Reprint. Jerusalem, 1962.

———. *Tefillah le-Mosheh*. Przemysl, 1892.

David ben Judah he-Ḥasid. *'Or Zaruᶜa*. MS JTSA 2203.

———. *Sefer Mar'ot ha-Ẓove'ot*. Edited by Daniel Matt. [*The Book of Mirrors*]. Chico, 1982.

de Leon, Moshe ben Shem Ṭov. *Sefer ha-Mishqal*. Edited by J. Wijnhoven. Ph.D. dissertation, Brandeis University, 1964. (Earlier corrupt edition: *Ha-Nefesh ha-Ḥakhamah*. Basle, 1608.)

———. *Sefer ha-Rimmon*. MS Brit. Mus. 759; MS Moscow 219; and MS Cambridge Add. 1516.

———. *Sodot*. MS Schocken 14, fol. 78–99.

———. *Ẓavva'at Rabbi 'Eliᶜezer*. In *Beit ha-Midrash*, edited by A. Jellinek, 3:131–40. Jerusalem, 1967.

de Vidas, Elijah. *Re'shit Ḥokhmah*. Jerusalem, 1972.

———. *Toẓe'ot Ḥayyim*. Jerusalem, 1985.

Donnolo, Shabbetai. *Sefer Ḥakhmoni*. Edited by D. Castelli as *Il Commento di Sabbetai Donnolo sul libro de la Creazione*. Florence, 1880.

Eleazar ben Judah of Worms. *Perush ha-Tefillot*. MS Oxf. Bodl. 1204.

———. *Sefer ha-Roqeaḥ*. Fano, 1505. Reprint. Jerusalem, n.d.

———. *Sodot ha-Tefillah*. MS Oxf. Bodl. 1595/96.

Eliezer ben Joel ha-Levi of Bonn. *Sefer RaVYaH*. Edited by S. Y. Cohen and E. Prisman. 4 vols. Jerusalem, 1965.

Epstein, Yeḥiel Mikhl. *Qiẓẓur Shenei Luḥot ha-Berit*. Jerusalem, 1969.

Ezra ben Solomon of Gerona. *Perush le-Shir ha-Shirim*. In Ḥ. Cheval, (ed.). *Kitvei RaMBaN*. Jerusalem, 1967. Vol. s: 473–518.

———. *TaRYaG Miẓvot ha-Yoẓe'ot me-ᶜAseret ha-Dibberot*. In Ḥ. Cheval, Ibid. Vol. 2:519–548.

Giqatilia, Joseph. *Shaᶜarei 'Orah*. Edited by J. Ben-Shlomo. 2 vols. Jerusalem, 1970.

———. *Sodot*. Printed in back of *Noᶜam 'Elimelekh*, Lwow, 1817. Also MS JTSA 1609 fol. 117a–20a; MS Vatican 214, fol. 64a.

Ḥayyaṭ, Judah. *Minḥat Yehudah* to *Maᶜarekhet ha-'Elohut*. See *Maᶜarekhet ha-'Elohut*.

Horowitz, Isaiah. *Shenei Luḥot ha-Berit*. 4 vols. Josefov, 1878. Reprint. 2 vols. Zikhron Yaᶜaqov, n.d.

Ibn Ezra, Abraham. *Sefer Re'shit Ḥokhmah*. Baltimore, 1939.

———. *Sefer Teᶜamim*. Jerusalem, 1941.

Ibn Gabbai, Meir. *ᶜAvodat ha-Qodesh*. Jerusalem, 1973.

———. *Derekh 'Emunah*. Warsaw, 1890. Reprint. Jerusalem, 1967.

———. *Tolaᶜat Yaᶜaqov*. MS JNUL Heb. octo 3913 (Adrianople, 1547); MS JTSA 1646 (late sixteenth century?); MS JTSA 1553 (late sixteenth century?); *Editio princeps*, Istanbul, 1560; Warsaw ed., 1876. Reprint. Jerusalem, 1967.

Ibn Makhir, Moshe. *Sefer Seder ha-Yom*. Lublin, 1876. Reprint. Jerusalem, 1969.

Ibn Ḥabib, Levi. *She'elot u-Teshuvot me-ha-RaLBaḤ*. Venice, 1565.

Ibn Makhir, Moshe. *Sefer Seder ha-Yom*. Lublin, 1876. Reprint. Jerusalem, 1969.

Ibn Sahula, Meir ben Solomon (attributed). *Be'ur Sodot ha-RaMBaN*. Printed as *Be'ur le-Ferush ha-RaMBaN* in *'Oẓar Mefareshei ha-Torah*. Jerusalem, 1973. (Also see Ibn Shuᶜayb.)

Ibn Shuᶜayb, Joshua. *Be'ur Sodot ha-RaMBaN*. As above.

———. *Derashot*. Krakow, 1596.

Ibn Shraga, Joseph. *Sod Qiddush le-Ma'alei Shabbeta'*. Printed in Abraham Elmalik, ed. *Liqquṭei Shikheḥah u-Fe'ah*, fol. 39a-b. Ferrara, 1556.

Isaac ben Samuel of Acco. *Sefer Me'irat 'Einayim*. Edited by Amos Goldreich. Jerusalem, 1981.

Jacob bar Sheshet. *Meshiv Devarim Nekhoḥim*. Edited by G. Vajda. Jerusalem, 1968.

Jacob ben Asher. *'Arba'ah Ṭurim*. Warsaw, 1860–69. Reprint. 8 vols. New York, n.d.

Jacob ben Jacob ha-Kohen of Soria. *Perush ha-Sefirot*. In G. Scholem, "Qabbalat he-Ḥakham R. Ya'aqov he-Ḥasid b. Ya'aqov ha-Kohen." *Madda'ei ha-Yahadut* 2 (1927): 227–40.

Jellinek, Adolf, (ed.). *Beit ha-Midrash*. 6 vols. Leipzig, 1853–78. Reprint. 3 vols. Jerusalem, 1967.

Joseph of Hamadan. *Sefer Ṭa'amei ha-Miẓvot/* Section 1 [*miẓvot 'aseh*]. Edited by Menaḥem Meier. Ph.D. dissertation, Brandeis University, 1974.

———. *Sefer Ṭa'amei ha-Miẓvot* [including *miẓvot lo ta'aseh*]. MS JTSA Mic. 1722.

Judah ben Samuel he-Ḥasid. *Sefer Ḥasidim*. Edited by R. Margaliot. 4th ed. Jerusalem, 1970.

———. Edited by J. Wistineztki, with additions by J. Freimann. Frankfurt am Main, 1924.

Judah ben Yaqar. *Perush ha-Tefillot ve-ha-Berakhot*. Edited by Sh. Yerushalmi. Second edition, Jerusalem, 1979.

Judah ha-Levi. *Sefer ha-Kuzari*. Translated by Yehuda Even-Shmuel. Jerusalem, 1972.

Karo, Joseph. *Shulḥan 'Arukh*. 10 Vols. Vilna, 1874/75.

Kol-Bo. Tel-Aviv, n.d.

Labi, Shimon. *Ketem Paz*. Djerba, 1940.

Levi Yiẓḥaq of Berdichev. *Qedushat Levi*. Jerusalem, n.d.

Ma'arekhet ha-'Elohut. Mantua, 1558. Reprint. Jerusalem, 1963.

Maḥzor Viṭri. Edited by S. Ish-Hurwitz. Berlin, 1897.

Mekhilta' de-Rabbi Ishmael. Edited by Jacob Lauterbach. 3 vols. Philadelphia, 1933–35.

Menaḥem Recanati. *Perush 'al ha-Tefillot*. MS JTSA 1898 (before 1525).

———. *Perush ʿal ha-Torah*. Jerusalem, 1961.

———. *Sefer Ṭaʿamei ha-Miẓvot*. Przemysl, 1888. Reprint. Brooklyn, n.d.

Midrash Rabbah. 2 vols. Vilna, n.d. Reprint. Jerusalem, 1965.

Midrash Tanḥuma'. Edited by Solomon Buber. 2 vols. New York, 1946.

Midrash Tehillim. Edited by Solomon Buber. Vilna, 1891. Reprint. Jerusalem, 1966.

Mishnat Shir ha-Shirim. Edited by Saul Lieberman. Appendix to G. Scholem, *Jewish Gnosticism, Merkabah Mysticism and Talmudic Tradition*. New York, 1965.

Mizraḥi, Elijah. *She'elot u-Teshuvot*. E.p. Istanbul, 1560–61. Second edition. Jerusalem, 1937–38.

Moshe ben Avraham of Przemsyl, *Maṭṭeh Mosheh*. London, 1958.

Moshe ben Jacob of Kiev. *Shoshan Sodot*. Partial ed., Koretz, 1784. Complete MS: Oxf. Bodl. 1565.

Moshe ben Maimon [RaMBaM.] *A Guide for the Perplexed*. Translated by Shlomo Pines. 2 vols. Chicago, 1963.

———. *Mishneh Torah*. Jerusalem, 1965.

———. *Moreh Nevukhim*. Jerusalem, 1960.

Moshe ben Naḥman [RaMBaN.] *Kitvei RaMBaN*. Edited by Ḥayyim Chavel. 2 vols. Jerusalem, 1967.

———. *Perushei ha-Torah le-R. Mosheh ben Naḥman*. Edited by Ḥayyim Chavel. 2 vols. Jerusalem, 1959–60.

Moshe Jonah of Safed. *Kanfei Yonah*. Defective edition. Koretz, 1786.

Naftali Hirz Treves. *Siddur Mal'ah ha-'Areẓ Deʿah*. Thiengen, 1560.

Perush le-Sefer ha-Temunah. See *Sefer ha-Temunah*.

Pesiqta' de-Rav Kahana'. Edited by B. Mandelbaum. 2 vols. New York, 1962.

Pirqei de-R. 'Eliʿezer. Edited by D. Luria. Warsaw, 1852. Reprint. Jerusalem, 1970.

Saadiah Gaon. *Book of Beliefs and Opinions*. Translated by S. Rosenblatt. New Haven, 1948.

———. *Sefer 'Emunot ve-Deʿot*. Jerusalem, n.d.

Sefer ha-Bahir. Edited by Reuven Margaliot. Jerusalem, 1952.

———. German Translator and Editor, G. Scholem. [*Das Buch Bahir*] Leipzig, 1923. Reprint, Darmstadt, 1970.

Sefer ha-Minhagim (from the school of Meir b. Barukh of Rothenburg). Edited by I. Elfenbein. New York, 1938.

Sefer ha-Peli'ah. Premysl, 1883.

Sefer ha-Qanah. Jerusalem, 1973.

Sefer ha-Temunah. Lemberg, 1892.

Sefer ha-Yeẓirah. Warsaw, 1884. Reprint. Jerusalem, 1965.

Sefer ha-Yiḥud (from the circle of Joseph of Hamadan). MS JTSA Mic. 1737.

Sefer ha-Zohar. Edited by R. Margaliot. 3 vols. Jerusalem, 1951.

Siddur Rabbenu Shelomoh mi-Germaiza'. Edited by M. Hershler. Jerusalem, 1971.

Siddur RaSHI. Edited by S. Buber. Berlin, 1911. Reprint. New York, 1959.

Siddur Rav ᶜAmram Ga'on. Edited by D. Goldschmidt. Jerusalem, 1971.

Siddur Rav Saᶜadiah Ga'on. Edited by S. Assaf, and B. Yoel. Jerusalem, 1941.

Sod ᶜIlan ha-'Aẓilut. Edited by G. Scholem. In *Qovez ᶜal Yad* n.s. 5 (1951): 67–102.

Sod ha-Shem. Printed in *Zohar Ḥadash*. Istanbul, 1740.

Tiqqunei ha-Zohar. Edited by R. Margaliot. Jerusalem, 1951.

Ṭrani, Moshe ben Joseph. *She'elot u-Teshuvot ha-MaBiṬ*. Lwow, 1861.

Untitled Commentary on the Prayers. MS Paris Hebr. 596.

Viṭal, Ḥayyim. *Sefer Ḥezionot*. Edited by A.Z. Aeschcoli. Jerusalem, 1954.

———. *Shaᶜar ha-Kavvanot*. Jerusalem, n.d.

Wertheimer, A., (ed.). *Battei Midrashot*. 2 vols. Jerusalem, 1980.

Yalquṭ Re'uveni. 2 vols. Warsaw, 1884. Reprint. Jerusalem, 1962.

Yalquṭ Shimᶜoni. 2 vols. Jerusalem, n.d.

Zohar Ḥadash. Edited by R. Margaliot. Jerusalem, 1953.

SECONDARY SOURCES AND MODERN WORKS

Agnon, S. Y. "A Whole Loaf." [*Pat Shelemah*]. In *Twenty-One Stories*. New York, 1970.

———. *Yamim Nora'im.* Tel-Aviv, 1973.

Altmann, Alexander. "Moshe Narboni's Epistle on Shiʿur Qomah." In idem, ed. *Jewish Medieval and Renaissance Studies* pp. 225–88. Cambridge, MA, 1967.

———. *Studies in Religious Philosophy and Mysticism.* Ithaca, 1969.

Baer, Seligmann. *Seder ʿAvodat Yisra'el.* Roedelheim, 1968.

Baer, Yitzḥak. *A History of the Jews in Christian Spain.* 2 vols. Philadelphia, 1961.

Baqal, Meir, (ed.). *Sefer Pitron ha-Ḥalomot ha-Shalem.* Jerusalem, n.d.

Bar-Ilan, Meir. *Sitrei Tefillah ve-Heikhalot.* Ramat Gan, 1987.

Baron, Salo. *A Social and Religious History of the Jews,* 2nd ed. 18 vols. to date. New York, 1952–83.

Barukh, Y. L., (ed.). *Sefer ha-Shabbat.* Rev. ed. Tel-Aviv, 1980.

Beit-Arie, Malachi. "Pereq Shirah: mova'ot u-mahadurah biqorṭit." Ph.D. thesis. Hebrew University, 1967. 2 vols.

Benayahu, Meir. "Le-Qorot ha-Yehudim be-Tiria." *Ẓion* 12 (1948): 37–48.

———. "Taqqanot Tiria." *Qoveẓ ʿal Yad* n.s. 4 (1946): 193–268.

Bension, Ariel. *The Zohar in Moslem and Christian Spain.* London, 1932.

Ben-Shlomo, Joseph. *Torat ha-'Elohut shel R. Mosheh Cordovero.* Jerusalem, 1965.

Bialik, H.N. "Gillui ve-Kissui be-Lashon." In *Divrei Sifrut.* Tel-Aviv, 1954.

Blau, Ludwig. "Die erste Auagabe von Meir ibn Gabbais *Derekh 'Emunah. Zeitschrift für Hebraische Bibliographie* 10 (1906): 52–58.

Bloom, Harold. *Kabbalah and Criticism.* New York, 1975.

Campbell, Joseph, (ed.). *Man and Transformation: Papers from the Eranos Yearbooks.* Princeton, 1972.

Carmi, T., (ed.). *The Penguin Book of Hebrew Verse.* New York, 1981.

Charlesworth, James, (ed.). *Old Testament Pseudepigrapha.* 2 vols. Garden City, NY, 1983–85.

Cohen, Arthur A. and Mendes-Flohr, Paul, (eds.). *Contemporary Jewish Religious Thought.* New York, 1987.

Cohen, Martin S. *The Shiʿur Qomah.* Lanham, MD, 1983.

Cooperman, Bernard Dov, (ed.). *Jewish Thought in the Sixteenth Century.* Cambridge, MA, 1983.

Dan, Joseph. "The Emergence of Mystical Prayer." In idem and Talmadge, F., (eds.). *AJS Studies in Jewish Mysticism,* pp. 85–120. Cambridge, MA, 1982.

———. Ḥugei ha-Mequbbalim ha-Ri'shonim. Jerusalem, 1980.

———. "Samael, Lillith, and the Concept of Evil in Early Kabbalah." *AJS Review* 5 (1980): 17–40.

———. *Torat ha-Sod shel Ḥasidei 'Ashkenaz.* Jerusalem, 1968.

Day, John. *God's Conflict with the Dragon and the Sea.* Cambridge, 1985.

Deikman, Arthur. "Deautomatization and the Mystic Experience." In R. Woods, (ed.). *Understanding Mysticism,* pp. 240–60. Garden City, NY, 1980.

de Lange, Nicholas. *Atlas of the Jewish World.* New York, 1984.

Douglas, Mary. *Natural Symbols.* New York, 1973.

———. *Purity and Danger.* London, 1966.

Eisenstein, J.D. *'Oẓar Dinim u-Minhagim.* New York, 1938.

Eisler, R. *Weltenmantel and Himmelszelt.* Munich, 1910.

Elbogen, Isaac. *Ha-Tefillah be-Yisra'el.* Edited and expanded by Joseph Heinemann. Tel-Aviv, 1972.

Eliade, Mircea. *Patterns in Comparative Religion.* New York, 1958.

———. *The Sacred and the Profane.* New York, 1959.

———. *The Two and the One.* New York, 1965.

Ellwood, Robert. *Mysticism and Religion.* Englewood Cliffs, NJ, 1980.

Fernandez, James. "The Performance of Ritual Metaphors." In J. David Sapir, (ed.). *The Social Uses of Metaphor,* pp. 100–31. Philadelphia, 1977.

Fine, Lawrence. *Safed Spirituality.* New York, 1984.

Finesinger, Sol. "The Custom of Looking at the Fingernails at the Outgoing of the Sabbath." *Hebrew Union College Annual* 12–13 (1937–38): 347–65.

Fishbane, Michael. "The Sacred Center." In idem and P. Flohr, (eds.). *Texts and Responses: Studies Presented to N. N. Glatzer,* pp. 6–27. Leiden, 1975.

———. "The Teacher and the Hermeneutical Task: A Reinterpretation of the Hermeneutical Task." *Journal of the American Academy of Religion* 43 (1975): 709–21.

Fishman, Talya. "Women and Torah Study." *Kabbalah: A Newsletter of Current Research in Jewish Mysticism* 2:2 (1987): 4–6.

Frazer, Sir James. *The Golden Bough*. 3rd ed. Volume 3: *Taboos and Perils of the Soul*. New York, 1935.

Freud, Sigmund. *Complete Works*. Edited by J. Strachey. 24 vols. London, 1953–74.

Friedberg, Ch. *Beit ᶜEqed Sefarim*. 2nd ed. 4 vols. Tel-Aviv, 1954.

Gaster, Theodor. *Festivals of the Jewish Year*. New York, 1953.

Geertz, Clifford. *The Interpretation of Cultures*. New York, 1973.

Gennep, Arnold van. *The Rites of Passage*. Translated by M. Vizedom and G. Caffee. Chicago, 1960.

Gilat, Yiẓḥaq. "Taᶜanit Shabbat." *Tarbiẓ* 52 (1982/83): 1–15.

Ginsburg, Elliot. "The Sabbath in the Kabbalah." *Judaism* 31 (1982): 26–36.

———. "The Sabbath in the Classical Kabbalah." Ph.D. thesis. University of Pennsylvania, 1984.

———. *The Sabbath in the Classical Kabbalah*. Albany, in press.

———. "Ẓelem 'Elohim: Some Thoughts on God and Person in Zoharic Kabbalah." In L.D. Shinn, (ed.). *In Search of the Divine*, pp. 61–94. New York, 1987.

Ginzberg, Louis. *The Legends of the Jews*. 7 vols. Translated by Henrietta Szold and Paul Radin. Philadelphia, 1968.

Goetschal, Roland. *Meir ibn Gabbai: Le Discours de la Kabbale Espagnole*. Leuven, 1981.

Goldenberg, Robert. "The Broken Axis: Rabbinic Judaism and the Fall of Jerusalem." JAAR 45, Supplement (1977): 869–82.

———. "The Jewish Sabbath in the Roman World." In W. Haase and H. Temporini, (eds.). *Aufstieg und Niedergang der Romanischen Welt*, II.19.1, pp. 414–47. Berlin, 1979.

Goldreich, Amos, (ed.). *Sefer Me'irat ᶜEinayim*. Jerusalem, 1981.

Gotthold, Ze'ev. "ᶜErev Shabbat." *Maḥanayim* 85–86 (1963): 14–26.

Gottlieb, Efraim. *Meḥqarim be-Sifrut ha-Qabbalah*. Edited by Joseph Hacker. Tel Aviv, 1976.

———. *Ha-Qabbalah be-Khitvei Rabbenu Baḥyya ben Asher.* Jerusalem, 1970

———. *Ha-Qabbalah be-Sof ha-Me'ah ha-Shelosh ʿEsreh.* Jerusalem, 1969.

Graetz, Heinrich. *History of the Jews.* 6 vols. Translated by Bella Lowy. Philadelphia, 1891–98.

Green, Arthur. "Bride, Spouse, Daughter: Images of the Feminine in Classical Jewish Sources." In Susannah Heschel, (ed.). *On Being a Jewish Feminist,* pp. 248–60. New York, 1983.

———, (ed.). *Jewish Spirituality.* Vol. 1. New York, 1986.

———. "The Zohar: Jewish Mysticism in Medieval Spain." In P. Szarmach, (ed). *An Introduction to the Medieval Mystics of Europe.* Albany, 1984.

Gries, Ze'ev. "ʿIẓẓuv Sifrut ha-Hanhagot ha-ʿIvrit be-Mifneh Me'ah ha-16 u-ve-Me'ah ha–17 u-Mashmaʿuto ha-Hisṭorit." *Tarbiẓ 56 (1987): 527–81.*

Gruenwald, Ithamar. *Apocalyptic and Merkavah Mysticism.* Leiden, 1980.

Guberman, Karen. "The Language of Love in Spanish Kabbalah: An Examination of the 'Iggeret ha-Qodesh." In D. Blumenthal, (ed.). *Approaches to Judaism in Medieval Times,* pp. 53–105. Chico, 1984.

Guttmann, Julius. *Philosophies of Judaism.* Translated by David W. Silverman. New York, 1964.

Ha-Cohen, Mordechai. "Minhagei Leil Shabbat." *Maḥanayim* 85–86 (1963): 28–41.

Hacker, Joseph. "Ha-Peʿilut ha-'Inṭeleqṭu'alit be-Qerev Yehudei ha-'Impiriah ha-ʿOthemanit." *Tarbiẓ* 53:4 (1984).

Ḥallamish, Moshe. *Le-Toledot ha-Qabbalah be-Teiman be-Re'shit ha-Me'ah ha–17.* Ramat Gan, 1984.

Heinemann, Issac. *Ṭaʿamei ha-Miẓvot be-Sifrut Yisra'el.* Vol. 1. 4th ed. Jerusalem, 1959.

Heinemann, Joseph. *Ha-Tefillah bi-Tqufat ha-Tanna'im ve-ha-'Amora'im.* 2nd ed. Jerusalem, 1966.

Heschel, Abraham J. "ʿAl ha-Ruaḥ ha-Qodesh bi-Ymei ha-Beinayim." In S. Lieberman, (ed.). *Sefer ha-Yovel li-Khvod Alexander Marx* [Hebrew Volume], pp. 175–208. New York, 1950.

———. *The Sabbath.* New York, 1951.

Idel, Moshe. "Infinities of Torah." In Geoffrey Hartman and Sanford Budick, (eds.). *Midrash and Literature.* New Haven, 1986.

———. *Kabbalah: New Perspectives.* New Haven, in press.

———. "The Land of Israel in Medieval Kabbalah." In L. Hoffman, (ed.). *The Land of Israel,* pp. 170–87. South Bend, 1986.

———. "The Magical and Theurgic Significance of Music in Jewish Texts from the Renaissance Period to Hasidism" [Hebrew]. *Yuval* 4 (1982): 33–63.

———. "Mysticism." In A. Cohen and P. Mendes-Flohr, (eds.). *Contemporary Jewish Religious Thought.* New York, 1987.

———. "Targumo shel R. David ben Yehudah he-Ḥasid le-Sefer ha-Zohar u-Ferushav la-'Alfa' Beita'." *ʿAlei Sefer* 8 (1980): 60–72; 9 (1981): 84–98; and 10 (1982): 25–35.

Idelsohn, I.Z. *Jewish Liturgy and its Development.* New York, 1960.

Jonas, Hans. *The Gnostic Religion.* 2nd ed. Boston, 1963.

Jung, Carl. *The Portable Jung.* Edited by J. Cambell. New York, 1971.

Karpeles, G. *Geschichte der Judischen Literatur.* Berlin, 1921.

Kasher, Menaḥem. *Ḥummash Torah Shelemah.* 18 vols. to date. New York, 1949.

Kasher, Menaḥem and Ashkenazi, Shmuel, (eds.). *Haggadah Shelemah.* Jerusalem, 1967.

Katz, Jacob. *Halakhah ve-Qabbalah.* Rev. ed. Jerusalem, 1985.

Katz, Steven T., (ed.). *Mysticism and Philosophical Analysis.* New York, 1978.

———. "The Conservative Character of Mystical Experience." In idem., (ed.). *Mysticism and Religious Traditions,* pp. 3–60. New York, 1983.

Kiener, Ronald. "Ibn al-ʿArabi and the Qabbalah." *Studies in Mystical Literature* 2 (1982): 26–52.

———. "The Status of Astrology in Early Kabbalah." *Meḥqerei Yerushalayim be-Maḥshevet Yisra'el* 6:3–4 (1987): 1–42, English section.

Klibansky, R., Saxl, F., and Panofsky, E. *Saturn and Melacholy.* London, 1964.

Lauterbach, Jacob Z. "The Origin and Development of Two Sabbath Ceremonies." *Hebrew Union College Annual* 15 (1940): 367–424.

Leach, Edmund. "The Symbolic Representation of Time." In W. Lessa and E. Vogt, (eds.). *A Reader in Comparative Religion,* 3rd ed., pp. 108–16. New York, 1972.

Leibreich, Leon. "An Analysis of U-Ba Le-Ziyyon." *Hebrew Union College Annual 21 (1948): 175–209.*

Levenson, Jon D. *Sinai and Zion.* Minneapolis, 1985.

Lewin, Benjamin. *'Oẓar ha-Ge'onim.* 12 vols. Haifa-Jerusalem, 1928–42.

Lieberman, Ḥayyim. *'Ohel RaḤeL.* Vol. 1. Brooklyn, 1980.

Lieberman, Saul. *Tosefta' ki-Fshuṭah* 10 vols. New York, 1955–67.

Liebes, Yehuda. "Ha-Mashiaḥ shel ha-Zohar." In *Ha-Raʿyon ha-Meshiḥi be-Yisra'el.* Jerusalem, 1982: 87–236.

———. "Peraqim be-Millon Sefer ha-Zohar." Ph.D. dissertation. Hebrew University, 1976.

Lincoln, Bruce. "Treatment of Hair and Fingernails among the Indo-Europeans." *History of Religions* 16 (1977): 351–62.

Marcus, Ivan. *Piety and Society.* Leiden, 1982.

Margaliot, Reuven. *Mal'akhei ʿElyon.* Jerusalem, 1945.

Marmorstein, Arthur. "David ben Jehuda Hasid." *Monatsschrift fuer Geschichte und Wissenschaft des Judentums* 71 (1927): 39–48.

Matt, Daniel, (ed.). *The Book of Mirrors by R. David ben Yehuda he-Ḥasid.* Chico, 1982.

———. "David ben Yehuda Heḥasid and his *Book of Mirrors.*" *Hebrew Union College Annual* 51 (1980): 129–72.

———. ed. and trans. *Zohar: The Book of Enlightenment.* New York, 1983.

Meier, Menaḥem. "A Critical Edition of the Sefer Taʿamey ha-Mizwoth Attributed to Isaac Ibn Farhi/Section I". Ph.D. dissertation. Brandeis University, 1974.

Moore, G. F. *Judaism.* 2 vols. New York, 1971.

Muẓapi, Ben Ẓion. *ʿOlamo shel Ẓaddiq.* Jerusalem, 1985/86.

Neusner, Jacob. *There We Sat Down.* Second edition, New York, 1978.

Noy, Dov. "Histakkelut ba-Ẓippornayim bi-Shʿat ha-Havdalah." *Maḥanayim* 85–86 (1963): 166–73.

O'Flaherty, Wendy D. *Women, Androgynes, and Other Beasts.* Chicago, 1980.

Oron, Michal. *Ha-Peli'ah ve-ha-Qanah.* Jerusalem, 1980.

Otto, Rudolf. *The Idea of the Holy.* 2nd ed. London, 1950.

Patai, Raphael. *Hebrew Goddess.* 2nd ed. New York, 1978.

———. *Man and Temple.* 2nd ed. New York, 1967.

Pieper, Josef. *Leisure: The Basis of Culture.* New York, 1952.

Polhemus, T. *Fashion and Anti-Fashion.* London, 1978.

Principe, Walter. "Mysticism: Its Meanings and Varieties." In H. Coward and T. Penelhum, (eds.). *Mystics and Scholars*, pp. 1–15. Waterloo, Ontario, 1977.

Rosenberg, Shalom. "Ha-Shivah le-Gan ᶜEden." In *Ha-Raᶜyon ha-Meshiḥi be-Yisra'el*. Jerusalem, 1982: 43–63.

Rosenzweig, Franz. *The Star of Redemption*. Trans. by W. Hallo. Boston, 1972.

Schechter, Solomon. *Studies in Judaism*. Philadelphia, 1908.

Scheindlin, Raymond. "Medieval Hebrew Love Poems." *Prooftexts* 5:2 (1985): 105–35.

Scholem, Gershom. "Bil'ar, Melekh ha-Shedim." *Maddaᶜei ha-Yahadut* 1 (1925/26): 112–27.

———. (ed.). *Das Buch Bahir*. Leipzig, 1923. Reprint. Darmstadt, 1970.

———. *Devarim be-Go*. Edited by Avraham Shapira. 2 vols. Tel-Aviv, 1976.

———. "Eine unbekannte mytische Schrifte des Mose de Leon." *Monatsschrift fuer Geschichte und Wissenschaft des Judentums* 71 (1927).

———. "Havdalah de-R. Aqiva." *Tarbiẓ* 50 (1982): 243–81.

———. *Jewish Gnosticism, Merkabah Mysticism and Talmudic Tradition*. New York, 1965.

———. *Kabbalah*. Jerusalem, 1974.

———. "Li-Ydiᶜat ha-Qabbalah bi-Sfarad ᶜErev ha-Gerush." *Tarbiẓ* 24 (1954): 167–206.

———. *Major Trends in Jewish Mysticism*. 3rd ed. New York, 1967.

———. *The Messianic Idea in Judaism*. New York, 1971.

———. "Mysticism and Society." *Diogenes* 58 (1967): 1–24.

———. *On the Kabbalah and its Symbolism*. New York, 1965.

———. *The Origins of the Kabbalah*. Translated by A. Arkush. Princeton, 1987.

———. *Pirqei Yesod be-Havanat ha-Qabbalah u-Semaleha*. Trans. by J. Ben-Shlomo. Jerusalem, 1967.

———. *Ha-Qabbalah be-Gerona. Jerusalem, 1963/64.*

———. *Ha-Qabbalah be-Provans*. Jerusalem, 1970.

———. *Ha-Qabbalah shel Sefer ha-Temunah ve-shel 'Avraham 'Abulᶜafiah*. Jerusalem, 1969.

———. *Re'shit ha-Qabbalah.* Jerusalem, 1948.

———. *Re'shit ha-Qabbalah ve-Sefer ha-Bahir.* Jerusalem, 1961/62.

———. *Sabbatai Ṣevi.* Trans. by R. J. Z. Werblowsky. Princeton, 1973.

———. "Sefer Ḥemdat Yamim le-Rabbi Shalem Shabbazi." *Kiryat Sefer* 5 (1927/28): 267–72.

———. "Sidrei de-Shimmusha' Rabba'." *Tarbiẓ* 16 (1945): 196–209.

———. *Urpsrung und Anfange der Kabbala.* Berlin, 1962.

———. *Von der mystichen Gestalt der Gottheit.* Zurich, 1962.

———. "Yediᶜot Ḥadashot ᶜal R. Yosef 'Ashkenazi ha-Tana' mi-Ẓefat." *Tarbiẓ* 28 (1958): 58–59 and 201–09.

———. *Zur Kabbala und ihrer Symbolik.* Zurich, 1960.

Sed-Rajna, Gabrielle. "De quelques commentaires kabbalistique sur le rituel dans les manuscrits de la Bibliothèque Nationale de Paris." *Revue des Etudes Juives* 124 (1965): 307–51.

Schutz, Alfred. *The Collected Papers.* Vols. 1–2. The Hague, 1962.

Sharf, Andrew. *The Universe of Shabbetai Donnolo.* Warminster, 1976.

Sharot, Stephen. *Messianism, Mysticism and Magic.* Chapel Hill, 1982.

Sperling, Avraham. *Sefer Ṭaᶜamei ha-Minhagim u-Meqorei ha-Dinim.* Lwow, 1895/96. Reprint. Jerusalem, 1972.

Steiner, George. *After Babel: Aspects of Language and Translation.* New York, 1975.

Steinsaltz, Adin. *The Thirteen-Petalled Rose.* Translated by Y. Hanegbi. New York, 1980.

Ta-Shma, Israel. "Be'erah shel Miriam." *Meḥqerei Yerushalayim be-Maḥshevet Yisra'el* 4 (1985): 251–70.

———. "Heikhan Nitḥabberu Sifrei ha-Qanah ve-ha-Peli'ah." In *Peraqim be-Toledot ha-Ḥevrah ha-Yehudit bi-Ymei ha-Beinayim u-va-ᶜEt ha-Ḥadashah* [Festchrift for Jacob Katz], pp. 56–63. Jerusalem, 1980.

———. "Tosefet Shabbat." *Tarbiẓ 52 (1982/83): 309–23.*

Talmadge, Frank. "Apples of Gold: The Inner Meaning of Sacred Texts in Medieval Judaism." In Arthur Green, (ed.). *Jewish Spirituality.* Vol. 1, pp. 313–55. New York, 1986.

Tigay, Jeffrey. "Shabbat." In *'Enẓiqloppediah Miqra'it,* Vol. 7:504–21. Jerusalem, 1981.

Tishby, Isaiah. *Ḥiqrei ha-Qabbalah u-Sheluḥoteha.* Jerusalem, 1982.

———. with Lachover, Fishel. *Mishnat ha-Zohar.* 2 vols. Jerusalem, 1957–61.

———. *Netivei 'Emunah u-Minut.* Ramat-Gan, 1964.

Trachtenberg, Joshua. *Jewish Magic and Superstition.* New York, 1939.

Turner, Victor. "The Center Out There: Pilgrim's Goal." *History of Religions* 12 (1973): 191–230.

———. *The Forest of Symbols.* Ithaca, 1967.

———. *The Ritual Process.* Ithaca, 1969.

Twersky, Isadore, (ed.). *Rabbi Moses Naḥmanides.* Cambridge, MA, 1983.

———. *Rabad of Posquieres.* Rev. ed. Philadelphia, 1980.

Urbach, Ephraim. *ḤaZaL: Pirqei 'Emunot ve-De'ot.* Jerusalem, 1971.

———. *The Sages.* 2 vols. Trans. by I. Abrahams. Jerusalem, 1979.

Vajda, Georges. *Récherches sur la philosophie et la kabbale dans la pensée juive du moyen age. Paris, 1962.*

Werblowsky, R. J. Zwi. *Joseph Karo, Lawyer and Mystic.* Oxford, 1962.

Wijnhoven, J. H. A. "Medieval Jewish Mysticism." In *Bibliographic Essays in Medieval Jewish Studies*, pp. 269–332. New York, 1976.

———. "The Zohar and the Proselyte." In Michael Fishbane and Paul Flohr, (eds.). *Texts and Responses: Studies Presented to N.N. Glatzer*, pp. 269–332. Leiden, 1975.

Wolfson, Elliot. *The Book of the Pomegranate: Moses De Leon's Sefer ha-Rimmon.* Atlanta, 1988.

———. "Left Contained in the Right: A Study in Zoharic Hermeneutics." *AJS Review* 11 (1986): 27–52.

Woods, Richard, (ed.). *Understanding Mysticism.* Garden City, NY, 1980.

Yaari, Avraham. "Sefer Pesaḥ la-Shem le-R. Ḥayyim ben Meir ibn Gabbai." *Kiryat Sefer* 9 (1933): 388–93.

Zaehner, R.C. *Zurvan: A Zoroastrian Dilemma.* Oxford, 1955.

Zborowski, M. and Herzog, E. *Life is with People.* New York, 1952.

Zerubavel, Eviatar. *Hidden Rhythms.* Chicago, 1981.

Zinberg, Israel. *A History of Jewish Literature.* 13 vols. Trans. by B. Martin. Cleveland and New York, 1972–78.

INDEX 1
Source Index to *Sod ha-Shabbat*

This index is designed to help locate those works that are either quoted in ibn Gabbai's *Sod ha-Shabbat* or paraphrased therein at some length. Parallel sources and brief textual allusions, while noted in my commentary, have been omitted here. Broadly speaking, three sorts of textual borrowing have been catalogued here:

(1) Acknowledged citations whose locator is provided in the text of *Sod ha-Shabbat*. Here I have simply directed the reader to the page in *Sod ha-Shabbat* where the citation appears.
(2) Acknowledged citations whose locator does *not* appear in *Sod ha-Shabbat*, but which has been provided in my commentary. Here I have directed the reader to both the relevant page in *Sod ha-Shabbat* and to the germane note number. The note number appears in parentheses after the page number citation.
(3) Unacknowledged borrowings. These quotations and close paraphrases are identified through the addition of an asterisk. (The asterisk appears prior to the page citation for *Sod ha-Shabbat*.) As in category 2 the reader is also directed to the note(s) in the commentary where the specific passage is identified and discussed.

A. BIBLICAL SOURCES

B. RABBINIC SOURCES

MISHNAH

BABYLONIAN TALMUD

C. MEDIEVAL HALAKHIC WORKS (cited alphabetically, by author)

D. KABBALISTIC SOURCES (cited in chronological order)

INDEX 2
Thematic Index to the Introduction, Notes to the Introduction, and the Commentary

This index is designed to help locate selected themes discussed in the introductory essay and in the commentary to *Sod ha-Shabbat*. The emphasis is on those subjects that might otherwise be difficult to locate: subjects which are not easily derived from the Table of Contents or from basic knowledge of the structure of the Sabbath day.